Linda Berg-Cross, PhD

Couples Therapy
Second Edition

Pre-publication
REVIEWS,
COMMENTARIES,
EVALUATIONS . . .

"*Couples Therapy* is a rich re-source for both the practicing clinician and the sophisticated layperson. Written in language that is accessible and jargon free, it is simultaneously scholarly—a treasure house of practical techniques and clinical wisdom consistently supported by references to empirical findings. Berg-Cross is holistic in her approach, integrating multiple perspectives ranging from the biological to the spiritual. Her clinical examples are readily recognizable and they consistently instruct. She provides vivid metaphors that have strong therapeutic utility and are by themselves a good reason for individuals, students, and therapists of any theoretical orientation to read this book."

Robert M. Prince, PhD, ABPP
Past President, Section V (Psychologist-Psychoanalyst Clinicians) of Division 39, American Psychological Association

"*Couples Therapy, Second Edition* is an exceptional text. It is lucidly written, rigorously researched, and seasoned with delicious flashes of wit. Berg-Cross organizes volumes of research in a clear but not simplistic manner. Even included are flow charts for therapists, guides to practical interventions, and questionnaires for patients. This is the type of reference one keeps by the desk, watching it become dog-eared and battered until the next revision is released.

I particularly appreciate the evenhanded manner in which Berg-Cross pulls from many theoretical orientations. No political pulls here, no snide remarks . . . just the thoughtful, often compassionate evaluation of a therapist/researcher walking a reasoned path through the maze. Couples therapists should consider this book a standard reference. However, I particularly recommend it to my colleagues who, like me, are exclusively private practitioners doing individual therapy in the real world. Berg-Cross gives easy access to recent research and directs us toward a richer understanding of the contexts from which our patients come to us."

Susan Farber, PhD
Clinical Psychologist,
Private Practice,
Boise, ID

"Highly readable, brilliantly organized, and rich in its breadth, this book is a great gift to the therapeutic community. In twenty-five years of clinical practice, I have seen more and more individuals coming to treatment with their significant other. Schools and theories of marital and family therapy have sprung up to meet the need. Here the reader can learn all of them in one place and, most important, see how to make use of all of them.

Dr. Berg-Cross steers clear of dense, obfuscating concepts as well as slick, quick-fix protocols, the Scylla and Charybdis of psychology writing. She describes with a great touch the pace and stages of change, both pathological and therapeutic, in couple relationships and in individuals in couple relationships."

Rob Clark, PhD
Private Practice;
Adjunct Clinical Supervisor,
Yeshiva University,
New York City

The Haworth Clinical Practice Press®
An Imprint of The Haworth Press, Inc.
New York • London • Oxford

Couples Therapy

Second Edition

HAWORTH Marriage and the Family
Terry S. Trepper, PhD
Executive Editor

Couples Therapy
Second Edition

Linda Berg-Cross, PhD

The Haworth Clinical Practice Press
An Imprint of The Haworth Press, Inc.
New York • London • Oxford

Published by

The Haworth Clinical Practice Press, an imprint of The Haworth Press, Inc., 10 Alice Street, Bing-hamton, NY 13904-1580

Cover design by Jennifer M. Gaska.

Library of Congress Cataloging-in-Publication Data

Berg-Cross, Linda.
    Couples therapy / Linda Berg-Cross—2nd ed.
       p.   cm.
    Includes bibliographical references and index.
    ISBN 0-7890-1453-X (hard : alk. paper)—ISBN 0-7890-1454-8 (soft : alk. paper)
    1. Marital psychotherapy. 2. Marital psychotherapy—Problems, exercises, etc. 3. Commu-nication in marriage. 4. Communication in marriage—Problems, exercises, etc. I. Title.

RC488.5 .B463 2001
616.89′156—dc21
                                                         00-050552

To my children
Sage Berg-Cross and Gypsyamber
and Warren D'Souza

ABOUT THE AUTHOR

Linda Berg-Cross, PhD, is Professor of Psychology at Howard University, in Washington, DC. She also maintains a family practice in Potomac, Maryland, and is active in supervising family and couples therapists. Dr. Berg-Cross is the author of *Basic Concepts in Family Therapy* (1987, 1999) and has published numerous research papers. She earned MS and PhD degrees from Columbia University. She is married with two children.

CONTENTS

Introduction

When love and skill work together, expect a masterpiece.

John Ruskin

This research-based, skill-oriented book is intended for therapists who work with either distressed couples or satisfied couples seeking marital enrichment. The book is also written for researchers and scholars in the field of couple psychology who are seeking an up-to-date synthesis of the most important research. Graduate students will find a helpful blend of theory and practice, one that broadens their ability to develop their own effective therapeutic style.

Because there is no one effective method for dealing with the diversity of woes at each marital stage, an integrative approach is needed—one that draws on multiple techniques, each chosen after carefully analyzing the types of marital issues that exist for a particular couple. Students reading this book will learn how couples must build and master four cornerstones of marital life. They will learn how and why couples develop dysfunctions in each area. They will, I hope, use the theories and research findings to build effective interventions of their own devising, and incorporate and modify the many illustrative therapeutic interventions offered herein.

THE ORGANIZATION OF THE BOOK

The four cornerstones that shape the structure of this book represent the four major areas of marital functioning.

Cornerstone 1 is resiliency. It focuses on creating an optimistic philosophy of life to prevent and minimize the potentially devastating effects that poorly managed anger, anxiety, and depression have on a relationship. This cornerstone structure can vary from highly resilient to highly vulnerable.

The resiliency cornerstone highlights how marital satisfaction is affected by one's thoughts about his or her mate and one's philosophy of marriage. Couples therapy, to be successful, must help clients realize how marital

1

satisfaction is regulated by personal theories about "what makes my mate tick." So often, general marital expectations and attributions about why a spouse did or did not behave in a particular way set one up for marital disappointments and despair. When a partner believes that the mate is being intentionally mean-spirited or selfish, the prognosis for the marriage is very poor. If a partner starts thinking about the spouse as motivated by love and compassion but thwarted in the execution of those sentiments, the marital relationship becomes pregnant with potential for positive changes.

Cornerstone 2 is social support. It focuses on creating family and community roles that enhance the partner relationship. The components of this cornerstone structure can include a wide assortment of stress relievers and stress generators. The social support cornerstone focuses on the culture and community—on how friends, family, and colleagues can serve to enhance a couple's appreciation of and bonding with each other. The text focuses on three important extramarital roles: parenting, in-law relationships, and the work world. Although these domains can interfere with potential marital bliss, great potential exists to use these ties to strengthen marriages.

Cornerstone 3 is adaptability. It focuses on creating communication patterns that resolve conflicts and deal effectively with crises. This cornerstone is characterized by varying degrees of interpersonal flexibility or inflexibility. The adaptability cornerstone is concerned with the influence of family dynamics on communication patterns between the partners. This includes the effects that our families of origin have on us, but it also includes the family dynamics that characterize one's current nuclear family and that are, at some level, affecting and being affected by the spousal subsystem. Family dynamics have an enormous influence on the ability and desire to communicate with one's husband or wife effectively. Thus, most marital and couples therapy programs focus exclusively on this level. Although effective communication is clearly critical for satisfying marital relationships, here it is embedded within three additional, interacting cornerstones.

Cornerstone 4 is self-fulfillment. It focuses on creating a spiritual connection with the world and with one's mate. This cornerstone is characterized by varying degrees of commitment and alienation. The self-fulfillment cornerstone is influenced by individual growth and development as well as by marital satisfaction. We are all seekers on a separate journey. When we marry, we hope that our partners will explore the territory we explore, walking the same paths and blazing the same trails. Rarely is this the case. Despite our need for sameness, security, and dependability, we all have a developmental need to grow independently and to learn to face our challenges with private strength and purpose. When a marriage can help the individual on his or her private road to self-fulfillment, it has, in a way, gone beyond the call of duty and on to some higher stage of marital bliss.

The four-cornerstone approach has strong clinical validity and recently received strong empirical support from Bradbury (1995), who analyzed the results of over 115 longitudinal studies that examined how marital quality or stability was predicted from some other theoretically relevant factor. He found four general factors that related to marital stability. These four factors overlap the current cornerstone model, and the similarities are quite striking.

Different types of researchers have focused on studying each of the four cornerstones. As the research in each cornerstone is reviewed, the reader will learn about the major theoretical orientations that have inspired the research. The resiliency cornerstone has been studied primarily by cognitive-behavioral theorists, the social support cornerstone by sociologically oriented theorists, the adaptability cornerstone by systems-oriented and psychodynamically oriented theorists, and the self-fulfillment cornerstone by humanistic-existential therapists and theologians. Each part begins with an introduction that describes the history and status of that particular theoretical perspective.

LEARNING AIDS USED IN EACH CHAPTER

This is not a one-idea book. Many ideas are presented here, related by the common goal of having people integrate social skills and personal growth into their marital relationships. This book is not filled with a multitude of easy suggestions (such as listening to your partner). It tries to give therapists a concrete idea of how to incorporate very complex and subtle behaviors and attitudes into a marriage.

The following didactic features will help therapists work with clients on each level.

Self-Exploration Exercises

At the end of each chapter are self-explorations that the therapist can use with couples. All of these self-assessment questionnaires meet the following four criteria:

1. They are in the public domain and are reproducible by therapists.
2. They have sufficient "face validity" so that the client can understand the results as well as the therapist.

3. They are brief.
4. They are easily scored.

Some of the exercises have been empirically validated; most have only face validity. The therapist should use these self-explorations to broaden and deepen assessments, never to categorize or summarize a couple.

Therapists may give these self-exploration exercises to their clients just as they appear, or they can all be tailored to fit particular client issues and needs. Remember, the exercises, unless noted, have not been scientifically validated. For this reason, no norms or interpretative score systems have been included. Instead, they should be used to help obtain more precise information about what clients are thinking, feeling, and doing in any particular area of inquiry.

The Therapeutic Dialogue

The therapeutic dialogues at the end of each chapter help couples define and prioritize realistic changes. The questions posed in each therapeutic dialogue explore three models of marriage: personal feelings and thoughts about one's own marriage, ideals about the perfect marriage, and information about couples in their cultural reference group. By comparing and contrasting specific aspects of the ideal marriage with cultural experiences (the marriages of friends, families, and coworkers), couples develop a sharper and more flexible evaluation of the strengths and weaknesses of their own marriage. By fully discussing positive role models in the couple's cultural community, the ideal marriage loses some of its absolute "shoulds," "musts," and "needs." Social comparison forces one's model of the ideal marriage to become more human, more fallible, and more resilient to daily stressors. By reducing the discrepancies between "how we are as a couple," "how our happily married friends function," and "how I want us to be," couples are motivated to make needed changes. A great deal of psychological evidence (Coopersmith, 1967) supports the notion that when the discrepancy between the self and the ideal is reduced, self-esteem and self-motivation are increased.

The mechanics of the therapeutic dialogue are limited only by the creativity of the therapist. Some therapists may choose to have couples use the therapeutic dialogue as stimuli for "journal-dialoguing" exercises. The usual procedure here is for couples to think about the topic or question posed, write for ten minutes on that topic, and then exchange writings and for ten minutes discuss their feelings about what they have read. (If individuals or couples really do not want to write, try having them speak into a tape recorder, in private, and then share the recording with their partners.)

The time allotted can vary from a "ten-ten" (ten minutes writing and ten minutes discussing) to "sixty-sixty" (sixty minutes writing and sixty minutes discussing). Couples can work on each set of dialogues over a period of several nights or several weeks. The therapist may also use the dialogue as a guide for a therapy session, in which he or she can help the couple explore and explicate the three models. Still another method is to have individuals work on different aspects of a model as part of individualized homework assignments. In each case, the goal is to have the couple be better able, at the end of the dialogue, to commit to realistic changes that will strengthen the marriage in a particular area.

Therapeutic Interventions

Each chapter has a series of suggestions on how therapists can implement the ideas presented within the therapy session. Again, these suggestions can serve as jumping-off points for clinicians to tailor an intervention to clients' particular needs. Most of the therapeutic interventions are based on theory or empirical research. Some are based on the author's own clinical experiences. However, the reader should keep in mind that no one therapeutic intervention works for all of the people all of the time. The therapeutic interventions are intended to stimulate creative applications by the reader to his or her particular couple.

Case Studies

Each chapter has case studies describing couples working on the issues under discussion. They are a combination of clinical case studies, diary entries, and self-exploration exercises from couples in marital-enrichment classes. All names and other relevant identifying information have been changed. In most cases, the case studies are combinations of many people's experiences.

Bibliotherapy and Videotherapy Recommendations

Therapists should feel free to share the recommended books and videotapes with clients. However, for bibliotherapy or videotherapy to be effective, it is important that the therapist recommend particular products for a specific reason and discuss and use the experience in therapy. Also, note that some of the books are highly technical and would be appropriate only for the most academically oriented couples. Therapists should be very familiar with the material that they are recommending to clients. Often, the books or videos serve as stimulus material for the next session.

Flowchart for Couples' Groups

Each chapter concludes with a group session outline that synthesizes the various points discussed into a flowchart, with activities spanning one to several sessions. It is one suggested model for therapists wishing to offer structured, weekly couple-enrichment groups to clients. However, therapists should creatively improve, change, and reorganize the material to fit their own needs.

Professional Development Questions

Integrative and thought-provoking questions are included at the end of each chapter. Instructors can use these to promote discussion in class, or the reader can use them to deepen his or her understanding.

WHICH CLIENTS WILL BENEFIT
FROM THE INFORMATION IN THIS BOOK?

As with all skill approaches, the more commitment and energy that couples put into analyzing, applying, and mastering the concepts and skills in each of the four cornerstones, the greater the benefits will be. However, the insights earned along the way are often personally painful, and at first, some of the new behaviors seem unnatural or awkward.

When individuals seek couples therapy, most often they are already in intense pain. The added tension and struggles that therapy presents make many couples flee after a few sessions because they sense that it is making the situation worse. Therapy seems to act like a magnifying glass in the early stages of assessment. Couples already recognizing that they are in deep trouble become preoccupied and continually focus on their weaknesses instead of their strengths.

The therapist needs to create a balance between assessing problems and assessing strengths; between instilling hope and offering insight. So as couples build better marriages, therapists must help them to put up with the same level of frustration and aggravation that comes with any new building. Those of you who have built a simple addition to your house or attempted to redecorate a room in your apartment will immediately recognize the unexpected havoc such small changes can bring and how all the errors loom larger than life. Like any renovation, working on a marriage is disruptive, often messy, and sometimes it is hard to remember why you ever started the project.

Couples therapy is most successful for couples who have made a commitment to remain married or in a committed relationship. A skill-based approach works best for those couples who have slowly drifted into a living arrangement that still provides some emotional stability, some practical help during difficult times, and a home base for the children. Although they are thankful for what they do have, they are yearning to make the marriage grow and prosper, deepen and sparkle. Couples who yearn for intimacy and cannot quite figure out what went wrong along the way will undoubtedly find that as they work with their therapist on exploring the areas discussed within the text, some light will shine on the lost path. When couples therapy is a last-ditch effort for those who are contemplating divorce or separation, the four cornerstone analysis can aid the participants in finding realistic answers to the all-important question: Is this marriage worth saving?

This book assumes that marriage can be a worthy path for self-development. Working on creating a good marriage is a morally high and enduring satisfaction. Working on the four cornerstones will not lead to carefree relationships in which people can double their pleasure and double their fun. But it will help couples label the challenges and opportunities in their relationships and give them the tools to grow emotionally and make difficult behavioral changes.

Although the text often refers to "married couples" and "husbands and wives," the subjects of this book encompass all of us who are in committed relationships (married or cohabiting). Although gay and lesbian couples face many unique challenges, the four cornerstones are just as critical for the success of their relationships. I hope the use of conventional terms provides easy reading and linguistic variety and does not limit the reader's appreciation of the diversity of healthy couple relationships that exist in our society.

REFERENCES

Bradbury, T. (1995). Assessing the four fundamental domains of marriage. *Family Relations, 44*(4), 459-468.

Coopersmith, S. (1967). *The antecedents of self-esteem.* San Francisco: Freeman.

PART I.

THE RESILIENCY CORNERSTONE: CREATING AN OPTIMISTIC PHILOSOPHY OF LIFE

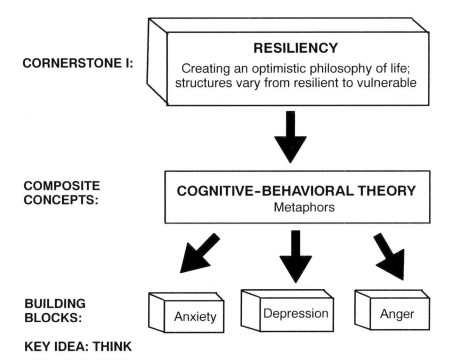

THEORETICAL ORIENTATION:
COGNITIVE-BEHAVIORAL

When I was a young man, I vowed never to marry until I found the ideal woman. Well, I found her—but alas, she was waiting for the ideal man.

Robert Schuman

The resiliency cornerstone is built on the coping skills and philosophy-of life that one uses to deal with adversity and stress both within and outside of the couple relationship. Analysis of this cornerstone reveals the type of schemas or guiding philosophies each partner uses to make sense of interpersonal encounters. Most important, the philosophy of life modulates one's affective experiences. With a positive philosophical outlook, a person remains emotionally available to constructively work on problems and attend to the partner's needs and points of view. This cornerstone assesses how thinking affects the couple experience.

Although personal resiliency examines positive philosophical strategies that strengthen the relationship, the cornerstone also harbors those personal vulnerabilities related to self-defeating, irrational, and counterproductive modes of thinking. These personal vulnerabilities in thinking lead to extremely destructive emotions—such as outbursts of anger or abuse, debilitating fears and insecurities that paralyze the relationship, and extreme depression and dysphoria. By carefully assessing and treating this cornerstone, couples therapists acknowledge that individual pathology and resiliency can greatly influence the couple relationship.

11

When did therapists realize the power of thought over emotions and behavior? Freud revolutionized our worldview when he proclaimed that neurotic symptoms were the result of human thought (Freud, 1916-1917). Before that, psychopathology was viewed as a disorder caused by demented mental processes that were not present in "normal" people. Freud showed that all people are subject to the same general rules that govern behavior and mental operations. When people are tormented by conflicting, unresolved, anxiety-provoking thoughts, their interpersonal behavior becomes disrupted and they act in seemingly irrational ways. The power of human thought to create irrational and abnormal behavior had been noted by the Greeks of antiquity, but its modern-day reintroduction by Freud permanently changed the way the everyday man or woman understands his or her own peculiar deviancies.

Although the basic premise, that thought affects human disturbance, continues to guide psychologists today, the type of thoughts that cause problems for people has been greatly expanded. No longer are taboo sexual fantasies the only thoughts that lead to trouble. All types of conscious and unconscious philosophies of human relationships can interfere with effective interpersonal relationships. Marital relationships are commonly disrupted by ways of thinking.

Cognitive theory provides a theoretically distinct approach for understanding and treating marital cognitions. The most effective theoretical elaborations and techniques derived from cognitive theory include rational emotive psychotherapy, restructuring and reframing skills, and the power of metaphoric devices. Rational emotive psychotherapy explores the power of thinking rationally and empirically; restructuring and reframing skills demonstrate the power of thinking from multiple perspectives and viewpoints; and metaphoric devices remind us that creative thought processes often unleash the most profound changes and insights. A brief discussion of each follows.

RATIONAL EMOTIVE PSYCHOTHERAPY

> By all means marry: If you get a good wife, you'll become happy; if you get a bad one, you'll become a philosopher.

> Socrates

Albert Ellis has been a leading force for over fifty years in explicating how irrational thoughts can lead to behavioral and emotional dysfunction in a marriage. Ellis began his career as a marriage therapist in the early 1940s. He soon became convinced that much marital discord occurred because individuals had deeply dysfunctional ways of thinking and could not live peacefully with themselves, much less anyone else. Ellis did not think that disgruntled partners, by and large, had interpersonal skill deficits. They most often justified not using the positive, pleasant social behaviors at their disposal by referring to intense, irrational feelings and unproductive philosophies of how their mates "should be" or "must be." They chose to act out their meanness, hurt, and anger because they felt such acting out was justified by the reality of the situation. They felt that the other person was "causing" their own poor behavior (Ellis and Harper, 1961).

Ellis began working with individuals, alone, without their spouses. He tried to teach partners that they were disturbed not by the actual behaviors or verbalizations of their mates but by their own biased, judgmental interpretation of those events. For Ellis, the "truth" of a situation is impossible to find. There is simply the wife's interpretation and the husband's interpretation. The key to marital happiness and personal fulfillment is to find and develop ways of thinking that embrace the relative nature of what is "true" in a flexible, self-affirming manner. Absolute, rigid philosophies block feelings of empathy and creative problem solving. Rigid thinking makes all conflicts an "I'm right and you're wrong" issue—an impasse.

Windy Dryden (1991) offers an excellent summary of rational-emotive couples therapy in his book *Reason and Therapeutic Change*. Most of the following discussion is based on that review. Within the rational emotive model, to resolve conflicts or live peacefully, each spouse needs to learn to avoid absolute judgments of "good" or "bad." People can learn to do this if they develop and accept rational philosophies that respect the autonomy and freedom of their spouses, the fallibility inherent in all human beings, and the daily unfairness of life as unavoidable givens in any marriage. So if a husband is ready to scream at his wife because she did not clean up the bathroom as promised, destructive conflict will be avoided if he consciously works to successfully convince himself of any of the following:

- His wife is a free person and no law of the universe states that she must do what he wants her to do.
- It is unfortunate and frustrating that she broke an agreement, but as humans, we are often unable to keep the promises we have made. It does not mean that she is a terrible person; it simply shows she is human.
- Even though it is unfair that the husband has to do the bathroom when he has already washed the clothes as he had agreed to, no one on earth lives a life in which things are always fair.

The outcome of this type of convincing self-talk is that the husband becomes emotionally ready to constructively negotiate with the wife, making her more likely to comply the next time such an agreement is sought.

Rational emotive couples therapists make a large distinction between couple disturbance and couple dissatisfaction. According to Dryden (1991),

> Couple dissatisfaction occurs when one or both partners are not getting enough of what they want from their partner and/or from being in an intimate relationship. Couple disturbance arises when one or both partners become emotionally disturbed about these dissatisfactions. Thus, they may make themselves anxious, angry, hostile, hurt, depressed, ashamed, guilty and jealous—emotions that usually interfere with the solution of couple dissatisfaction problems. In addition, when one or both partners are emotionally disturbed, they generally act in a self- and relationship-defeating manner, thus perpetuating couple disturbance. Rational emotive couples theory states that, assuming they have the necessary constructive communication, problem solving and negotiation skills, couples are likely to solve their dissatisfaction problems on their own. However, once couples are disturbed about their relationship, unless their emotional problems are dealt with, relationship problems usually remain, no matter how skillful one or both partners are in communicating, solving problems and negotiating workable compromises. (p. 183)

There are two main reasons for couple dissatisfaction: relationship myths and valid incompatibilities. Among the more popular myths that American couples grow up with are the following eight fairy tale truisms:

1. Romantic love should last forever in a good marriage
2. My partner should be able to understand what I want and need without my having to tell him or her
3. For sex to be good, it has to be spontaneous and full of emotional abandonment
4. If my partner is good enough to me, it will make up for other feelings of inferiority or inadequacy that I have
5. My partner will always be on my side in an argument or conflict
6. If our sex life isn't satisfying, that is proof that there isn't enough love in the relationship
7. In a good marriage, the partners will never disagree
8. Marriage will enhance my life without any great penalties, costs, or deprivations

Irrational thinking processes based on these myths are usually present when either partner makes absolute demands and commands. Couple disturbances occur when objectively unsatisfying marital interactions or actions occur and the spouse starts saying to himself or herself that (1) the other partner *must* not act that way, that it is *awful* and *horrible* if he or she continues to act that way, (2) one *cannot stand it* if the situation remains unchanged, and (3) the spouse is *bad* and *worthless* if he or she refuses to change. All of these thoughts are treated as devout personal religious tenets. Unfortunately, such thinking serves only to aggravate the spouse and increase the likelihood that he or she will intensify the noxious behaviors causing the marital dissatisfactions in the first place.

Learning to think rationally involves acknowledging that it is valid to have expectations of and desires for one's spouse. It is not appropriate or useful to escalate these desires into demands or to transform expectations into orders. By making irrational demands on one's partner, one is guaranteed to feel irrational anger. When both partners base their anger on the narcissistic belief that the other is the one who is wrong and who is a terrible person, couple disturbance gets perpetuated and exacerbated in a vicious cycle. Both partners are so busy damning each other that they have no energy to take responsibility for their own thoughts, expectations, and judgments.

For psychologically rich marriages, couples must take responsibility for creating a philosophy of marriage that allows them to tolerate and appreciate their partners, while expressing themselves and their own needs for personal growth.

When it becomes apparent that both husband and wife are locked into couple disturbances, it is very important to see them separately and terminate joint sessions. When one spouse cannot speak freely in front of the other or can do nothing but blame the other and demand that he or she change, individual sessions are mandatory. In the individual sessions, it is vital to flesh out a rational philosophy of marriage, one that is based on individuals' taking responsibility for what is in their control, accepting what is not under their control, and learning to tell the difference. Like the alcoholic who has lost all control over drinking, the maritally disturbed person has lost all control over thinking patterns. But thinking patterns can be changed and molded by self-choice. It is one of the few things, ultimately, that is truly under our personal control and will. After the blaming and demands are under control, joint sessions should be resumed.

The first step in developing a rational philosophy is to learn to monitor the effects that different types of self-talk have in distressing situations. The ABCs of rational emotive counseling are well known to most clinicians:

"A" refers to the activating event that causes an argument or gets one angry.

"B" refers to the self-talk or beliefs that the person has concerning that event.

"C" refers to the emotional and behavioral consequences of the particular beliefs that were embraced.

Such accepting, nonjudgmental thinking could lead clients to accept all different types of abusive relationships. Therapists should always be wary of conveying a conservative "learn to accept whatever life gives you" attitude. Instead, the goal should be to evaluate many different interpretations of the situation to see which ones carry equal emotional or rational validity.

RESTRUCTURING AND REFRAMING MARITAL PERCEPTIONS

It is man that makes truth great, not truth that makes man great.

Confucius

Despite the utility of learning to make rational, nondamning judgments, most distressed couples must also discover more creative ways to think about their marital quandaries. They need to "reframe" the problems so that they no longer seem to be insolvable problems. That is, they need to learn how to reach more optimistic conclusions from any one particular "take" on a situation. So instead of blaming partners for bad intentions, individuals need to come up with theories to explain why things are the way they are, presuming that the spouse has the best of intentions. These new theories invariably include the limitations imposed by the environment or by the "victimized" spouse who is building the new, nonblaming theories.

To stop jumping to black-and-white, dichotomous conclusions, couples need to entertain new information or ideas that will naturally change their perceptions. Just as a person suddenly sees the three-dimensional characters pop out of a computer-generated image, seeing a situation from a totally different perspective automatically leads to different feelings and judgments. Thus, couples need to cast their conflict in a different mold so it appears in a novel shape with new meanings that automatically elicit new emotions and different beliefs. Simple rational emotive brainwashing needs to be complemented by a change in perceptual consciousness—a different way of understanding the drives, stressors, frustrations, and rewards operating within the relationship. The husband whose wife is uninterested in sex may learn to reframe the situation from one in which he is being sexually neglected to one in which his wife is being inadequately stimulated. Or the wife whose husband is perpetually forgetting to do his household chores can reframe the situation from one in which his priorities are egocentric and selfish to one in which her constant mothering and Wendy-like behavior encourages him to be an endearing Peter Pan. Or the wife whose husband pays more attention to the children than to her may need to realize that she also pays more attention to the children than to her husband and she herself is setting the standard for spousal neglect. All of these reframes shift a spouse-blaming situation into a self-blaming situation. These types of reframes are particularly potent because a person who is alarmed or ashamed of his or her own behavior is motivated to change.

If it is possible to create alternative meanings for events in a marriage, how does one decide on the right interpretation of the many specific frustrations and tribulations involved in intertwining two or more lives? Is the flood in the basement caused by the wife's throwing tampons down the toilet a reason for outrage or for compassion? Indeed, at a deep, philosophical level, it is very hard to judge what specific events are ultimately "good" or "bad" for a marriage, much less what is the best way to react to any specific disaster. A marital philosophy that accepts that there are multiple possible outcomes, some detrimental and some productive, to any marital event, leaves breathing room for tolerance between the couple.

In happy marriages, spouses do learn to look on the bright side of things as much as possible. Indeed, they end up giving credit to their partners when an outsider would not do so. Happily married couples tend to idealize their spouses. For example, Hall and Taylor (1976) found that nonclinic spouses attribute more positive traits to their spouses than they do to themselves. They saw their spouses as relatively superior to themselves. Schriber, Larwood, and Peterson (1985) found that happily married spouses attribute more responsibility to themselves for conflict than to their spouses. They are also more likely to explain positive behaviors by referring to enduring positive personality dispositions in their spouses than when they are trying to explain their own positive behaviors.

Unhappily married couples, on the other hand, seem unable to give partners the benefit of the doubt. A recent review of the literature (Bradbury and Fincham, 1990) indicated that there is a general finding that, compared with satisfied spouses, dissatisfied spouses make attributions that cast the partner in a negative light. If something bad happens, it is because of some negative personality trait or some negative intention of the partner. Karney and colleagues (1994) confirmed that maladaptive attributions were related to the level of negative feelings toward one's mate but showed that those attributions remained unrelated to the level of negativity reported by the partner. Thus, it does not seem to matter whether or not the partner is angry. Even when he or she is happy with the mate, if the mate is angry, the attributions will be damaging. Common observation validates this research and reinforces the general thrust of the resiliency cornerstone: It is not enough to have people love us; we have to think well of them to have a chance at a good reciprocal relationship.

Getting distressed couples to make lemonades out of the lemons in their marriage is no easy task. It is very challenging to get distressed couples to give their partners the benefit of the doubt, drop their own defensiveness, and develop a loving philosophy. At first, distressed partners think they are being asked to be naive, saintly, insincerely sweet, or even worse, blind to the realities of life. Therapists can get couples to connect with this philosophy by telling parables or stories that illustrate the faulty logic of making simplistic, absolute judgments. For example, I will often remind couples that without the tornado, Dorothy would have never found the Land of Oz, or that without being prisoner of the Beast, Beauty would have never found her true love. Was the tornado a bad event? Was being caught by the Beast really a disaster for Beauty? Such fairy tales persist in popularity because they retell a universal truth—things are often not as they appear. No one knows if today's storm may not be the stuff of tomorrow's rainbow. Each couple can creatively foretell the future by optimistically interpreting their current crises. In their cockeyed optimism, they are likely to be just as accurate as the doomsayers about the long-term outcomes of any particular negative event. The bonus here is that the optimists will get the added value of bonding together and building bridges of marital fortitude when their attributions become kinder and they look for the silver lining hidden in each cloud.

But how else can we change "perception" and create these reframes or new philosophies for couples? The most skilled family therapists in the world are those who can find the right reframe for the right family at the right time in its development. Therapists can help distressed couples recast their problems by teaching them to unleash the power of metaphor and give meaning to their lives.

METAPHORS

Metaphors entail describing one thing in terms of another thing. Usually a metaphor uses some concrete sensory experience (something you have seen, heard, touched, or felt) to convey an abstract idea. When one builds a metaphor for communication, the result is more than either the first term or the second term—it gives birth to a new idea. So if a man says that his "marriage is at the end of a long marathon," I have an image of his marriage that expands my ideas about both marriages and marathons. This new combined image is more textured than either idea was before I heard the metaphor.

Marital experiences are so complex and convoluted that couples often have a difficult time describing what is wrong or what they want from the relationship. The feelings associated with marriage are so strong that simple descriptions of who said what to whom are almost always misleading for someone trying to understand what went wrong during a particular argument. When couples are encouraged to use metaphors to describe and analyze their experience, they gain new understandings and new possibilities for initiating change in the relationship.

Finding the right metaphor for the right couple at the right time is similar to hearing a song for the first time and knowing that it was there, all the time, waiting to be heard (Siegelman, 1990). It describes the experience better than an objective replay of the experience could do. The shades of feelings that can be explained by metaphor allow the client to experience intense feelings and allow the therapist to share the experience.

When the "right" metaphor is used, the creative insight it brings shifts attention so that the problem is perceived in a totally new way. The wife who tells her husband that he makes her feel "like an unchallenging, unpopular golf course that is used only when the other clubs are closed" is far more likely to find a way to bring the game over to her territory than the wife who simply says she wants and needs her husband to spend Saturday mornings with her.

I have used the following metaphors successfully in my own practice. Although they can be used with many different couples, the therapist needs to use them as a creative, jumping-off point, altering and expanding the ideas as needed. These particular metaphors were chosen because they can be used to help couples deal with anxiety, depression, and anger—the three areas of emotional distress discussed within the cognitive cornerstone in the following three chapters.

THE MARRIAGE TAX

There is an old saying that "The only two things you can't avoid are death and taxes." The humor in this quote comes from recognizing that it is as futile to resist paying taxes as it is to resist ever dying.

One powerful way of dealing with the hard-to-swallow aspects of a spouse's personality is to assume that each person has to pay a marriage tax to reap the benefits of the union. The marriage tax includes all the odious interactional obligations required to keep peace within the marriage and the nasty, annoying habits that spouses refuse to change. If spouses are willing to accept these sacrifices without resentment or fanfare, they are paying their marriage tax in an appropriate way. The more a partner wants to get out of a marriage, the larger the taxes he or she should be willing to pay. After all, it would not be the first time that one got what one paid for!

This traditional American mind-set toward paying taxes is ultimately very constructive. People are constantly seeking to reduce the amount of taxes that they have to pay. Yet very few people become clinically obsessed and totally focused on fighting taxation. There are many rational taxes that are overwhelmingly supported by the populace (libertarians may be excluded): to pay for road maintenance, police, and education. Other taxes are more controversial. Many people are worried about taxes being used to support wars, foreign aid policies, personally abhorrent artists, or biomedical procedures with which they have ethical qualms. Still, for society to function, each person must pay for all the taxes levied. We pay for the privilege of belonging to the society. The social contract makes us support the total system. The marriage tax works similarly.

Couples presented with the idea of a marriage tax will often doubt the validity of the analogy. The counterargument is that some people are just lucky; they have such workable marriages with seemingly little sacrifice or compromise. Why does it seem that others have to pay so few taxes for such a great marriage? Therapists can respond to this observation by revealing how "luck" is nothing more than an accepting attitude toward objectively odious aspects and demands of the relationship. Many of the so-called lucky people have simply developed a positive, consistent, disciplined way of evaluating how they are influenced by the difficult (that is, negative) aspects of relationships. They accept that life requires burden sharing. There is no free ride. Marital therapy groups are highly effective in getting couples to see the many burdens that affect every marriage.

Clients need to evaluate the emotional and physical costs of their marriage. What are the costs? How much time do they spend ruminating, arguing, or worrying about these hated activities? If a husband hates the way his wife demands that he call if he is going to be even five minutes late, he should be calculating the cost of this behavior in terms of a personally devised tax code. If it drives him crazy that in-laws are allowed to drop in unannounced and spend a few hours, he should compare that tax to an equally abhorrent tax he must pay in the civil realm. When clients think about these interpersonal obligations as part of a marriage tax, they will find their anger dissipating and their coping skills gaining muscle.

CHOOSE AN IDENTITY: BE A DUCK OR A SPONGE

In life, we can be ducks or sponges. A sponge absorbs all of life's miseries, as though in a deep and endless well. A duck lets life's problems slide off its back, touching it but never penetrating the core. This is a very simple and potent metaphor, and clients usually have an easy time deciding how much of the time they are a sponge and how much a duck.

This simple metaphor is very effective in helping couples let go of grudges and reduce the amount of anger they carry around with them. The therapist asks them how they would have handled a variety of problems during the week if they had been ducks rather than sponges. As each incident is examined, the virtue of duckhood as an attitude is strengthened. At times, I have given both husband and wife a duck feather to keep in their bag to remind them that they need to let the little daily spats between them fall out of consciousness. They should never let the daily humdrum problems of life penetrate to their core if they can help it. When duck feathers do not work, I have even resorted to giving couples a little sponge that expands when wet and asked them to keep wetting it every time they feel injured, hurt, or upset by something that their mates do to them. After they have counted the number of times during the week that they filled themselves up with dripping anger, the motivation to be a duck suddenly increases quite a bit.

THE ART OF A SUCCESSFUL MARRIAGE

Ikebana is the Japanese art of flower arranging. Ikebana, unlike the Western floral tradition, is concerned with how mass (the flowers) is related to space (the area surrounding the flowers). The flowers and greens are obviously important, but the empty spaces between the flowers and greens are also all-important for the Japanese. Ikebana requires that all the masses be well balanced by aesthetic spaces. The arrangement must have three movements reflecting the general landscape: there must be a background, middle ground, and foreground.

Many individuals find it helpful to think of the art of marriage as analogous to the art of Ikebana. So much time and effort are spent focusing on the mass: what he said and she said, what he did and she did, how much sex and the type of sex. Yet the spaces in a marriage are just as important. By spaces I mean what goes on in between and around the conversations and the interactions. When husband and wife are trying to discuss a problem, are they sitting so that they can hear each other easily and see each other? Is there competing noise from the television or CD player? Are children interrupting, is the phone ringing, or is cleaning underway at the same time? Is each partner filled with extraneous thoughts and inner conversations while the problem is being addressed? Or does the "space" between the conversation enhance the partner's problem solving and flow together as in a painted scene?

Understanding the contextual art of marriage illuminates some of the most mysterious moments in married life. How many husbands do not understand why their wives get angry and nasty because they are joking around and being lighthearted when dirty dinner dishes clutter the kitchen counter? Or wives who want their husbands to be erotically aroused by them but wear the same flannel pajamas to bed each night for months on end? The Ikebana of marriage involves removing distractions and adding surrounding elements that highlight the context.

The three significant areas of a general landscape are analogous to the three significant areas of a marital interaction: the background refers to the behaviors and interactions that have just preceded the current interaction; the middle ground refers to the current interaction; and the foreground refers to the anticipated behaviors and interactions that will follow the event. The best sexual encounter can be ruined by keeping one's mate waiting another fifteen minutes until a television show ends or by jumping out of bed afterward to finish a report that is due in the office the next day.

Therapists might despair to use this analogy with clients because it is so idealistic and hard to achieve. It is difficult enough to get a good conversation going without worrying about the surrounding context, what went on before, and what is going to happen afterward. However, I would contend that although therapists who can get clients to attend to these aspects may have fewer attempted healing interactions, they will have many more successful ones.

REFERENCES

Bradbury, T. and Fincham, D. (1990). Attributions in marriage: Review and critique. *Psychological Bulletin, 107*(1), 3-33.
Dryden, W. (1991). *Reason and therapeutic change.* London: Whurr.
Ellis, A. and Harper, R. (1961). *Creative marriage.* New York: Lyle Stuart.

Freud, S. (1916-1917). *A general introduction to psychoanalysis.* New York: Boni and Liveright.

Hall, J. and Taylor, S. (1976). When love is blind: Maintaining idealized images of one's spouse. *Human Relations, 29*(8), 751-761.

Karney, B., Bradbury, T., Fincham, F., and Sullivan, K. (1994). The role of negative affectivity in the association between attributions and marital satisfactions. *Journal of Personality and Social Psychology, 66*(2), 413-422.

Schriber, J. B., Larwood, L., and Peterson, J. L. (1985). Bias in the attribution of marital conflict. *Journal of Marriage and the Family, 47*(3), 717-721.

Siegelman, E. (1990). *Metaphor and meaning in psychotherapy.* New York: Guilford.

Chapter 1

Anger and the Couple Relationship

Marriage is an arrangement by which two people start by getting the best out of each other and often end by getting the worst.

Gerald Brenan

THE HEADS AND TAILS OF COUPLE ANGER: SELF-IMPOSED AND RETALIATORY ANGER

Heads or tails, couple anger is a coin with two distinct sides, each of which can make one a winner or a loser. The present analysis focuses on how destructive ways of handling the two sides of marital anger can be reminted so that both types of anger become a positive force in the couple's relationship.

The negative "head" of anger arises from our own thoughts. It is judgmental and self-imposed. It occurs when an individual makes absolute, negative judgments about his or her partner. For example, deciding that "My husband is selfish" or "My wife is a nag" will quickly generate angry feelings. This type of anger is imposed by "self-talk" and can be dissipated by more rational, positive "self-talk."

Two types of negative self-talk provoke self-imposed anger. First, anger emerges when spouses try to be mind readers and believe that the hurtful behaviors of their spouses are related to evil intentions. Perfectly rational people often develop spousal paranoia: A mysterious force makes them confident that their spouses are purposefully hurting them, demeaning them, or ignoring them. Such mind readers find it extremely difficult to reality test or to discuss their theories with their spouses. They appear to be constantly busy finding clues that support their conspiracy theory and allergic to direct questioning or entertaining the validity of alternative theories.

Second, self-imposed anger can erupt when the perceived thoughts, feelings, and behavior of a spouse are contrary to the expected and desired thoughts, feelings, and behaviors. Couples are happy when each spouse conforms to the loftiest expectations of the other and livid when expectations are blatantly negated. Unfortunately, much self-imposed head anger arises because of an inability to accept inevitable differences between husband and wife and because of poorly based, grand expectations about how a spouse "should" be. Years of shared experiences sensitize couples to how annoying or tiring that caring for another person can be. The result is anger directed at the spouse, most often for irrational reasons.

The reasons for self-imposed anger have to do much more with our own limitations than with any faults in our mates. Head anger is most often imposed because a spouse is a separate person, with his or her own needs and ways of being, and not the idealized image of that person that was constructed and nurtured to meet the partner's needs and ways of being. When the shadow falls between the dream and the reality, we feel cheated and angry.

The "tail" of anger is a retaliatory anger. When people are the victims of direct or indirect spousal anger, they retaliate with their own angry feelings. The ability to constructively react to spousal anger is a complex skill. One must weigh and negotiate different points of view. In addition, there is a strong, compelling need to emotionally protect oneself from feelings of shame, guilt, and rejection with immediate counterattacks.

The inability to openly and constructively respond to spousal anger, when it occurs, leads into a valley of unforgivable hurts. The hurt partner, who is the target of spousal anger, either counters with an outward attack or internalizes the anger and becomes withdrawn and depressed.

Self-disclosure and negotiation are most needed at these times, by both partners, but people need a secure holding environment to take such self-affirming steps. Attacking partners need to learn how to recover from situations in which they were the provoker, and hurt partners need to learn how to constructively deal with the felt retaliatory anger.

Reactions to retaliatory anger are determined by many factors, including (1) the degree to which the anger is justified, (2) how it is expressed, (3) the intensity and nature of the anger, (4) the historical significance of the anger, and (5) one's level of skill in dealing with anger. Resolution of retaliatory anger often requires us to change ourselves and admit personal limitations because our partners are justified in their feelings of disappointment and rage. This is much more taxing than trying to convince someone else why he or she should change to meet the righteousness of our own views. At other times, resolution of retaliatory anger requires defusing skills and tactful negotiation and assertiveness skills.

This chapter begins with a discussion of self-imposed anger and the methods of controlling such anger. Afterward, the intricate causes of retaliatory anger will be reviewed along with methods for constructively dealing with this type of anger.

SELF-IMPOSED ANGER

It is not bad enough that spouses have to provoke each other in both subtle and hostile ways. Most people go around provoking far more damaging marital anger right in their own minds. This occurs in different ways. The five most common provokers are irrational thoughts, partner desynchronicities, needs for control, feelings of jealousy, and time demands and fatigue. Each will be discussed in turn.

Cognitive Fixations (Repetitive Self-Talk)

Most useful models of self-defeating behavior postulate that people have some type of prerecorded, irrational thoughts playing subconsciously all of the time. This personal "Muzak" can affect feelings much more than the feel-good Muzak being piped throughout the malls of America. Most people are not conscious of this obsessional, self-imposed, unexamined, verbal Muzak until they conscientiously and painstakingly start monitoring themselves and the thoughts that are recurring throughout the day. When listening to the private inner voice, individuals become shocked and dismayed at how their inner records are surprisingly infantile, demanding, and absolute.

Continued monitoring allows people to notice a near universal relationship: When one plays verbal records that are absolute and degrading of themselves and others, the end experience is anger.

Whether one is using cognitive behavior therapy, rational emotive psychotherapy, dynamic insight therapy, or gestalt techniques to alter irrational thinking, the basic change mechanism remains the same. People become aware of self-defeating thoughts as well as the interrelationships between thoughts, emotions, and behaviors. They then begin to systematically test the rationality or usefulness of the self-defeating thoughts they have identified. Finally, the long, difficult task of reprogramming philosophies, self-concepts, and attributions is undertaken to effect a lasting change in how life is experienced.

Some irrational beliefs are more likely to create intense anger than others. For example, consider how the following irrational beliefs can conjure up intense, angry feelings in a marriage situation (Lohr, Hamberger, and Bonge, 1988).

"I Need Constant Approval" versus "I Can Satisfy Some of the People Some of the Time"

The first group of anger-arousing, irrational beliefs revolves around the idea that those closest to you must always approve of you. Subconsciously, people think, "It is necessary for my spouse to always admire me," "It is necessary for my spouse to always see me as capable and competent," and "My spouse can never find me acting inappropriately." By demanding constant approval from intimate others, one is doomed. Who has ever received universal approval twenty-four hours a day—day after day?

When the goal is to satisfy the partner some of the time and openly work with criticism the rest of the time, effort is refocused. Instead of defending oneself, a person practices self-evaluation. Negative reactions can be rationally evaluated for their veracity when a person is expecting that his or her spouse will have a significant number of valid negative reactions to one's behavior or desires over the course of time. Successful marriages require partners who acknowledge their own limitations and fallibilities. Acceptance of personal fallibilities helps slay the anger monster lurking behind every gesture of spousal disapproval.

"Others Are Causing All My Unhappiness" versus "I Am Responsible for My Own Happiness"

The second group of anger-arousing beliefs suggests that husbands and wives are the primary cause of each other's unhappiness. These are beliefs that lead to blaming someone else for our sorrow and woes instead of taking self-responsibility. Here, the unconscious record playing says things such as, "My spouse is the cause of my unhappiness," "My spouse is the cause of our family problems," and "My spouse starts all of our arguments."

Obviously, blaming problems on another person makes anger and hostility more justifiable. Unfortunately, most one-way blaming in marriages is not justified. Problems in marriage are interactional—it's what she does that provokes him to react, which then provokes her to react (and, of course, what she did to start the chain was a reaction to him!). When spouses stop blaming each other and accept that they must deal with the situation life has dealt them, they can begin to interact as allies.

"My Life Should Be Problem Free" versus "Life Is Rarely Fair for Anyone, Including Myself"

The third group of beliefs is tied to ideas of entitlement and overly high expectations. These are the narcissistic ideas of grandiosity and specialness. Repeating unrealistic ideas, such as "I hate to fail at anything," "I should be the most competent of all husbands," or "I should be able to cheer my wife up when she is down," sets people up for disappointment. High expectations are motivating, but they also are brutal to self-esteem when individuals continually fail to reach their predetermined goals. Constant rejection, particularly that which is self-inflicted, creates tension and anger.

A stoical philosophy helps a marriage—a philosophy stressing that adversity strikes in an unpredictable fashion and we are responsible only for that which is in our control.

"People Are Victims of Chance and the Environment" versus "People Can Successfully Work on Making Their Situation Better"

A fourth group of beliefs concerns how much influence individuals feel they can have on changing their current situation. If spouses believe that they are trapped in miserable marriages with intractable partners, anger will drip from them like sweat in the August Texas sun. Hopelessness "tapes" have thoughts recorded on them such as "It is almost impossible to overcome the influences of the past" or "My spouse will never forgive how I have treated him [her]." When you feel that you are trapped by your past, the present and future are very frustrating.

"It's Better Not to Think About Difficult or Hurtful Situations" versus "It's Better to Think Through Bad Situations and Implement Change"

The last group of beliefs focuses on overly anxious concerns and problem avoidance. When uncertain and worried, the marital partner has the opportunity to provide reassurance and security. At some point, excessive worry excludes the partner from being able to successfully help the spouse prepare for the unknown and unpredictable. Worried spouses who believe that there is no solution within their control minimize the protective factors of resourceful mates. Gaining strength from a mate is undermined if people subconsciously tell themselves, "I don't have the energy to confront my problems," "I have no control over my own happiness," or "I worry all the time about what will happen if my spouse leaves me."

Worrying erodes the ability to think of creative alternatives and live with the ambiguity that is part and parcel of married life. This issue is discussed in great detail in the chapter on anxiety. Many investigators believe that individuals who continually use these kinds of sentences on themselves are unconsciously prompted, or feel justified, to be verbally and even physically abusive (Bradbury and Fincham, 1993; Epstein, 1986).

Desynchronicities in Daily Habits

We all like to be around people who share our basic tempo of living, enjoy the rituals we enjoy, and believe in the same causes as ourselves. When partners experience significant desynchronicities in important daily

habits, tensions build and hard-core bargaining is required for both partners to be able to "live and let live."

Consider the case of Mary and Van. Mary valued personal hygiene. She
took a daily shower before and after work, brushed her tongue and flossed
three times a day, ironed her underwear, and did her nails twice a week. Van
was well groomed but very relaxed in his hygiene. Some days he did not
shower, he wore his slacks two or three times before laundering them, and he
cleaned under his nails only when he was going out. Mary and Van had a
number of problems, but the desynchronicities were the ones they constantly
wanted to talk about in therapy. Van wanted Mary to stop being obsessive;
Mary wanted Van to take pride in his appearance. People in love should
surely be able to change these minor types of behaviors to please one another.
Shouldn't they?

Yet efforts to change spousal behaviors of this sort are most often met with
significant resistance and outrage. The sentiment is, "Yes, this habit is a trivial
thing, so why can't you accept how I am?" As discussed elsewhere in this
text, people are happier when they marry someone who is a kindred spirit to
them when it comes to biological rhythms, style of thinking, tolerance for
ambiguity, and need for novelty. Many of us are not so lucky. When people
get married, they romantically believe that their interests will flow together as
naturally as two streams emptying into a common river. Time and experience
lead couples to realize that there are gaping areas of difference between them.
Their differing interests and styles often diverge as sharply as a river forked
by a mountain range.

Many of the differences that create conflict between husbands and wives
are gender typed. Although empirical data often present a more complex,
subtle set of sex differences, the stereotypes ring true to a great number of
people. For example, men want more passionate, nonverbal sex, regardless of
what has occurred between the spouses during the day. Women want sexual
intimacies to evolve from talking, philosophizing, and sharing. They resist
being swept away by an out-of-context-for-the-day physical feeling. Women
tend to be more liberal in their politics; men more conservative (Evatt, 1992).

THERAPEUTIC INTERVENTION 1:
CHANGING IRRATIONAL THOUGHTS

Helping husbands and wives uncover their irrational thoughts is a tricky
business. The first goal is to fully explore what a person is feeling in a
given marital conflict situation. Then, when the therapist is lucky, she or he
can simply reflect on what the internal dialogue of the client might be when

(continued)

(continued)

he or she has that feeling and hope the person buys into it. More often, however, clients need to go over a number of marital scenarios with the therapist and explore what semiconscious taped message seems to run across a number of different situations. Some therapists have a checklist of irrational thoughts and ask husbands or wives to check off which thoughts might be applicable each time they are experiencing intense anger toward their spouses. Other therapists have found it useful to tape-record the couple discussing a conflictual topic and then go over the tape, sentence by sentence, seeing which irrational thoughts and cognitive distortions might be fueling the argument.

Once a therapist has delineated the irrational thoughts fueling the intense, destructive emotions in the marriage, he or she needs to help the client empirically test the validity of those irrational beliefs and, over time, replace them with more rational self-talk. This sounds very artificial, but in practice, it is a most intense type of real-time, deep self-analysis. The primary questions being asked are these: "How do I choose to understand the reality of my situation?" "Am I using all the information available to me to come to my conclusions?" "Are there equally valid versions of reality in this situation?" "Why is it so important for me to view this situation in a particular way, given that it has fairly negative consequences on my relationship with my spouse?" "Am I overgeneralizing?" "Am I stuck in a dichotomous all-or-nothing type of thinking?"

The biggest problem therapists have in applying cognitive restructuring strategies is a tendency to rush through the assessment and restructuring phase in a half hour and hope to see results. Uncovering irrational thoughts and practicing more productive philosophies takes many hours of therapeutic discussion, discovery, and support. It also takes many hours of practice outside of therapy. Clients must be taught to trace how specific situations appear to trigger specific emotions. Then, the interpretation of the situation that actually led to the felt emotions needs to be uncovered. Often the interpretative schemas are related to rules we learned as a child. For example, dependent spouses often learned as children that they were not capable of doing things for themselves. When their spouses make them do things on their own, they get angry because they are telling themselves, "I cannot survive without you. I am too incompetent." Challenging and testing such pervasive belief systems are time-consuming but essential for managing marital anger.

CASE STUDY 1: THE RELATION OF MARITAL DISTRESS TO IRRATIONAL THOUGHTS

Paul and Lucy had both been married previously. Paul had two children in college, but he was close to neither of them. Both children had sided with the mother in a long and nasty divorce. Lucy had a very supportive,

(continued)

(continued)

friendly divorce when her husband of ten years, Gary, acknowledged that he was a homosexual and felt that he could no longer live in the guise of a heterosexual relationship. Lucy and her ex had two children, who were eight and six at the time she married Paul.

Paul and Lucy came to therapy thinking of a divorce after only two years of marriage. The main problem was that they spent all of their time fighting about the children. Paul had very high expectations and standards of housekeeping. Obviously, the children greatly frustrated Paul's need to maintain a clean and tidy house. Also, he always wanted to go out with Lucy and leave the kids with Gary. He felt Lucy was overprotective. Paul was always angry and quick to shout. When he was upset, everyone in the family had to stay away from him, lest they become the target of an unrelenting attack.

It very quickly became apparent that Paul was making himself angry much of the time by thinking irrational thoughts. Paul was seen individually for a few sessions during which the tenets of cognitive behavioral therapy were explained to him, and he realized that the following five thoughts were with him twenty-four hours a day: "Each person has a finite amount of love, and Lucy loves her children more than me." "All children are unappreciative and brats." "My stepchildren must acknowledge and appreciate everything that I do for them." "I cannot bear being rejected by my stepchildren." "The children are the cause of all the problems that I have with my wife."

The irrational nature of each of these thoughts was refuted by logic and natural experiments. Paul was encouraged to devise small tests of appreciation to see if the children would acknowledge anything positive that he did for them. He was shocked that when he brought home a doll that his daughter had been asking for, she hugged him, kissed him, and made a beautiful thank-you poem that she put on his pillow.

Lucy and Paul tried to develop a schedule of sacred times when they would be available for each other. After 9:30 p.m. on Mondays, Wednesdays, and Fridays became intimate times that they both fondly anticipated and enjoyed. Although Lucy and Paul were seen for less than three months, they continued to come in on a crisis basis for the next three years, whenever they had a "scary" fight. Mostly, these sessions served as a forum for processing the fight and provided a ritualized opportunity for both to profess their love and commitment for each other.

Commonly reported communication differences between men and women include the following: Women tend to be other focused; men tend to be self-focused. Men tend to talk about things; women tend to talk about people. Women talk more in private; men dominate conversation in public. Men are more decisive than women. Women cry about five times as much as men. Men are less willing to seek assistance (e.g., to ask for directions when lost on a car trip). When it comes to people's problems, men tend to give advice, whereas women give empathy. In general, women need more closeness and men need more distance in a relationship (Evatt, 1992; Gray, 1992; Tannen, 1990).

There are also biologically based desynchronicities. Women find their way through the world using landmarks (e.g., "Turn right at the supermarket"); men find their way using vectors (e.g., "Go southwest for two miles"); women are more sensitive to odors and to touch; men have better dexterity; and women, from the time they are infants, have more eye contact when they speak (Pool, 1994).

Who would not want a life mate who shares these daily inclinations? Who would want the friction of adapting on these basic dimensions? Yet all married people encounter such desynchronicities and must deal with the consequent anger (Evatt, 1992).

Please keep in mind that these gender differences can easily become stereotypes, and even when they are based on statistically true differences between the sexes, there are always great numbers of people who are not in accord with the gender stereotypes. Although it is essential for diagnostic purposes to understand commonly reported gender conflicts, the therapist must not accept or perpetuate the status quo (e.g., just because a phenomenon is prevalent does not mean it is healthy). Deciding what are desirable couple interactions must be dictated by ideologies that are meaningful to both partners and free of chronic covert or overt subjugation.

The Need to Control and Change Our Partners

Modern relationships are founded on mutual trust, the idea that the mate really does want to please and be agreeable. Given this assumption, it is very frustrating when requests for change are met with blank stares or disapproval. Folks start off thinking that asking someone to hang his or her coat in the closet is an easy, reasonable request. They end up feeling that their spouses are embarking on personal vendettas to torture them because six years later, the spouses are still draping the coat on the living room chair. Sometimes, it is indeed a personal vendetta (see passive-aggressive ploys discussed later). More often, though, changing one's behavior requires a lot more than a willingness to please. It requires time, attention, discipline, motivation, and reinforcement. Attempts to effect changes in specific behaviors require careful, concerted, agreed-on strategies in which one very small behavior at a time is worked on. Good marriages require partners who choose their battles carefully. If a spouse has ten behaviors that push all the mate's anger buttons, together they must choose one that both agree is a priority change item. Then, for the meantime, they must both work on accepting and tolerating the other nine.

THERAPEUTIC INTERVENTION 2: CLARIFYING COUPLE DIFFERENCES AND PRIORITIZING AREAS OF CHANGE

Husbands and wives are often relieved to find that many of their conflicts and desynchronicities are grounded in prevalent gender-based differences. It makes their marriage more "normal" and decreases feelings of failure. It is often a helpful exercise to have both partners make a list of all the differences between them that lead to problems. They then, individually, rank those differences from the most troublesome to the least troublesome. The therapeutic conversation analyzes which differences are idiosyncratic and which are rooted in biological, cultural, or familial differences. Note that rather than seeking the "true" cause for each difference (e.g., biological, cultural, familial, or idiosyncratic), the dialogue is directed toward exploring many possible plausible explanations.

These hypothesized causal explanations, in turn, help generate more realistic expectations about the likelihood of change and the effort involved in making such changes. When both partners come up with different explanations, which is often the case, it becomes necessary to generate many different solution paths to make sure that both people think the intervention will lead to changed behavior. For example, if the reason Paul does not make the bed is that he is clinically depressed, the effort to change will be dramatically different than if the reason is that no one in his family ever made the bed or because he feels that it is not his job to make the bed.

Anger is aroused when a mate does not change quickly enough or dramatically enough. Spousal education involves learning that when one spouse is asking the other to change in order to please the other, real motivation is slow to arouse, progress is uneven, and change is long in coming. Each portion of the change process must be attacked gradually, methodically, and repeatedly.

Jealousy Creates Anger

Another potential source of self-imposed anger is jealousy. Twenty years ago, jealousy between spouses was instigated, primarily, by flirting or being intimate with someone of the opposite sex. Infidelity is still a major cause of jealousy in marriage. However, other equally common targets of jealousy now include the workplace, exercise regimens, the children, civic responsibilities, and the computer.

Jealousy is a combination of feelings, including possessiveness, fear, abandonment, loss of connection, humiliation, and entitlement. Buss (1994) builds a very persuasive argument that, in our species, jealousy is a natural and evolutionarily important psychological mechanism specifically designed to alert one to potential threats to the relationship. Women have

THERAPEUTIC INTERVENTION 3: MAXIMIZING MOTIVATION TO MAKE PARTNER-PLEASING CHANGES

Motivation to change requires a six-step process. The person being asked to change must understand the following:

1. Why it is important that he or she change
2. What is troubling about the behavior or attitude
3. How the partner would respond to a change
4. How the partner can help facilitate a change
5. What other incentives would motivate a change
6. The costs and benefits involved in changing the behavior

Successfully changing a maritally noxious behavior requires many conversations focused on each of the six steps. Often, it is useful to start this six-step discussion as part of a therapy session and let the couple finish off on their own. The ranked difference list developed in the previous therapeutic intervention can help pinpoint noxious behaviors that would be most amenable to change and meaningful to both partners.

evolved to become jealous when commitment and emotional attachment have been threatened (because childbearing and child rearing make them dependent). Men have evolved to become jealous when the partner's sexual fidelity is threatened (because they have no other way to ensure the paternity of their offspring). Buss's research (Buss et al., 1992) confirms that such sex differences exist and can be measured psychologically and physically. When 511 college men and women had to rate their distress over a sexual infidelity situation and an emotional infidelity situation, "fully 83 percent of the women found their partner's emotional infidelity more upsetting, whereas only 40 percent of the men did. In contrast, 60 percent of the men experienced their partner's sexual infidelity as more upsetting, whereas only 17 percent of the women did" (p. 128). Physiological measures, such as galvanic skin response and heart rate, also indicated that men were more distressed over sexual infidelities and women more distressed by emotional infidelities. Obviously, both types of jealousy exist in men and women, and Buss is exploring only the relative importance of each type. In a clinically jealous partner, male or female, it is critical to examine both types of jealousy in detail.

When jealous feelings are acknowledged, they can motivate couples to reach out and build a bridge that brings them closer to each other. The threatened partner can find ways of building more self-sufficiency and trust while seeking bonding activities with his or her spouse. At these times, jealousy can be a very productive emotion. If jealousy simply triggers feelings of abandonment and frustrated dependency, the resulting anger will have little chance of being channeled into productive resolution areas.

Pittman (1989), in his book *Private Lies*, notes that jealousy is often a subliminal reaction to a lie. "People who are truly intimate know when they are being lied to, even if they can't precisely identify what the lie is. A lie will make one's mate feel distanced" (p. 73). Again, it is the feeling of being on separate sides of an increasing chasm that creates feelings of jealousy.

Jealousy can frighten, anger, or offend the receiving spouse. Most spouses feel that they have earned the respect and trust of their partner. Feelings of jealousy imply that the trust has not been earned—they have not proved to their mates that they are committed or faithful to the relationship. On the receiving end, a partner may feel strangled by the constant intimacy requirements of a jealous spouse. Living with the incessant questioning and suspicions of a jealous spouse, men and women fear that all their personal liberties are under attack.

Many mental health experts do not buy the evolutionary argument and have concluded that all jealousy is maladaptive. They do not think marriage should require a shutting down of all intense feelings and concerns for other people and activities. However, in most prototype models, the marital union is valued as the first among equals. Spousal obligations and needs are considered equally as important as self-obligations and needs. Competing interests, devotions, and particularly other people can threaten the sanctity of trust imbued in these marital values. Only when the spouse sanctions the deinvestment of "couple" energy is self-growth mutually consistent with marital happiness.

Extreme and constant feelings of jealousy are a sign of serious problems. The extremely jealous spouse is an extremely angry spouse. Spouses who experience repetitive waves of jealousy usually have one of two problems. First, they may be in a very destructive relationship where the provoking partner is not committed to the relationship. The provoking partner may be absorbed in his or her nonmarried life, unable to confront the failure of the marriage. The provoking partner may be sadistically enjoying retaliating for previous hurts by ignoring the partner. Alternatively, the jealous spouse may have severe personality problems that are being played out. The suspected spouse may be committed to the marriage, but these extremely jealous partners are frustrated in their attempts to find personal satisfaction or meaningfulness outside the marriage. They fall back on wanting their spouses to be there for them all of the time, fulfilling all of their needs. Unable to sustain self-esteem through self-validation, work, or extended family, they constantly need reassurance from their spouses. Unfortunately, in such cases, the suspected spouse can quell the fears and insecurities of the other for only the briefest periods of time. The cycle of jealousy and blame will begin again at the slightest hint of personal distress.

The most universal reason for jealous feelings is that the offending partner is no longer interested in being married but cannot come out and say so. Unable to express their true desires to leave the relationship, they act out their disinterest and withdrawal in all other ways imaginable. They continue to prod and emotionally punish the spouse, waiting for the mate to reject them and take the responsibility for ending the marriage.

Jealousy is always felt when one spouse is emotionally exiting the relationship and the other still wants to hold on. If the partner who is exiting is guilty or afraid to be honest with his or her spouse, the tendency is to label the mate's jealous feelings as "crazy" or "delusional." The more compromising the situation that the jealous spouse exposes, the more indignant the guilty spouse becomes. The accused partner constantly makes desperate attempts to protect himself or herself from the anger and responsibilities that would erupt if the validity of the jealous claims came to light. The therapist must often help jealous spouses to acknowledge the reality of their feelings. They should be encouraged to act on their feelings without the sought-after "confessions" of their rejecting, cold partners. Such confessions are hungered after, as individuals seek to assign blame and create plausible explanations and justifications for their feelings. But most seasoned marital therapists will verify that unfaithful spouses deny until they are literally "caught with their pants down" and even then, may continue to deny it! Oddly enough, when an ignored spouse denies any psychological maltreatment, the absence of jealousy or anger makes the deinvested spouse even nastier because it deprives him or her of the socially acceptable excuse of leaving an openly cantankerous marriage.

Handling jealous feelings requires the therapist to assess the validity of the accusations. Most often, individual sessions will reveal the extent to which the accused spouse admits culpability as well as the extent and nature of the distortions of the jealous spouse. If the husband is jealous of the time and energy that the wife is spending on her parents, the therapist must assess if the husband is promoting a cutoff or if the wife is overly enmeshed with her family of origin. His view and her view are joined by the therapist's view. Ideally, this gives a new multidimensional perspective to the problem instead of a simple polarization of views.

Time Demands and Fatigue Provoke Anger

The stress of dual-career couples has been well documented. Many couples purposely arrange their work schedules to minimize concordant work times so that they reduce the need for outside day care. This leaves

---

THERAPEUTIC INTERVENTION 4:
WORKING THROUGH JEALOUSIES AND THE MEANING OF INDEPENDENT ACTIVITIES AND INTERESTS

The therapist should help the couple recognize when their anger is provoked by jealousy. If one spouse feels betrayed and a general lack of commitment from the other, the diversions and activities of the other must be appreciated in terms of the effect on the relationship, as well as the benefiting individual. For example, talking to Mom daily may be very re-assuring and allow the young wife to give more to her husband, not less. The husband may be jealous for no objective reason. Conversely, emotional dependency on parents may make it more difficult for the young wife to turn to her husband for support and comfort, an emotional dependency that many husbands value. In this case, the husband's jealous feelings would be valid.

Therapists can help couples analyze the benefits and costs of trouble-some noncouple activities and interests. The benefits of privacy and extra-marital friendships and hobbies must be weighed against the moral, con-tractual, and emotional costs of such activities. Every couple must look outside the marriage for many of their needs for human companionship. Otherwise, the marriage is suffocated by impossible demands. Yet personal needs must be balanced by relationship needs, the time available for self-gratification balanced against the time available to function as a couple.

When the jealous feelings appear to be ill founded, the therapist can defuse the irrational anger by helping clients understand the self-defeating thoughts associated with their irrational jealousy. These thoughts include, "I am a very powerless person who needs my mate to live a successful life," "My spouse finds me the least interesting activity in town," and so on.

Therapists should always be sure to assess whether either spouse is experiencing jealousy about the partner's hobbies or civic involvements. For example, many a marital therapy session has focused on the anger and jealousy of golf widows, women whose husbands always put a golf game ahead of a marital responsibility. Some of these men are not threatening their marriage with their golf game; they still have plenty of time to socialize with their wives and carry out their parental and house-caring responsibili-ties. Far more men, though, must come to grips with the fact that working on a good marriage interferes with working on a good golf game.

---

many couples with virtually no time to interact during the week. The relationship is glued together, they hope, by a few hours of activity during the weekend.

How much time do couples need together to create a lasting, bonded marriage? Obviously, wide individual differences exist, but daily contact is needed by most couples. Couples who find one hour each day to be together have adopted one of the most potent, therapeutic marital aids.

Related to the time constraints is the amount of fatigue that people feel. When people are tired, they are more irritable. A well-rested person is less easily imposed on than a very tired person. Most couples learn that heavy, difficult discussions should not take place as soon as people return from work. After work, a cool-down and rest-up period is needed. It may be snoozing on the couch or taking a bath. More likely, it is rushing kids to after-school activities and making dinner. Still, an evening recharge of some type is needed if anger management is a goal in the marriage.

Many couples become so angry toward their spouses, for so long, over so many topics, that they are afraid to use any of the positive strokes so critical for congenial living. For them, the therapist might need to orchestrate a "behavioral exchange" to break the impasse.

RETALIATORY ANGER

When one partner acts out angry feelings by attacking the spouse, the recipient immediately feels defensive and upset. This feeling of anger that arises in response to a unprovoked attack (in the proximal sense) by one's partner is what I call "retaliatory anger." Retaliatory anger is very difficult to control, and equally difficult to express constructively unless individuals are very focused and self-disciplined.

Head anger is distinguished from retaliatory anger in that head anger is due to irrational judgments and retaliatory anger is due to rational judgments. Head anger is very idiosyncratic. Mary might believe that her husband does not love her enough because he refuses to go where she wants for vacation, but outsiders would usually feel that this is a sign that negotiation is lacking, not love. In other words, regarding head anger, other people would not be upset by what upsets you. In retaliatory anger, objective outsiders feel that the anger is justified. Also, with head anger, the focus is on the personal feelings of rage, regardless of whether or not the spouse is treated fairly. In retaliatory anger, the focus is on how personal

---

**THERAPEUTIC INTERVENTION 5:
THE BEHAVIORAL EXCHANGE**

Behavioral exchanges were one of the first techniques popularized by marital therapists (Stuart, 1980). There are many variants to the technique, but the essential features involve creating the opportunity for pleasurable interactions between couples who have become chronic bickerers, always carrying a marital anger chip on their shoulders.

(continued)

(continued)

To create a behavioral exchange, each partner draws up a list of easy-to-do, partner-initiated activities that would generate pleasure and closeness. The lists are exchanged, and additional activities may be suggested by the initiating spouse. The recipient spouses must agree that the activities would be meaningful and pleasurable to them. The possibilities are unlimited, but typical items on lists include (1) watches my favorite TV show with me, (2) lets me have time to read a book, (3) helps me with the dishes, (4) initiates sex, (5) initiates cuddling without the intent of sex, (6) calls me at work, (7) kisses me good-bye in the morning, (8) compliments me on how I look, and (9) is willing to visit relatives and have a relaxed time. Once there are a dozen or so items on the list, each partner must agree that he or she will initiate three of the activities during the week.

This simple exercise is very effective in creating positive interactions between chronically angry partners and in breaking down historically fortified barriers toward intimacy. Although people most often cannot immediately forgive and be nourishing in a spontaneous manner, they can carry through on a goodwill assignment to bring pleasure to their mates. Once each partner is the recipient of some positive expression of caring, he or she expresses appreciation, and new windows of opportunity open with a fresh breeze of optimism.

feelings of rage are inappropriately vented onto the spouse and how the recipient spouse becomes a victim.

Let's first examine the factors fostering retaliatory anger. Once in touch with the wellsprings, therapists will be able to compassionately understand retaliatory anger in their clients.

Like head anger, retaliatory anger can become a chronic condition. Most individuals hold onto retaliatory anger because to forgive is to swim against the tide of self-respect. Forgiveness might well signify that the retaliatory anger was somewhat overblown and inappropriate. Yet much marital anger is appropriate and justified (e.g., the spouse was objectively treated in a way that was thoughtless, hurtful, the cause of great inconvenience, etc.). When feelings of anger are justified reactions to a partner's inappropriate anger expressions, they become retaliatory. To keep their claim on reality, people keep their retaliatory anger, hoping that their mate will one day see the wrongfulness of the situation with the same accuracy and clarity that they themselves do (even if it is ten years later).

Holding onto retaliatory anger, however, is not a passive activity. It is played out in many different nasty and devious attitudes, innuendoes, and behaviors. All of these passive-aggressive, intimidating, controlling, or verbally insulting behaviors have the direct effect of creating a dynamic interaction in which retaliatory anger in one spouse begets retaliatory anger in the other spouse. One partner's anger confirms the propriety of the other's retaliatory anger and another coin of marital angst gets pressed into service.

Buss (1991) came up with a list of 147 upsetting, spouse-provoking behaviors. All of these behaviors can give rise to retaliatory anger. The most anger-provoking marital behaviors fell into clusters, including behaviors such as condescension (when a spouse treats a partner as stupid or inferior), possessiveness, unfaithfulness, inconsiderateness, moodiness, alcohol and drug abuse, physical self-absorption, sexual withholding, and emotional constriction. Many others have found similar sets of provokers. The following discussion centers on the anger provokers I have found to be most common and conflict producing.

Criticism (Condescending)

Criticism is the act of correcting or finding fault with someone else's actions, behaviors, words, or feelings. Marital criticism carries at least four potent covert messages. First, it lets the criticized spouse know that his or her mate is angry. Second, it makes clear that the spouse is being held responsible for certain errors. Third, marital criticism carries the holier-than-thou implication that the criticizing spouse would not have committed such an error. And most damaging, open criticism implies that the error is undoubtedly indicative of a larger, more ominous, negative personality trait exhibited by the spouse. When people feel their own personalities and intentions are being challenged, the natural and unavoidable response is to feel threatened and become angry themselves.

What happens in most marriages is that each spouse swears that his or her criticisms are meant only as informative feedback, a way of communicating and sharing what is really troubling. He or she does not mean to insult the other, put himself or herself one-up in the situation, or attack the core being of the mate. The partner is just too sensitive to criticism. It is unclear why spouses are so defensive about their "metacommunications," but, clearly, the tone used, words chosen, facial expressions, and context all play an important role in letting the recipient of the criticism feel a sharp pain.

Historical Attacks Provoke Anger

Children make one another cry by name-calling or even by laughing at one another. Most people can still remember the anger and humiliation of being the recipient of such uncalled-for, thoughtless attacks as children.

In marriages, name-calling and ridicule still provoke hurt and anger. But attacks on past behaviors and mistakes make the blood pressure soar and the will to negotiate disappear. How many times does one have to be reminded that it was he or she who chose to go on vacation to Yellowstone during the raging fires and to visit San Francisco during the earthquake? How could that ever help anyone decide where to vacation over the coming summer? Is it really necessary to remind a spouse that drinking coffee in the car is what caused the great car accident of 1990? Will he or she suddenly stop drinking coffee in the car with this 751st reminder?

Spouses know all of the psychological sore spots; that is what makes the relationship so vulnerable. Dragging out the past can immediately push one partner into an emergency flight path out of the conversation. Eventually, bringing up the same old situational offenses can push both partners into an automated conversation with a repetitive script that has no personal investment. Couples simply experientially leave the situation and let the prerecorded argument run its course.

THERAPEUTIC INTERVENTION 6:
LEARNING TO DEAL WITH CRITICISM

Weisinger and Lobsenz (1981), in *Nobody's Perfect: How to Give Criticism and Get Results,* describe a simple two-step strategy for profiting from spousal criticism. The first step requires that the person criticized should ask questions and not give explanations. This sounds easy, but very few of us genuinely try to find out exactly how we have failed the other person—we are too busy defending ourselves against any attack. But when the criticism seems very important to a spouse and she or he is a valid observer, it can make all the difference in the world to ask two simple questions: "How do you think I should do it?" and "What are your suggestions?" In the second stage, these two questions, when responded to, require the simplest of follow-ups—"Thank you for sharing that with me." and "I'll think about it." In the two-step procedure, the criticized partner cannot add any explanations. One only asks questions and gives the follow-up comments noted. If this is said without sarcasm or retaliatory anger, the interaction is a success.

In a session, therapists can direct clients how to responsibly respond to criticism by modeling being the subject of criticism with one of the spouses or by coaching the spouse who is the recipient of criticism. In-session practice, therapist and spousal feedback, and the experience of successful criticism interactions before expecting the couple to try it out at home.

(continued)

(continued)

A second suggestion for handling spousal criticism offered by Weisinger and Lobsenz is not to take each and every criticism to heart. Couples must make allowances for each other when they are stressed, worried, depressed, overworked, or tired. People are never at their best at these times. It just is not that personal an insult to be criticized by a distressed spouse.

The third and most energizing strategy is to try to change so that the criticism is no longer valid. All individuals are capable of growing and changing. Adapting to live peacefully with a mate is self-serving and self-enhancing. It is a personal victory, not a personal failure.

The therapist may repeatedly have to present these three new positive reactions to criticisms. Essentially, the three strategies listed above come down to three choices: the choice to listen and understand the criticism, the choice to dismiss the criticism, and the choice to accept the criticism and decide to change. Most individuals have gotten used to fighting criticism with countercriticism and rationalizations. These alternative procedures take some getting used to, but they reap invaluable rewards.

THERAPEUTIC INTERVENTION 7: RESPONDING TO HISTORICAL ATTACKS

Individuals who refuse to use historical attacks have gained a good deal of fair-fighting dignity. When one is the recipient of historical attacks, the most effective solutions involve

1. Learning to ignore such remarks,
2. Responding to such attacks during "nonfight times" or by putting his or her feelings into a letter or onto a tape,
3. Acknowledging to the partner the (partial) "truth" in the attack.

Many clients can benefit from having an individual session in which they practice dealing with historical attacks.

Neglect or Self-Centeredness Can Provoke Anger

Neglect is a universal anger provoker in marriages. Did you forget your husband's birthday? Did you forget to call your wife and tell her you would be late coming home? Did your husband go out and buy himself a new leather attaché case the same day he told you there was not enough money to fly home to your cousin's wedding? Does your wife choose to spend the weekend shopping with friends, regardless of your plans? All of these are situations in which one spouse feels neglected by the other. All are situations in which the spouse has acted in a self-centered way, seemingly taking his or her mate out of the cockpit and putting the partner into some recess of the baggage hold.

Passive-Aggressive Actions Can Provoke Anger

Sometimes, one spouse gets angry and no one else can understand the reason for the anger. The supposedly offending partner appears so calm, in control, and courteous. Only by knowing the subcontext and circumstances can the therapist understand the angry and aggressive intent behind the actions. Father Gallagher (1978), the major developer of the Marriage Encounter Movement, describes the passive-aggressive partner as operating like a magnifying glass over a pile of straw in the noonday sun. When the fire starts, it is not the magnifying glass that started the fire but the circumstances. Passive-aggressive spouses are magnifying glasses. They know how to make conversation and criticism go hand in hand. They will introduce touchy subjects at inappropriate times, use the silent treatment to punish, forget little things that are important to the other person, answer honest questions with provoking questions, and blatantly meet their own needs at the expense of their partner's needs. The classic example is the spouse who "must" go running after work and leaves his or her spouse to pick up the kids, make the dinner, and do the frantic afterwork errands. The "healthy" running spouse is amazed at why anyone would be upset by someone's being disciplined enough to take good care of his or her health.

Emotional Constrictiveness Can Provoke Anger

A full and meaningful marriage has partners who share a wide range of emotional experiences with each other. If a husband and wife routinely share anger, joy, grief, boredom, sadness, and humor, their marriage will be intimate and grow stronger. When one spouse decides to emotionally withdraw or has never learned to share emotionally, marital strife often ensues unless subcultural values provide alternative outlets. In most societies, it is more common for the man to be emotionally constricted, but in the United States, there are a significant number of marriages in which the wife is less able to share emotions than the husband. When wives are emotionally constricted, husbands classify them as "frigid" because sexual withdrawal is almost always a dominant feature of the constriction.

When the husband is emotionally constricted, the wife usually chalks it up to "the male personality thing" and stops pushing for this type of intimacy. Indeed, Deborah Tannen's (1990) best-selling book, *You Just Don't Understand*, is based on the premise that emotional constrictiveness among men is a cultural difference and not a sign of developmental arrest. I disagree. Men who are in satisfying marriages look forward to sharing a wide range of emotions with their wives—in the same mother tongue with the same nonverbal cues and a large array of idiosyncratic but well-understood nuances of communication.

Shame and Spouse-Provoked Anger

So far, the discussion has concentrated on justified retaliatory anger, when one spouse is the butt of criticism, passive-aggressive ploys, or emotional constrictiveness on the part of the other spouse. But many times, the anger-arousing triggers are effective because they awaken a significant degree of shame in the target spouse. The defense against the shame is the anger. Individuals feel shame when they are attacked and

---

CASE STUDY 2: THE ANGER-PROVOKING SPOUSE

Barry and Linda had married in their early twenties. Linda had been a flight attendant but quit when she married. Barry wanted his wife home with him every evening. Linda also couldn't bear the separations at that time and happily shifted to a job at the local hospital. Within a year, Linda began to miss the freedom, excitement, and respect that she had enjoyed with her last job. She felt constantly harried and constricted. Every time she suggested a job change, Barry started criticizing her. He would say that she didn't know how to create a good home or appreciate all that they did have. Eventually, she started having children and quit work to be a full-time homemaker.

With the arrival of children, Barry quickly became unable to share any of his feelings or thoughts with Linda. He came home, played with the kids, and watched TV. The only time he touched Linda was in bed as a direct prelude to sexual intercourse. Linda could not stand his emotional constrictiveness. Her anger seethed all day and night, and once a week, usually on the weekend, she confronted him. He usually listened for a minute and then walked out of the room. Then he ignored her for the rest of the night or became totally absorbed in a book or a game with the children. At times, Linda felt he did little things to retaliate for her outbursts, such as refusing to get out a video that she was looking forward to seeing or making fun of her friends.

The other trigger that really got to Linda was that Barry did not help with any of the housework. He felt that because he was the sole breadwinner, her job was to cook, clean, pay the bills, do the repairs, and organize the

(continued)

(continued)

kids' activities. If they were going to have people over for the evening, Barry would be sure to come home from work or his weekend exercise routine just when the guests arrived. When Linda tried to get Barry involved, he simply stated that he was not going to do it and she should just get used to that fact.

After three children and ten years of marriage, Linda was angry nearly all of the time. Eventually, she started a children's birthday party business and her increasing contact with families with young children convinced her that she needed to be in therapy. The other women she met seemed so carefree and happy with their husbands and their lives. She realized, for the first time, that she had been getting less than she felt she deserved from her marriage.

Linda was in therapy only a month when Barry decided to come and see what "she was wasting all the money on." Barry showed a complete denial of any anger or distancing. He thought if Linda could only stop taking life so seriously, they would get along fine. He admitted that he didn't want to do any housework and felt justified that the traditional division of labor was fair in their case. Barry agreed to come to therapy on a crisis basis, but he had no interest in committing himself to regular sessions. The therapist and Linda started to include Barry by writing a five-minute synopsis of what went on in each session and asking his opinion on issues that would have been explored had he been present. Barry liked this no-pressure inclusion and slowly began to realize that Linda's despair was real. He also slowly stopped ridiculing her moods and started reassuring her.

When Linda asked for his help in developing a new expanded business brochure, Barry energetically labored with her for over a month to get the brochure exactly how she wanted it. This was an emotional turning point in the marriage.

Linda became more assertive and confident. She learned to explain, in a nonprovoking manner, why she was asking for Barry's help with housework. Her major point was that housework was an expression of her commitment to the marriage and family. She steadfastly refused to accept it as her "job." She wanted Barry to express his commitment by joining in the housework or some comparable activity. She felt a little cooperation on his part could greatly improve her moods.

Slowly and without ever admitting he was changing, Barry started asking her what he could do for her around the house so that she could "stop seeing the shrink." Sometimes he did what she asked, but often he did not. When he didn't, they both tried to joke about it.

Now, Linda felt that he was on her side. She knew he was becoming aware of what she was feeling, and this made all the difference in the world to her. Six months after therapy started, Linda stopped coming and arranged for her and Barry to come together for a seasonal checkup. Over the two years that I continued to see them, the marriage strengthened considerably. Barry started balancing the attention he gave the children with the attention he gave his wife. Disagreements, although still frequent, were almost always resolved amicably before the night was over.

belittled because they are prone to feel deserving of criticism. They believe, because of their own perfect self-prototypes, that they should be better able to meet the needs of a mate, be more tolerant, be more efficient, and so forth. In other words, as spouses criticize each other, they unconsciously join in and start criticizing themselves.

How does personality affect the use of retaliatory anger strategies? Buss (1991) found that personality greatly affects how we respond to anger-provoking situations in our marriages. Consider someone with the following personality description: agreeable, conscientious, emotionally stable, intelligent, and energetic. Do you think this person would have a high-intensity anger explosion if his or her spouse decided not to plant the garden on Saturday, even though a joint decision had been made a week before? Well, that person might well be angry, but probably someone with that personality picture would just try to renegotiate a new date or maybe go and plant the garden alone. He or she probably would not get into a drag-out, moralistic, name-calling brawl over it. Nor would that person slink off to the bedroom and refuse to talk for a few days. Another spouse who was critical, lax, emotionally labile, and not oriented to thinking problems through in a careful, rational manner might well react with one of these two negative extremes.

Probably, even more important than general personality traits are the strategies each person develops to deal with conflict in the marriage. Some individuals are conflict avoiders and some are conflict engagers. Krokoff (1991) found that men or women who had a predisposition to generate conflicts and pick at the details had marital satisfaction deteriorate over a three-year period of observation. Women (but not men) who were predisposed to deny, ignore, or tolerate conflict had increasing improvements in marital satisfaction over that same three-year period. Although this study points to the virtues of female tolerance, clearly women should not put up with any type of abuse or suppress anger to a point that it is unhealthy (e.g., likely to lead to depression, somatic symptomatology, or loss of self-esteem).

THE THREE WORST WAYS TO RESPOND
TO SPOUSAL AGGRAVATION

Expressing anger is unavoidable in a marriage. Although it can ruin an evening and make weeks seem like years, the expression of anger is one of the most important ways we have of growing in a marriage and resolving conflictual issues that could tear the spiritual fabric of the marriage to shreds. Indeed Gottman and Krokoff (1989) reported, in an unreplicated study, that although disagreement and anger exchanges were related to unhappiness and marital conflict at the time they were occurring, they were predictive of improved marital relationships in the long run. Couples who were arguing and fighting at the beginning of the study were more likely to report an increase in marital happiness three years later.

However, these researchers found three modes of anger expression that did not lead to improved marital satisfaction: defensiveness (which includes making excuses, whining, and denying responsibility), stubbornness, and withdrawal from interacting (stonewalling). Spouses who express their retaliatory or self-provoked anger with these three strategies are doomed for difficult times (for a further discussion of these strategies, see pp. 320–322).

Some spouses are so avoidant or defensive that they never provoke fights and put up a shield of virtuousness. Gallagher (1978) describes this type of person quite aptly:

> He takes credit for having poured oil on troubled waters for whatever length of time they've not had a fight, and he throws up his hands in disgust that the other person can't control himself [herself]. He looks on his spouse as too volatile, too emotional, too easily upset, or too sensitive. But it isn't that simple. I have to take an honest look at why it is that I never seem to start the fights. Maybe the reason is negative. Maybe I don't care much what happens . . . Maybe my spouse is concerned with what is going on between us and the only way to get me to talk and reveal what is going on inside me is to start a fight . . . Maybe I've put up such a mask of perfection—acting the cool, calm and collected type—that it takes a sledge hammer to get through to me. . . . Oh, a superior attitude is an excellent way to push the other person's temperature up to the boiling point. (p. 98)

For some men, the withdrawal is a coping mechanism to prevent impulsive, aggressive retaliatory behavior. Discussing conflicts literally causes their blood to boil and if they stay in that situation, they explode. Measuring cardiovascular, neuroendecrine, and immunologic changes during a fifteen-minute conversation, Miller (1999) found definite physiological changes indicative of stress and anger among men who were characterized as cynical and hostile on personality tests. Their heart rate and blood pressure (systolic and diastolic) increased. Even more shocking was an increase in natural killer cells and cyctotoxic T cells during the conflict discussion. Thus, among a certain group of hostile men, there are clear indications that they can become "physiologically compromised" by discussing marital problems. This highly aroused physiological state accompanied by feelings of intense anger increases the probability of all types of physical and verbal abuse. Maybe this explains why men are generally so avoidant of discussing marital conflicts— they are trying to avoid their own physiological upset and increasingly hostile interactions. They are not intentionally trying to "dis" the wife, as so many women interpret husband avoidance.

The demand and withdraw pattern is exasperating for any couple, but in some couples it appears intimately related to patterns of physical violence and extreme verbal abuse. Men who batter seem to be both more demanding and more withdrawing than nonbattering men (e.g. "I want you to clean this kitchen, now. Take off that disgusting shirt. And don't dare bother me tonight"). Women who were battered were more demanding than women who were not battered (e.g. "Tell me where you are going. Clean up the kitchen. Don't start drinking"), but they were not any more withdrawing (Berns, Jacobson, and Gottman, 1999). Perhaps it is the increased female demands that contribute to the men's loss of control and the maddening male withdrawal pattern. Or it may be the demands and withdrawal of the men that prompt the increase in female demands. This vicious circle probably has no particular starting point. If, however, this circular model is correct, it would make good sense to teach men how to reduce withdrawing and both sexes how to reduce demands.

Very rarely does withdrawal from marital conflicts work in the long term. In the short term, though, it is often essential to avoid making matters worse. If someone feels that he or she is going to be physically violent or verbally abusive, it is imperative to withdraw—for a while. However, people who habitually leave the scene when conflict erupts only raise the pressure inside the spouse's bottled need for dialogue. Spousal anger often turns into blind rage when withdrawal is a habitual response to conflict.

Stubbornness and the refusal to concede the merits in the spouse's viewpoint are also damning responses to spousal anger. Some couples try to deal with their differences maturely and rationally by just expressing the differences and trying to live with them. They feel that this is often the best compromise when the inevitable differences between people begin to emerge. Such communication is invaluable. Virtually all mental health professionals stress how important it is to communicate. However, communicating is a necessary but not sufficient ingredient for marital stability. That is, one can share and understand until the stars fall out of the sky, but if he or she is consistently unwilling to change, to compromise, to try something new, the anger will not be used constructively. To be successfully married is to agree to change, to grow, and to compromise.

**THERAPEUTIC INTERVENTION 8:
DEVELOPING INSIGHT INTO DESTRUCTIVE
METHODS OF RESPONDING TO ANGER**

A helpful exercise is to have clients look over the entire list of anger provokers and repeatedly ask themselves, "How often do I respond with defensiveness when I am treated like this?" "How often do I become stubborn?" "How often do I withdraw and refuse to enjoy the rest of the day?" Once a husband or wife breaks through the denial and sees how she or he is responding in a destructive manner, that person will be motivated to try some of the positive strategies discussed in the next section.

POSITIVE WAYS TO RESPOND TO SPOUSAL ANGER

Love is an act of endless forgiveness, a tender look that becomes a habit.

Peter Ustinov

There are at least four different positive strategies for spouses to use when responding to spousal anger.

Respond to Anger by Disclosing Vulnerable Feelings

Expressing the effects of spousal anger directly is much healthier than expressing it indirectly. When one spouse is criticizing the other, it is far better for the criticized spouse to say how hurt and offended he or she is than to start counterattacking. Even when this strategy does not lead to spousal change, it helps the attacked spouse center himself or herself and not fall into the shame trap described earlier.

Humor

Laughter is the cure for many of life's miseries. Sharing the comic nature of a conflict is often one of the most effective responses to anger, but mostly when the humor is contagious and can be shared by the anger-initiating spouse. It takes a great deal of practice to use humor effectively. The offending spouse must never bear the brunt of the humor; it should always be directed at the situation or circumstance. The most important skill is learning to see the irony in a situation.

Empathy

When a spouse is the recipient of the other's anger, it is helpful to try to step into the partner's angry shoes. The recipient should assume that the

---

THERAPEUTIC INTERVENTION 9:
THE LOVE LETTER TECHNIQUE

John Gray (1992) has developed a structured letter-writing technique that helps couples bypass explosions of destructive anger. It involves the angry partner's taking the responsibility to walk himself or herself through the negative feelings and onto the path of positive feelings. The "safe" emotional release of hostility, coupled with a focus on the positive aspects of the relationship, allows the angry partner to freely communicate without a hidden hurtful agenda.

The technique begins with a time-out: The angry spouse goes off alone to collect his or her thoughts. The person imagines that the partner can hear him or her writing the letter with perfect love and understanding. The letter is composed of five paragraphs—each touching on five important but hard-to-share emotions: anger, sadness, fear, regret, and love. The first paragraph is about why he or she is angry, hurt, or frustrated. The second paragraph is about why the angry spouse is sad or disappointed. This is followed by a paragraph about one's fears and then a paragraph about one's feelings of embarrassment, regret, or apology. The last paragraph is about love and feelings of appreciation or positive wishes. The last step in the letter writing involves having the angry partner write a response to his or her own letter. In the response letter are all the phrases and thoughts that the angry partner longs to hear: "I understand . . .," "I'm sorry . . .," and "You deserve so much for . . ."

After this exercise, many individuals feel no need to give the letter to the partners. If a person does give it to the partner, the air has been cleared and one is open to dealing with the initial instigating problem in a cooperative and supportive way.

---

anger is justified. He or she should think about the reasonableness of the anger instead of the unreasonableness of it. For example, if a wife refuses to have sex on a particular night, a husband might simply call it a nasty payback and sulk. The wife would then be well served by talking to him about how she felt used or neglected during the past day or week. She may talk about her fatigue. But then, with empathy, she should talk about how she knows that he feels neglected. She should let him know that she can understand how his hurt is being translated into anger.

Empathy is not simply understanding the other person. It is a lot more complicated. Empathy is the ability to successfully share that feeling with the person with whom one is trying to be empathic. The experience of an empathic other can mellow an angry spouse and create forgiveness in the spouse experiencing retaliatory anger.

Time-Out

Sometimes the best thing we can do when another tries to provoke us is to leave that person alone. Get out of the room or, in an extreme situation,

---

THERAPEUTIC INTERVENTION 10:
CHANGING NONVERBAL COMMUNICATION

So often, empathy is disrupted not by what is said but by how it is said. Voice quality is full of complex emotional information that influences interactions. Vocal characteristics can convey a whole range of feelings: dominance, submission, sympathy, anger, sadness, indifference, and joy. Couples are even able to differentiate a truly felt smile from a smile that hides anger by the different muscle groups that are used in each situation. Disagreements escalate into arguments because each partner tunes into the hostile tone and nonverbal threat before processing the rational words that start the conversation. Empathy, likewise, is often sabotaged by nonverbal expressions of impatience, scorn, or ridicule (Greenberg, 1988).

Thus, teaching couples what they sound like in an argument or when they are trying to be empathic is a lesson with long-term benefits. The easiest way to do this is with a tape recorder. Have couples discuss a topic that is distressing to the wife for three minutes and then a topic that is distressing to the husband for three minutes. Then have them discuss an area of mutual distress for three minutes. When they listen to the tape recording, let them analyze their own vocal cues and emotional innuendoes. Were they supportive and empathic? Were they nonverbally open to solving the mutual problem? Then, let them practice the same conversations again and again, until they can do it without a destructive nonverbal cutting edge. Sometimes, they have to pretend to be someone else, perhaps a TV character, before they can enact a nondestructive interaction. Once it is on tape, there is concrete, positive proof that they can learn to put away a passive-aggressive conversational style and more genuinely support each other as well as resolve their mutual problems.

---

out of the house. No one should have to be psychologically or verbally abused—no matter how subtle that abuse may be. In this case, the message must be clear: "I will not allow you to treat me this way. I must leave until you are in a better mood."

A time-out is a surprisingly complicated procedure to teach couples because the goal is to make the behaviors guiding their interactions "rule"-bound instead of "stimulus"-bound. That is, couples gain control by disciplining themselves to carry out a series of unfamiliar, difficult proscribed behaviors in a highly provoking situation. They are carrying out these rules to ensure their emotional and physical well-being, just as many people must learn to take foul-tasting medicine each day to ensure their health. Time-out requires not doing the most natural behaviors and inhibiting learned reactions. For this reason, therapists need to help couples create a new philosophical discipline that will guide future behavior in the relationship.

TYPES OF ARGUMENTS BETWEEN COUPLES

It is clear that anger and fighting are important though painful elements of a successful, growing marriage. Without fights, there is less involvement. Thoughts and feelings are hidden. Openness and honesty disappear. By buying peace, many couples sell off the sought-after closeness. Much like what happens in the story "The Gift of the Magi," the sacrificing of personal values for the other leads to useless gifts. However, not all arguments are the same. Couple conflicts fall into four different categories (Lloyd, 1990).

Squabbles are little, unavoidable scraps that occur because we are living with someone who is not a clone of ourselves. If a husband leaves a party earlier than the wife wanted to, she may be upset and feel that he ruined a good evening. She may get a little miffed, but he doesn't feel well and doesn't care. By the time they both wake up, the issue is forgotten.

Squabbles cover new topics as they come up. They aren't very intense. People calmly state their dissatisfaction and are willing to leave it at that. Squabbles are healthy and unavoidable. They allow people to reaffirm their separateness while at the same time agreeing that the union is far more important than the current differentness. They allow issues to be brought up and remain unresolved. This is important because power plays can be minimized when different views are tolerated and the issues aren't all that important to either party.

Indeed, couples who are violent report having significantly fewer squabbles than do nonviolent couples. It is as though these partners are incapable of letting a minor disagreement drop without a resolution. Instead, the argument and its intensity escalate as a solution is sought (Lloyd, 1990). Thus, the more dysfunctional the marriage, the more therapists will have to attend to squabbles, exploring how they trigger dysfunctional anger reactions. Therapists shouldn't waste time resolving scraps with highly functioning couples, but, rather, should normalize their occurrence and function when brought up in therapy.

Problem-solving conflicts are the most common type of argument among satisfied couples. An issue comes up and both partners have different ideas of how to proceed. After sharing points of view and negotiating, a solution is agreed on. These conflicts can provide invaluable information about what works in the marriage. The solution strategies used in problem-solving conflicts can often be creatively applied to dealing with other types of conflicts. Therapists need to spend as much time learning what works for a particular couple as learning what characterizes their chronic conflicts.

Stable, heated arguments are recurrent arguments that typify a developmental stage in the marriage. Arguments about how to budget money, sharing household chores, and child-rearing problems often fall into this category. These are the types of problems that can lead to violence and the use of inappropriate expressions of anger. Solutions are often minisolutions or unattainable. They do not address the core of the issue, they may be difficult or impossible to implement, and there is no sense that the solution used one week would be usable the next week.

These stable, heated arguments are the most important to address in the therapeutic situation. The therapist should proceed to examine family-of-origin issues related to these developmental areas, how power issues are being played out in this arena, and needed areas for education.

Same old issues refers to the type of conflicts that occur with regularity throughout a marriage. Like a pair of worn socks, they have outlasted their usefulness, but it is somewhat comforting to go through the routine. For example, some couples may fight over how long they will stay at each relative's house during the holiday season—every holiday season the same arguments will occur. The issues and priorities never seem to change, and although there are some minor changes in the resolutions of these issues from year to year, they are more the same than different.

Same old issues are highly significant indicators of the major narratives driving the marriage. Family-of-origin issues come back to haunt individuals in their same-old-issue fights. These fights also highlight couple tensions about the extent to which they should fuse or individuate. Resolving and discarding the need to fight over the same old issues is usually a prime therapeutic goal for couples seeking long-term marital therapy. Being liberated from same-old-issue arguments leads to a more mature, spiritual, and supportive relationship.

Therapeutic strategies for resolving same-old-issue arguments include family-of-origin sessions, sharing family-of-origin experiences with the spouse, developing safety cues and safety hatches to signal the onset of such an argument or a predetermined way of ending such an argument, and chiseling out philosophical, shared resolutions to the "real" issues behind such arguments.

ANGER AND VIOLENCE

Lack of anger management skills is directly related to violence between couples. And physical violence is much more frequent than commonly

THERAPEUTIC INTERVENTION 11:
SCRIPTING NEW ROUTINES

Many couples have fought so often for so long over so many topics that they are resistant to using the positive verbal strokes they use in their everyday life outside of the marriage. For them, the therapist might need to help script new routines.

Chronically angry couples have usually gone a long time without saying anything expressively supportive, tender, or revealing to each other. Leslie Greenberg (1988), in his emotionally focused therapy, suggests using "verbal experiments" that promote contact between the partners, to re-experience deeper, fuller levels of emotional expressiveness. For me, these verbal experiments entail scripting new verbal routines for the partners.

The scripting procedure involves accessing the emotional experience underlying interactional positions. If a husband is sexually approaching his wife only in the middle of the night, his emotional experience might be fear of rejection if he approached her when they were both fully conscious. To see if this "fits," the therapist instructs the husband to look at his wife and say, "I'm afraid of your sexual rejection." He may have to say it several times, with coaching, looking at his wife eyeball to eyeball. He then is given the time and space to reflect on what, if anything, he felt when he was saying those words. If the words did not evoke any emotions, did alternative explanations or words come to mind during this period? If the words did evoke strong emotions, what type of symbolic image could capture that feeling? Perhaps it will be an image of a dying star or two lions in heat but in separate cages. Recently, I had a verbally abusive female client who, after she told her husband, "I deserve to be able to depend on you," said she had a vision of herself as being the planet Earth without gravity. Her husband immediately said, "I was pulled into another galaxy by an unknown force. Don't worry. I'm going home to anchor our lives again." Obviously, a rare, but wonderful, therapeutic moment.

Many vulnerable and tender statements can be potent when working with angry couples. Consider the following high-powered scripts: "I miss you." "I'm afraid that I need you too much." "I'm afraid of you." "I hide when I am with you and that makes me sad and angry." "I disagree." "I need space." "I need someone to hold me and reassure me." Therapist empathy can guide the therapist to find the right script. The question for the therapist is, "If I were in this marriage, acting this angry, what would I really be feeling or experiencing?"

assumed. In fact, many, many couples who are in therapy work on a variety of issues without ever penetrating and dealing with the violence that occurs in the marriage. Mostly, this happens because therapists have not directly assessed for the frequency and intensity of violence in the relationship or they have used inadequate screening measures. In a study of couples entering couples therapy, O'Leary, Vivian, and Malone (1992) found that only 1.5 percent of the husbands and 6.0 percent of the wives listed physical aggression as a presenting problem on an intake question- naire. However, 46 percent of the husbands and 44 percent of the wives (or 56 percent of the couples) indicated that physical abuse or violence was occurring when asked in an individual interview. Thus, every couple needs to be queried about when violence occurs and how it is handled. The following discussion leans toward the more severe types of marital abuse, but the concepts are equally applicable to the whole spectrum of violence that occurs between couples.

Physical, Verbal, and Psychological Abuse

The National Coalition Against Domestic Violence defines battering as:

> a pattern of behavior with the effect of establishing power and control over another person through fear and intimidation. . . . Battering hap- pens when batterers believe they are entitled to control their partners, when violence is permissible, when violence will produce the desired effect or prevent a worse one, and when the benefits outweigh the consequences. (Landes, Siegel, and Foster, 1993, p. 111)

Thus, battering includes not only physical assaults but psychological, emotional, economic, and sexual abuse. It also extends to behaviors de- signed to produce fear, isolation, intimidation, and control. It can vary from having one's pet tortured to having personal possessions damaged and even to being shot and killed.

In an ideal society, spousal abuse would be considered totally unaccept- able at all times. There are many cultural factors in the United States, however, that promote abuse, including inequality at home and at work, low self-esteem, abuse of alcohol and drugs, personality disorders, and historical and religious traditions that subordinate women. And, unfortu- nately, many subgroups of Americans still openly condone and promote the subjugation of women (Chin, 1994).

Of course, the taboo nature of abuse has not been associated with a low incidence of occurrence. Verbal, psychological, sexual, and physical abuse are fairly common in American homes. Severe, repeated violence may occur in as many as one in fourteen marriages (Dutton, 1988). Statman (1990) reports that there are more cases of marital violence in the United States each year than there are muggings, rapes, and car accidents com- bined. Also, male-instigated marital violence tends to escalate over time, both in frequency and intensity (Walker, 1989). Avis (1992) reported that an average of thirty-five incidents occurs before a woman seeks protection from the legal system. Indeed, women are in most danger of being killed by their husbands after they separate from them (Walker, 1989).

The focus of most domestic violence programs has been on treating men because their physical violence is far more likely to result in physical injury to the wife. Most men who are assaulted by their wives do not report the assault and do not perceive the assault as damaging.

There is great debate over whether one gender is more responsible for provoking violence. Straus's (1994) analysis of the 1985 National Family Violence Survey of Women indicated that gender was not a significant factor in predicting who provoked the initial violence: The husband was the only violent partner in 25.9 percent of the cases, the wife was the only violent partner in 25.5 percent of the cases, and both were violent in 48.6 percent of the cases. Even looking at severe assaults that include punching, kicking, and attacking with weapons, the results were similar: Wives were the sole provokers 29.6 percent of the time, husbands were the sole provokers 35.2 percent of the time, and both were provokers 35.2 percent of the time. Although it is possible that among couples in which both were assaulted, the wife was acting in self-defense the majority of the time, we must still deal with the observation that domestic violence is perpetuated by women as well as by men. Straus collected his data using the Conflicts Tactics Scale, a self-report measure that asks the frequency of using nineteen different behaviors, which vary on a violence continuum, when resolving conflicts in intimate relationships. The behaviors range from the use of reasoning and discussion (three items) to the use of verbal threats or insults (six items) to minor physical violence such as slapping and pushing (four items) to major physical violence, including beating up the partner or using a weapon to injure the partner (six items).

However, recent work has criticized Straus, Gelles, and Steinmetz's (1980) reliance on paper-and-pencil questionnaires as a way of assessing symmetry in marital violence (Dobash et al., 1992). After all, the motives, meaning, context, and consequences of violence are essential in understanding the phenomena (e.g., a wife who shoots her husband after he tries to rape her is qualitatively different from a husband who shoots his wife for talking to an old boyfriend).

Recent research tends to confirm that male aggression is usually the primary problem. Jacobson and colleagues (1994) have studied one group of violent husbands in a more contextual format and have found the wife to be the real victim in nearly all cases. On the basis of self-reports of violent arguments, they found that once the argument began, there were no wife behaviors that could successfully suppress husband violence and the husband's violence escalated independent of whether or not the wife was violent. The wife escalated in violence only in response to the husband's emotional abuse or increased physical violence.

It appears that a significant distinction also needs to be made between mild acts of violence (e.g., shoving, grabbing, slapping) and severe acts of violence (e.g., hitting, punching, striking) (Pan, Neidig, and O'Leary, 1994). In about half of all general marital clinic cases, mild violence is evident when directly assessed, although even here the wives report a more negative psychological impact from such violence than do the husbands (Vivian and Langhinrichsen-Rohling, 1994). However, severe violence appears to be a unilateral process in which wives are more likely to be "highly" victimized than are husbands. These cases represent 30 percent to 40 percent of the general marital cases seen at the clinic where the study was conducted. Like Jacobson and colleagues (1994), Vivian and Langhinrichsen-Rohling found that women tend to use severe physical aggression in self-defense, when they are the target of physical aggression and coercion (including sexual coercion). Husbands tend to use physical aggression as a way of forcing their agenda (Cascardi, Langhinrichsen, and Vivian, 1992; Langhinrichsen-Rohling, Neidig, and Thorn, 1995).

Male violence is a greater social problem, if for no other reason than that it does result in far more severe and frequent physical and psychological injury. Consider that police records show that over 90 percent of all violent crimes between spouses were directed at women by husbands or ex-husbands, whereas only 5 percent were directed at husbands by wives or ex-wives (cited in Kurz, 1994). The wide discrepancy between survey data and data obtained from the legal system attests to the devastating effects of male violence. This observation must be tempered by the recognition that police have a strong bias to arrest the male even when the female is the perpetrator or the male has more significant injuries.

Most men who physically abuse their wives have clinically identifiable personality disorders and show symptoms of depression. They appear to have many of the irrational beliefs described previously, circulating unconsciously in their brain, like a never-ending CD. The personality picture that emerges of the "typical batterer" is someone who demands unconditional love and approval. While this is a general trait, it particularly increases with his partner. He is often oversensitive to any rejection or criticism by his partner. He may develop blaming and irrational beliefs, overgeneralizing from small instances of carelessness on his spouse's part. He may find it necessary to rectify his wife's "insulting" behavior by blowing up to "teach her who is boss." This angry, controlling outburst only causes the wife to be more rejecting. Hence, a repetitive cycle begins that ultimately causes the relationship to deteriorate, resulting in an abyss of negative cognitions, affects, and behaviors (Lohr, Hamberger, and Bonge, 1988).

This classic picture of a batterer reveals a man with low self-esteem and high power needs, someone who demands perfection from himself and perfect loyalty from his spouse. The disappointment of unfulfilled dreams and expectations makes these men lose self-respect and feel as though they will be failures forever. The batterer blames his wife for his situation and feels justified, though guilty, about his abuse. Although Lohr and colleagues are undoubtedly describing one prominent type of batterer, researchers in domestic violence are researching other relevant types of abusers. For example, Hamberger and Hastings (1986) found three personality disorders prevalent among the men attending a domestic violence abatement program. They were schizoid-borderline, narcissistic-antisocial, and possessive-dependent-compulsive. Each personality type would probably respond to a different type of therapeutic intervention.

Some researchers have tried to develop predictive models of spousal physical aggression. The best predictor is, not surprisingly, a history of physical violence. Marital violence exists on a continuum, however, and victims of less extreme forms of violence (verbal aggression and shoving) are statistically at risk for more extreme forms of violence over the course of time. Conversely, couples who have been extremely violent with one another nearly always engage in the less extreme forms of violence as well (Sugarman, Aldarondo, and Boney-McCoy, 1996). This points out how important it is to treat minor forms of marital violence as serious lapses of control that will not be tolerated.

Other significant predictive factors of marital violence include a general history and acceptance of aggressive behavior: witnessing parental violence as a child, living with an aggressive partner, and severe relationship conflicts (O'Leary, 1993). Additional research indicates that youth, having a low income, alcohol and drug problems in either spouse, marital conflict, and depressive symptomatology in either spouse all significantly increase the risk of physical aggression in a marriage (Pan, Neidig, and O'Leary 1994; Sugarman et al., 1996). Like many suggested "causes" of marital violence, factors such as depression, alcoholism, and marital conflict can also be conceptualized as the "results" or "effects" of marital violence.

In addition, keep in mind that when using checklists to "tag" potentially abusive couples, the frequency of violence appears to capture the problem more than the most severe incident reported. Thus, a couple who reports frequent pushing and cursing of each other is more likely in need of treatment for marital violence than a couple who reports no violence whatsoever, except one slap that recently occurred during a heated argument (Hamby, Poindexter, and Grey-Little, 1996).

The Michigan Coalition Against Domestic Violence (1988) lists seventeen high-risk behaviors that therapists can use to assess the likelihood that a client spouse is abusive or at risk for being abusive. The clinical signs deepen the research findings and include the following:

1. Jealousy (a sign of possessiveness and lack of trust)
2. Controlling behavior (such as time away from home, money, friends, etc.)
3. Quick involvement (marriage was a whirlwind romance, impulsive job decisions, etc.)
4. Unrealistic expectations
5. Isolation (cuts spouse off from friends and family)
6. Blames others for problems
7. Blames others for feelings (makes women feel responsible for his happiness)
8. Hypersensitivity (easily insulted)
9. Cruelty to animals or children
10. "Playful" use of force in sex
11. Verbal abuse
12. Rigid sex roles
13. Dr. Jekyll and Mr. Hyde (sudden changes in personality and mood)
14. Past battering
15. Threats of violence
16. Breaking or striking objects
17. Any force during an argument

Ideally, women who are physically abused need to (1) physically leave the home, and (2) not return until the husband is successfully engaged in a treatment program and the couple is in marital therapy.

Psychological Entrapment and Abused Women

Although in cases of extreme physical abuse, women may, at times, turn to sheltered housing, nearly half will return to their abusive spouses. Of those who return home, over half will be beaten by their husbands again within a short time period (Landes, Siegel, and Foster, 1993). Because so many women are abused by men, the question becomes, "Why don't they leave?" "Doesn't staying in an abusive situation indicate collusion with the arrangement?"

To understand why women stay in abusive situations, it is important to consider four questions.

What Are the Consequences of the Spousal Violence?

Although the long-term consequences are devastating for the couple, in the short term, a period of violence usually cycles with a period of extreme remorse and regret, a honeymoon period in which the relationship is all "lovey-dovey." This honeymoon effect serves to reinforce the violent episode and makes the abused partner hope that if only she or he can "learn how to keep the partner in a good mood," violence can be avoided.

How Much Has the Woman Invested in the Relationship and What Have Been the Outcomes of Those Investments?

All individuals must invest both time and energy in a marriage. However, as marital conflicts arise, individuals can choose to put varying degrees of energy into resolving specific problems. Some spouses choose their battles so carefully that very few conflicts propel them into a resolution mode. For others, each disagreement is the occasion for long, persistent attempts at persuasion and negotiation. Research by Bauserman and Arias (1992) has shown that abused wives are more likely than nonabused wives to be committed to staying in the marriage when they feel that they are investing energy to try to solve their problems. Even though the problems persist, up to a point, effort reinforces and justifies continued effort. Through the phenomenon of "effort justification," these women are "entrapped" in the marriage by their own efforts to improve it. When they are giving so much and getting so little back, they need to justify their effort by clinging to the overall importance of the relationship.

How Optimistic Is She That Her Partner Will Change?

When women are caught in the entrapment cycle, they need to keep increasing their efforts to the point that they are willing to see the futility of their efforts. They need to try solutions that are costly in terms of time and energy. Then, they need to evaluate the success or failure of those attempted solutions. When a women has repeatedly put high-cost effort into marital solutions and failed, she becomes motivated to leave the relationship. It is as though high-cost efforts that result in failure break down the optimistic expectation that the relationship will eventually change for the better once a person tries hard enough. If the woman halfheartedly just tries

to "keep the peace" and smooth things out on a daily basis, effort justification and entrapment are more likely.

Indeed, Bauserman and Arias (1992) found that abused women's commitment decreased as their failed efforts increased. Thus, entrapment is
more likely to occur when the costs are low. Abused women who made
occasional failed efforts at conflict resolution may be more committed to
their marriages because the costs of staying in the marriage may appear
less salient.

What Are the Alternatives to Living with Her Husband?

Understandably, women with workable housing alternatives are far
more likely to leave an abusive husband than those who are trapped with
no place to go. When parents live nearby and are receptive to helping, the
woman is more likely to leave. If the woman has the financial resources to
get her own place, her desire to leave can become a reality. If she is able to
care for her children successfully, without her husband, she is still more
likely to leave.

Even when a women resists moving out, therapists should provide them
with the telephone number of the National Domestic Violence Hotline:
1-800-333-SAFE. This group can direct victims to their closest shelter and
provide critical support in a crisis.

Research on Treatment of Marital Violence

Although abuse tends to be a recurring problem, in a significant minor-
ity of cases, marital violence spontaneously ceases (Margolin and Fernandez, 1987). Indeed, in a three-year longitudinal study of 772 nonclinical
couples, more than one-third of the men who had been violent in the year

---

**THERAPEUTIC INTERVENTION 12:
PROGRAMS FOR ABUSIVE SPOUSES**

First, Control the Violence

When couples are physically, verbally, or psychologically violent with
each other, this becomes the first and primary focus of treatment. Sometimes, it is difficult to persuade the couple that nonviolence should be the
first therapeutic goal. Treatments for abusive spouses generally concur
that it is critical to have a period of supportive confrontation if one or both
spouses deny the importance of the abuse. The confrontation consists of
exposing the abuser to the reported history of abuse and the crisis nature
of the current situation.

(continued)

(continued)

When violence is ongoing, particularly if it is used to subjugate and control the partner, the couple must be seen separately in therapy. Aggressive partners must take responsibility for their behavior and must get to the point where they are motivated to control themselves. Unfortunately, all too often, men who batter feel that "the bitch deserved it." With this mind-set, violence is destined to recur. Breaking this belief pattern has proven to be enormously difficult (see treatment discussion below).

Women need to be seen separately, also, at this point, to help them seek protective services if they desire them, and to prevent "paybacks" for speaking honestly within the session. When a wife has separated and is trying to keep her whereabouts a secret, joint sessions can lead to stalking by the husband and put the woman in extreme danger.

When violence is ongoing and puts the spouse in imminent risk of losing her life or well-being, the therapist has a legal responsibility to report the problem to the police. This is true regardless of the women's desire to minimize the problem or protect her mate. Therapists need to keep detailed notes of their recommendations and actions to make sure that they are not liable for failure-to-warn malpractice suits.

Researchers are still trying to ascertain at what point conjoint couples' treatment is most appropriate. However, at a minimum, it seems necessary that both individuals feel comfortable with conjoint treatment, that the woman is not fearful of speaking her mind in front of her mate, and that neither partner has an active alcohol or drug abuse problem or an active bipolar or psychotic disorder that is not controlled by medication.

Therapeutic Intervention 12a: Assessing Violence. Walker (1989) suggests exploring the following three scenarios with all victims of abuse:

- Describe the first time your spouse was violent.
- Describe a typical episode when your spouse gets violent.
- Describe the worst episode of when your spouse was violent.

Besides assessing if the violence has been escalating, the therapist becomes more aware of the range and character of the abuse.

Therapeutic Intervention 12b: Creating a Safety Plan. When working with women or men in danger of extreme abuse, it is important to help them develop a "safety plan" that will allow them to leave the house when they feel threatened and before any violence erupts. Usually, a safety plan has the following ingredients: (1) having an extra set of keys to the car that are hidden and accessible, (2) having some extra money, (3) knowing where one can go (which hotel, relative, friend, etc.), (4) having a plan for keeping the children safe, (5) having friends or neighbors whom one can call who can come over on short notice, and (6) knowing who to call after arriving at the designated safety point. The safety plan empowers the victim and provides short-term protection until a more basic solution is in place.

(continued)

(continued)

Next, Confront the Alcohol and Drug Use

The national epidemic of drug use and alcohol abuse is permanently intertwined with the epidemic of marital violence. In a tragically illuminating study (Stith, Crossman, and Bischof, 1991) thirty-nine men who were enrolled in a batterer program were compared to fifty-two men enrolled in an alcohol treatment program. The two groups were virtually indistinguishable. Of the batterers, 64 percent were alcoholics, and 59 percent of the alcoholics were batterers. The two groups were virtually alike in terms of level of marital stress, level of sex role egalitarianism, and history of childhood violence. The overwhelming overlap between the two groups strongly suggests that all treatment programs for batterers address substance abuse problems and that all alcohol programs address family violence issues.

Indeed, programs that address both issues have reported some success. O'Farrell and Choquette (1991) found that before a spouse-involved alcohol treatment program, both the husbands and wives in their study were reporting violence rates five times as prevalent as the national norm on the Conflicts Tactics Scale. One year after treatment, the wives' scores were no different from the national norm and the husbands' use of violence was now only twice as frequent as that reported in the national norm.

Then, Work on the Relationship

When the violence is under control, conjoint therapy is increasingly the treatment of choice. This is a controversial recommendation, and there are many therapists who believe that if there is any physical violence in a relationship, the violent partner must be held legally responsible, the victim protected, and remediation done only on the violent individual. They believe it is inappropriate to ever reframe violence as an interaction problem treatable by couples therapy. Yet if a couple is going to stay married, therapy will be much more successful if it addresses the violence in context as well as individual dynamics.

Of course, in the sessions, strong emotions can be easily triggered. Then, abusive behavior can erupt within the session. This is never, to my knowledge, a positive experience. To help prevent violence within a session, many therapists have ground rules that permit and encourage clients to leave the office if feelings become too intense.

prior to the initial survey ceased or interrupted their violence and showed concomitant reductions in their use of psychological aggression (e.g., verbal insults and threats) during that time. This same study found that over half of the men who had been violent in the first year of the study were involved in either persistent or inconsistent patterns of wife assault.

None of the men in this study were given any treatment for their violent behavior (Aldarondo, 1996).

Although the most recent comprehensive review of treatment effectiveness suggests that we have not yet devised a singularly effective treatment (Rosenfeld, 1992), many individual treatment evaluation findings indicate that programs that deal with issues of power, family dynamics, communication patterns, and problem-solving techniques hold promise for motivated couples (Harrell, 1991; Petrick, Petrick, and Subotnik, 1993). With both treatment and legal interventions, surveys indicate that approximately one half of marital violence can be significantly reduced over a three-year period (Woffordt, Mihalic, and Menard, 1994).

Even more dramatic success rates have been reported by the Institute for Family Services in Somerset, New Jersey, where 75 percent of all court-mandated clients who complete the program never repeat the same offense (Wylie, 1996). Although many argue that rigorous outcome studies have not been conducted on this program, it has a unique combination of therapeutic components that merit increased attention. The institute's program relies almost entirely on a group therapy format with open communication and no privileged information. Many laypeople (former clients, mostly) serve as sponsors and cotherapists, much like in the AA model of treatment, although individual sponsors are not assigned, to foster reliance on the community instead of a single person. Most striking is that the program relies heavily on a strident political advocacy program that educates the men about the use of power in our society. Men are guided into this area by exploring topics such as how their partner communications are shaped by male-female power differentials just like their communications with their boss are shaped by boss-employee power differentials. This didactic feminist message is delivered in the context of highly emotional and honest male-bonding relationships.

Last, the role of the legal system in preventing abuse has also been studied. Some research indicates that being arrested is a strong deterrent to recurring abuse, even if charges are not pressed. Similarly, Rosenfeld (1992) found that differences in recidivism rates between subjects in treatment and those just arrested and detained were quite small.

LEARNING AIDS

Therapeutic Dialogue (Anger)

Therapists working with angry, married clients should explore the following areas:

1. Ideally, how would each partner like to handle his or her angry feelings?
2. Ideally, how would each partner like to cope with the other's anger?
3. What are the interactions and situations in the marriage that make the client angry?
4. What are the interactions and situations in most people's marriages that make them angry?
5. What are the similarities and differences between your client's situation and the average couple he or she knows?
6. What are the coping options available to the client when he or she is angry?
7. What are the successful coping mechanisms used by people close to the client in similar situations?
8. What can the client do to create more options for how to handle anger?
9. How were angry feelings dealt with in the husband's family as a child?
10. How were angry feelings dealt with in the wife's family as a child?
11. How does the client think the average family he or she knows handles angry feelings in the family? What constructive solutions has he or she seen in other families?
12. What can the couple do in their interactions with each other to broaden the options available to them when they are angry?
13. How realistic are each of the ideal images of handling anger? How can the ideal image be modified to make it more attainable?

Self-Exploration 1: Partner Anger Inventory

Rate all questions on the following scale:

0	1	2	3	4	5
Not at all		Moderately angry		Extremely angry	

(Add any additional items that get you angry and are not on this list. Be sure to rate them on the same scale.)

1. How angry do you get when discussing money issues with your partner?
2. How angry do you get when your partner questions you about your feelings?
3. How angry do you get when you feel your mate is acting silly or immature?

4. How angry do you get when your partner is disappointed with you?
5. How angry do you get when your partner has an advantage or an easier time because of his or her gender?
6. How angry do you get when he or she is intolerant of your short-comings?
7. How angry do you get about the differences in your salaries?
8. How angry do you get if your partner doesn't consult you before making a big decision?
9. How angry do you get when the kids are acting up?
10. How angry do you get when your partner goes someplace without you?
11. How angry do you get if you have to watch the children while your partner goes out?
12. How angry do you get when your partner's friends or family intrude on your privacy?
13. How angry do you get when chores are not done on time?
14. How angry do you get when your mate appears to enjoy someone else's company more than yours?
15. How angry do you get when the house isn't clean?
16. How angry do you get if your partner seeks out other people's opinions rather than yours?
17. How angry would you get if your mate was unfaithful to you?
18. How angry do you get when your mate drinks too much?
19. How angry do you get when you see your partner reaching his or her goals quicker than you are reaching yours?
20. How angry do you get when family or friends side with your partner instead of you?
21. How angry do you get about how your mate dresses?
22. How angry do you get when you are asked to do additional chores?
23. How angry do you get about demands for communication?
24. How angry do you get about demands for sex?
25. How angry do you get about the tone of voice used by your partner?
26. How angry do you get when your mate embarrasses you?
27. How angry do you get when she or he points out your mistakes?
28. How angry do you get when your mate spends money without telling you?
29. How angry do you get when your partner implies that you are not doing enough for him or her?
30. How angry do you get when your partner openly disagrees with you in public?

31. How angry do you get when your partner does not cooperate with you?
32. How angry do you get when your partner ignores you and pays attention to the children?
33. How angry do you get when you are feeling ill?
34. How angry do you get when she or he gets angry at you?

To determine your overall level of anger, add up all your scores and divide by 34 (or the total number of items if you added your own). If, for example, your total score was 102, your mean score would be: $102 \div 34 = 3$. This score would indicate that you are generally "moderately angry" with your partner.

Then, compare your average score with your partner's average score (adjusting for any added items). Next, discuss each item with a rating of 3 or greater, explaining why you get angry in that situation. When your partner is explaining his or her ratings, do not comment on what your spouse is feeling or defend yourself. You may, however, ask two questions: "Would you tell me more about it?" and "How could I realistically change to make it easier for you and me to deal with this particular situation?"

Self-Exploration 2: Marital Effort Scale

It is often helpful to ask spouses in anger-ridden or abusive relationships how much energy they put into trying to solve or prevent marital problems related to each of the following areas. Items are rated on a 5-point scale on which 1 = no effort, 2 = some effort, 3 = moderate effort, 4 = large effort, and 5 = very large effort.

1. Participating in decisions about spending money
2. Household chores
3. Paying attention to his or her appearance
4. Having meals ready on time
5. Keeping family members out of your affairs
6. Hitting each other
7. Screaming at each other
8. Getting together with his or her friends for the night
9. Getting together with my friends for an evening or afternoon
10. Frequency of sex
11. Looking too attractive
12. Not looking attractive enough
13. Getting the children to behave
14. Problems with in-laws

15 Working too much
16. Watching TV
17. Sleeping too much
18. Spending time with the children
19. Agreeing on disciplining strategies
20. Deciding what to do on holidays or with leisure time

Add any other items that represent areas in which enormous effort is being expended to make the marriage work.

Couples who are doing this exploration need to compare their scores, item by item. There is no logical way to "add up" the items and get a total score. Rather, any item with a rating of 3 or greater is important to discuss. Is this an area where more effort or a different type of effort is needed? What are the costs and benefits of the current strategies being used to effect change? Are there totally new ways to go about asking for or motivating a change? Perhaps this is an area in which change is very unlikely and one needs to concentrate on increasing his or her own tolerance levels.

Sample Workshop Flowchart Intended for Groups of Four or Five Couples Working with Anger

I. Psychoeducational Strategies
  A. Explaining the difference between the two heads of anger: self-imposed anger and retaliatory anger
  B. The role of self-talk in creating self-imposed anger
    1. The illusion of fusion inevitably leads to frustration and anger.
    2. Desynchronicities and gender differences between spouses provoke anger.
    3. Jealousy provokes anger.
    4. Control needs provoke anger.
    5. Time demands and fatigue provoke anger.
    6. Shame provokes anger.
  C. The role of spouse-provoked or retaliatory anger provokers
    1. Criticism
    2. Historical attacks
    3. Neglect
    4. Passive-aggressive actions
    5. Emotional constrictiveness
  D. The cycle of physical, verbal, or psychological abuse

II. Self-Explorations (Done by couples in private and shared before re-joining the group)

III. Therapeutic Dialogue (Done by couples in private and shared before rejoining the group)
(Proceeding in the order presented, both partners respond to each question before going on to discuss the next question.)
In group, the therapist explores with couples how relationship goals can be achieved by modifying overly ambitious, pie-in-the-sky expectations. Using information about their current situation and the realities seen among friends and family, couples fine-tune expectations so that they are achievable and motivate rather than discourage attempts at change.

IV. Therapeutic Interventions
Work with a couple in front of the group and apply one or more of the therapeutic interventions. Share rationale during demonstrations. Let group discuss additional interventions.
A. Changing irrational thoughts
B. Clarifying couple differences and prioritizing areas of change
C. Maximizing motivation to make partner-pleasing changes
D. Working through jealousies and the meaning of noncouple activities and interests
E. Explaining and planning a behavioral exchange
F. Learning how to deal with criticism
G. Responding to historical attacks
H. Developing insight into destructive methods of responding to anger
I. Using the love letter technique
J. Changing nonverbal communication
K. Scripting new routines
L. Entering programs for abusive persons

V. Finding Motivation and Time to Make the Changes
Group discussion

Bibliotherapy

Borcherdt, B. (1989). *Think straight! Feel great! 21 guides to emotional self-control.* Sarasota, FL: Professional Resource Exchange.
Dotty, B. (1994). *One hundred things we can do about anger and violence.* Reading, CA: Bookery.
Lerner, H. (1985). *Dance of anger.* New York: Harper and Row.

Statman, J. (1990). *The battered women's survival guide: Breaking the cycle.* Dallas, TX: Taylor.

Videotherapy

Scenes from a Marriage. (1973). Directed by Ingmar Bergman. A probing and honest look at the frustrations of marriage.
Shoot the Moon. (1982). Directed by Alan Parker. A story of marital infidelity and what went wrong.
War of the Roses. (1989). Directed by Danny DeVito. A dark comedy about the extremes of marital anger and revenge.
Who's Afraid of Virginia Woolf? (1966). Directed by Mike Nichols. Angry, bitter conversations between couples who are unable to forgive, forget, and move on.

Professional Development Questions (Anger)

1. Can you think of a potent metaphor or simile that would help couples graphically understand the effect that "self-imposed anger" or "retaliatory anger" has on a marital relationship?

2. Make your own list of irrational expectations that couples have for each other and that provoke "self-imposed anger." Go over the list with a couple and see how many of the items are arguably "rational" things to be upset about from another person's perspective.

3. What is the best way to respond to anger in a spouse? How can the recipients of spousal anger learn to calm their partners without being abused? What is the best way for a therapist to work with this problem?

4. How can a therapist assess the presence of spouse abuse? What is the best way to present a treatment plan to the couple that will reduce psychological, verbal, or physical abuse? Do you believe that it is best to treat the abusive partner separately or as a couple?

REFERENCES

Aldarondo, E. (1996). Cessation and persistence of wife assault: A longitudinal analysis. *American Journal of Orthopsychiatry, 66*(1), 141-151.

Avis, J. (1992). Where are all the family therapists? Abuse and violence within families and family therapy's response. *Journal of Marital and Family Therapy, 18*(3), 225-232.

Bauserman, S. and Arias, I. (1992). Relationships among marital investment, marital satisfaction, and marital commitment in domestically victimized and nonvictimized wives. *Violence and Victims, 7*(4), 287-296.

Berns, S., Jacobson, N. and Gottman, J. (1999). Demand-withdraw interaction in couples with a violent husband. *Journal of Consulting and Clinical Psychology, 67*(5), 666-674.

Bradbury, T. and Fincham, F. (1993). Assessing dysfunctional cognitions in marriage: A reconsideration of the Relational Belief Inventory. *Psychological Assessment, 5*(1), 92-101.

Buss, D. (1991). Conflict in married couples: Personality predictors of anger and upset. *Journal of Personality, 59*(4), 663-688.

Buss, D. (1994). *The evolution of desire: Strategies of human mating.* New York: HarperCollins.

Buss, D. M., Larsen, R. J., Westen, D., and Semmelroth, J. (1992). Sex differences in jealousy: Evolution, physiology, and psychology. *Psychological Science, 3,* 212-233.

Cascardi, M., Langhinrichsen, J., and Vivian, D. (1992). Marital aggression: Impact, injury, and health correlated for husbands and wives. *Archives of Internal Medicine, 152*(6), 1178-1184.

Chin, K. (1994). Out-of-town-brides: International marriage and wife abuse among Chinese immigrants. Special issue: Family violence. *Journal of Comparative Family Studies, 25*(1), 53-69.

Dobash, R. E., Dobash, R. P., Wilson, M., and Daly, M. (1992). The myth of sexual symmetry in marital violence. *Social Problems, 39*(1), 71-91.

Dutton, D. (1988). *The domestic assault of women: Psychological and criminal justice perspectives.* Toronto: Allyn & Bacon.

Epstein, N. (1986). Cognitive marital therapy: Multilevel assessment and intervention. Special issue: Rational-emotive couples. *Therapy, 4*(1), 68-81.

Evatt, C. (1992). *He and she: 60 significant differences between men and women.* Berkeley, CA: Conari.

Gallagher, C. (1978). *Love is a couple.* New York: Doubleday (Image Books).

Gottman, J. and Krokoff, L. (1989). Marital interaction and satisfaction: A longitudinal view. *Journal of Consulting and Clinical Psychology, 57*(1), 47-52.

Gray, J. (1992). *Men are from Mars, women are from Venus: A practical guide for improving communication and getting what you want in your relationship* (First edition). New York: HarperCollins.

Greenberg, L. (1988). *Emotionally focused therapy for couples.* New York: Guilford.

Hamberger, L. and Hastings, J. (1986). Personality correlates of men who abuse their partners: A cross-sectional validation study. *Journal of Family Violence, 1*(4), 323-341.

Hamby, S., Poindexter, V., and Grey-Little, B. (1996). Four measures of partner violence: Construct similarity and classification differences. *Journal of Marriage and the Family, 58*(1), 127-139.

Harrell, A. (1991). Evaluation of court ordered treatment for domestic violence offenders. Prepared for the State Justice Institute, Miami, FL.

Jacobson, N., Gottman, J., Waltz, J., and Rushe, R. (1994). Affect, verbal content, and psychophysiology in the arguments of couples with a violent husband. *Journal of Consulting and Clinical Psychology, 62*(5), 982-988.

Krokoff, L. (1991). Communication orientation as a moderator between strong negative affect and marital satisfaction. Special issue: Negative communication in marital interaction: A misnomer? *Behavioral Assessment, 13*(10), 51-65.

Kurz, D. (1994). Physical assaults by husbands: A major social problem. In R. Gelles and D. Loseke (Eds.), *Current controversies on family violence* (pp. 88-104). Thousand Oaks, CA: Sage.

Landes, A. B., Siegel, M. A., and Foster, C. D. (Eds.). (1993). *The information series on current topics: Domestic violence, no longer behind the curtains.* Wylie, TX: Information Plus.

Langhinrichsen-Rohling, J., Neidig, P., and Thorn, G. (1995). Violent marriages: Gender differences in levels of current violence and past abuse. *Journal of Family Violence, 10*(2), 159-176.

Lloyd, S. (1990). Conflict types and strategies in violent marriages. *Journal of Family Violence, 5*(4), 269-284.

Lohr, J. M., Hamberger, L. K., and Bonge, D. (1988). The nature of irrational beliefs in different personality clusters of spouse abusers. *Journal of Rational-Emotive and Cognitive-Behavior Therapy, 6*(4), 273-285.

Margolin, G. and Fernandez, V. (1987). The "spontaneous" cessation of marital violence: Three case examples. *Journal of Marital and Family Therapy, 13*(3), 241-250.

Michigan Coalition Against Domestic Violence. (1988). [Unpublished raw data.]

Miller, G. 1999. Psychosocial mechanisms of natural killer cell mobilization during marital conflict. Dissertation Abstracts International Section B: The Science and Engineering. Vol 59(9-B): 5100

O'Leary, K. D. (1993). Controversies regarding psychological explanations of family violence. In R. Gelles and D. Loseke (Eds.), *Current controversies in family violence.* Newbury Park, CA: Sage.

O'Leary, K. D., Vivian, D., and Malone, J. (1992). Assessment of physical aggression in marriage: The need for a multimodal method. *Behavioral Assessment, 14*(1), 5-14.

Pan, H., Neidig, P., and O'Leary, K. (1994). Predicting mild and severe husband-to-wife physical aggression. *Journal of Consulting and Clinical Psychology, 62*(5), 975-981.

Petrick, N. D., Petrick, R. E., and Subotnik, L. S. (1993). The prediction of completion of treatment for male abusers: A pilot study. *Family Violence and Sexual Assault Bulletin, 9*(2), 20-27.

Pittman, F. (1989). *Private lies: Infidelity and the betrayal of intimacy.* New York: Norton.

Pool, R. (1994). *Eve's Rib: Searching for the biological roots of sex differences.* New York: Crown.

Rosenfeld, B. D. (1992). Court ordered treatment of spouse abuse. *Clinical Psychology Review, 12*(2), 205-226.

Statman, J. (1990). *The battered women's survival guide: Breaking the cycle.* Dallas, TX: Taylor.

Straus, M. (1994). Physical assaults by wives: A major social problem. In R. Gelles and D. Loseke (Eds.), *Current controversies on family violence* (pp. 67-88). Thousand Oaks, CA: Sage.

Straus, M., Gelles, R., and Steinmetz, S. (1980). *Behind closed doors: Violence in the American family.* New York: Doubleday.

Stuart, R. (1980). *Helping couples change: A social learning approach to marital therapy.* New York: Guilford.

Sugarman, D., Aldarondo, E., and Boney-McCoy, S. (1996). Risk marker analysis of husband-to-wife violence: A continuum of aggression. *Journal of Applied Social Psychology, 26*(4), 313-337.

Tannen, D. (1990). *You just don't understand: Men and women in conversation.* New York: William Morrow.

Vivian, D., and Langhinrichsen-Rohling, J. (1994). Are bidirectionally violent couples mutually victimized? A gender sensitive comparison. *Violence and Victims, 9*(2), 107-124.

Walker, L. (1984). *The battered women syndrome.* New York: Springer.

Walker, L. (1989). Psychology and violence against women. *American Psychologist, 44*(4), 695-702.

Weisinger, H., and Lobsenz, N. (1981). *Nobody's perfect: How to give criticism and get results.* New York: Stratford.

Woffordt, S., Mihalic, D., and Menard, S. (1994). Continuities in marital violence. *Journal of Family Violence, 9*(3), 195-225.

Wylie, M. S. (1996). It's a community affair. *Networker,* (March-April), pp. 58-66.

Chapter 2

Depression and the Couple Relationship

> The great thing about marriage is that it enables one to be alone without feeling loneliness.
>
> Gerald Brennan

Clinically depressed people find it hard, if not impossible, to be giving, involved, and fun spouses. They are also unresponsive to their partners' efforts to provide them with comfort and reassurance. The lack of energy, interest, and optimism associated with a depressive episode is very stressful to a marriage. The relationship is increasingly stressed the longer the depression lasts and the more severe the depression. Most marriages with a depressed partner have more than their share of marital problems that can be traced directly to the depression.

On the other hand, unhappy, distressed relationships can provoke a clinical depression in one or both of the partners. Thus, an emotionally unsatisfying marital relationship can incite or exacerbate clinical depression, which, in turn, can further stress a marriage. Consider the amazingly high concordance rates between depression and marital dissatisfaction: If someone is in a troubled, unhappy marriage, there is a 50 percent chance that one of the partners is clinically depressed (Beach, Sandeen, and O'Leary, 1990).

All of the studies cited in this chapter focus on couples in which one spouse is dealing with a clinical depression as determined by DSM-IV criteria. Although some of the findings may be applicable to couples who are having a nonclinical, fleeting case of the blues, the goal is to learn about the special problems facing distressed couples who are also dealing with a significant depressive illness.

Therapists need to assess which is causing more pain and distress—the depression or the marital distress. If the problems seem relational and the

---

Author's note: This chapter was co-authored by Seren Cohen.

depression seems to be linked to couple conflict, withdrawal, or sharp attitudinal differences between the spouses, then traditional couples therapy would be indicated. When depression persists in a highly functional marriage, and the marital problems seem more related to the negative consequences that depression has on intimacy, then spouse-assisted therapy (in which the nondepressed spouse becomes an adjunct therapist—working with the therapist to alleviate the depression) is indicated. In most cases, however, the therapist will be treating a dual diagnosis (depression and marital distress).

This chapter begins by focusing on how troubled marriages can provoke depression in one or both of the partners. The second part of the chapter focuses on how to inoculate nondepressed spouses and how they can be used in spouse-assisted therapy to help their partners.

MARITAL DISTRESS PROVOKES AND MAINTAINS DEPRESSION

Marital interactions have been shown to play an important role in the etiology, maintenance, and treatment of some depressions. Consider the following statistics:

1. In 1987, Weissman showed that the risk of having a major depressive episode was twenty-five times higher for both men and women in discordant marital relationships than it was for individuals in harmonious marital relationships.
2. Although in the general population, women are far more likely to be diagnosed as depressed than are men, among those experiencing marital distress, men and women are equally at risk for depression.
3. In a 1978 study of working-class women in England, Brown and Harris found that 38 percent of women without an intimate, confiding relationship with a husband or boyfriend developed psychiatric symptoms of depression following a stressful life event. Only 4 percent of women with a supportive, intimate relationship developed depressive symptomatology.
4. A 1983 study by Birtchnell and Kennard tried to assess the influence that marriage can have on one's mental health. They examined 240 healthy married women in Sussex, England, and compared them with 240 depressed women in a local hospital. All the women were given detailed life interviews, personality tests, and tests for depression and psychological distress. Results showed a strong association between marital satisfaction and mental health. Of the depressed women,

34 percent were in negative marriages compared with 8 percent of the healthy women. The quality of marital interactions between the two groups differed, with significantly more of the depressed women perceiving themselves as receiving less affection than they gave (43 percent compared with 28 percent) and perceiving their husbands to be the dominant partner (63 percent compared with 41 percent).

The relationship between marital dissatisfaction and depression is obvious when one considers how similar both conditions are to each other. Subjectively, both marital distress and depression present with a variety of negative emotional states. Both are accompanied by anger, low mood, lack of motivation, perceived helplessness, and hopelessness. Behaviorally, both conditions are associated with social skill deficits, poor communication and problem solving, and reliance on aversion and coercion to express and satisfy needs. Cognitively, both distressed couples and depressed individuals believe that the problems are too big to be solved or too rigid for change.

Given the large overlap in symptomatology, how can one determine which came first? Does depression cause marital distress or does marital distress cause depression?

Much of the evidence cited above suggests that marital discord contributes to the development of depression (Brown and Harris, 1978). Most impressive are the studies that demonstrate that in happy marriages, individuals are better able to withstand stress and less likely to succumb to depression (Weissman, 1987). In addition, the Birtchnell and Kennard (1983) study found that the differences in marital distress between depressed and normal mood women occurred because the healthy women in the community had terminated their unsatisfying marriages. These results strongly suggest that leaving a poor-quality marriage could improve mental health. Indeed, the mental health of the divorced women from bad marriages improved to the level of mental health found among women from good marriages after the women from the bad marriages got a divorce. This pattern was true for both the patients and the community women, further supporting the relationship between positive marital relationships and mental health.

WHAT CAUSES DEPRESSION?

About one in twenty Americans (over 11 million people) will become depressed this year. The lifetime risk for major depressive disorder is over 8 percent for men and over 23 percent for women (Depression Guideline Panel, 1993). A large proportion of these people are married.

The scientific consensus is that although biological and genetic factors can place a person at risk for developing depression, psychological factors are critical in provoking and maintaining most depressive episodes (Depression Guideline Panel, 1993). The three most popular psychological theories of depression (cognitive behavioral theory, psychoanalytic theory, and interpersonal theory) all have direct treatment implications for treating depression in a marital context.

Cognitive behavioral theory offers the most popular explanation of depression and emphasizes the effect of thoughts on behavior and motivation (Wright, Thase, Beck, and Ludgate, 1993). According to Beck (Beck, 1967; Beck et al., 1979), three cognitive distortions are at the core of depression: arbitrary inferences, overgeneralization, and magnification/minimization. These distortions lead people to feel hopeless about the past, present, and future. The cognitive patterns of depression are deeply ingrained and seem perfectly true and sensible to the depressed person. Therapy focuses on identifying the patient's underlying beliefs and the "thinking errors" that lead to self-defeating behaviors. These are "tested" like hypotheses in day-to-day settings and in therapy sessions. The individual learns to monitor his or her thought content and to keep challenging its validity.

Arbitrary inference, the first cognitive distortion, refers to the process of drawing arbitrary, negative conclusions from experiences. The wife who gets depressed because her husband bought a used car rather than a new car might feel that he is implicitly giving her the message that she is not contributing enough to the family with her part-time job. This is an arbitrary inference that may be true but is not necessarily true. By examining the truth or falsehood of such statements in couple sessions, the depressed partner can learn to recognize his or her tendency to use arbitrary inferences.

Overgeneralization refers to a pattern of making broad, overarching conclusions based on single events. For example, if a person is having a terrible day, disappointing others and himself or herself, it is an overgeneralization that tomorrow and the day after will be just as dismal. But that is precisely the type of overgeneralization that the depressed person continually makes. The biggest overgeneralization seen in the therapy of depressed couples is that the marriage is incapable of changing for the better and that the depressed partner is incapable of being loved and admired for his or her contribution to the marriage. The hopelessness for change can be countered in the therapy session by reviewing how the couple has had to change in the past to deal with crises or opportunities, discussing other couples they know who have made significant changes, and pointing out how coming to therapy is a major new change, symbolic of the couple's commitment to make other needed changes.

Magnification and minimization refers to a pattern of thought in which one exaggerates the import of negative events and minimizes the effect of positive ones. When a husband spends the whole week thinking and hurting about how his wife called him an "emotional midget" and never daydreams or remembers the movie they went to that week, the room they painted over the weekend, or the enjoyable sex they had the night before, he is engaging in the magnification-minimization process of distorted thinking. When a wife dwells on the dinners that turned out inedible and minimizes the one that everyone enjoyed, the same process is at work.

One's self-esteem is always more wounded by failure than it is bolstered by success. But for the depressed person, this imbalance is grossly exaggerated so that the positive events are given almost no weight at all. Learning to monitor and acknowledge small, daily successes and learning to contain the meaning of daily failures are two important therapeutic goals. This learning takes place on the individual level and the couple level. An easy therapeutic intervention is to get the couple to try to reverse the weightings they give to positive and negative events. The evening out that ended in disaster should be minimized, whereas the successful fund-raising booth that they manned at the school fair should be maximized.

In psychoanalytic theory, it is more the content of the thoughts and their accompanying affect that produce depression than the processes generating the thoughts. Traditional psychoanalytic theory emphasizes how loss of love and emotional insecurity are key variables in depression. More recent approaches emphasize the loss of self-esteem and defensive reactions. The reaction to loss, however, remains the core cause of depression in analytic theory. Most often, the losses experienced in early life dramatically affect the development of personality. By understanding the personality organization of a person, one can trace how fear of rejection has been handled in the past and how fear of rejection is currently being handled in the marriage.

Loss of partner love, partner security, or self-validation from a partner often causes people to turn their angry feelings of abandonment inward, onto themselves. Losing love becomes like losing a part of the self. Feeling that a partner has rejected them or lost interest in them creates a profound feeling of loss. The severity and nature of the current loss interacts with other losses in the client's history to determine the severity of the reaction.

The rejecting partner creates, over time, in the depressed mate, a self-denigrating mate. The pain from the loss is turned inward in the form of self-hate or self-anger. Rejected partners are afraid to direct anger outward toward rejecting spouses, who may abandon them completely or further destroy their self-esteem.

The aims of psychoanalytic therapy are always to change the personality structure and not simply to alleviate the symptoms. People must approach the marriage with a cognitive and emotional openness that does not distort the mate's intended messages. Psychodynamic therapy emphasizes that insight (understanding how one learned to react in a certain way), working through the transference (how feelings for the therapist reveal feelings about other authority figures in one's life), and corrective emotional reactions (accepting the support, love, and forgiveness of a spouse within a session) will lead to an improvement in interpersonal trust, coping mechanisms, and the ability to experience a wide range of emotions.

In psychodynamic couples work, spouses learn to discuss how their own imagoes (internal representations of loved ones from early childhood) affect how they process the rejection they feel from their spouse. By disclosing, sharing, and reprocessing what is happening "to me in my marriage" and differentiating it from what happened "to me in my childhood" or to "my parents in their marriage," individuals learn to take responsibility for their own current relationships.

Lewinsohn's social skill model cites interpersonal behaviors as both potential causes and cures for depression (Lewinsohn, 1987; Lewinsohn, et al., 1984; Schmaling and Becker, 1991). This approach stresses the importance of role transitions, loss, grief, and conflict in the etiology and treatment of depression. Patients are encouraged to evaluate their interactions with others, especially how they isolate themselves from supportive relationships. Interpersonal theory draws on interpersonal cognitions (cognitive theory) and reactions to loss (psychodynamic theory). Conceptually, its uniqueness lies

---

THERAPEUTIC INTERVENTION 1:
THREE VITAL ASSESSMENT QUESTIONS

To assess the extent to which interpersonal or intrapsychic issues are promoting or exacerbating a client's depression, the following three questions cover the major theoretical underpinnings of depressive affect:

1. What thoughts of your marriage or your partner are most distressing to you? What keeps going round and round in your head about your spouse and the state of your marriage? (Cognitive behavioral questions)

2. What type of losses have you experienced over the past year or two? What type of disappointments have you experienced? Have any dramatic changes occurred in your family situation or your family of origin's situation? (Psychodynamic questions)

3. What are the most rewarding times and interactions that you have with your spouse these days? How about in the past? What are the most anxiety-provoking, anger-provoking, or depressing interactions that you have with your spouse these days? What are the types of interactions you are wishing for? (Interpersonal questions)

on stressing current interactions and the meaning that various self-generated interpersonal behaviors have on others.

The three theories have much overlap, but some clear theoretical differences are evident among them. Integrating the theoretical outlooks of diverse clinicians, at least three factors seem to mediate the relationship between depression and marital dissatisfaction. They are personality traits, external stressors, and coping style. How might each of these contributory factors interact with marital life to promote depression?

COMMON PERSONALITY TRAITS AND DEPRESSION IN MARRIAGE

Dependency and introversion are two well-known traits that have been empirically shown to predispose individuals to depression. Whether these traits are acquired through developmental learning, based in biological predispositions, or the result of a combination of both is unclear. What is clear, however, is that persons with relationships characterized by dependency or introversion are at greater risk for depression. If the initial assessment reveals either or both of these traits in either spouse, a detailed evaluation for depressive symptomatology is warranted.

Dependency refers to a pattern of depending on others for assurance of self-worth. It may be expressed in many ways. It may be found in the husband who must dominate his wife, always being "right" and "calling the shots." Although seemingly the powerful partner, he is, in reality, dependent on his wife's acquiescence to validate his leadership role. It may also be seen in the wife who invests her self-worth entirely in caring for others, limiting her own growth and horizons.

When threatened, dependent persons may defend themselves by clinging or by making increasing demands on their spouses for support. Conversely, they may also deal with threatened loss of support by denying their dependency needs and becoming aloof or dominating.

Either way, spouses are defending their self-esteem. Unable to bounce back from setbacks as easily as others, dependent spouses react quickly and intensely to frustrations and disappointments in the marriage. They rely heavily on the positive emotional support of their mates to see them through and assure them that they are "OK." Thus, people prone to depression are more dependent on the positive emotional support of their spouses. The increased reliance is accompanied by an increased sensitivity to rejection when their spouses disagree with, criticize, or ignore them. Because their heightened sensitivity exposes them to increased levels of rejection, loss, and disdain, they are at an increased risk of depression.

Research also suggests that depressives have a tendency to be more introverted than the general population. It is hypothesized that introverts have a lower threshold of nervous system arousal (they get upset more easily) and can quickly find social interactions taxing and aversive. Ironically, although dependent people experience more interpersonal needs than do independent people, if they are also introverted, they socialize less and find it harder to receive the emotional support they need.

EXTERNAL STRESS
AND DEPRESSION IN MARITAL RELATIONSHIPS

In a controlled study of life events and depression (Paykel et al., 1969), researchers compared life events preceding the onset of a depression with life events of control subjects drawn from a random epidemiological survey sample of 185 depressed patients and 938 community controls.

Three results highlight the relationship between the threat of negative life events and depression. First, depressed patients reported three times the number of negative life events than did community controls. Because the life-stress scales measured concrete events (e.g., job loss, marital divorce or separation, illness or death), it was unlikely that the result represented a distorted bias of negative response set among the depressed.

Second, the study evaluated the nature of precipitating events. Events were categorized in two forms: exits and entrances. Exits included events involving the departure of a significant other from one's everyday life. Entrances involved the introduction of a new person into the social field. Results showed that in the six months preceding depression, depressed persons experienced five times the number of exits than did community controls. In order of frequency, such exits included deaths of family members, marital separations, divorce, and children's leaving home due to school, marriage, or the draft (which was in effect at the time). Note that all of these exits are family related.

Third, the dominant areas of life precipitating depressive episodes were in the areas of marital and family life. Marital disruption was identified as the primary stressor in 33 percent of depressions and family stressors in 11 percent. The next most dominant area related to health and included serious personal illness, illness of a family member, pregnancy, and childbirth. Together, these areas of marriage, family, and health composed 66 percent of precipitating stressors.

COPING STYLES AND DEPRESSION IN MARRIAGE

There are adaptive and maladaptive coping styles. Adaptive coping styles refer to problem-solving approaches that are active, results oriented, and aimed at removing or reducing the source of stress. Maladaptive coping styles are usually emotion-focused behaviors and include hostile confrontation, emotional discharge, or the seeking of emotional support. Depressives engage in more emotion-focused behaviors.

Take the typical marital problem of equitably distributing household responsibilities. Adaptive coping styles would include having a "meeting" to assign chores, expressing what each spouse perceives as "fair" and negotiating a compromise, working on lowering expectations of what the spouse can realistically contribute, working on expressing appreciation for the contributions the spouse does make, and so on. Maladaptive coping styles would lead one to shout, refuse to talk to the spouse, withhold sex and affection, cry, or be verbally abusive. Maladaptive strategies, by definition, do not help in resolving the problem; they usually help to make the problem worse.

In a study of coping resources and depression, Husaini and vonFrank (1985) surveyed 675 individuals; measures included a telephone interview and two self-report responses taken seven months apart. Instruments included the Holmes and Rahe Life Stress Scale, the Center of Epidemiological Studies Depression Scale, and scales of social support and personal competence. In this community sample, the authors observed the following relationships: First, people who felt that they were in control and responsible for the outcome of the marital disagreement were less depressed and used more adaptive coping strategies. Second, the affective quality of social support, not the quantity of social support, was correlated with lower levels of depression. Third, an external locus of control (feeling that one was not in control and could not affect the outcome of the marital disagreement) was a stronger predictor of depression than social support. Thus, the first line of protective defense against depression may be a sense of personal control and mastery.

Ross and Mirowsky (1990) approached the question of the importance of personal control in a second study. On the basis of the same epidemiological sample, the authors assessed four alternate levels of personal control and associated these with depression.

People at the first level of personal control, "instrumentalists," defined themselves as generally responsible for both positive and negative outcomes in their lives. The second and third levels were characteristic of "self-blamers" and "self-defenders," respectively. Self-blamers attributed responsibility for negative events to themselves; positive events were attributed to the responsibility of others. Self-defenders reversed the process, essentially attributing to themselves responsibility only for the positive. The fourth group, "fatalists," accepted no responsibility for any outcomes.

Those with a sense of responsibility for both successes and failures, instrumentalists, composed 64 percent of the sample population. This group also showed the lowest level of depression in the population. Self-defenders and self-blamers, comprising 17 percent and 11 percent of the population, respectively, had the highest levels of depression. Fatalists, evident among 8 percent of the sample, had levels of depression significantly higher than instrumentalists but below the self-defenders and self-blamers. These results, in general, point to the importance of a sense of personal control and responsibility.

During the assessment phase, it is helpful to explore if each partner is an instrumentalist, self-defender, self-blamer, or fatalist. For example, self-defenders will be blaming the partner, the jobs, the children, or the in-laws for all of the problems. Self-blamers will be castigating themselves and their own ineptitude. By methodically approaching the issues at a stylistic level (e.g., "You seem to be the type of person who feels that no matter what is going wrong, it was up to you to make sure it was going right"), therapists can help spouses can get in touch with their personal control style. They then can see how they are using it, perhaps inappropriately, in a variety of marital situations and conflicts. Also, knowing the two groups most prone to depression should sensitize the therapist to look more closely for depressive symptomatology in these groups.

THERAPEUTIC INTERVENTION 2: ASSESSING FEELINGS OF PERSONAL CONTROL AND EFFICACY

A good diagnostic dilemma to give each partner to assess his or her feelings of efficacy is the following: Pretend that this weekend you return home to find that while you were out with a friend, the house burned to the ground with all of your possessions. Your spouse was cooking when a fire started in the pan. Your spouse ran to get the fire extinguisher, which was kept in the stairwell. When she or he returned, the kitchen was already engulfed in flames and spreading. Tell me all the things you would do and what your spouse would do in the first twenty-four hours after the fire. Who would decide what needs to be done? What do you think those decisions would be?

The answers have a lot of face validity and indicate the type of social supports that individuals think are available, the degree of energy and hopefulness that they feel, and whether they are instrumentalists, fatalists, self-defenders, or self-blamers. After analyzing their responses to the disaster dilemma, ask how they would have responded to this situation two years ago. This will give an indication of how damaged the feelings of efficacy have become during the depressive episode.

(continued)

(continued)

When a client feels little or no control, the therapist must help the couple plan a graduated series of empowering actions and decisions. The first assignments may be as simple as deciding whether to go to the movies or rent a video. More difficult assignments could include deciding what type of car to buy or how to handle the social demands being made by a relative.

THERAPEUTIC INTERVENTION 3: SCULPTING

Another good way to get depressed spouses to communicate their pain is to use a sculpting technique. In sculpting, each partner is asked to place both individuals in statuesque poses that capture the feelings and psychological distance between the couple (Sherman, 1993). The therapist may need to model some possibilities to break through initial inhibitions. Modeled poses can include standing far apart but trying to hold hands; standing crouched, like wrestlers on a mat, ready to attack each other; or holding onto each other for dear life. Once the poses are fixed, each person describes what he or she feels like in that particular pose. After both partners have sculpted their view of the relationship, they are again invited to create another scene, this time one that would describe their ideal relationship. Differences and similarities in the scenes are discussed. The ideal sculptures serve as goalposts to guide both the therapist and the couple in picking effective interventions.

Another, slightly more complicated variation of the sculpting technique calls for each spouse to represent both partners in terms of a symbolic animal or object. This usually works best when the therapist is helping the couple crystallize the dynamics within a specific conflict situation. Usually, the interpretation of feelings is obvious and the therapist can move immediately toward using the sculpture to metaphorically summarize the problem (Sherman, 1993).

CASE STUDY 1: INDIVIDUAL AND COUPLE TREATMENT OF DEPRESSED WOMEN

Linda and Joey, both Mexican Americans in their late fifties, had been married for five years. They both had previous marriages of a long duration, with grown children, and were both recently divorced. During their five-year marriage, Joey's mother had died and his brother and son had committed suicide. Linda had had a mastectomy and had been cut off without explanation from her only child, a daughter. The daughter was 1,000 miles away, attending college, and refused to answer any phone

(continued)

(continued)

calls or letters for the past two years. She simply said she needed to be away from both her parents and was finally acknowledging how angry she was about how both of her parents had acted during their divorce. The daughter didn't come home on vacations and communicated only when she needed money.

Joey was a very successful computer salesman, with a salesman's personality. He was always trying to find a way to cope with their current crisis and still smile. He loved to tell jokes, complimented his wife all the time, and felt blessed for what life had given him. Linda, on the other hand, was a very sour person. She felt that she had been used as a maid in her first marriage and treated in a sexually demeaning way. She thought her divorce settlement was a gross injustice and that it was an unfair burden to have cancer. She looked at her husband's good humor as an unrealistic, immature response to tragedy and felt it belittled her more "human" reactions.

Linda and Joey came for therapy because Linda was uncertain if she could continue in the marriage. She cried almost every day, and when she was not crying, she was screaming. Each day, she became more and more intolerant of Joey's habits. She felt she could not survive without him because of the many tasks he did around the house and because he was so accepting of her. At the same time, his upbeat nature made her want to scream, and she felt totally misunderstood and victimized.

Linda was already on medication when she came to therapy. The focus of the marital sessions was on helping Linda feel that she had more control in her marriage. Although Joey was an excellent housekeeper and cook, Linda felt that whenever he complimented himself on a job well done (which he did all the time), she was indirectly being made to feel inadequate. Linda didn't care if the bed was made. Joey's pride in his perfect hospital corners made her angry because it implied that bed making was very important and she should care whether or not the bed was made. Linda was happy to eat something from Taco Bell or a can of Campbell's soup for dinner, whereas Joey prided himself on preparing well-balanced, visually attractive meals. Joey was hurt that Linda did not appreciate what he was lovingly and willingly doing for both of them.

To help Linda gain control, for a period of one month, she was put in charge of making a list of the chores she felt they needed to complete each week. She also divvied up the assignments. Most important, she had the job of rating how well each job was done with a five-star rating system. Joey's job was to compliment his wife twice as much as he complimented himself. Linda was surprised that not only could she do the chores she assigned to herself, but she did them well. Joey was surprised at how often he was tooting his own horn for no particular reason.

Linda had three individual sessions in addition to twelve marital sessions that were centered on learning new and more effective coping strategies. Linda had been a carefree, positive type of person until the bitter

(continued)

(continued)

divorce from her first husband. She felt that she had turned into an "ugly monster" when she realized that life was not fair. She thought that all her positive behaviors had been extinguished due to lack of reinforcement. The ugly monster was a very unattractive person, but at least she had the joy of expressing her abject misery. Therapy focused on the existential issues of meaningfulness and responsibility. We focused on questions such as the purpose of motherhood, the meaning of love, the impact that physical pain has on coping resources, and finding purpose when our ultimate destiny is death. Other conversations concerned the responsibilities she had toward herself and her husband. As Linda came into her own philosophy of life, she started pretending to be her old self, making light of her daily tribulations. She tried to please the people with whom she had daily contact. At first, she felt the pretend exercises were appreciated by those around her but were, essentially, very artificial and hokey. Soon, however, she felt less depressed and had more energy. She became openly thankful that her husband had stood by her and started planning a weekly fun excursion for the two of them. When therapy ended, the ugly monster was still a frequent visitor, but she was no longer the main character in Linda's self-image.

THE PROTECTIVE NATURE OF SOCIAL SUPPORT

Social support comes in many forms and from many different places. It comes from within the marriage—from the physical, emotional, economic, and spiritual giving of one partner to the other. Support also comes from friends, family members, and colleagues who form the couple's extended community.

Whatever the source, whatever the function, support that comes with care and positive feelings is especially powerful. Evidence consistently shows that support can provide us with a protective "buffer" from life's bumps and stressors. It has a direct, positive effect on well-being and reduces our vulnerability to depression.

In a 1986 study, Beach, Arias, and O'Leary studied the relationship of marital satisfaction and social support to depression. The researchers predicted that marital satisfaction and couples' social "networks" could both predict depression, and they both did.

The study included 268 married adults; on the average, couples had been married nineteen years. Instruments measured marital satisfaction, depression, social networks, and social support. There were strong correlations between both marital satisfaction and social support to depression. The quality of the marriage and the frequency of social contact outside the marriage were both related to depressive symptomatology. That is, depressed individuals were those who had unhappy marriages and few friends outside the marriage.

Among unhappily married couples, the risk for depression was two times higher than that of the maritally satisfied. It was also twice as high among those who were socially isolated compared with those who were socially "connected" to friends and activities outside the marriage. Among those who were both socially isolated and unhappily married, the risk of depression was thirteen times greater.

Thus, even with a spouse who is a "supportive best friend," people need friends outside the marriage for the marriage to "breathe." Being limited to one good friend can be very depressing for the average person and put crazy demands on a marital partner to be all things at all times. A rich and varied social life allows each partner to constantly infuse the marriage with new information and allows the "person" in the marital union to remain a unique individual.

Also, having a mate who is a dependable, take-charge type does not necessarily mean that one is receiving adequate support. Billings and Moos (1982) found that the affective quality of the marital support was more important than the quantity of support that a spouse offered in predicting relapse after a serious depressive episode. For example, it was much more protective to have a wife who emotionally supported the husband through a period of unemployment with reassurance and esteem boosters than to have a wife who economically supported the husband by getting a second job and cutting out want ads for him.

THERAPEUTIC INTERVENTION 4:
EQUITY IN MARRIAGE—CREATING A LONG-TERM VIEW

Depressed spouses often feel that they are not carrying their weight in the relationship. They feel like a burden to their spouses and are ashamed of their neediness. Their dependency only reinforces their feelings of worthlessness.

Because their perceptions of being overbenefited may be quite accurate, the therapist has to help the couple reframe such an imbalance as temporary. If people stay married for fifty years, one might expect that for twenty years the wife will be overbenefited, for another twenty the husband will be overbenefited, and they may have concurrent equity for only ten years. The fear of forever being overbenefited can be alleviated if the depressed spouse is committed to personal growth and if they both acknowledge that external events create continual crises that push for changes in the relationship. It is a way of thinking that stresses living comfortably in the now, mindful of the flow and changes that always define a human life.

CASE STUDY 2:
LEVEL OF SUPPORT
AND THE DEPRESSED PARTNER

Kristen and David have been married for eight years. Kristen is Swedish and was brought up a devout Catholic in the outskirts of Stockholm. David is Jewish and lived in several large Eastern cities while growing up. Kristen was pregnant when she got married and converted as a condition of the marriage. Both Kristen and David are in their early thirties, but both had been told throughout their adult lives that they were infertile. When Kristen became pregnant, they were both overjoyed and both unhesitatingly decided to get married. They had a son, and within ten months of the first child had a set of twin boys as well.

Kristen had been a well-known international fashion model prior to her pregnancy and gave up work after having children. David was a magazine editor based in New York City but had taken a different publishing job in Washington, DC, shortly before Kristen got pregnant. When Kristen settled in Washington, she knew no one. Her entire social life depended on David.

Kristen was overwhelmed with the chore of raising three young children without any assistance. Her entire family still lived in Sweden, and all of her modeling friends in the United States were based in New York. David worked long hours and traveled to New York at least once a week. Seven or eight times a year, he traveled abroad for a week or more. Kristen's conversion to Judaism was also disorienting because she knew nothing of the religion or the culture. This had recently become an issue as the children started attending Hebrew school and they had joined a synagogue. Kristen said she felt conspicuous and rejected by the few women she had tried to approach.

Kristen had a bout of depression in her early teens and recognized the symptoms over the past year. She was losing her appetite, and, although she had finally gotten back into modeling shape, she felt terrible all the time and had no energy. She felt that she was an inadequate mother and in danger of losing her husband because she "was such a loser." She was not interested in sex. She worried all the time that the three boys were being too aggressive and hyperactive. She doubted her parenting skills and felt that David had a much more natural way with them. With David gone so much of the time, she often felt that she was a zombie. She thought about dying and the ultimate purposelessness of life, but she had never seriously developed a suicide plan. Kristen said that a lousy mother was probably better than no mother at all.

Both David and Kristen had ten individual sessions. David's sessions focused on teaching him how to be a resourceful spouse. He was given books explaining depression and was encouraged to "court" his wife as much as possible. David loved the idea of dating his wife once again and immediately started planning romantic and interesting Saturday nights for the two of them.

(continued)

(continued)

Kristen's tiredness and lack of sexual energy were reframed. Instead of the problems being due to Kristen's "depression," they began to see that David's long hours and inability to carry any of his home or child care responsibilities required Kristen to work overtime. David was encouraged to take on a minimum, regular, weekly, five-hour child care shift, during which time Kristen would be free to go out or stay at home uninterrupted. They also decided to read some books on Judaism together so that they would start to share some common bonds in that area.

Kristen's individual sessions were devoted to helping her network in the community and meet some women friends. She was encouraged to have a coffee for the other women in the neighborhood who were home with small children. She decided to volunteer at a local community center and offer classes in modeling. She began going to a yoga class that offered baby-sitting and made a very good friend in that class.

A year later, Kristen was well integrated into the community and was very happy with her marriage, herself, and her life situation.

CHARACTERISTICS OF MARRIAGES
WITH A DEPRESSED PARTNER

Are the interactions of unhappily married couples with a depressed partner unique? How are they different from the unhappily married who do not suffer from depression?

Research indicates that unhappily married couples with a depressed partner are unique both in terms of the quality and type of interactions. In a meta-analysis of sixteen studies done in the 1980s, Beach, Sandeen, and O'Leary (1990) found that unhappily married couples with a depressed partner showed four distinct characteristics when compared with unhappily married couples that showed no signs of depression: a greater frequency of depressive behaviors, a lower level of marital cohesion, a greater lack of symmetry in relationships, and a greater level of hostility.

A Greater Frequency of Depressive Behaviors

It is not too surprising that depressed people are found to act more depressed. However, it is important to keep in mind that spouses are the most frequent recipients of the depressed partner's symptomatology. The spouse of the depressed person has to constantly look at a downturned grimace, hear the pessimistic conversations, listen to the personal self-degradation, and live with a low-energy partner who is not interested in sex and is full of everyday regrets. There are also often long, weepy periods and a variety of psychosomatic complaints. Conversations with a depressed spouse seem invariably to be filled with negativity about the past, present, and future.

Clearly, depressive behaviors change the affective tone and the quality of marital relationships. Given the frequency with which such interactions plague the maritally distressed and depressed, they are important areas of intervention.

A Lower Level of Marital Cohesion

Cohesion is the sense of togetherness or belonging that makes couples feel like a team. The 1988 study by Beach, Nelson, and O'Leary found that the level of cohesion in marriages differentiated discordant depressed from discordant nondepressed wives with the discordant, depressed couples showing significantly less cohesion than the discordant, nondepressed couples. This is especially striking because nearly all unhappy couples suffer from low feelings of cohesiveness. To find significant differences between these two groups indicates how alienated the maritally distressed/ depressed couples must feel. Billings and Moos (1982) also found that families with low levels of cohesion showed higher depressive symptomatology. Similarly, Monroe and colleagues (1986) found that the cohesion subscale of the Dyadic Adjustment Scale (DAS) predicted symptoms of depression. Depressed couples who are struggling with marital issues need to focus on ways to develop methods of building cohesion and initiating caring gestures for each other.

A Greater Lack of Symmetry in Relationships

Depressed, unhappy couples often show an "imbalance" in their relationship: The needs of one partner become primary at the expense of the other. One study (Hautzinger, Linden, and Hoffman, 1982) found that depressed persons often evaluate themselves as being "worse off" in some way than their spouses. Their spouses tend to agree. Verbalizations of both partners frequently focus on the depressed spouse's feelings and symptoms rather than discussing marital problems or real concerns.

A 1979 study by Merikangas, Ranelli, and Kupfer further supported the asymmetry in the interaction of depressed, discordant couples. In this study, depressed female inpatients showed a strong tendency to change their opinions to those of their partners following discussion. As their depression improved, the balance of opinions became more even.

If depressed spouses are encouraged and helped to be assertive, they are less likely to withdraw when conflicts emerge between the partners. Healthy confrontations are more likely to lead to conflict resolution and to lower the probability of spiraling into the valley of constant avoidance.

A Greater Level of Hostility

Several studies have shown that spouses of depressed persons often feel hostile during and after marital interactions (Arkowitz, Holliday, and Hutter, 1982; Kahn, Coyne, and Margolin, 1985). The longer the individual has been in distress, the more likely the nondepressed spouse is to engage in aggressive behaviors (Beach and Nelson, 1989; Nelson and Beach, 1990). In addition, there is evidence that relapse rates for depression increase significantly when the nondepressed partner shows high expressed emotion and is critical (Hooley and Hahlweg, 1985; Hooley and Teasdale 1989). Also, depressed spouses often have periods of hostile outbursts and rejection.

These characteristics, studied by more dynamically oriented therapists, are described as an "insecure attachment style" (Roberts, Gotlib, and Kassel, 1996).* With the proper temperament and parenting, infants who become securely attached to a parent seem to develop into adults who have warm, interdependent, and responsive relationships. Insecurely attached children respond to their parents' comings and goings with ambivalence or avoidance and seem to develop into adults who have similar problems with their mates. Anxious-ambivalent individuals desire extreme closeness but alternate between hostility and dependency when the partners act in an unpredictable or unsupportive manner. Avoidant individuals are uncomfortable with closeness and tend to shut down and retreat when the partners act in a rejecting manner. They do not know how to seek comfort and security from their mates. It is assumed that as children these adults had similar experiences with their parents.

Insecurely attached people want their partners around to make them feel more secure (Feeney and Kirkpatrick, 1996). However, when their partners are rejecting, distant, or depressed, they become highly emotional and dysfunctional. Thus, individuals with insecure attachment styles are at

---

*Ainsworth et al. (1978), described three classic attachment styles based on how infants responded to the return of their mothers after a brief separation. The healthiest relationship was a secure attachment, in which the baby was happy to see the mother. There were two types of insecure attachment that were associated with interpersonal dysfunctions. In the avoidant attachment style, the child ignored the mother's return. In the ambivalent attachment style, the child was alternatively angry and clingy with the mother on her return. These attachment styles appear to be quite stable over time and are now being studied in terms of adult development and their influence on adult relationships.

high risk for frustrating and tumultuous relationships. The good times are very rewarding. It is just that the smallest hint of separation or rejection from the partner cannot be tolerated. It is immediately personalized and made into catastrophy, leading to the characteristics of depression, hostility, inequality, and lack of cohesiveness.

However, it is unlikely that these insecure traits, per se, cause depression in the at-risk partner or the provoking partner. Rather, it is probable that these traits cause people to interpret their experiences in a negative manner, and these thoughts lead to their depression. That is, how one thinks about one's relationship affects whether or not one is at risk for depression. The marker for a dysfunctional thinking style, however, is noted by the characteristics of an insecure attachment style. Insecure attachments are characterized by these thinking patterns, "I need the approval of my partner to be happy," or "If I fail in the eyes of my partner, then I am a failure as a person."

Roberts, Gotlib, and Kassel (1996) have indeed confirmed that the different adult attachment styles are related to different types of attitudes and cognitions. Insecurely attached adults have far more dysfunctional attitudes that directly affect their self-esteem and increase their level of depression. The model, developed through a statistical path analysis, suggests that insecurity in adult attachment is related to negative thinking about the self. The negative thoughts lower self-esteem, which then acts as a more proximal cause of depressive symptoms. This relationship holds true regardless of the level of depressive symptoms or the degree of neuroticism.

Therapists working with insecurely attached couples need to be alert for both forms of despair—the angry feelings "buried" in avoidance as well as direct, unmodulated outbursts. Anger awareness and skills in conflict resolution can become specific intervention targets.

EFFECTIVENESS OF MARITAL THERAPY IN TREATING DEPRESSION

Given these characteristics, research shows that discordant depressed couples benefit from therapies that focus directly on the marital relationship. Individual cognitive therapy reduces depression but not marital discord. Conjoint marital therapy can reduce both.

In a 1991 study (Townsley et al.), researchers tried to uncover the underlying factors that make conjoint therapy more effective than individual cognitive therapy. Individual cognitive therapy assumes that depressive cognitions pervade all relationships, including marital ones. Change the depressive cognitions through individual therapy and behaviors will change. This will provide the spouse with some new stimuli to react to, and through new, self-initiated interaction cycles, the couple will develop an improved relationship. Conjoint marital therapy assumes that cognitions related to depression in marital discord are not the same as those related to generalized depression.

The study included fifty women seeking marital therapy and copresenting with depression. A series of instruments assessed their marital adjustment as well as their attributional style for explaining positive and negative events (i.e., assigning blame). The study also measured the level of depressogenic cognitions (i.e., making catastrophies, overgeneralizing, and personalizing) and beliefs about relationships. A statistical analysis showed that the frequency and form of depressogenic cognitions (pessimism about past, present, and future) were not significantly related to marital adjustment. Three factors, however, did relate to marital adjustment: attributional style for assigning responsibility and blame, dysfunctional beliefs about relationships, and a negative-hostile style of communicating.

This study suggests that the cognitive variables addressed in standard, individual cognitive therapy may not be adequate in treating marital dysfunctions. If true, marital therapy should be more effective than traditional, individual therapy in treating depression effected by marital conflict.

Research of therapy outcomes supports the superiority of marital therapy. In a 1990 study, O'Leary, Riso, and Beach compared therapy outcomes for forty-one unhappily married and depressed women who were randomly assigned to one of three treatment groups: individual cognitive therapy, marital therapy, and a wait-list control. A majority of subjects (70 percent) believed that marital discord preceded their depressions.

At outcome, women who received conjoint therapy showed reductions in, or elimination of, depression, and increased marital satisfaction. Those who received individual cognitive therapy showed reduced depression but increased marital discord; this population was also more vulnerable to depressive relapse. Presumably, if the dysfunctional aspects of the marital relationship are not corrected, the roots of the depression still exist and just regenerate.

ENLISTING THE AID OF A RESOURCEFUL SPOUSE

Most marital therapy efforts for depressed persons have focused on conjoint marital therapy. The focus of the sessions is on the problems in the marital relationship. However, there is good reason to believe that spouses can also be used in "spouse-assisted" therapy to help the partner work through the depression. This is particularly true when the marital distress is moderate or low. Spouse-assisted therapy involves conjoint meetings in which couples work through marital dysfunctions, but it also stresses teaching specific skills to "well" spouses so they can better cope with their depressed partners. In the process of helping "treat" the spouse, many of the dysfunctional interactions may be inhibited and the marriage recalibrated to a mutually satisfying mode. Of course, all spouses with a depressed partner can potentially help their partners deal with the depression, regardless of the amount of distress in the marriage. Also, engaging husbands or wives in this type of therapy is much easier than engaging them in conjoint marital therapy, in which their behaviors and attitudes are framed as part of the spouse's problem.

THERAPEUTIC INTERVENTION 5: STRATEGIES FOR RESOURCEFUL PARTNERS WITH A DEPRESSED MATE

The following is a tentative list of skills, attitudes, and interactions that could be of use to the resourceful spouse. Possible therapy interventions to achieve these goals are also listed.

Psychoeducation and Bibliotherapy

Spouses need to be educated about the etiology, nature, course, and treatment of depression. Every client and spouse should be given a copy of the NIMH pamphlet on depression or a comparable fact sheet on depression. These brochures are available through the Government Printing Office (see the Bibliotherapy at the end of this chapter).

Generalization Tactics for Coping with a Depressed Partner

Explore how the client has dealt with other depressed family members and friends. Therapists mistakenly assume that when one is coping with a depressed spouse, this is the first, up-close experience of living with a depressed person that the spouse has had. Rarely is this true. Most people have known someone in their family of origin, a close peer, or a work colleague who was clinically depressed. Some have had personal experiences with depression. Recognizing and remembering the other depressed people in the spouses' lives gives them a sense of mastery and "normalizes," a little, the stresses and strains of the current crisis. Many times, the idea of recovery is not real until the spouse remembers other personal instances of people who were depressed and worked through it. The therapist should work with this information to instill hope and discover new attitudes and interactions that could prove helpful in the current situation.

Reframing the Depression to Include the Well Partner's Contribution

Resourceful, nondepressed spouses must acknowledge that their behavior or attitudes may be contributing to and exacerbating the depression

(continued)

(continued)

in their spouse. This means acknowledging that depression is not solely the partner's problem; rather, the depression is a symptom that may be reduced or alleviated by improving the quality of the marital relationship. Nondepressed partners must realize that they need to change and that they are not the victim of an unhappy spouse but may be an active contributor to a marriage with unhappy aspects.

When clients enter therapy, they tend to believe that the symptoms and the dysphoria are within them. They do not believe other people can influence or contribute to the course of the illness. Indeed, what depresses them most is that they feel powerless to change themselves. Even when clients take a more systemic view of their own problems, their spouses invariably continue to define the problem as belonging to their partner. Strong personality traits are used to describe the client's problems: She or he is too lazy, too insecure, too quick too judge, too pessimistic, and so forth. The job of the therapist is to get rid of these personality labels and focus on the interactions between the couple. Under what conditions does the client get more talkative or smile? What marital interactions will make her or him withdraw, stop talking, or become tired?

Having Both Partners Engage in Pleasurable Activities

Nondepressed spouses must continue doing some of the activities that they find restorative for themselves. However, they need to find time to facilitate and support the depressed spouse by engaging him or her in pleasurable activities. That may mean that resourceful spouses need to watch the children or do the errands alone while their mate exercises, goes to visit a friend, finishes a home repair, or enjoys reading a book without disturbances. Supporting pleasure-seeking activities is a long-term commitment of the resourceful spouse. It is not unreasonable to expect that resourceful spouses will be coaching their mate for a period of six months or more in how to enjoy themselves.

The therapist should help the spouse schedule his, her, and "their" activities. Begin by asking the depressed spouse what activities bring him or her pleasure. Try to get eight or nine listed. Then ask for a list of activities that the nondepressed spouse finds pleasurable. Finally, generate a list of activities that the couple has enjoyed doing together in the past or would probably enjoy doing together in the future. Once all three lists are made, make a schedule of the week's activities and help resourceful spouses put in at least three pleasurable periods: one for themselves, one for the depressed partner to do alone or with others, and one that the couple can do together. The scheduling may take an entire session to do thoroughly, but it is very important in orienting the couple toward change.

It is important that the couple acknowledge that the partner's illness is placing extra demands on the healthy spouse. The nondepressed partner has a right to have his or her needs met, even though there is a desire and commitment to help the depressed spouse. Unfortunately, conflict is in-

(continued)

(continued)

evitable because helping the depressed spouse often means that we are unable to have our own needs met. On a Saturday morning, the husband cannot work on his golf game if he must hang around doing family chores with his wife. Searching for answers on how much sacrifice is necessary and how much self-care is indulgent is a highly personal and threatening issue. Yet resolving this issue is essential for the therapeutic dialogue with a resourceful spouse, because marital conflicts over emotional commitment and equity are the cause of much marital depression.

Stressing an Attitude of Commitment in the Resourceful Partner

Encourage the partner to have a consistently loving and respectful attitude. It is critical for the restoration of self-esteem and shifts the positive transference from a therapist to the more appropriate love object—the partner.

Attitude is more important than a specific set of behaviors. This is not surprising. The same phenomenon has been found between parents and children. Children fare best when their parents have a loving attitude toward them and are a consistent force in their lives. Love and consistency are far more important than whether a parent is strict or lenient, playful or serious, a nature enthusiast or a couch potato. Similarly, in a marriage, partners are most content when they sense a loving attitude in a consistently available mate. This attitudinal presence is far more important than whether the spouse is attitudinally dissimilar on a number of dimensions, a shouter, a worrier, or a crier.

The resourceful spouse always has to guard against abusive or passive-aggressive behaviors that serve as "paybacks" for the grief caused by the depression. When Juliet and Roy came to sessions, Juliet always made a mockery of how Roy was so quiet and incapable of communicating. Although she felt that she was simply giving a factual account of the frustrations of living with a depressed husband, her tone and choice of words always sounded punishing. No wonder her husband did not want to talk to her!

Each person in a marital relationship is responsible for cultivating a loving attitude. Love is not a responsive feeling that spontaneously appears when someone is sensitive or responsive to our needs (this usually has a lot more to do with feelings of gratitude). Love is a self-cultivated feeling. It is our own private understanding and respect for the life path of the other. When we stretch our life view to encompass the rich path of conflict and disappointment faced by a mate, then we learn to love that person. We come to see his or her life as clearly as our own.

Discovering the secret of marital love is much like discovering the joys of a secret garden. By going beyond our own needs, joys, and sorrows and carefully rewalking the paths reserved for our husband's (wife's) footsteps, we find the seeds of love. The seeds of love are watered by our creativeness in piecing together the logic of the path and the beauty

(continued)

(continued)

inherent in that spot. The love is fertilized by using and mixing in experiences in our own lives to appreciate the experiences in our mate's life.

Love in a marriage is constant work. It does not come naturally and it does not come easily. It comes from abandoning, for moments, one's own sense of self to experience one's soulmate. Love is the result of experientially sharing your partner's sense of self. It is the result of that moment of fusion, frustrated by the reality that it is momentary. It is almost always bittersweet.

When one spouse feels "loved," in this sense, by the other, then many behavioral insensitivities are ignored and many differences of opinion and attitude are accepted. Spouses who feel loved, in this sense, have no doubt about the commitment their mate has made toward them.

Networking Clients or Partners with Their Religious Community If Appropriate

Despite the fact that we are one of the most religious of the industrialized countries, religion is a very confusing topic for many Americans. Yet when in trouble, it is very natural to seek spiritual guidance and inspiration. Depression is still, in many ways, a sickness of the soul. Spouses may find that they need spiritual support to help deal with their depressed mates. I do not believe that therapists are spiritual healers in the same way as representatives of organized religions. Priests, ministers, monks, imams, and rabbis connect the person to the cosmos through a community of ritual and supportive people.

Many Americans are uncomfortable seeking support from their church when they are in crisis unless they have been advised to do so by an outside professional. Also, clients or spouses who have left the church of their childhood often want or need permission to try another spiritual household. Nonbelievers often yearn to find humanistic communities that can help fill the spiritual void. The therapist needs to regard religious institutions as strong community resources and encourage clients and spouses to explore such options if they so desire.

When exploring the spiritual resources available, keep in mind that this can potentially be a very divisive issue for couples. Attending the "wrong" church, aversion toward having a spouse seek religious support, or reducing the amount of "couple time" are all toxic issues that can reduce the value of church or synagogue involvement.

Helping the Resourceful Partner Sharpen His or Her Debating Skills

Some resourceful spouses can engage in the tricky business of analytic, change-oriented dialogues with their partner. By that, we mean that when the depressed persons are drawing negative inferences, resourceful spouses can help them to see the arbitrary and self-defeating nature of their thinking. For example, Sam, was a depressed forty-five-year-old who was persuaded by his wife to go to the annual family reunion. As they were

(continued)

(continued)

driving home, his wife, Myrna, was sharing her evaluations of how everyone had fared over the past year. Sam said, "I was so quiet and boring; I'm sure they are all hoping I stay home next time." Myrna then started pointing out the few interactions she did see Sam engage in while he was at the picnic. Although she agreed he was not going out and initiating many conversations, she pointed out all the other folks who simply sat in the shade and waited for the others to mill around them. She helped him to see that his behavior was no different from many of the others at the reunion. Sam started to feel better. Even if Sam had been a total deadweight during the day, that would be no reason to assume that no one wanted him to come next year. Indeed, they might be most anxious to see him next year, to see if his mood had improved at all!

An important therapeutic intervention is to instruct the resourceful spouse in the art of reframes, or how to make lemonade out of lemons. The main idea is to teach these spouses to be optimists and to give them ideas on how to elicit optimistic statements from their partners that can be socially reinforced. When a depressed client makes a pessimistic statement, the spouse can ask for the one small shred of evidence that would make the pessimistic outlook erroneous. Good-humored modeling and nudging of the "positive spin" can give both client and spouse hope. It also will illustrate to them, again and again, how powerful thoughts are in controlling moods.

The resourceful spouse must avoid projecting a "Pollyanna" attitude that all is always well with the world. This has the consequence of alienating the depressed spouse even more. The optimism has to be tempered by the actual stressors and hardships that confront the couple.

Encouraging Resourceful Partners to Use Touch

Resourceful partners should be encouraged to use nonsexual touch to reassure their mates. Hugging, holding, stroking, and nonsexual massage are all strengthening and calming for a depressed person.

Many couples have gotten into a bind where all touch is related to sex. It is awkward for resourceful spouses to start using nonsexual touches because they are unaccustomed to this and because they hunger for sexual touch. Remember that because depression is accompanied by a lessening or deadening of libido, most marriages with a depressed person have a sexually frustrated spouse. Resourceful spouses should be encouraged to continue expressing when they are interested in having sex, even if that is every night. At the same time, they should never pressure their partner into having sexual relations. The nonsexual touches should be clearly defined as that and never used to "trick" a partner into having sex. The resourceful spouse may need to masturbate more often or ask for the depressed spouse to pleasure him or her or try to use the abstinent period as an opportunity to be intimate in noncoital ways. Therapists can use bibliotherapy and direct instruction on how to use touch therapeutically.

(continued)

(continued)

Having the Resourceful Partner Acknowledge and Share the Loss Experience

As discussed earlier, quite often depression is due to loss—loss through death, relocation, unemployment, illness, or arguments. Resourceful, non-depressed partners are willing to remember with their mates, remembering the good times and the bad times. They will openly share the sadness for things undone and the fact that none of us can go back in time, only forward.

When appropriate, the spouse should help the depressed partner tie up loose ends in regard to the loss. Writing letters, making amends, and finding ways to gain closure all help people deal with loss. Some spouses need to learn to empathize with their partner's loss. Practice in a joint session with reflective listening skills is often very valuable. Other times, empathy can be enhanced by having the couple work on a metaphoric image of the loss. For example, the image of a sweet chocolate bunny rabbit being left to melt in the afternoon sun captured the feelings of helplessness experienced by a couple where the husband was severely depressed after being fired and unable to find comparable employment. From this image, they developed metaphors about needing to "seek some shade for protection," "remain cool," and know that the evening will surely come and save him.

Encouraging Self-Sufficiency in the Depressed Partner

Because the depressed spouse is likely the more dependent spouse, their partners need to take steps to encourage self-sufficiency and confidence.

Resourceful spouses may, together with their mate, make a list of decisions and activities that the mate would like to be able to do independently. Together, the list of "I want to try . . ." can be tackled in a graduated fashion; the least threatening or difficult actions or decisions should be focused on first. When they have been successfully mastered, more difficult tasks can be set. For example, David and Lisa may decide that Lisa really wants to be able to decide what video they should watch that evening, go to visit her sister 300 miles away for a week (leaving the children with David), and take on an extra, particularly attractive consulting job that would require her being away one evening every two weeks. Together, they decide that this month Lisa will choose all the videos and next month take the trip to visit her sister. When she gets back, if the consulting job is still available, she will try it if all is proceeding as it should be.

Developing and Maintaining Marital Rituals

Because marriages with a depressed partner tend to be less cohesive, the resourceful spouse does need to overcompensate and help the marriage sustain a sense of "we-ness." Doing daily chores together, planning rituals, having some recreation time together each week, making plans for the future, and talking about common daily concerns are five classic ways of maintaining a sense of closeness when one person in the marriage is going through a temporary depression.

CASE STUDY 3:
THE RESOURCEFUL WIFE
AND THE WORKING METAPHOR

Michael, a fifty-three-year-old recovering alcoholic, had been married previously and had a twenty-six-year-old daughter from that marriage. He had been married to his current wife for sixteen years, and they had a fourteen-year-old daughter. Michael and Anita came to treatment when Anita was at her wit's end because she was married to the "living dead" and just could not take it anymore.

Michael had his own beauty supply business but had not managed it well. He continued to try to expand his client base but was not currently meeting the family's expenses. He refused to take an active part in solving the family's financial crisis and just kept trying, unsuccessfully, to get new clients.

Michael had acknowledged his own drinking problems only within the past year, as the result of his eldest daughter entering a rehab program based on Tough Love principles. Michael and his ex-wife were actively involved in the program, and Michael was forced to face his own addiction. For the past year, he had attended AA meetings and remained abstinent. Anita felt very much out of the loop because she was not the biological mother of the eldest daughter and was not involved in the recovery process. Michael also kept her out of his AA family. Although Anita attended Al-Anon meetings and totally supported Michael's recovery efforts, she still felt isolated.

Michael had an excellent but adolescent relationship with his fourteen-year-old daughter. The daughter adored him, and Michael reciprocated by spending all his at-home time helping her prepare for her equestrian competitions.

The couple's problems were significant: They rarely had sexual relations, and when they did, it was Anita who initiated them. They were quickly slipping into bankruptcy. Anita was trying to work with the lawyers without Michael's help. Michael slept a lot and was uninterested in doing any couple activities.

Anita was a confident, fun-loving, extroverted person who only wanted to make things right with Michael. She loved him deeply and was totally committed to the marriage. She was frustrated that although she was willing to "do anything," nothing she did seemed to make it right. Michael also professed deep love and commitment for Anita. However, he did not label himself as depressed. He said he was always a serious and quiet person. This had always been a problem between him and Anita. He felt he was justified to feel despondent about his life. He agreed he was a terrible husband but was unable to follow through on any suggestions for increased participation in his marital life.

Originally, Anita's gregariousness and optimism were the catalyst for getting married and having a child. Being around Anita was exciting and

(continued)

(continued)

interesting. Within a short time, however, Michael began to feel pressured to be someone that he knew he would never be. Anita was the night person who loved impromptu get-togethers with friends and neighbors. Michael was a morning person who liked going jogging during the early daybreak hours. Michael began to feel that the personality differences between them were unbridgeable. Anita did too much, talked too much, and thought too much for him.

First, treatment consisted of educating Michael about the benefits that antidepressant medications could have in his case and overcoming a strong antimedication bias. Michael eventually went for a medication evaluation. After taking Prozac for two months, he decided it was not making a significant difference.

Anita was a psychiatric nurse who worked with depressed people and was a natural "resourceful spouse," so little work was needed in that area. She was optimistic, willing to listen, filled with ideas for activities, and able to share in an intimate and open manner.

The most important parts of therapy were the joint marital therapy sessions. After a few sessions, two main marital issues emerged: Michael's long-buried resentments over Anita's assumption that he would be the primary breadwinner and Anita's feeling that his privateness and quietness were passive-aggressive maneuvers to get back at her for unvoiced slights. Over the course of several sessions, Anita admitted that for many years she had relied on Michael to financially support the family but realized that in the future they would have to share that burden. She related her dependency on Michael to a desire to have the security she never felt as a child growing up in a chaotic, abusive, alcoholic home. Michael began to see how he had to give Anita some clear clues as to what he was feeling so that she would not interpret his habitual withdrawal as a personal attack.

Through a series of metaphoric exercises in which Michael and Anita symbolically represented their chronic interaction problems, Michael came to appreciate that Anita's feelings of personal rejection and punishment were reasonable reactions. He did not intend to inflict such feelings on her but realized that he was making it extremely difficult for her to avoid such feelings. One of the most powerful images was the dinner table image that they constructed as a couple. Anita was pictured as a giant, electronic appliance with blinking emergency lights and whistles going off in all directions. Michael was pictured as a little boy, hiding under a chair that was covered with a blanket and trying, one by one, to pull hundreds of wires out of the appliance so that it would turn off before it blew up. He was pulling the wires out with a remote control device so that if anyone came home, he would not be blamed for breaking the machine. The fact that the symbolism is obvious is not as important as that it provided a correctable, working image for the couple that blamed neither person for the problem.

(continued)

(continued)

Therapy lasted six months. When the couple terminated therapy, they were still unsure if they would be able to successfully remain married. However, they were able to enjoy some time together and work on limited family issues together. By the end of therapy, Michael's depression had lifted significantly and he had found a job with a well-established company at a good salary. He reported feeling more optimistic and was able to think more clearly.

LEARNING AIDS

Therapeutic Dialogue (Depression)

Therapists working with depressed, married clients should explore the following areas:

1. What in the marriage makes the client depressed?
2. What in most people's marriages makes them depressed?
3. What similarities and differences are there between your clients' situation and the average couple they know?
4. What coping options are available to the client?
5. What coping options are available to people the client knows in similar situations?
6. What can the client do to create more options?
7. How were depressive affect and behaviors handled in the client's family as a child?
8. How were depressive affect and behaviors handled in the spouse's family as a child?
9. How does the client think the average family he or she knows handles depressive affect and behavior?
10. What can the couple do in their own relationship to create more options when people have feelings of depression?
11. Ideally, how would the client like to handle feelings of depressive affect?
12. Ideally, how would the client like the spouse to handle feelings of depressive affect?
13. Ideally, how would the spouse like to handle the client's feelings of depressive affect?
14. How realistic are each of these ideal images? How can the ideal image be modified to make it more attainable?

Self-Exploration 1: The Resourceful Spouse Scale

This exercise lets spouses communicate how supportive and resource-ful they perceive their spouses to be. In general, therapists should focus on those areas in which the partner feels less than a "3" (a moderate amount) of resourcefulness or supportiveness.

Rate how often you agree with the following statements using the scale below:

1 = not at all
2 = a little
3 = a moderate amount
4 = very frequently
5 = all the time

1. My partner can handle problems that come up in my life.
2 My partner is able to take care of himself or herself.
3. My partner loves me and cares about me.
4. When I am sad or worried, I can tell my partner.
5. After talking problems over with my partner, I feel calmer.
6. When life gets rough, I can count on my partner.
7. Our relationship is very important to my partner.
8. We make important decisions together.
9. We share responsibility for our life together.
10. My partner tries to "work things out with me" so that I get what is most important to me.
11. When I tell my partner I am angry, my partner listens to me.
12. To make our life better, my partner has had to give up what was important to him or her.
13. My partner knows how to contain his or her worry and not let it get in the way of our relationship.
14. We laugh a lot together.
15. My partner has forgiven me for things I have done.
16. My partner has taught me a lot about life.
17. Our relationship enriches my spiritual life.

Note:

Items 1 and 2 tap perceived competency of the mate.
Items 3-7 tap attachment feelings.
Items 8-13 tap the perceived problem-solving skills of the spouse.
Items 14-17 tap feelings of positive commitment.

Low scorers (mean of less than 3) are feeling the absence of a supportive, resourceful spouse. Individual sessions with the nonresourceful spouse are often helpful in overcoming resistance toward change. When both spouses are low scorers, negotiating small acts of friendship provides a good starting point.

Sample Workshop Flowchart Intended for Groups of Four or Five Couples Working with Depression

I. Psychoeducational Strategies
   A. What causes depression?
   B. Common personality traits and depression
   C. External stress and its role in depression
   D. Coping styles and depression
   E. The protective nature of social support
   F. Characteristics of marriages with a depressed partner
      1. Greater frequency of depressive behaviors
      2. Lower level of marital cohesion
      3. A greater lack of symmetry in relationships
      4. A greater level of hostility

II. Self-Exploration (Done by couples in private and shared before rejoining the group)
   A. The Resourceful Spouse Scale

III. Therapeutic Dialogue (Done by couples in private and shared before rejoining the group)
   Proceeding in the order presented, both partners respond to each question before going on to discuss the next question.
   In group, the therapist explores with couples how relationship goals can be achieved by modifying overly ambitious, pie-in-the-sky expectations. Using information about their current situation and the realities seen among friends and family, couples fine-tune expectations so they are achievable and motivate rather than discourage attempts at change.

IV. Therapeutic Interventions
   Work with a couple in front of the group and apply one or more of the therapeutic interventions. Share the rationale during demonstrations. Let the group discuss additional interventions.
   A. Three vital assessment questions
   B. Assessing feelings of personal control and efficacy
   C. Sculpting
   D. Equity in marriage: creating a long-term view

E. Strategies for resourceful partners with depressed mates
1. Psychoeducation and bibliotherapy
2. Generalization tactics for coping with a depressed partner
3. Spouse-assisted therapy reframing the depression to include the well partner's contribution
4. Having both spouses engage in pleasurable activities
5. Stressing an attitude of commitment
6. Networking clients, partners, or both with their religious community, if appropriate
7. Helping the resourceful partner sharpen his or her debating skills
8. Encouraging the resourceful partner to use touch
9. Having the resourceful partner acknowledge and share in experience of loss
10. Encouraging self-sufficiency in the depressed partner
11. Developing and maintaining marital rituals

V. Finding Motivation and Time to Make the Changes
Group discussion

Bibliotherapy

Barker, P. (1993). *A self-help guide to managing depression.* New York: Chapman and Hall.

Branson, K. and Babcock, D. (1992). *I don't know who you are anymore: A family's struggle with depression.* New York: Legendary.

Burns, D. (1990). *The feeling good handbook.* New York: Dutton.

Hinchliffe, M. (1978). *The melancholy marriage: Depression in marriage and psychosocial approaches to therapy.* New York: John Wiley. (Professional book)

Sholevar, P. (Ed.). (1994). *Transmission of depression in families and children: Assessment and intervention.* Northvale, NJ: Jason Aronson. (Professional book)

U.S. Department of Health and Human Services. Public Health Service. (1993). Depression is a treatable illness: A guide for patients (AHCPR Publication No. 93-0553). Rockville, MD: Author.

Williams, M. (1993). *The psychological treatment of depression: A guide to the theory and practice of cognitive behavior therapy.* New York: Routledge.

Videotherapy

Death of a Salesman. (1986). Directed by Volker Schlondorff. Beaten down by life, a salesman finds no solace in his home and family.

It's a Wonderful Life. (1946). Directed by Frank Capra. Hollywood's best
    example of how philosophy of life affects depression and holds the
    cure.
When a Man Loves a Woman. (1994). Directed by Luis Mandoki. A won-
    derful portrayal of a resourceful spouse who helps his alcoholic wife.

Professional Development Questions (Depression)

1. How would you decide if spouse-assisted therapy, couples therapy,
   or individual psychotherapy were most appropriate in treating someone with depression?

2. How persuasive is the evidence that an unhappy marriage can pre-
   cipitate a depressive episode? What ethical responsibility does a
   therapist have to explore the marital relationship when a person
   comes in for individual psychotherapy to treat depression?

3. What factors make for a resourceful spouse? Which do you think
   would be the easiest to teach someone and which the most difficult?
   Why?

4. Very often, the partner of a depressed spouse is pushing for the depressed spouse to take medications, although the depressed spouse is
   very resistant to being medicated. What couple dynamics might be increasing the resistance of the depressed spouse toward taking the
   medication? What couple dynamics might be fueling the partner to
   pressure for medication? How might the therapist address these dynamics in the session?

REFERENCES

Ainsworth, M., Blehar, M., Waters, E., and Wall, S. (1978). *Patterns of attach-
    ment.* Hillsdale, NJ: Lawrence Erlbaum.
Arkowitz, H., Holliday, S., and Hutter, M. (1982). "Depressed women and their
    husbands: A study of marital interaction and adjustment." Paper presented at
    the annual meeting of the Association for Advancement of Behavior Therapy,
    Los Angeles, November.
Beach, S. R., Arias, I., and O'Leary, K. D. (1986). Relationship of marital satis-
    faction and social support to depressive symptomatology. *Journal of Psycho-
    pathology and Behavioral Assessment, 8*(4), 305-316.

Beach, S. R. and Nelson, G. M. (1989). "Marital discord and depression: Is depression associated with a distinct type of marital discord?" Paper presented at the 97th meeting of the American Psychological Association, New Orleans, August.

Beach, S. R., Nelson, G. M., and O'Leary, K. D. (1988). Cognitive and marital factors in depression. *Journal of Psychopathology and Behavioral Assessment, 10*(2), 93-105.

Beach, S. R., Sandeen, E. E., and O'Leary, K. D. (1990). *Depression in marriage.* New York: Guilford.

Beck, A. T. (1967). *Depression: Causes and treatment.* Philadelphia: University of Pennsylvania Press.

Beck, A. T., Rush, A. J., Shaw, B. F., and Emery, G. (1979). *Cognitive therapy of depression.* New York: Guilford.

Billings, A. G. and Moos, R. H. (1982). Life stressors and social resources affect posttreatment outcomes among depressed patients. *Journal of Abnormal Psychology, 94*(2), 140-153.

Birtchnell, J., and Kennard, J. (1983). Does marital maladjustment lead to mental illness? *Social Psychiatry, 18*(2), 79-88.

Brown, G. W. and Harris, T. (1978). *Social origins of depression: A study of psychiatric disorders in women.* London: Tavistock.

Depression Guideline Panel. (1993). Depression in primary care: Vol. 1. Diagnosis and detection (AHCPR Publication No. 93-0550). Rockville, MD: U.S. Department of Health and Human Services.

Feeney, B. and Kirkpatrick, L. (1996). Effects of adult attachment and the presence of romantic partners on physiological responses to stress. *Journal of Personality and Social Psychology, 70*(2), 255-270.

Hautzinger, M., Linden, M., and Hoffman, N. (1982). Distressed couples with and without a depressed partner: An analysis of their verbal interaction. *Journal of Behavior Therapy and Experimental Psychiatry, 13*(4), 307-314.

Hooley, J. M. and Hahlweg, K. (1985). The marriages and interaction patterns of depressed patients and their spouses: Comparing high and low EE dyads. In M. J. Goldstein, I. Hand, and K. Hahlweg (Eds.), *Treatment of schizophrenia: Family assessment and intervention.* Heidelberg and Berlin: Springer-Verlag.

Hooley, J. M. and Teasdale, J. D. (1989). Predictors of relapse in unipolar depressives: Expressed emotion, marital distress, and perceived criticism. *Journal of Abnormal Psychology, 98*(3), 229-235.

Husaini, H. and vonFrank, A. (1985). Life events, coping resources and depression. *Research in Community and Mental Health, 5*(1), 111-136.

Kahn, J., Coyne, J. C., and Margolin, G. (1985). Depression and marital disagreement: The social interaction of despair. *Journal of Social and Personal Relationships, 2*(3), 447-461.

Lewinsohn, P. A. (1987). *Depression prevention: Research directions. The series in clinical and community psychology.* Washington, DC: Hemisphere.

Lewinsohn, P. A., Antonuccio, D. A., Steinmetz, J., and Teri, L. (1984). *The coping with depression course: A psychoeducational intervention for unipolar depression.* Eugene, OR: Castalia.

Merikangas, K. R., Ranelli, C. J., and Kupfer, D. J. (1979). Marital interaction in hospitalized depressed patients. *Journal of Nervous and Mental Disease, 167*(11), 689-695.

Monroe, S. M., Bromet, E. J., Connell, M. M., and Steiner, C. (1986). Social support, life events and depressive symptoms: A one–year prospective study. *Journal of Consulting and Clinical Psychology, 54*(4), 424-431.

Nelson, G. M. and Beach, S. R. (1990). Sequential interaction in depression: Effects of depressive behavior on spousal aggression. *Behavior Therapy, 21*(2), 167-182.

O'Leary, K. D., Riso, L. P., and Beach, S. R. (1990). Attributions about the marital discord/depression link and therapy outcome. *Behavior Therapy, 21,* 413-422.

Paykel, E. S., Myers, J. K., Dienelt, M. N., Klerman, G. L., Lindenthal, J. J., and Pepper, M. P. (1969). Life events and depression: A controlled study. *Archives of General Psychiatry, 21*(6), 530-550.

Roberts, J., Gotlib, I., and Kassel, J. (1996). Adult attachment security and symptoms of depression: The mediating role of dysfunctional attitudes and low self-esteem. *Journal of Personality and Social Psychology, 70*(2), 310-320.

Ross, C. E., and Mirowsky, J. (1990). Control or defense: Depression and sense of control over good and bad outcomes. *Journal of Health and Social Behavior, 31*(1), 71-86.

Schmaling, K. and Becker, J. (1991). Empirical studies of the interpersonal relations of adult depressives. In J. Becker and A. Kleinman (Eds.), *Psychosocial aspects of depression* (pp. 169-185). Hillsdale, NJ: Lawrence Erlbaum.

Sherman, R. (1993). Marital issues of intimacy. *Individual Psychology, 49*(3-4), 318-329.

Townsley, R. M., Beach, S. R., Fincham, F. D., and O'Leary, K. D. (1991). Cognitive specificity for marital discord and depression: What cognitions influence discord? *Behavior Therapy, 22*(4), 519-530.

Weissman, M. M. (1987). Advances in psychiatric epidemiology: Rates and risks for major depression. *American Journal of Public Health, 77*(3), 445-451.

Wright, J. H., Thase, M. E., Beck, A. T., and Ludgate, J. W. (1993). *Cognitive therapy with inpatients: Developing a cognitive milieu.* New York: Guilford.

Chapter 3

Anxiety and the Couple Relationship

Never underestimate people's ability not to know when they are in pain.

Art Garfunkel

ANXIETY: WHAT ARE THE SYMPTOMS?

Although epidemiological studies indicate that the majority of individuals with generalized anxiety disorder are women (55 to 65 percent), all ages and sexes are at risk (Brown, Barlow, and Liebowitz, 1994). Consider that Himmelfarb and Murrell (1984) found an astonishing 17 percent of elderly men and 21.5 percent of elderly women living in the community had sufficiently intense anxiety that could benefit from some medication or psychotherapeutic intervention.

Indeed, within most marriages, anxiety is as stressful and distressing as anger or depression. Many people still do not use the term anxiety. They simply say they have a case of the nerves, are overly sensitive, or act neurotic.

Anxiety is multifaceted. Distinct physiological reactions, thoughts, and feelings are associated with it (Barlow, 1988). The physiological indicators include heightened muscle tension and agitation, irritability, restlessness, easy fatigability, and feeling "keyed up." The experiential component of anxiety is usually more distressing. People feel as if they cannot stand being in their own bodies. They cannot concentrate or pay attention to the task at hand. They are consumed with trying to reduce their discomfort but are unable to think clearly about what is triggering their anxiety or how they can desensitize themselves to the anxiety-arousing cues. Behaviorally, a person may exhibit trouble sleeping, a poor attention span, quick distractibility, and fidgetiness (Marten et al., 1995).

Anxious thoughts are fairly easy to describe. They are simple and involve lots of worry: "This won't work out." "Something terrible is going to happen." "I am going to be unable to cope." "I'm afraid of going crazy." Often, it does not get more sophisticated than that. Thus, the beliefs most strongly associated with anxiety may include nervousness, a sense of uneasiness, unpredictability, and a shaky, equivocal sense of control (see DSM-IV; American Psychiatric Association, 1994). Anxious people avoid fully confronting their feared scenarios and rehearsing ways of coping with possible disasters. Instead of confronting and working through possible problems, they constrict their thinking to repetitive, simple "what if" queries that magnify and focus on their sense of powerlessness (Borkovec and Inz, 1990).

The symptoms may vary somewhat from person to person, but almost everyone can recognize what it means to be jittery, on the edge of a nervous breakdown, chronically insecure, or anxious.

THE EXISTENTIAL MEANING OF ANXIETY

The basic problem is man's anxiety in time, e.g., his present anxiety of himself in relation to his past and his parents (Freud); his present anxiety over himself in relation to his future and his neighbors (Marx); and his present anxiety over himself in relation to eternity and God (Kierkegaard).

W. H. Auden

Anxiety, luckily, is not like being pregnant. You can have varying degrees of anxiety. It can be as slightly noticeable as a day-old mosquito bite or as consuming as a red-alert, nuclear attack threat. For all of us, the intensity of our anxieties ebbs and flows over hours, days, and months. In most societies, people want to get rid of this chronically unsettling mixture of apprehension, physiological arousal, and fear, regardless of its intensity. However, anxiety is very adaptive and is at the very root of what it means to be human. The ability to be anxious is one of the distinguishing features of our species.

Anxiety is universal and unavoidable. It occurs whenever we need to change: when we have to stop doing something we have come to think is "our way of doing things" or when we have to learn a new way of behaving or thinking. Because a good marriage involves constant change and growth, it involves anxiety. To reject new opportunities to get closer or have a more dynamic marriage may seem foolhardy and paradoxical. But to choose a new behavior, attitude, or interaction means that we are giving up the security of the known for the uncertainty of the unknown. Making such choices affirms our uniqueness, our aloneness, and our lack of control. It makes us existentially anxious (Fischer, 1988; Fromm, 1941).

Married life is filled with such existential, anxiety-arousing choices. For example, a wife may have the opportunity to take an interesting class, but it meets two nights a week and would severely limit the amount of time that the couple spends together. She is nervous about how it would affect the relationship, so she chooses not to take the class. A husband wants to try a different type of foreplay but is afraid of how his wife will react to his request. He chooses to keep the desire a secret. In both of these cases, the anxiety associated with change is avoided but so also is the potential for learning and growing with one's spouse.

In our working definition, anxiety is the mix of rational and irrational fears that we project onto the future. Any situation that creates change provokes some measure of anxiety. It is healthy to recognize when changes are imminent so we can prepare and adapt. Unfortunately, many people get so overwhelmed by the messenger (anxiety) at the door that they never read the message. It is healthy in a marriage to acknowledge both the message and the messenger. Lucky is the couple who can mutually acknowledge their apprehensiveness, with excitement and optimism riding on the back of the anxiety.

Another way of saying this is that anxiety is the feeling we get when we fear change. It is the conscious recognition that although the future is unknown and unknowable, we want to maintain continuity, purpose, and an even flow. Many believe that not all change involves anxiety, only change that threatens some core value. The threat can be to physical life, of course, but in today's world, the threat is more often to one's psychological life (one's loss of freedom or meaningfulness or security). To be anxious, then, is to be motivated and mobilized to protect one's identity (May, 1950).

Anxiety provides the necessary vigilance needed for preservation of self. It allows the unique identity of each person to be self-directed instead of conditioned, solely, by outside forces. Thus, if a wife feels that time away from her husband threatens her core value of being a committed wife, she will feel far more anxiety about taking a course than if she feels that they will still have ample time to be together. The husband who feels that discussing his sexual fantasies would threaten his core value of respecting his wife's modesty will feel more anxiety than if he simply would be embarrassed by a seemingly unusual desire.

COUPLE ANXIETY AND THE USE OF DEFENSE MECHANISMS

The Greek figure of Medusa is the icon of anxiety. Her hair is full of writhing serpents reaching upward and outward. Medusa symbolizes the irrational forces in the world that can get us even if we are mindful and focused. She is not the symbol of rational fears but, rather, that unexplainable fear that can materialize at any moment. She symbolizes the dark and devouring forces of Earth that threaten our identity. In the Medusa legend, whoever looked at Medusa turned to stone. In our personal lives, anxiety is the most frightful of all emotions and freezes us so that we cannot behave, think, or feel the human range of experience—it is as though we were made of stone. Our Medusas are both internal and external. She is the collapse of security when our mate is insensitive to our needs. She is the void we feel when we ponder the meaning of our overstructured, underexamined life. She is the feeling we get after trying to teach our three-year-old how to go to the potty and we continue to hit a brick wall.

Because anxiety is aroused when our values are threatened, not only does change provoke anxiety, all types of spousal rejection do so as well. Whenever a spouse is insulting or demeaning, the core value of being worthy of spousal approval and respect is threatened. An intimate loving partner is extremely affirming of our values, likes, and dislikes. This is what makes it easy to be intimate. Thus, when a spouse speaks honestly of differences in values and priorities, the first reaction is to feel threatened and anxious. That on-the-edge feeling makes people want to explain and defend themselves, to sway their partners' judgments and decisions. They want to be reassured about their basic worthiness. Couples need to learn how to balance the need to reassure each other with the need to honestly bring differences to the table for discussion. The only way to do this successfully is to learn how to recognize and manage marital anxiety.

When anxiety becomes severe enough, both men and women use a variety of psychological defense mechanisms to deal with it. Men are more likely to deal with anxiety by using alcohol and drugs (repression or suppression) or seeking thrill and adventure activities (displacement) (Monti et al., 1989). Women are more likely to deal with anxiety by getting depressed, somaticizing the anxiety into real physical complaints, or seeking the comfort of the family of origin (regression) (Vanfossen, 1986).

Members of either sex can become overly dependent on their spouses (identification), overschedule their free time (avoidance), seek the comfort of religion, or structure their lives by using multiple rituals to avoid strange situations. All of the defense mechanisms work by creating the illusion that change can be avoided—that the psychological identity (e.g., values, desires, aspirations) of the person is not being threatened—or by limiting one's perceptions of the available choices.

Neuroticism or emotional instability has been the most consistent personality predictor of marital instability (Hafner and Spence, 1988; Kelly and

Conley, 1987; Kim, Martin, and Martin, 1989). Think about it. The largest single predictor of whether a marriage will end in a divorce is the mental upset and instability of each of the partners. Because a large portion of "neuroticism" is usually anxiety and insecurity, an anxious spouse is likely to be in a high-risk, unhappy marriage. But why? What is the path by which anxiety comes to wreak havoc on a marriage? The chains linking anxiety and marital happiness are many, but the focus here is on the six major couplers discussed next.

PROVOKERS OF ANXIETY IN MARRIAGE

Worry is interest paid on trouble before it falls due.

W. R. Inge

Existential Questioning and the Search for a Meaningful Life

First marriages may appear to occur at a mature age in this county. After all, the average age for a man to get married is 26.3 years and the average age for a women is 24.1 years (U.S. Bureau of the Census, 1994). Even so, most individuals are not "fully formed," in a societal sense, when they take their marriage vows. They are still groping for career choices, negotiating adult relationships with parents, and experimenting with life as an adult. After marriage, individuals continue to change and grow at a rapid pace.

Because marriage is one of the biggest decisions people make, many assume that they are committing themselves to maintaining the status quo. "Till death do us part" is supposed to be like it is during the honeymoon period. With that cultural fantasy, no wonder couples are shocked by how much each of them can change after only a few years. Decade after decade, new challenges, choices, and opportunities keep confronting a person. All of these burdens and opportunities are accompanied by fear, apprehension, and change.

Anxiety conflicts are, at root, existential reactions to the need for change. Existential anxieties deal with universal themes such as the inevitability of loss, the experience of a separate consciousness, the yoke of personal responsibility, the awareness and acceptance of our own mortality, and the search for a meaningful life. If we marry in our twenties and stay married till our fifties we are grappling with these developmentally triggered issues for much of married life (Yalom, 1980).

A meaningful life occurs when we have our own identity and values, a sense of order and coherence about our existence. Each person's meaning of life is unique. It does not come from reading a book or having the right type of childhood. It must be discovered by living, by discovering meaning along the path of experience. Having a meaningful life does not necessitate having a happy life, particularly when the personal meanings include values such as self-sacrifice, duty, and obligation.

No one can escape the search for meaning in one's life. It is a midlife developmental task that emerges as surely as the infant's need to learn to walk or talk. The search for meaning creates anxiety because, to find what is meaningful to us, we have to risk following our private callings. Very often, adult children lack the freedom to follow their private callings because they still feel psychologically intimidated by their need to please their own parents. A woman who may want to stay home with her children feels pressure from her parents, who sacrificed to send her to law school to have a full-time career. A man who may want to play with a jazz band on the weekend is inhibited by his father's feeling that such behavior is a stupid escape and a good way to lose a wife.

Even after individuating from their family of origin, people may be too frightened to risk following their private callings because they fear the ire and disrespect of their spouses. One partner cannot explore new values and lifestyles easily if his or her spouse is critical and nonsupportive. We each want our spouses to be stable so that we can explore and take risks. We panic when our anchors pull up and drift out to unknown waters. If we stay on board, we may be extremely unhappy because we have no control over where we are headed. If we stay on shore and let our spouse explore, we are deserted.

The combination of not knowing who we are and being afraid that trying on new identities will cause friction within the family creates the existential anxiety of meaninglessness during the marital years. The jokester who wants to try to be more serious, the thin woman who does not want to try to keep her girlish figure, and the workaholic who wants to suddenly make do with a part-time job may all feel harsh, unrelenting waves of anxiety as they fear upsetting the family equilibrium for some unknown, value-changing persona.

Another related source of existential anxiety involves coming to grips with our responsibilities. Each generation defines, however loosely, the obligations for the men and women in that generation. Our generation has been particularly polarized about adult responsibilities. Some say we have a responsibility to stay home with our children; others say we have a responsibility to develop ourselves in the greater work world. Many say we each need to pay our own way, but no one has told us what is too little to pay or when we have paid enough. As adults, we are confused about how much comfort we are entitled to and how much sacrifice is appropriate; we are unsure if we should constantly shed our interests and friends in favor of new experiences or if we should bask in the safety of well-known routines. Couples are always coping with how independent, interdependent, or dependent they should be with one another at various phases of their lives.

Conventional Passages (Choice Points) Cause Existential Anxiety

In our particular sociological epoch, a large number of choices faced by married couples still follow a predictable, developmental pattern. In the early years, decisions have to be made about how interdependent each spouse will be with his or her family of origin, how much time each will devote to work and hobbies and how much time each will devote to the other, how the finances will be handled, where they should live, when they should move, how much they should save and for what purposes, and if and when to have children.

For the overwhelming majority of couples who end up parenting, the everyday choices involved in raising children are overwhelming. Parents are held accountable by society for raising pleasant, responsible little people. Tantrums, aggression, rejection, illness, and intellectual and physical deficiencies are all problems that parents feel they must respond to. But how? The choices are endless. There are questions of schooling, camps, day care, religious training, chores, privacy, boundary setting, rule setting, and recreation. Older children present us with even more choices.

With too many choices confronting us, it is impossible to adequately evaluate all of the alternatives and feel confidence in our selection. Most of us, most of the time, make important decisions based on the flimsiest of information. Deciding where to live, how much to spend on a house, or which job field to enter is more complicated than ever before. Understandably, we become anxious about having to make such decisions and anxious about having to live with the consequences of the decisions.

Midlife Crises and Anxiety

Midlife crises cause many divorces. The dentist who decides he wants to be a social worker, the homemaker who decides she wants to hit the road with a high-powered sales job, and the husband who decides he wants to date young women and nurture his erotic potential are all classic examples of midlife crises. In the book *Turning Points,* Ellen Goodman (1979) discusses how the midlife search for meaning occurs when one senses the passing of the sand through life's hourglass. The recognition that the dreams of youth and young adulthood were not fulfilled or were not what they promised to be creates a sense of panic.

Marital therapy for a midlife crisis requires a mix of existential searching and spousal flexibility. In existential therapy, the focus is on the basic questions that confront each human: What does it mean to be free? What types of freedom are important to me? For whom am I responsible and what are the limits of my responsibility? How can I deal with the fact of my ultimate aloneness on this earth? How can I deal philosophically with my own mortality (Yalom, 1980)?

The answers to these questions are, of course, not as important as the journey one goes on in an attempt to answer them. In existential psychotherapy, individuals review their lives like scathing book critics. They also have the option of writing the sequel or the next chapter. In fact, they are encouraged to do so. The challenge for all humans seeking fulfillment is to work with the hand that has been dealt, not to simply throw down the cards and leave the game.

Accepting the idea that one can write a new chapter instead of dropping out and making a whole new story is essential for a positive marital reconciliation in such midlife crises. Once the angst-ridden partner is ready to embrace the rewrite, the observing partner must be willing to coproduce the production. What often happens, unfortunately, is that couples enter a midlife crisis at similar times and find each other unwilling to make the changes desired so much by the other. This is the true psychological definition of irreconcilable differences.

THERAPEUTIC INTERVENTION 1: NOVEL-IN-PROGRESS TECHNIQUE FOR RESOLVING MARITAL CRISES

The use of storytelling is gaining increased popularity as a therapeutic intervention. When couples reach a major choice point and are at odds on how to proceed, it is often helpful to have them compose two orthogonal stories of their marital history (adapted from Bateson, 1993). In the first version, the couple tries to tell their life story by emphasizing the continuity in their relationship—how one event naturally and predictably led to another in a clear, inevitable pattern. This is usually easy to do—it is the type of story couples tend to use to make sense of their experience. In the second version, the couple tries to construct a marital history following on this statement: "After lots of surprises and choices, or interruptions and disappointments, we have arrived someplace neither of us ever could have anticipated." Sometimes, the stories become dichotomous: One version

(continued)

(continued)

stresses the predictability of life, whereas the other stresses its unpredictability; one is the story of choices that have been made, whereas the other is the story of chance occurrences with which one has had to deal; one has a theme of optimism, the other a theme of pessimism. By having couples realize that there is more than one plausible story to explain the history of their marriage, they can creatively try to "write" the midlife crisis into the script by coauthoring and merging various versions.

For example, a woman who wanted to take a weekend job to learn new skills was struggling because her husband felt she was distancing herself from him at a very low point in their relationship when they most needed time together. Two stories evolved about this marriage, differentiated by the fact that one story traced all of the personal sacrifices they had made to stay together this long, and in the other story, they focused on how each of their personal triumphs had strengthened their commitment to work for a closer, better marriage. Then, in session, they created the next chapter to each story. The chapter added to the first story was based on the wife's not taking the job (the sacrifice story). The chapter added to the second story was based on the wife's taking the job (the cup-runneth-over story). They agreed it was up to them to write either of these chapters or go on to write still other chapters.

CASE STUDY 1: CHOICE POINTS AND THE FLYING GASTROENTEROLOGIST

Midlife crises tore apart the marriage of Julia and Evan. Julia was a South African woman from a very wealthy family. She had attended the best boarding schools and gone to a prestigious small liberal arts college in the States. There she met Evan, a bright, middle-class, premed student from Missouri.

They married the week after graduation and went off for a six-month trip around the world. When they returned, Evan prepared himself for the beginning of medical school. Evan's father was a dentist who had always wanted to be a doctor. The next best thing was for Evan to become one. Evan was the only son, fulfilling a father's dream. He was also excited about med school and hoped to do public health work after graduating. Julia got ready for her graduate school career in clinical psychology.

Julia's parents' money allowed them to buy a spacious condo near the campus. Julia's parents were temporarily living in the same city where Julia and Evan attended school, and the two couples often went together for an evening out or a weekend trip. Julia's five years in school were consumed by her studies and Evan. When she graduated, Evan still had

(continued)

(continued)

his residency to do. She took a part-time job so that she would be able to do things with Evan on the rare times he was available. During this period, she got pregnant for the first and only time. Her baby died at birth, and she had a hysterectomy.

Over the next seven years, they adopted two children. Evan did a fellowship after his residency and then spent a year on a public health project. He worked hard and was the rising star. Julia was the ideal mother and wife and put her career on the back burner—working one day a week at a community mental health clinic. They had ample help in the house, and the children had a full-time nanny. Around this time, suddenly all funds in South Africa were frozen and Julia's parents could no longer subsidize the couple. Julia could not help the family maintain the style to which she and Evan had become accustomed.

Evan panicked. He could not imagine going to an office every day and doing gastronenterology. The changing financial picture occurred right before Evan's father died from a six-month bout with brain cancer. When he was first diagnosed, a very emotional scene occurred between Evan and him, where he implored Evan not to throw his life away trying to make money or being tied to his work. He was regretful that he had pushed Evan to become a doctor. Evan's panic became chronic. He decided not to join a group practice. He stayed home, paralyzed. Julia pressured him to do something because they desperately needed money. She took a full-time job, and after a year of "exploring his options," Evan decided to fly a small plane for corporate travelers. He thought this would make him happy.

Julia demanded that they go to therapy because she could not live with that decision. They attended only three sessions. Evan announced in the second session that he wanted a divorce. He did not want Julia's pressures to be his pressures, and his quest for happiness was different from hers. He felt that the children needed parental time, and economics was of little consequence. Julia was crushed, but by the third session, Evan had gotten a lawyer and refused to attend any more therapy sessions. Julia was seen in therapy throughout the divorce process. Recently, she sent me a letter saying that she had remarried three years after the divorce. Evan lived a simple life and had not remarried but was a wonderful father. They all got together for family celebrations and holidays. Julia was now thankful to Evan for realizing so early that they wanted different lives and for making it possible for them both to achieve their goals.

Illness

The health psychology literature is consistent in demonstrating that illness is both a cause and consequence of family dysfunction. On one hand, acute and chronic illnesses place stressors and strains on all members of the family (Sperry and Carlson, 1992). Economic hardships become coupled with changes in social interactions and intimacy expectations for the sick as well as the healthy spouse (Burns-Teitelbaum, 1996). Anxiety can permeate the entire family. On the other hand, chronic family stress, caused by a child or a spouse, can contribute to compromised immune function, somatization responses, and the breakdown of coping responses to ongoing medical conditions.

Patterson and McCubbin (1983) cite how the following hardships affect the marital relationship and the children when there is an ill spouse:

- There is invariably a marked increase in strained family relationships, characterized by overprotectiveness and worry about the ill spouse alternating with rejection, anger, and depression concerning the illness and its costs. Often, acting out and depression are evident among the children. The increased vulnerability of the ill spouse can make that person a convenient scapegoat, absorbing the blame for the current problems between other family members.
- Many times, family rituals are lost as the ill member can no longer fully participate.
- The family structure is altered with the burden of increased tasks and time commitments. The treatment regimen, hospital and doctor visits, and so on, all take their toll on both spouses.
- Very often, an increase in financial burden occurs as health insurance does not give adequate coverage and the income of the ill spouse is reduced or lost.
- Sometimes the family is faced with the need to relocate so that the ill spouse is in a better climate, near medical facilities, or in a house with features adapted to his or her disability.
- Social isolation occurs because of fatigue, less discretionary income, and an inability to continue old social rituals.
- Grieving is a natural and unavoidable hardship for spouses who face disabling or terminal illnesses.

Clearly, this list just touches the surface of the problem. Demographic and cultural variables, such as age, ethnicity, personality, and history, all affect the meaning of illness and its impact on the interpersonal relationships in the family.

Overall, however, illness causes anxiety and stress in the marital partner as well as the ill partner. Research reviews on how spouses adjust to cancer in their partner conclude that stress is the highest when the prognosis is poor because the cancer has metastasized or the partner is in a terminal stage. The extent of caregiving required from the healthy spouse, the duration of the illness, and the patient's distress also affect the spouse's stress level. If the cancer survivor adjusts well to his or her posttreatment status, the spouse also tends to adjust well. In general, women are more worried and emotionally depleted by their husband's illness than vice versa (Sales, Schulz, and Biegel, 1992).

Do not be misled to think that only life-threatening conditions have a significant influence on the marital relationship. Andrews, Abbey, and Halman (1991), for example, found that the stress of infertility had profound effects on the marital relationship. The researchers interviewed 157 couples in their homes for over an hour. All had tried to conceive, unsuccessfully, for over a year, but none had yet tried the most advanced infertility treatments such as in vitro fertilization or gamete intrafallopian transfer. A continuum of stress was experienced by the couples. High-stress couples reported being very taxed by the tests and treatments recommended by the doctors, missing work because of doctor's appointments, feeling overburdened by keeping track of ovulation, and feeling that their lives had changed because of the fertility problems. Indeed, couples who reported these stressors did have negative marital consequences in four distinct areas: They had greater marital conflict, they felt less sexually attractive, they felt more sexually inadequate, and they were now having sexual intercourse less frequently. Low-stress couples did not experience hassles and anxieties because of the infertility, and they also did not report experiencing the marital problems experienced by the stressed couples.

Gender differences in illness frequency and expression are also the cause for much havoc in relationships. First, women tend to have many more illnesses than men, visit the doctor more often for comparable symptoms, and be restricted to the bed more often. Although women appear to be hormonally protected from cardiovascular disease until menopause, they are at greater risk for sex-specific conditions than are men. Men, on the other hand, have more of the severe health problems of all types and die, on the average, five to seven years earlier than women. The major explanation for this paradox is constitutional. "Women bend and men break" is the working metaphor.

The greater health problems of women are accompanied by other gender differences of a more psychological nature. Women are more sensitive to bodily discomforts than men, tend to rate symptoms as more serious than men, and are more likely to label symptoms as illness. In brief, women tend to be more anxious than men about their health. Contrary to expectations, women who have multiple roles (mother, spouse, employee) are no more likely to be ill than women with one or two roles. Indeed, the health risks seem to be lower for men and women who are involved in multiple, active roles.

Despite the complexity of the topic, two general observations must be made on the relationship between anxiety and spousal illness. First, the anxiety that accompanies physical disability, illness, and disease makes effective communication very difficult. The first reaction of most people is to deny and suppress negative information about their ill health. They look to their spouses to confirm their wellness—not their sickness. If their spouse becomes overly concerned, they feel smothered and feel that the future is very ominous. If their spouses are too casual or not concerned, ill persons may feel abandoned and that they are not getting the support they need to make the best decisions for their treatment. Because anxiety interferes with the hearing and processing of much new information, couples need to discuss a new illness frequently and repeatedly.

The most important help that the well spouse can offer is to "normalize" the life of the ill spouse and keep as many routines and enjoyments in place as possible. The more couples do things together as a unit, the less likely that anxiety will reach a debilitating level. The most helpful "attitudinal" stance is to maintain hope, attachment, optimism, faith, and courage. As always, it is helpful to look outside the family for social support and information on how to handle problems. Businesses, for example, prodded by federal legislation, are beginning to help well family members support their loved ones. Under the Family and Medical Leave Act (FMLA) of 1993, firms that employ at least fifty people within a seventy-five-mile radius are required to offer eligible employees (those who have worked over 1,250 hours in the previous year) up to twelve weeks of unpaid leave to care for a sick family member. Ideally, smaller companies or businesses offer similar policies on a voluntary basis.

When one spouse has a chronic, disabling illness, the well spouse needs to build a beautiful memory fortress with a large moat that protects the preillness relationship from the difficult present situation. This may involve the classic defense mechanism of "splitting." It involves romanticizing the good aspects of the relationship while minimizing or denying the hardships. With a memory icon of "the wonderful marriage" and "the wonderful spouse" cemented in consciousness, the well spouse can continue to be both committed and loving. Recent research suggests that well spouses who forget the negative experiences that occurred within the marriage are the most likely to "be there" when the going gets rough and least likely to feel unduly burdened. It is as though they are saying, "Life was wonderful until this happened. He (or she) gave me so many wonderful years. We were one spirit and I cannot separate us now."

In a study of spouses who were caretaking mates with Alzheimer's disease, the most stress was experienced by those who had the least positive memories of the marriage and their spouse. Those who were able to forget the bumps and idealize the spouse were able to give because they felt their own cup runneth over (O'Rourke and Wenaus, 1998). What is unclear is if a wonderful marriage is the only force that can strengthen couples for the hard times or if an individual's ability to rewrite the relationship in glowing terms is also a sufficient factor.

Although illness does create anxiety, in the patient as well as in the healthy spouse, it can have many positive effects on marriage. When partners become ill and homebound, they have more time to talk with their mates and be of help. Mates have a chance to be supportive, and patients have a chance to be openly thankful. Joint problem solving is often involved as family members discuss the meaning of symptoms, the choice of remedies, and the reallocation of resources during the illness. Illnesses, particularly temporary illnesses, provide a unique opportunity for bonding and family cohesion.

More serious illnesses also force most couples into a closer, more intense relationship. Carter and Carter (1993) studied twenty spouse pairs in which the wife had a single mastectomy for Stage I/II cancer at least 2.5 years prior to the testing. As individuals, both husbands and wives who had lived through a mastectomy were not any more depressed or anxious than control participants after 2.5 years. As a couple, however, those who weathered a mastectomy were significantly closer to each other and far more willing to adapt to situational pressure than were control couples. In fact, the closeness was so extreme, it was in the unhealthy range, where they were in danger of giving up their individual identities for the sake of a "couple" identity. In addition, their high adaptability, which may have been very appropriate during the medical crisis, lingered on like an anxious coping response, for fear that any routine would be unpredictably shattered.

It appears that when one partner is faced with a serious illness or problem, the marriage does not get too strained if, together, both partners are willing to label the experience as "our problem." The sharing of a negative experience is profoundly strengthening to a relationship. If the primary sufferer says, "No, this is my cross to bear," the partner is marginalized and feels impotent. If the partner says, "I feel for you, but this is your problem and ultimately you are going to need to find the answers," the partner puts himself or herself in the role of consultant and is divorced from the opportunity of a deeper fused relationship. Studies have shown that the challenges made to a couple's relationship when the woman is given a diagnosis of breast cancer are most successfully met by those couples who believe and act as though the cancer is "our problem" (Skerrett, 1998).

Many of these points were well illustrated in the popular TV program *Thirtysomething,* in which there was a yearlong portrayal of a personal ordeal with ovarian cancer. Sharf and Freimuth (1993) conducted an analysis of twenty episodes of this show. The take-home messages of the show were that cancer is a disease that affects the entire family, there is a need to destigmatize people who get cancer, and communication within the family is one of the most effective coping strategies for dealing with the stress of illness. Pretty good advice from prime-time television.

In summary, anxiety, with or without illness, can interfere with marital communication, sexual desire, marital satisfaction, and effective problem solving. No wonder a good cognitive-behavioral therapy program that helps couples lower their anxiety levels can have widespread impact on the marital system.

Recognizing the endemic impact of anxiety, clinicians are trying to treat a variety of problems in which anxiety is only a secondary contributor, to see if reduced levels of anxiety can have a positive clinical impact on the primary problem. For example, researchers in Germany have devised a program to help idiopathic infertile couples increase their chances of conception by lowering their anxiety about the problem (Tiscjem et al., 1999). The goals of the program were to reduce thoughts of helplessness, foster problem solving to increase timed intercourse and lower marital distress. The techniques included psycho-education, cognitive restructuring, and communication skills. The whole focus of the program was to reduce the anxiety about infertility and let couples focus on taking control of the aspects of the situation that were in their control (e.g., how they were relating to each other, how they were following medical directives, etc.). The live birth rate that resulted from this six-month program was higher than what would be expected from looking at epidemiological data. However, due to the lack of real control groups, it is a program in need of replication before we get too excited about its therapeutic potential.

CASE STUDY 2: ANXIETY AND ILLNESS

Kim and George were Asian Americans and had been married for twenty-five years. They had two adult sons and a daughter in college. Both had good incomes, and they lived an enviable lifestyle: season tickets to the opera and the symphony, exotic vacations twice a year, few household responsibilities, nonstressful jobs, and common interests. They were best friends who had many vibrant ties with their extended family and community.

Their troubles began some eleven months prior to seeking treatment when Kim developed a terrible case of cystitis. She felt constant pressure

(continued)

(continued)

on her bladder and had to urinate every fifteen to thirty minutes. Her tests kept coming back "negative," and she was told it was probably stress related. The problem got much worse whenever they had sex. Kim began to get very nervous whenever she was not near a bathroom, and even the thirty-minute car ride to work was an ordeal. She avoided any physical contact with George, lest he wanted to have sex with her. George was supportive for the first six or seven months. Then he began worrying about whether they were ever going to have sex again. He felt that Kim had become self-absorbed and obsessed about the cystitis. She no longer was interested in what was happening with him. Often, she would break into tears while lying in bed or watching TV. She kept on saying that George could not understand and that she needed to be alone. George started to withdraw and developed a cool, removed manner. Kim felt that it was the beginning of the end of her marriage and called for an appointment.

Treatment consisted of conjoint marital sessions, with four major foci. First, George was given support and empathy for the ordeal that he was experiencing. The effects of illness on a family unit were explained in detail, and Kim, for the first time, realized that this illness had affected both of them. It was not merely that George had lost his tolerance and empathy. Rather, the illness was affecting the routines and interactions he needed and had come to depend on. He felt powerless to help Kim. He was very frustrated and stressed by seeing Kim suffer and not knowing how to help.

Second, George was given guidelines on how to be a supportive husband through this crisis period. In particular, he and Kim talked about ways that he could help her from dwelling on the problem. One effective method they found was for George to work with Kim on a "honey-do" list (a list of household chores for one's "honey") whenever Kim seemed distant or preoccupied. After the list was completed, he would be willing to work on the jobs (buy the necessary materials, call for estimates, begin preparing a room for painting) as long as Kim was willing to go along and help him. George also reorganized the CDs and took "control" of a dozen favorites. Whenever Kim was weepy or crying or at her wit's end, George took out the CD and made tea. George was a great husband, and Kim was a responsive, thankful wife. Both strategies worked well, and within four to five weeks their sense of closeness was returning.

Third, Kim's aunt called one day and shared how her own intercystial bladder irritations had gone undiagnosed for five years. Kim decided once again to seek help from another urologist. Direct bladder investigation revealed that indeed she did have an intercystial bladder: a chronic irritation of the lining of the bladder. This condition is different from cystitis, is not due to an infection, and does not appear on the cultures normally taken for cystitis. There are no surefire cures for this problem, and many people go through years of misdiagnosis or stress diagnoses before discovering their problem. Luckily, self-help groups were just being organized in Kim's home state, and she became actively involved in trying to learn to control

(continued)

> *(continued)*
> this disease. Knowing the medical/biological problem was much more reassuring than trying to reduce "stress" in all areas of life.
>   Fourth, the sex problem was dealt with by having them enjoy some noncoital sex for a period of weeks. Then they started using a condom when they were having sex. Kim was careful to urinate after each encounter. The problem was controlled but flared up from time to time. Whether it was due to sex or something else was unclear. Kim had mentally decided to take whatever precautions she could and then try to enjoy her sexual life.

LONELINESS

If you are afraid of loneliness, do not marry.

Chekhov

Despite Chekhov's proclamation, married people are, generally, less lonely than unmarried people (Gove, Style, and Hughes, 1990). Nevertheless, as many as 25 percent of couples in at least one study reported dealing with long periods of loneliness (Barbour, 1993). Today, loneliness occurs for two reasons. First, with so many couples working different times and traveling on their jobs, family time is often reduced to less than a few hours a week. The recreational downtime for one spouse often does not coincide with the downtime of his or her mate for weeks on end. Wanting the comfort of a spouse and not having him or her available makes one very lonely. Second, as the culture has encouraged married people to cultivate their own interests and hobbies, midcareer marriages are often composed of partners with little in common besides children, a common residence, and shared relatives (not to minimize the strength of these three golden bonds). For many couples, the healthy drive for self-actualization becomes a sword of marital alienation and loneliness.

The most endemic type of marital loneliness has been coined "LTL (living together loneliness)" (Kiley, 1989). Living together loneliness is defined as "a person's emotional response to a perceived discrepancy between expected and achieved social contact from any particular person or persons" (p. 23). Kiley posits that as society has shaped couples to expect intimacy, sharing, and emotional belonging with their spouses, the incidence of LTL has increased proportionately.

Generically lonely people feel generally left out, as if there is no one they can turn to. They feel isolated from others and believe that no one really knows them well. Married persons with LTL may have friends and family with whom they share great confidences and intimacies, but if they expect such sharing from their spouse and it is not forthcoming, they still feel lonely. These clients are lonely because they feel isolated and left out from their spouses' lives. They do not feel that their spouses are intuitively in pace with them or know the deeper parts of their being. Because they expect this intense level of connection from their partners and it is not forthcoming, they experience profound feelings of loneliness.

The feeling of loneliness is a mixture of many other feelings—bewilderment, isolation, agitation, depression, and exhaustion—but the feeder emotion is extreme anxiety. Different combinations of feelings may predominate, depending on the developmental stage of the person. On one hand, a newly married man may feel completely bewildered as his new wife is busy planning her career instead of their weekend. He may experience shock and surprise that he, of all people, is in this situation. On the other hand, a serious illness in a person married for twenty years or more may be complicated by a resulting depression that occurs because one feels that he or she does not have a supportive spouse.

Both external and internal causes of marital anxiety can directly lead to LTL. Leading external causes include the aforementioned time squeeze of married couples, geographical mobility and its dissociating effects, and demanding, critical, and avoidant spouse behaviors. Leading internal causes include the inability to personally distinguish between selfishness and feelings of powerlessness. When couples desire to be filled with meaningful interactions and instead feel devastating emptiness, they go through a process of analyzing the appropriateness of their own expectations. Are they simply dependent persons or empty wells, or are they constantly seeking more than their partners deliver? Are they justified in expecting a rich and rewarding interaction with their spouse? Will they ever be able to elicit the responses they so desperately want, or are they impotent to effect change?

The therapist working with LTL clients needs to help them find their personal answers to these questions. Usually, clients need to learn to be more assertive, increase their level of self-disclosure, and acknowledge the emotional limitations of their partners at this point in their marriage. Many a divorce occurs because LTL clients conclude, after many hours of searching, that they want and deserve more than they are getting from their current relationship.

Although LTL is a very common expression of marital anxiety, more extreme clinical problems are associated with LTL. For example, agoraphobia, the fear of leaving home, has been conceptualized, in part, as a marital solution for lonely wives who are dependent on their husbands for company and support. The more disabled they are by their anxiety to do errands, visit friends and relatives, or develop hobbies outside the home, the more they must rely on their husbands to accompany them on such trips. They flee the feeling of aloneness and feel safety only when their spouses or trusted friends are with them. When the spouse does the required chaperoning, the agoraphobia is reinforced and the fear of aloneness recycles. Because many men and women who live alone have agoraphobia, the role of a codependent spouse is clearly not a sufficient or necessary part of the disorder. Among couples, however, it does seem to exacerbate if not directly contribute to such problems.

Overscheduling of Activities

> It haunts me, the passage of time. I think time is a merciless thing. I think life is a process of burning oneself out and time is the fire that burns you. But I think the spirit of man is a good adversary.
>
> Tennessee Williams

Very often, couples feel anxious because they chronically do not "have time" to get their list of activities accomplished. Self-esteem is so linked to reportable activities in our society that sitting and talking is considered by many to be wasteful and superfluous, a simple luxury that they cannot afford. Taking time to meaningfully relate to another person becomes anxiety arousing because it means not getting important things done—things that will maintain our self-respectability.

Couples have lost control over time, and many have become like senseless machines. All of their job, community, and consumer-oriented obligations have hidden the basic intimacy obligations that they have to themselves and each other. No time is left for the important people in one's life. The more frightened people are by their inability to use their time "correctly," the more paralyzed they become by time. Many begin to experience insomnia, which is, existentially, the fear of surrendering to timelessness. In the classic neurotic paradox, people stay up hour after hour worrying that they will not have enough time the next day to accomplish all their required tasks (Steiner and Gebser, 1962).

Along with insomnia, self-scheduled sleep loss is also rising among couples who are trying desperately to get all the required activities into a day by reducing the amount of sleep that they need (as though they could control how much sleep their body requires). Some studies indicate people are sleeping, on the average, two hours less a night than just twenty years ago! Loss of sleep is a leading cause of anxiety and should not be lightly dismissed.

Whether the sleep loss is from insomnia or from disciplined, self-imposed sleep deprivation, the effects are similar: increased anxiety, irritability, or depression (Ebert, 1993; Samkoff and Jaques, 1991; Wehr, 1991).

At the opposite extreme are people so tired from all their extraspousal commitments that all they do when they have time together is sleep. They just cannot keep going, and rather than talk, go out, or have sex, they collapse. The old couch potato is often someone who is simply taxed to the max, getting recharged for the next daily marathon of scheduled activities.

The Time Crunch and Household Responsibilities

It has been repeatedly demonstrated that, currently, women try to fit a lot more scheduled activities into the day than do men. In the 1988 National Survey of Families and Households, women performed an average of thirty-three hours of housework per week, not counting child care. Men averaged fourteen hours a week. Despite the disparity of time, women continue to do most of the traditionally defined female household tasks and men do most of the traditionally masculine tasks, such as taking care of the cars, doing household repairs, and providing snow and lawn care. The three tasks most likely to be shared were assigning chores, making money decisions, and arranging for home repairs (Mederer, 1993). It is generally agreed that men's jobs are much less stressful than women's because they have a well-defined beginning and end, involve personal discretion as to when the task should be performed, and have a leisure component within the task. Cooking dinner, for instance, has to be performed every day at specific times when people are most in need of some relaxation and when children are most in need of supervision and reassurance. Mowing the lawn occurs less frequently, and the timing, more or less, is at the discretion of the mower. For these reasons, when the division of labor is made more equitable, women, particularly working women, report much greater satisfaction in the marriage (Robinson and Spitze, 1992).

The overall statistics, however, hide very important trends in household equity. For example, in 18 percent of dual-career households and 16 percent of single-career households, men contribute over twenty hours a week to household chores. In 10 percent of these families, men do as much housework as their wives (Mederer, 1993).

The time spent on chores is only one aspect of family labor. Unfortunately, it is often the only one considered by researchers or couples. Just as important is the orchestration of family work: deciding what is a necessary job, creating standards for the completion of chores, and making sure that they are done in an acceptable manner. So behind every bit of family productivity, there is someone who defined the task, was the catalyst for doing the chore, and oversaw its completion. Taking Johnny to the dentist may take one hour. Finding the right dentist, getting the needed X-rays, and freeing Johnny from other pressing after-school obligations may take an additional four hours. The orchestration hours are dictated by external demands and usually interfere with other ongoing activities. Whether one is orchestrating home maintenance (e.g., getting an exterminator for termites), care of household members (e.g., doing laundry, cooking, shopping), or transactional matters (e.g., paying bills, getting information for a vacation), preparing for the task and mopping up the mistakes are far more taxing than the actual task. These orchestration tasks are dominated by females and provide them with both enormous power and enormous stress in the marriage (DeVault, 1991).

Time, Commuting Marriages, and Anxiety

Currently, over one million dual-career couples work and live in different geographic areas. They cohabit as a couple only on available weekends and vacations. Many traditional couples wonder what this lifestyle is like and if they should consider such a change. Forces such as an ever-increasing number of women in the workforce, a tight economic market, limited job mobility, and midlife career changes make such geographically separated marriages likely to increase. Indeed, it is estimated that 72 percent of dual-career couples face the issue of geographic separation for the sake of career commitments and advancement (Bunker et al., 1992).

Nearly half of all commuting couples live one to four hours apart, by car. More than a third, however, live over eight hours apart from each other. A very small percentage of commuting couples even work on different continents! Couples try to see each other on a regular basis. Seventy percent of couples spend all weekends together, and another 20 percent get together at least monthly. Commuting lifestyles are most popular among those without children (Anderson, 1992).

Bunker and colleagues (1992) examined the quality of life of women and men in two types of dual-career families. Ninety commuting dual-career couples and 133 single-residence dual-career couples were compared on measures of marital satisfaction and stress. The benefits of a commuting lifestyle were much as would be expected. Commuting couples had fewer competing demands on their time during the work week, had the opportunity for intense concentration and more time at work, were able to devote themselves to their chosen job in a chosen location, and they experienced greater job satisfaction. Although commuting marriages are higher on job satisfaction, the rest of one's life seems to suffer. Stressors include concerns about fidelity, missing one's partner, loss of emotional support, and a sense of discord that comes from comparing their nontraditional lifestyle to traditional marriage. The financial strain not only comes from separate residences but from travel costs, increased child care costs, and long-distance phone calls. Not surprisingly, commuters were less satisfied with their partners and with family life. They also were less satisfied with life as a whole—managing to be single and married at the same time and still feeling that life was lacking a sense of completeness.

The benefits of living together were both emotional and economic. Daily interaction fostered interdependency, intimacy, and coherence in family life. Informal conversations and daily rituals were emotionally nurturing and critical for what many seek in a marriage. However, the daily living obligations put a great stress on work obligations and personal time. Traditional dual-career couples experienced a greater stress overload than commuter couples. They felt they had more to do and less time to do it. Thus, marriages of commuters with two households, travel time, and needs to negotiate from afar still give people, in general, more time to get their personal priority items accomplished than does the traditional arrangement.

Bunker and colleagues (1992) also examined how the experience differed for the partner who lived in the primary residence and the partner who was the commuter. It did not seem to matter if you were the commuter or the home-based person. The stresses on the marriage were similar and the benefits appeared to be the same.

This study raises the intriguing idea that traditional couples might benefit from compartmentalizing their time schedules more than they consider "normal." The more important message of the study is that you really cannot have it all. When someone wants a rewarding family life and a challenging career, he or she needs to consciously decide which one will take priority to make it work.

Economic Hardships

Money disagreements have always been a leading cause of anxiety and marital unhappiness. In part, this is because money is required to satisfy the most important and basic human needs, such as food, shelter, comfort, and health care. When these needs are not fulfilled, anxiety is triggered because one's very survival is threatened. But money also causes anxiety because it is used to hurt and control one another in marriage. Ideas about the purpose of money are very idiosyncratic and deeply entrenched. Understanding the husband's and wife's attitudes toward money is the first step toward financial mental health in a marriage.

Money issues vary on two dimensions (Mellan, 1994). The first dimension covers how responsible or irresponsible a person is with money. It defines how able he or she is to budget, to work extra if needed, to save, to delay gratification, and to avoid using money to buy friends and respectability. The second dimension covers how considerate or inconsiderate a person is with money. It defines how able he or she is to spend money with genuine concern for the feelings and welfare of others. The resulting four quadrants classify the financial management styles of most people.

1. *Responsible, considerate people are very successful in handling money issues within their nuclear families.* They are willing to chart a reasoned course of fiscal safety and take the needs of all family members into account. We all would love to marry people in this quadrant.

2. *Responsible, inconsiderate people are seen as very authoritarian.* They put money away from their check on a weekly basis but then feel they have the right to buy whatever they want with the savings. Persons in this quadrant may take a bonus and buy an expensive personal toy, believing the money is "extra," even though other family members have competing desires or needs. The spouse of a responsible, inconsiderate money manager feels insignificant.

3. *Irresponsible, considerate persons blow their paychecks.* These people are immature and a source of great frustration and anxiety.

4. *Irresponsible, inconsiderate persons are very self-centered and constantly hurt or anger their partners.* They are totally incapable of monitoring their spending or budgeting. At the same time, their impulsive spending is all centered on themselves. Maybe they like to gamble or play at expensive golf courses or dress in expensive clothes. Whatever the desire, they are focused on the self.

Regardless of money type, one of the most potent dictums, worth repeating again and again when money is an issue, is that "Financial freedom is the result of decreased spending, not of increased income." Money problems are often resolved better by examining priorities about material possessions, travel, and generosity than by searching frantically for ways to earn more money. One very helpful book that guides couples in such a reevaluation is J. Dominguez's (1992) book *Your Money or Your Life.*

Social Disgrace, Failing Expectations, and Anxiety

Marriage is like paying an endless visit in your worst clothes.

J. B. Priestly

Shame is a major provoker of anxiety in marriages. Shame is the feeling of self-disgust or self-disappointment that occurs when we cannot meet

THERAPEUTIC INTERVENTION 2:
THE MONEY INTERVIEW—ASSESSING
RESPONSIBILITY/IRRESPONSIBILITY
AND CONSIDERATENESS/INCONSIDERATENESS

The following questions are important when interviewing couples about money issues:

- In what ways do you think you are materialistic? In what ways are your best friends materialistic? Your spouse? How much do you value the acquisition of material goods?
- How fiscally responsible are you? How fiscally responsible are members of your family of origin? How fiscally responsible are your best friends? Your spouse? Ideally, how fiscally responsible would you like to be?
- How self-indulgent are you when it comes to money? How self-indulgent are the members of your family of origin? How self-indulgent are your best friends? Your spouse? Ideally, how self-indulgent would you like to be?
- How much is financial success part of your definition of personal success or success as a family? How does your spouse evaluate personal success? How was success evaluated in your family of origin? Ideally, how would you like to evaluate personal and family success?

The desire to maintain a certain, socially approved standard of living is the primary reason that unhappily married couples stay together in a world in which divorce is a socially accepted option. Financial stress is largely a subjective phenomenon: Middle-class couples who experience relatively minor changes in their financial condition can experience the same amount of financial stress as the unemployed, out-of-benefits worker who has lived that way much of his or her life. Economic hardship is an objectively traumatic event, but personal meaning systems, to a certain extent, determine how any one individual adjusts to changed circumstances.

When money problems beset a couple, they need to focus on teamwork and developing a common agenda to meet their goals. Unfortunately, when money is tight, people tend to feel very hostile toward the outside world for withholding the rewards they feel they deserve or need. They take this societal anger and project it onto their spouses. They get angry at their spouses because they are not able to buy a new car or take a vacation or send the children to the best schools. Of course, hostility in one spouse is most often reciprocated by the other. Money fights are often the most nasty and mean-spirited of arguments (Dortch, 1994).

When there is a family-owned business, the issues of money become even more complicated (Kaslow, 1993). Many multigenerational pressures exist, and parents often feel that their adult children are being too risky with the company's investments. Desires to break free of parental control over

(continued)

(continued)

finances cause many adult children to flee the family business. The power arrangements in the business determine the kinds of stressors that are experienced. If all the family members are equal partners, the most important interactions are those used to resolve disagreements. When one family member is the owner and the others are employees, issues of fairness, promotions, transferring of power, and appropriate compensation are perennial causes of anxiety and arguments. For example, if the wife is the bookkeeper in the husband's automobile repair shop, the wife may not even draw her own salary because it is all "in one pot" anyhow. However, over time, the lack of compensation will lead to low self-esteem, fears about not having a retirement fund or Social Security, and anxiety because she has no real control over the shape or nature of the practice. Therapists working with families in family-owned businesses spend much time containing anxiety by creating clear boundaries and making the work environment a more formal arrangement.

---

our own standards and expectations. Arnold Buss (1961), one of the world's experts on shame, says that with shame,

> there is inevitably a sharp drop in self-esteem, as the person verbally attacks himself or feels let down by himself. Shame is the only variety of social anxiety that always involves a decrease in self-esteem. There are intense feelings of regret or mortification, which are hard to verbalize. The ashamed person wishes he could sink into the earth, away from those who have observed his shameful behavior. He assumes that their low opinion of him matches his own. (p. 149)

In marriage, our partners are privy to all of our public selves and much of our private selves. When we fail, we see ourselves as inferior, less intelligent than others who set similar goals, less capable of fulfilling our dreams. If we feel this way about ourselves, we assume that deep down our partners must judge us in a similar manner. This feeling of social exposure and rejection creates concomitant feelings of shame and anxiety (Christensen, Danko, and Johnson, 1993; Gilbert, Pehl, and Allan, 1994).

Consider the three major sources of shame and how hard it is to hide these from a spouse. The first and most prominent cause of shame is failure experiences: When we are not promoted at work, receive a less than glowing evaluation, cook a special dinner that comes out inedible, or invest savings in a surefire deal that goes down the drain, we have pinned our hope of success on the prickly cactus of failure. It hurts.

The second cause of shame is more subtle: disappointment. We all have hopes of fulfilling the expectations of significant others. We want to be able to give our partners what they need and desire from us. When we cannot meet their expectations, we have failed.

The most intense shame comes about when we feel that we have acted immorally—lying, stealing, cheating, engaging in taboo sexual fantasies, infidelity, or cruelty. These acts are so difficult to acknowledge that spouses will continue to lie about them even after they are presented with incontrovertible evidence. The classic case is the denial that occurs when wives or husbands first confront their spouse with evidence of affairs. Characteristically, cheating spouses are filled with shame and do two things: They deny any wrongdoing whatsoever, and then they accuse their partner of paranoia and evil intentions. This projection of failed expectations and shame-inducing rhetoric is always later experienced as crueler than the actual infidelity by the betrayed partner. The faithful remember how weak the adulterer was and how willing to hurt in order to delay the inevitable day of disclosure. However, the lying and absurd defensiveness that occurs in such situations is the only way to control unbearable feelings of shame and anxiety in the wrongdoer.

Powerlessness Creates Shame, Which Creates Anxiety

Efficacy is the psychological term used to describe feelings of personal empowerment. It is the sense of having control over one's life. Powerlessness is the extreme opposite feeling. It is things happening to you over which you have no control. With feelings of powerlessness come deep feelings of anxiety. Powerlessness is a necessary ingredient for the experience of anxiety, but it is also sufficient to bring on that experience. Studies have shown that when monkeys are exposed to intense electrical shocks, monkeys who can control the timing of the shocks hold up much better than those who are passively linked recipients to the in-control monkeys' shocks. The analogy to marriages is clear: Partners who can control the timing, frequency, and intensity of painful events (e.g., deciding which bills to pay, determining if and how much overtime to work, when to accept travel assignments, etc.) hold up much better than the partners who are passively linked to "in-charge" spouses.

Much of what happens in life is clearly not under anyone's control. The Alcoholics Anonymous prayer "Grant me the serenity to accept the things I cannot change, courage to change the things I can, and wisdom to know the difference" is as important to successful marriages as it is to successful sobriety. Whenever one person seeks to assign blame for every problem that confronts the marriage, the other partner will be chronically anxious.

MALADAPTIVE RESPONSES TO ANXIETY: ALCOHOL USE, ANXIETY, AND THE MARITAL RELATIONSHIP

Recent insights into the causes of alcoholic dependence and abuse have highlighted the role of anxiety. Alcohol is a depressant, and anxious individuals find alcohol an effective form of self-medication. When one drinks, social anxieties are lessened, worries and obsessions fade in intensity, and the pain accompanying chronic low self-esteem is dulled. For a while, it solves more problems than it creates. However, alcohol dependence and alcohol abuse soon begin to take their toll on the drinker and his or her family. Drinking too much interferes with virtually every important couple function, from sexuality, to communication, to work. Alcohol problems have long been a major mental health problem in the United States and have wrecked countless millions of marriages and families.

Alcoholism is now defined as one of many drug problems—a "substance dependence" disorder. The DSM-IV criteria for substance dependence requires that a person demonstrate at least three of the following symptoms:

- Tolerance (a need for markedly increased amounts of the substance to achieve the desired effect)
- Withdrawal (an aversive physiological reaction to the absence of the drug)
- Taking the drugs in a larger amount or over a longer period than was intended
- A persistent desire or unsuccessful efforts to cut down or control substance use
- Spending a great deal of time obtaining the substance, using the substance, or recovering from its effects
- Reducing important social, occupational, or recreational activities
- Persistent use even though it causes recurrent physical or psychological problems*

For a substance abuse diagnosis, the criteria for dependence, do not have to be met. Instead, the individual has to show at least one of the following:

- Failure to fulfill major role obligations at work, school, or home
- Use of the substance in situations where it puts oneself or others at risk (e.g., driving while intoxicated)
- Legal problems or interpersonal problems caused or exacerbated by the substance.

---

*Reprinted with permission from the *Diagnostic and Statistical Manual of Mental Disorders,* Fourth Edition. Copyright 1994 by the American Psychiatric Association.

Although drinking patterns and problems begin during the teenage years and usually predate marriage, the horror alcohol abuse has caused marriages has focused attention on how drinking is exacerbated and maintained by the marital system. In the alcohol treatment literature, two types of marriages develop when one or both partners have alcohol problems (Steinglass, 1987). In the first type, one spouse has difficulty with alcohol. The well spouse recognizes the seriousness of the problem and seeks to protect the rest of the family from its harmful effects and openly confronts the alcoholic about the nature of the problem. Usually, by the time the couple comes to therapy, the nondrinking spouse has threatened to leave unless some changes occur.

The second type of marriage has "alcoholic couples," in which both partners are implicated in the maintenance of the problem, even if only one of them is the drinker. The relationship is organized around alcohol, and both the drinker and his or her codependent spouse must take responsibility for the lifestyle that they have created. This is the pattern found among couples who have been married a number of years and when the drinking has become a major force in their relationship and family life.

Alcoholic couples usually have a very skewed division of responsibilities. When "wet," the alcoholic spouse is unable to fulfill obligations to spouse or children. The wet spouse is then regulated to a child status by the nondrinking spouse and is not expected to take on any adult responsibilities. The nondrinking spouse agrees to pay the bills, go to the bank, talk to the relatives, and entertain the children because the drinking spouse cannot be relied on. When the spouse is "dry," she or he may temporarily try to take on parental and spousal tasks and, in fact, may often do so very successfully during these periods.

Among alcoholic couples, daily routines and important family rituals are both affected. Sometimes, the family just knows that the drinking will ruin most holidays and celebrations at some point. Other families will devise elaborate plans to make sure that the drinking does not interfere with those occasions (e.g., after Christmas morning, the children spend the day with grandparents to assure that their day is not ruined by a ranting, disgruntled parent). Either way, instead of focusing on the birthday or the Thanksgiving dinner, the focus is on the drinking and its consequences.

Theoretically, the nondrinking spouse is inextricably helping to maintain the status quo just as much as the drinker. In a fair number of family systems, the willingness to act as the single sober parent leads to a great deal of inner satisfaction. Sooner or later, they begin to thrive on it. Consequently, one of the keys to aiding the recovery of the addict is the readiness of the sober spouse to give up the role of the single parent and return to (or take on for the first time) the role of marital partner or coparent. (Goldberg, 1989, p. 83)

THERAPEUTIC INTERVENTION 3: BREAKING THROUGH DENIAL IN A SPOUSE WITH AN ALCOHOL PROBLEM

Among couples with an alcoholic member, the problem in couples therapy is getting the alcoholic to stop denying that she or he has a problem. This can usually be accomplished in one of three ways: First, the therapist can ask drinking spouses to keep a diary, noting what they are drinking and how much they are drinking. Over the course of a month, this diary gives everyone a visible window into the drinking pattern. Sometimes, drinking spouses are amenable to simply agreeing to limit their drinking to a certain amount at certain times. Although they do not consider the drinking a problem, they are willing to change that behavior if other changes in the marriage will ensue. The nondrinking spouse gets the changes without the drinking spouse ever having to "admit" to a problem. When neither of these strategies works, one can propose that the drinking spouse submit himself or herself to an independent evaluation by an expert. Of course, in this case, the therapist must have a working relationship with an expert alcohol counselor so that the referral process is smooth and the results of the evaluation are known to be valid. Even if the drinking spouse resists this assessment offer, the nondrinking spouse can be encouraged to attend Al-Anon meetings to see if she or he can find help and support (Karpel, 1994).

THERAPEUTIC INTERVENTION 4: ASSESSING ALCOHOL PROBLEMS WHEN BOTH PARTNERS INITIALLY DENY A PROBLEM

In therapy, alcoholic couples will often both deny that alcohol is a problem in the marriage. Therapists can try to assess the influence of alcohol by asking the following ten questions:

1. Do you ever have any arguments over drinking or other drug use? Please describe them.
2. How much do each of you drink on a daily basis?
3. How much can you drink before getting tipsy? (large tolerance is problematic.)

(continued)

(continued)

4. Does anyone in the family (or in the family tree) have a drinking problem?
5. Under what circumstances do each of you drink a little too much?
6. What is the longest each of you has gone without a drink this year?
7. What are the benefits of drinking for each of you?
8. How do the children react after you have had too much to drink?
9. What health problems have you experienced due to your drinking?
10. What is the difference in your arguments after one of you has been drinking?

In addition, anyone suspected of alcohol dependence or abuse should be given the Michigan Alcoholism Screening Test (Selzer, 1971) to give the therapist an objective reading of the problem.

When alcohol appears to be a major maladaptive coping style within the marriage, the therapist usually best serves the couple by openly sharing that assessment. Then the therapist needs to provide the couple with information on Al-Anon, Alcoholics Anonymous, and other treatment options available within their community. Depending on the severity of the alcohol problem, the therapist has to make a judgment call if couples treatment can succeed without adjunctive treatment for the alcohol problem. Almost always, the answer is no. This information should not be shared after only one session, for the couple has not had time to bond with the therapist and will be unlikely to accept the assessment. However, after three or four sessions, as the priorities of change needed in the marriage are becoming formalized, identifying alcohol problems becomes essential for the success of treatment.

Although this section has focused on alcohol as a maladaptive response to anxiety, it is clear that many types of substance abuse (e.g., marijuana) fall into this category. Much of the information that applies to alcohol problems applies to other types of substance abuse problems.

CHARACTERISTICS OF THE ANXIETY-REDUCING SPOUSE

When one partner is chronically anxious, the spouse is soon at risk for developing his or her own reactive problems. It is difficult to remain calm and relaxed when constantly exposed to someone who is agitated and upset. In addition, dealing with an anxious spouse requires an enormous amount of time, energy, and resources. Nonanxious spouses become overwhelmed by the amount of attention their anxious spouse needs and are frustrated when their investment does not immediately yield a change. Anxious spouses need reassurance that goes beyond a hug and a few words. It may require hours of patient listening and working through an issue that the nonanxious spouse feels is ridiculous to begin with.

Research has shown that couples who have a low rate of affectional exchange are more likely to experience anxiety (Bell, Daly, and Gonzalez, 1987; Zimmerman et al., 1994; Zimmerman and Christa, 1991). This is not at all surprising. Just think about how a frightened, scared child will jump into his or her parent's arms and after a few strokes, hugs, and moments of body comfort be off running around the playground as confident as can be. Recall from your introductory psychology course the baby monkeys studied by Harlow (1971). The monkeys were raised on wire mesh, artificial mothers who had only a towel around their middle to provide contact comfort. Yet, when a cootie bug was placed in the monkey's cage, the baby monkey would get hysterically anxious and rush to be tactually reassured by the cloth mother. After clinging to the cloth mother for some moments, the monkeys started to explore the cootie bugs and were quite quickly taking off legs and antlers with unabashed interest. This need for comfort contact remains active in adults. Most of the intimacy rituals that couples have involve some degree of touch. Consider the following affectionate behaviors that often occur independent of drives toward coitus: rubbing backs, necks, shoulders, and feet; combing someone's hair; holding hands, snuggling close together on the couch; lying intertwined while sleeping; and taking baths together. Although touch helps, talk is also a very effective anxiety reducer. There are strong individual and gender differences, however, in how effective either touch or talk will be for any one person.

Men are less willing than women to share a number of feelings, including anxiety, anger, depression, and fear, even though most men are more disclosing to their wives than to their friends and family. Within a marriage, however, men have a much easier time telling their wives what makes them angry than what makes them worried. The male hesitancy to disclose worries makes it difficult for husbands to help reduce their wives' anxiety (Berg-Cross, Kidd, and Carr, 1990). Unable to acknowledge the unsettling effect of anxiety, they tend to use defense mechanisms such as reaction formations and denial. For example, wives often worry about whether their children will be accepted by others. Husbands most often pooh-pooh this concern, making the wives feel alone, irrational, and even more anxious.

When people are anxious, they need to be around other people. The affiliative needs of anxious people were dramatically displayed in a classic study by Schacter and Singer (1962), who showed that people who thought they were going to be receiving injections chose to wait with others more often than people who thought they were simply going to do a memory task. Later research showed that it was not just any person who would help us cope with our anxiety; we want to be with others who are in the same situation. This is one reason why self-help groups are so beneficial.

In marriage, we want to be near our spouse when we are anxious, but we want our spouse to have the same concerns that we have. If one is worried about being able to pay the mortgage and the spouse is not at all concerned, being together will only exacerbate one's fears. If, however, the spouse not only does understand one's concerns but has similar concerns, a person is strengthened. One feels calmed down, better able to cope. Living with an anxious spouse puts great strains on the well spouse and the marital relationship. Increasing evidence, however, supports that marital interactions can incite, exacerbate, and maintain anxiety-related symptoms. A number of comparative treatment research projects show that distressed couples indicate that conjoint marital therapy is better than relaxation therapy or individual psychotherapy for treating agoraphobia. Hafner (1992) and Emmelkamp and colleagues (1992) have reported success using spouse-aided therapy specifically to treat married men and women who suffer from agoraphobia. The goal of the treatment is to work on the marital problems that are directly linked to the presenting problem. Hafner and Spence (1988), for example, report the case of a young, married, male professor who was having panic attacks that interfered with his functioning at work. Over the course of several years, the symptoms multiplied; he became obsessive-compulsive and was finally unable to continue working full-time. His wife, who had been firmly committed to being a full-time homemaker, was forced to take a part-time job as a stenographer while the husband took on some of the home and child-rearing responsibilities. The wife was initially very resentful about having to lose her role as homemaker, but as soon as the husband was relieved of the total burden of being a breadwinner his symptoms began to disappear. Over the course of therapy, the wife was helped to see the advantages of role sharing, and the couple finally agreed that both would carry the economic burden and share the home responsibilities. The husband became more well, and within eight months of beginning therapy, he was symptom-free.

THERAPEUTIC INTERVENTION 5:
PARTNER-AS-COTHERAPIST INTERVENTIONS

Besides the problems within the relationship that seed or fuel anxiety, worries arise from nonmarital concerns and domains. In both instances, the spouse sometimes can serve as a very effective cotherapist (Schmaling and Jacobson, 1988). The following can be effective cotherapy strategies for spouses.

(continued)

(continued)

Confront the Fear

The spouse can help the mate reappraise and confront the situation. Instead of avoiding possible catastrophes, the focus is on reaffirming the skills and resources that are available to cope with likely misfortunes and hardships. For instance, a wife may feel very anxious about not working part-time while her children are little, fearing that the family will not be able to make ends meet. Her husband can reinforce this fear or he can help his wife by making a budget with her, enumerating the methods they each have of saving money and cutting expenses.

Helping the partner face the fear involves understanding it oneself. Misunderstandings are very common, and most spouses underestimate how much their worries are shared and overestimate how much awareness the partner has of the mate's level of distress (Pickersgill and Beasley, 1990). Therapists sometimes find a big payoff in finding ways to help the cotherapist spouse to understand the experience of the suffering spouse.

Reduce Partner's Stress

The anxiety-dissipating spouse can work to eliminate the traumatic events that relate to anxiety. For example, the wife who is overly anxious about being able to pay the bills needs a husband who is willing to take a lunch from home instead of buying it each day. The husband who is overly anxious about keeping the house clean needs a wife who is willing to work with him on a system so that it can be kept clean. The strategy here is not to willy-nilly follow along and wholeheartedly reinforce the partner's irrational fears and restrictive demands. Rather, the goal is to create a base of cooperative, relevant, anxiety-reducing activities that bond the partners so that needless worry can be discussed in a supportive atmosphere instead of a defensive, hostile, "I'm right—you're wrong" atmosphere. This notion of stress reduction is central to most integrative models of generalized anxiety disorder (Barlow, 1988).

Create Quiet and Calm

Anxiety-dissipating spouses will find it useful to spend time creating quiet and calm with their mates. Anxiety has such a strong, physiological component and causes such a constriction of problem-solving skills that until the spouse is physiologically relaxed, little cognitive restructuring is possible. It is impossible to effectively communicate and help a spouse when his or her autonomic nervous system is in high gear.

The one physiological measure that consistently distinguishes anxious from nonanxious individuals is muscular tension (Marten et al., 1995). Multiple types of activities are used by couples to "chill out." The activities could involve meditating together; back, head, or foot massages; relaxing while listening to music; or hiking without talking.

Talk About the Future

In a marriage, the most effective stress inoculation strategies are usually long, extended conversations about the roadblocks and stressors that

(continued)

(continued)

are likely to be met farther down the path. Being informed of and anticipating the difficulties about to befall a couple, allow them to rehearse their coping strategies. Much as a small shot of a virus can alert the immune system and inoculate a person against a future all-out attack by the virus, so also can anticipation of future difficulties pad the psyche from damaging, out-of-control feelings due to a stressful event. This was first experimentally shown over forty years ago, in a study that demonstrated that patients who had elected to have surgery and who were informed about the unpleasant consequences they could expect suffered fewer postoperative setbacks than did patients who did not receive this preparatory information.

Spouses can help inoculate each other from a variety of stressors by serving as the supportive cast in a variety of rehearsal situations. Many job problems are successfully resolved because people have repeatedly practiced approaching the boss or co-worker with their spouse before the curtain has actually risen.

Change the Conversation

Helpful spouses prevent their mates from "overthinking." Although planning, rehearsing, problem solving, and extended conversations are all important to reassuring the anxious mate, there is a point at which thinking about the issue will only make it worse. This is particularly true in situations in which there is a limit to how reasoning can help provide an answer. Questions such as, "Why am I not able to handle our financial pressures with ease?" or "How do I know that I will not become mentally ill or get a disabling disease?" or "Why did God let our child die?" have no logical answer. The only way not to feel anxious about such questions is not to think about them. In these situations, anxious people need to learn to meditate (and keep their minds empty), or they need to learn how to feed their minds with kinder, gentler images and questions. For example, instead of dwelling on the possibility of getting a disabling disease, a person should concentrate on what he or she can do during the day to promote good health.

Indeed, many therapists have found that overthinking about the frightening world situation feeds personal anxieties. I know therapists who find that anxious patients do much better when they are restricted from reading the paper and from watching the news on the television. The bad news, fearful news diet heightens sensitivity to negative outcomes. On the edge and vigilant, self-worries are a natural extension of local and community worries. The focus is to teach couples to focus on problems within their control (Craske, Barlow, and O'Leary, 1992).

It is often a difficult judgment call to differentiate between what is a viatal anxiety-reducing conversation and what is a repetitive, go-nowhere talk. I have found that a half hour is a reasonable amount of time to achieve a

(continued)

(continued)

calming effect from any one conversation. If the partner's mood has calmed, additional conversation may be productive. If not, it is probably time to change the conversation channel, assuring the anxious partner that tomorrow he or she will again be available to talk through the trauma. For example, when a couple experiences the death of a child, the grieving talk can go on for months or even years before the pain is contained.

Selectively Encourage the Support Network

The anxiety-dissipating spouse knows that she or he needs to enlist the help of friends and family. Most helpful spouses have fantasies of omnipotence. Their love is so great and their intentions are so pure that they and they alone will be able to help their spouse "snap out of it." Virtually never is this the reality. Real life requires a dense network of social support as well as a high-quality network.

For example, research has shown that pregnant women experiencing negative life events had 57 percent more birth complications when they lacked social support than women in similar situations who had good support systems. Thus, the anxiety-dissipating spouse learns which relatives and friends to share with and how to receive support without crossing boundaries of confidentiality. Not surprisingly, when spouses can share the same social network, they are more satisfied with the marriage (Barrera and Balls, 1983).

Keep in mind that all friends do not make equally good sounding boards. Before encouraging a client to use a particular person for social support, inquire about that person's style of interacting. Barrera and Balls (1983) found that if a wife disclosed a marital conflict to a friend who was very interfering, she felt even more distant from her husband afterward. If the confidant was supportive, then the marital relationship was strengthened.

During periods of extreme stress, the social network is essential for most families. During the Persian Gulf War, for example, the most successful coping mechanisms for dealing with the mate's absence included seeking out friends for social support, avoiding unproductive worrying by diverting time and energy toward helping others and the troops, and focusing on maintaining one's own health by eating well and exercising (Figley, 1993).

Seek Medical Consultations

Anxiety-dissipating spouses listen carefully to their mates and do not let psychological explanations muddy the possibilities of needing to be checked out medically. Many somatic problems have anxiety as a symptom. These include drug reactions, metabolic disorders (e.g., hyperthyroidism, hypoparathyroidism, Cushing's disease, Addison's disease, hypoglycemia, and pheochromocytoma), neurological problems (e.g., cerebral ischemia, cerebral vascular insufficiency, postconcussive syndrome, multiple sclerosis,

(continued)

(continued)

and hepatolenticular degeneration), cardiovascular diseases (e.g., coronary heart disease, congestive heart failure, and mitral valve prolapse), Meniere's disease, and sleep apnea.

Schedule Pleasant Events

Anxiety-dissipating spouses schedule a pleasant couple event into every day. It may be as simple as playing a well-loved CD, watching a sitcom, or picking up a favorite ice cream for dessert. When the shared enjoyment is nested in a loving, relaxed context, the daily pleasure pill is a potent anti-anxiety medication.

Structure Family Time

The anxiety-dissipating spouse helps to structure the family time. Brown, O'Leary, and Barlow (1993) report using three major strategies to organize the anxious client. First, they teach clients to delegate responsibility. Instead of trying to do everything, the client defines success by getting others to do their fair share. Second, clients are taught how to be assertive and say "no" when they feel they are being treated unfairly or are being pressured to do something that they would prefer not to do. Third, they are taught to develop lists and master time management skills. So if the husband is anxious about the family vacation plans, the supportive wife is one who will help him delegate by asking to take on planning tasks, encourage him to be assertive by stating his bottom-line concerns ("I do not want to spend more than $75 a night—and I do not want to be pressured into spending more"), and facilitate time management by mapping out the day-to-day agenda as well as the budget with her husband. Once the situation is structured enough to lower the anxiety level to tolerable limits, alternative options and exigencies for emergencies can be discussed.

LEARNING AIDS

Therapeutic Dialogue (Anxiety/Nervousness)

1. What events in your marriage make you anxious?
2. What events in your marriage do you believe make your mate anxious? Where are the similarities and differences between the two of you?
3. Among your friends, which situations trigger the most anxiety/ nervousness? The least anxiety/nervousness?
4. Would you like a life without worry and apprehension? What would be the costs of such a lifestyle?

5. In an ideal marriage, how would your spouse deal with your anxieties?
6. In an ideal marriage, how would you deal with your spouse's anxiety/nervousness?
7. What are some realistic goals you could develop to better deal with your own anxieties and your spouse's anxieties?
8. What types of rejection or criticism make you most nervous? Why are you particularly vulnerable in these areas? Are there any historically meaningful events that can help you understand your reactions?
9. What types of rejection or criticism make your spouse most nervous?
10. Why is he or she particularly vulnerable in these areas? Are there any historically meaningful events that can help you understand his or her reactions?
11. How do your different friends react to rejection, burdens, and the unknown?
12. Ideally, how would you like to deal with rejection, burdens, and the unknown?
13. Is there any way you can alter your ideal method of handling your worries?
14. How much of a risk taker are you? What would happen if you increased the level of risk taking in your relationship with your spouse?

Self-Exploration 1: Situational Nervousness

Rate how nervous you feel in each of the following situations.

1 = Not at all nervous
2 = Somewhat nervous
3 = Very nervous

1. It is Sunday night and there are five loads of dirty clothes in the laundry room—with no clean underwear for work Monday
2. After work, you have to go to the dentist and the supermarket and do a carpool before making dinner
3. You have to go on a trip for work but have not yet found all the baby-sitters needed for your children
4. Getting ready for Christmas
5. Cooking Thanksgiving dinner for the family
6. Deciding which elementary school to send your child to

7. Deciding which car to buy
8. Deciding where to take your summer vacation
9. Deciding how to cut family spending
10. Realizing you do not have enough money to cover the month's bills
11. Having to take on a part-time job two nights a week
12. Losing your job
13. Disappointing your spouse because you didn't get an anticipated raise
14. Disappointing your spouse because your mother-in-law is angry with you
15. Disappointing your spouse because you are unable to buy something that he or she really wants
16. Your spouse's being ill
17. Your being ill
18. Your spouse having a chronic illness
19. Your having a chronic illness
20. Illness in one of your children
21. Feeling trapped in your neighborhood
22. Feeling trapped by your circle of friends
23. Feeling trapped by your job
24. Feeling trapped by family obligations
25. Feeling trapped by parenting obligations
26. Feelings of loneliness

Couples should compare their individual reactions to each item as well as their total scores. They can then use this self-exploration as a stimulus for discussing how feelings of anxiety might affect the marriage. No norms are available, and this is not intended to differentiate clinical and nonclinical levels of anxiety.

Sample Workshop Flowchart Intended for Groups of Four or Five Couples Working on Anxiety

I. Psychoeducational Strategies
   A. Symptoms of anxiety
   B. Anxiety as a reaction to threat—the existential definition
   C. The Medusa metaphor
   D. The six provokers of anxiety in marriage
      1. Existential decisions and meaningfulness
      2. Illness
      3. Loneliness
      4. Overscheduling of activities

     5. Economic hardships

     6. Social disgrace and failing expectations

   E. Characteristics of a supportive spouse

II. Self-Exploration (Done by couples in private and shared before re-joining the group)
The Worry Scale

III. Therapeutic Dialogue (Done by couples in private and shared before rejoining the group)
(Proceeding in the order presented, both partners respond to each question before going on to discuss the next question.)
In group, the therapist explores with couples how relationship goals can be achieved by modifying overly ambitious, pie-in-the-sky expectations. Using information about their current situation and the realities seen among friends and family, couples fine-tune expectations so that they are achievable and motivate rather than discourage attempts at change.

IV. Therapeutic Interventions
Work with a couple in front of the group and apply one or more of the therapeutic interventions. Share the rationale during demonstrations. Let the group discuss additional interventions.
   A. Novel-in-progress technique for resolving marital crises
   B. The money interview: assessing responsibility/irresponsibility and considerateness/inconsiderateness
   C. Breaking through denial in a spouse with an alcohol problem
   D. Assessing alcohol problems when both initially deny a problem
   E. Partner-as-cotherapist interventions
     1. Confront the fear together
     2. Reduce partner's stress
     3. Create quiet and calm
     4. Talk about the future
     5. Change the conversation
     6. Selectively encourage the support network
     7. Seek medical consultation
     8. Schedule pleasant events
     9. Structure family time

V. Finding Motivation and Time to Make the Changes
Group discussion

Bibliotherapy

Andrews, G. (1994). *Treatment of anxiety disorders: Clinician's guide and treatment manuals.* New York: Cambridge University Press. (Professional book).

Berent, J. (1994). *Beyond shyness: How to conquer social anxieties.* New York: Fireside.

Felder, L. (1993). *When a loved one is ill: How to take better care of your loved one, your family, and yourself.* New York: Plume.

James, L. R. and James, J. (1994). *So you're injured, what next?* Wilmington, DE: Zenobia James. (Tells couples how to deal constructively with illness and disability).

Peurifoy, R. (1995). *Anxiety, phobias, and panic: Taking charge and conquering fear.* New York: Warner.

Ross, J. (1994). *Triumph over fear.* New York: Bantam.

Videotherapy

Husbands and Wives. (1992). Directed by Woody Allen. Another great Allen movie on the strains put on marriages over time.

A Woman Under the Influence. (1974). Directed by John Cassavetes. Dated, but details the emotional breakdown of a married woman.

Zelig. (1983). Directed by Woody Allen. The story of a human chameleon who desperately wants to fit in.

Professional Development Questions (Anxiety)

1. This chapter discusses six provokers of anxiety in marriage. What would be the easiest way to assess which of these provokers are troublesome to a particular couple? Are there other important provokers you can think of to assess?

2. What is a simple way to explain to couples the influence that anxiety can have on their relationship? How would you explain what anxiety is, what provokes it, and how partners can help each other deal with it?

3. What advice would you give a holistically oriented internist or oncologist about how to reduce the influence of an illness on the couple and how to use the spouse to promote recovery?

4. How might the economic hardships associated with unemployment spread to provoke anxiety in the other areas? What type of preven-

tion program might help couples better weather the devastating anxieties associated with unemployment?

REFERENCES

American Psychiatric Association. (1994). *Diagnostic and statistical manual of mental disorders* (Fourth edition). Washington, DC: Author.

Anderson, E. (1992). Decision-making style: Impact on satisfaction of the commuter couple's lifestyle. *Journal of Family and Economic Issues, 13*(1), 5-21.

Andrews, F., Abbey, A., and Halman, L. (1991). Stress from infertility, marriage factors, and subjective well-being of wives and husbands. *Journal of Health and Social Behavior, 32*(3), 238-253.

Barbour, A. (1993). Research report: Dyadic loneliness in marriage. *Journal of Group Psychotherapy, Psychodrama, and Sociometry, 46*(2), 70-72.

Barlow, D. H. (1988). *Anxiety and its disorders: The nature and treatment of anxiety and panic.* New York: Guilford.

Barrera, M. and Balls, P. (1983). Assessing social support as a prevention resource: An illustrative study. *Prevention in Human Services, 2*(4), 59-74.

Bateson, M. D. (1993). Composing a life. In C. Simpkinson and A. Simpkinson (Eds.), *Sacred stories: A celebration of the power of stories to transform and heal* (pp. 39-53). New York/San Francisco: Harper.

Bell, R. A., Daly, J. A., and Gonzalez, M. (1987). Affinity-maintenance in marriage and its relationship to women's marital satisfaction. *Journal of Marriage and the Family, 49*(2), 445-454.

Berg-Cross, L., Kidd, F., and Carr, P. (1990). Cohesion, affect, and self-disclosure in African-American adolescent families. *Journal of Family Psychology, 4*(2), 235-250.

Borkovec, T. D. and Inz, J. (1990). The nature of worry in generalized anxiety disorder: A predominance of thought activity. *Behavior Research and Therapy, 28*(2), 153-158.

Brown, T. A., Barlow, D. H., and Liebowitz, M. R. (1994). The empirical basis of generalized anxiety disorder. *American Journal of Psychiatry, 151*(9), 1272-1280.

Brown, T. A., O'Leary, T. A., and Barlow, D. (1993). Generalized anxiety disorder. In D. Barlow (Ed.), *Clinical handbook of psychological disorders* (pp. 137-189). New York: Guilford.

Bunker, B., Zubek, J., Vanderslice, V., and Rice, R. (1992). Quality of life in dual-career families: Commuting versus single-residence couples. *Journal of Marriage and the Family, 54*(2), 399-407.

Burns-Teitelbaum, N. (1996). In sickness and in health. *Working Women,* March, 61-72.

Buss, A. H. (1961). The psychology of aggression. New York: John Wiley.

Carter, R. and Carter, C. (1993). Individual and marital adjustment in spouse pairs subsequent to mastectomy. *American Journal of Psychotherapy, 21*(4), 291-299.

Christensen, B. J., Danko, G. P., and Johnson, R. (1993). Neuroticism and the belief that one is being scrutinized and evaluated by others. *Personality and Individual Differences, 15*(3), 349-350.

Craske, M. G., Barlow, D. H., and O'Leary, T. A. (1992). *Mastery of your anxiety and worry.* Albany, NY: Graywind.

DeVault, M. L. (1991). *Feeding the family: The social organization of caring as gendered work.* Chicago: University of Chicago Press.

Dominguez, J. (1992). *Your money or your life.* New York: Penguin.

Dortch, S. (1994). Money and marital discord. *American Demographics, 16*(10), 11-14.

Ebert, D. (1993). Human sleep, sleep loss, and behavior. *British Journal of Psychiatry, 163*(1), 263-264.

Emmelkamp, P. M., Van Dyck, R., Bitter, M., Heins, R. (1992). Spouse-aided therapy with agoraphobics. *British Journal of Psychiatry, 160*(1), 51-56.

Figley, C. (1993). Coping with stressors on the home front. *Journal of Social Issues, 49*(4), 51-71.

Fischer, W. F. (1988). *Theories of anxiety.* Lanham, MD: University Press of America.

Fromm, E. (1941). *Escape from meaning.* New York: Holt, Rinehart, and Winston.

Gilbert, P., Pehl, J., and Allan, S. (1994). The phenomenology of shame and guilt: An empirical investigation. *British Journal of Medical Psychology, 67*(1), 23-36.

Goldberg, M. (1989). Individual psychopathology from the systems perspective. In G. Weeks (Ed.), *Treating couples: The intersystem model of the Marriage Council of Philadelphia* (pp. 70-84). New York: Brunner/Mazel.

Goodman, E. (1979). *Turning points.* Garden City, NY: Doubleday.

Gove, W. R., Style, C. B., and Hughes, M. (1990). The effect of marriage on the well-being of adults: A theoretical analysis. *Journal of Family Issues, 11*(1), 4-35.

Hafner, R. J. (1992). Anxiety disorders and family therapy. *Australian and New Zealand Journal of Family Therapy, 13*(2), 99-104.

Hafner, R. J. and Spence, N. S. (1988). Marriage duration, marital adjustment, and psychological symptoms: A cross-sectional study. *Journal of Clinical Psychology, 44*(3), 309-316.

Harlow, H. F. (1971). Learning to love. Santa Barbara, CA: Albion.

Himmelfarb, S. and Murrell, S. (1984). The prevalence and correlates of anxiety symptoms in older adults. *Journal of Psychology, 116*(2), 159-167.

Karpel, M. A. (1994). *Evaluating couples: A handbook for practitioners.* New York: Norton.

Kaslow, F. W. (1993). The lore and lure of the family business. *The American Journal of Family Therapy, 21*(1), 1-16.

Kelly, E. and Conley, J. (1987). Personality and compatibility: A prospective analysis of marital stability and marital satisfaction. *Journal of Personality and Social Psychology, 52*(1), 27-40.

Kiley, D. (1989). *Living together, feeling alone: Healing your hidden loneliness.* Englewood Cliffs, NJ: Prentice-Hall.

Kim, A., Martin, D., and Martin, M. (1989). Effects of personality in marital satisfaction: Identification of source traits and their role in marital instability. *Family, 16(3),* 243-248.

Marten, P. A., Brown, T. A., Barlow, D. H., Borkovec, T. D., Shear, M. K., and Lydiard, R. B. (1995). Evaluation of the ratings comprising the associated symptom criteria of DSM-III-R, generalized anxiety disorder. *Journal of Nervous and Mental Disease, 181*(11), 676-682.

May, R. (1950). The meaning of anxiety. New York: Ronald.

Mederer, H. (1993). Division of labor in two-earner homes: Task accomplishment versus household management as critical variables in perceptions about family work. *Journal of Marriage and the Family, 55*(1), 133-145.

Mellan, O. (1994). *Money harmony: Resolving money conflicts.* New York: Walker.

Monti, P., Abrams, D., Kadden, R., and Cooney, N. (1989). *Treating alcohol dependence.* New York: Guilford.

O'Rourke, N. and Wenaus, C. (1998). Marital aggrandizement as a mediator of burden among spouses of suspected dementia patients. *Canadian Journal on Aging, 17*(4), 384-400.

Patterson, J. I. and McCubbin, H. I. (1983). Chronic illness: Family stress and coping. In C. R. Figley and H. I. McCubbin (Eds.), *Stress and the family: Volume 2. Coping with catastrophe* (pp. 21-36). New York: Brunner/Mazel.

Pickersgill, M. and Beasley, C. (1990). Spouses perceptions of life events within marriage. *Personality and Individual Differences, 11*(2), 169-175.

Robinson, J. and Spitze, G. (1992). Whistle while you work? The effect of household task performance on women's and men's well-being. *Social Science Quarterly, 73*(4), 844-861.

Sales, S., Schulz, R., and Biegel, D. (1992). Predictors of strain in families of cancer patients: A review of the literature. *Journal of Psychosocial Oncology, 10*(2), 1-25.

Samkoff, J. and Jacques, C. (1991). A review of studies concerning effects of sleep deprivation and fatigue on residents. *Academic Medicine, 66*(11), 687-693.

Schacter, S. and Singer, J. (1962). Cognitive, social, and physiological determinants of emotional state. *Psychological Review, 69*(2), 379-399.

Schmaling, K. B. and Jacobson, N. S. (1988). Recent developments in family behavioral marital therapy. *Contemporary Family Therapy: An International Journal, 10*(1), 17-29.

Selzer, M. L. (1971). Michigan Alcoholism Screening Test: The quest for a new diagnostic instrument. *American Journal of Psychiatry, 127*(12), 1653-1658.

Sharf, B. and Freimuth, V. (1993). The construction of illness on entertainment television: Coping with cancer on *Thirtysomething. Health Communication, 5*(3), 141-160.

Skerrett, K. 1998. Couple adjustment to the experience of breast cancer. *Families, Systems, and Health, 16*(3), 281-298.

Sperry, L. and Carlson, J. (1992). The impact of biological factors on marital functioning. *American Journal of Family Therapy, 20*(2), 145-156.

Steiner, H., and Gebser, J. (1962.) *Anxiety: A condition of modern man.* New York: Dell.

Steinglass, P. (1987). *The alcoholic family.* New York: Basic Books.

Tiscjem. C., Florin, I., Krause, W., and Pook, M. (1999). Cognitive-behavioral therapy for idiopathic infertile couples. *Psychotherapy and Psychosomatics, 68*(1), 15-21.

U.S. Bureau of the Census. (1994). Current population reports. (Series P-20, No. 478). Washington, DC: Government Printing Office.

Vanfossen, B. (1986). Sex differences in depression: The role of spouse support. In S. E. Hobfoll (Ed.), *Stress, social support, and women: The series in clinical and community psychology* (pp. 69-84). New York: Hemisphere.

Wehr, T. (1991). Sleep loss as possible mediator of diverse causes of mania. *British Journal of Psychiatry, 159,* 576-578.

Yalom, I. (1980). *Existential psychotherapy.* New York: Basic Books.

Zimmerman, T., Bertagni, P., Siani, R., and Micciolo, R. (1994). Marital relationships and somatic and psychological symptoms in pregnancy. *Social Science and Medicine, 38*(4), 559-564.

Zimmerman, T., and Christa, L. (1991). The Ryle Marital Patterns Test as a predictor of symptoms of anxiety and depression in couples in the community. *Social Psychiatry and Psychiatric Epidemiology, 26*(5), 221-229.

PART II.

THE SOCIAL SUPPORT CORNERSTONE: CREATING FAMILY AND COMMUNITY ROLES THAT ENHANCE THE PARTNER RELATIONSHIP

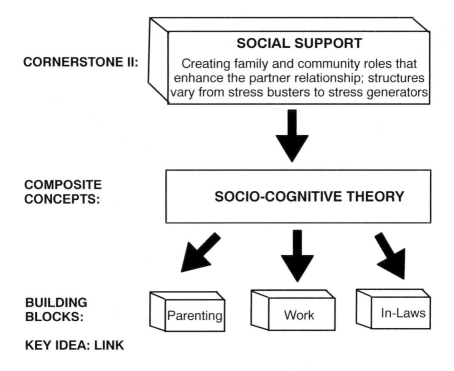

CORNERSTONE II:

SOCIAL SUPPORT

Creating family and community roles that enhance the partner relationship; structures vary from stress busters to stress generators

COMPOSITE CONCEPTS:

SOCIO-COGNITIVE THEORY

BUILDING BLOCKS:

Parenting   Work   In-Laws

KEY IDEA: LINK

THEORETICAL ORIENTATION: SOCIOCOGNITIVE

The social support cornerstone is built upon the positive, synergizing effects that our other relationships can have on the couple relationship. Inasmuch as no one person or endeavor can satisfy all our needs, it is essential to have multiple interests, commitments, and obligations. In our culture, our primary relationships, beyond that of our mate, are with our jobs, our children, our extended family, our interests and hobbies, and our civic involvements. Although these roles can and should enhance a relationship, in today's world they are very often the source of extraordinary stress. Whether it is parents who feel that they are not giving enough time to their children, adult children who are overwhelmed with responsibilities to aging parents, or workers who are burdened by impossible job demands, this cornerstone is often a source of multiple stressors for a couple.

The science of psychology is a little more than 100 years old. Until a few years ago, psychology was historically distinguished from sociology in that psychology was the study of how mind and body shaped and controlled feelings, cognitions, and interpersonal relationships, and sociology was the study of how culture and environment controlled feelings, cognitions, and interpersonal relationships. Now, the fields have become intermingled. The mix of sociological and psychological theory is perhaps one of the best examples of how cross-disciplinary research has recreated new domains of acceptable inquiry for both disciplines.

The current discussion is limited to how the new hybrid sociopsychological theories explain marital conflicts, growth patterns, and potential for

change. The approach seeks to make sense of the personal and interpersonal problems that arise in marriage in the context of the limitations and
problems of the larger society. In large part, the theoretical framework we
will be drawing on is based on the work of Nathan Hurvitz and what has
been termed the sociocognitive approach (Hurvitz and Straus, 1991).

The sociocognitive theories of marital distress claim that the economic
and social problems of society affect marital and family conflicts, distress
levels, and possible coping responses. For example, the depression and
rage felt by a wife whose husband is an alcoholic is due, in part, to
society's promotion and tolerance of alcoholism. Economic barriers to
women's financial independence, and society's failure to provide safe
havens for women and their children are additional factors affecting marital distress. Focusing on the power allocation or depression in the family
may help the couple, but clearly, the problem needs to be understood and
treated in the context of the wider society.

Cultural trends have a profound influence on work life, parenting, and
relationships with extended family. All of these roles and relationships are
intertwined with the spousal relationship.

THE CULTURAL INFLUENCE OF WORK
ON MARITAL RELATIONSHIPS

The sociocognitive approach focuses on how the stable social arrangements of a society affect couples. No social arrangement is more powerful
in affecting marriages than how the nation allocates jobs, goods, and
services. The fact that most people need to commute over thirty minutes,
twice a day, in a car or on public transportation, to get to their jobs has a
profound influence on the tempo and stress of modern marriages. As a
society, we have lately become very conscious of this environmental stressor. Many people are experimenting with home-based work and seeking
less glamorous employment closer to their homes in an effort to shift from
the financial rewards of a "good job" to the emotional rewards of a "good
family life."

Couples are forced to deal with such role conflicts on a daily basis,
particularly the conflict between being a good provider and worker and
being a good spouse and parent. We are all in a cultural catch-22. Not only
can devotion to one role interfere with devotion to the other role, but
failure to succeed in one role often makes success limited in the other role.

People who work in high-stress environments have more spillover of
work-related issues into their home life than do others. Particularly when
the couple is already in conflict over an issue (child care, finances, or
whatever), it is easy to triangulate the work situation into the relationship

and focus the arguments on how the job demands prevent a normal home life. When one spouse is overinvolved and overstressed at work, the other spouse becomes jealous. How can so much energy and commitment be expended for work and none for the marriage? This resentment polarizes the couple even further, as they see the hostility as a threat to their career or needed emotional support (Borum and Philpot, 1993).

Thus, among the people who report experiencing spillover, the most common experience is negative work-related feelings affecting the family. Feelings such as tension, anger, guilt, worry, and disappointment surround people as they walk into their homes. As most Americans know, the "fussy" hour of babies (usually 5 p.m. to 7 p.m.) now extends to all members of the family, particularly work-weary adults.

THE CULTURAL CHANGES IN PARENTING AND THEIR EFFECT ON FAMILY LIFE

Another important concept in sociocognitive theory is social stratification. This refers to the societal system in which families and individuals are hierarchically arranged in such a way that power, wealth, prestige, and privilege are clearly distributed according to well-understood and accepted social rules. For example, until recently, parents were considered to hold power over their children, even their adult children, until such time as the parents were mentally or physically disabled by old age. Parents deserved respect and were privileged because they were the parents. This cultural expectation has had a profound effect on marital relationships because adult children need to find ways to repay the emotional debt they owe their parents while still preserving their own sense of autonomy.

Nowadays, social stratification between parent and child is breaking down. At one end of the economic ladder, children are being raised by grandparents and day care workers, and on the other end they are being raised by nannies. Adult children now demand that their parents respect them to the same degree that they respect their parents. They often do not feel a great emotional debt, nor do they feel that the parents should be privileged. Add to this the many stepparent relationships that occur in America and parent-child relationships become ever more baffling.

In a sobering, critical analysis that explores this societal shift in parenting, David Elkind (1994) has concluded that as narcissistically oriented adults have become parents, they have exploited their children to further their own nonchild pursuits and goals. Despite the increasing need for children to master time-intensive skills and receive extensive emotional support if they are to successfully compete in a complex world, parents have steadily decreased the amount of guidance and protection they are willing to offer their own children. In this new family imbalance, Elkind sees children as exploited and vulnerable. In a way, he is saying that we are becoming a society of adult-centered parents with erratic control over our children.

In his book, *Ties That Stress,* Elkind (1994) traces how family feelings have shifted from a strong child-centered focus to an adult self-centered focus. This can be seen in many of the societal shifts that have occurred over the past twenty years. First and foremost, there has been increasing societal stress on women fulfilling themselves in the nonmaternal role whenever their capabilities and inclination permit. In essence, women have been pushed to seek social affirmation and self-esteem from the paid work arena. Second, there has been a shift toward "consensual" love being the primary criterion for marital commitment. Most men and women believe in receiving the same intensity and expressions of love that they offer to their spouses. Consensual love does not make room for the marital notion of "sacrifice"—it is labeled as "being used." Equity reigns, and altruism is vilified and demeaned as "enabling." This shift toward preserving the family only when the parents are still "romantically" in love with each other has been coupled with the idea that divorce is a "right" of unhappy adults.

Along with the shift in feelings toward marriage, a shift has occurred in the behaviors that define family life. There is very little family togetherness, at least in a sense that is meaningful to children. Many children do not eat meals with their parents or see them for any significant part of the day. Increasingly, vacations are even isolated so that one can take the children on a holiday and never have to talk to them or see them for more than a few moments. The media is a blizzard of societal mirrors reflecting an "every person for himself or herself" family lifestyle. The horror of *Married with Children* and *The Simpsons* is that people intuitively understand that they are more like those families than like the family in *Little House on the Prairie.*

Elkind (1994) suggests that this basic change of focus has robbed children of a carefree period of innocence. Instead, children of today are expected to be competent and sophisticated. Children are "dating" in third grade and sexually active by junior high. They are expected to deal responsibly with birth control and emotionally charged topics such as death, infidelity, and financial problems. Many are expected to be financially self-supporting (in terms of spending money) by the time they are eight or ten years old.

All of these stresses have taken their toll on today's youth. They are frightened, acting out, and exhibit a pseudoprecocious maturity. In their unhappiness and panic, they disrupt the family and couple systems further, trying to right the balance.

Some contemporary family therapists maintain that a viable spousal relationship is bought at the expense of a healthy family balance. There is just not enough time in today's world to be a good parent and a good spouse. Parents take vacations alone, not so much to desert their children as to reconnect as a couple. Yet a strong parental relationship may serve as the best foundation for a meaningful spousal relationship that can stand the test of time. For this to happen, the "me first" or "we first" philosophy must be replaced, or at least balanced, with a "them first" orientation.

CULTURAL AND RELIGIOUS DIVERSITY AND ITS EFFECT ON IN-LAW RELATIONSHIPS

Just as changes in society have influenced our sense of obligations to and entitlements with children, they have also affected our in-law relationships. Albert Ellis is purported to have once said that we are all not lucky enough to marry orphans. Indeed, many of the thorniest marital problems are directly linked to conflicts and expectations about in-law interactions. The in-law relationship, long prominent in the actual arrangement of "who" or "what type" one would marry, still exerts primordial pressures on the married couple. Although an American ethos dictates no interference in the lives of married children, interdependencies with the family of origin are culturally encouraged, psychologically inevitable, and essential for spiritual and existential development. With the increasing cultural, religious, and ethnic diversity among married couples, however, the issue of how to happily live with in-laws who have alien social backgrounds has taken on increased importance.

CULTURAL CONFLICTS AND THE WEDDING CEREMONY

The issue of religious, ethnic, or cultural group loyalty is most often confronted in the early stages of cross-cultural or interfaith romances. Children know the "type" of person they are supposed to marry. When children deviate widely from the familial expectation, it is often part of an ongoing attempt to individuate themselves from their parents. By marrying someone whom the parents do not approve of, the child asserts his or her separateness and independence of the parents (Davidson, 1992; Sung, 1990).

Couples in love frequently feel that the bond they have with each other will supersede any cultural or religious bonds they may have. If their cultural/ethnic/religious identity is weak, they may truly feel more "existentially" comfortable with their loved ones than with others of their own background. If their cultural/ethnic/religious identity is strong, they often feel their partners will naturally come to love what they love, to appreciate the heritage that is so beautiful and bountiful in their own lives.

The marriage ceremony itself is most often the first traumatic and conflict-ridden event for the in-law relationship. Disparate backgrounds are brought to the fore in unrelenting bas-relief. Despite the deep divisiveness that occurs as one tries to create appropriate and meaningful intercultural marriage ceremonies, all too many couples rationalize that these differences are confined to the marriage ceremony and are not predictive of future everyday differences.

Psychologically mature couples can use the marriage ceremony to endear themselves to their in-laws, taking advantage of a unique "critical period" in the transformation of the family structure. Most families are willing to make adaptations during this period of dramatic change that they would be highly resistant to at other times. Friedman (1985) compares the wedding ritual to "hinges in time." On the hinges of time, weddings can make it possible for families to restructure their relationships and heal old wounds. The hinge can also swing in the doorway of powerful family divisions, causing wounds that take decades to heal. The wedding is an important time to set the tone for how cultural differences will be handled in the new family. Most couples have to await the birth of a child to have another such adjustable hinge in time.

In *The Intermarriage Book,* Petsonk and Remsen (1994) give a number of general suggestions on how to "merge" interfaith weddings. Among the many suggestions for helping the two families begin to intertwine are the following: Have the couples share a glass of wine with both sets of parents during the ceremony to signify the merging of two families; the person officiating the ceremony can offer special blessings to a couple who were able to overcome their cultural differences and fall in love with the unique person they have chosen; the woman can give flowers to her mother- and father-in-law; the man can give flowers to his mother- and father-in-law; after the bride and groom kiss, "plants" should begin a round of applause; and each family should have an assigned special ambassador whose job it is to make the other side of the family feel welcome. Such recommendations could be invaluable but must take place in the wider context in which in-laws are working on basic areas of compatibility/incompatibility.

Greenstein, Carlson, and Howell (1993) stress that throughout the marriage, interfaith couples need to find solutions instead of avoiding their problems. Rigid positions are usually futile, but principled negotiation that separates the person from the problem can lead to mutually satisfying decisions about the family's spiritual life.

When culturally diverse individuals marry, the in-law relationship is burdened with the developmental need to choose, consciously or unconsciously, how much each person is going to assimilate from the in-law culture into his or her own cultural identity. Therapists working on in-law issues need to be aware of how cultural identities develop over time as well as how their own cultural identity may influence their assessment and treatment of the in-law relationship. A series of interview studies guide the following discussion, but only future empirical work will confirm just how important these factors are in cross-cultural and interracial marriages (Berg-Cross and Cohen, 1993).

COPING STRATEGIES CHARACTERISTIC OF INTERCULTURAL IN-LAW RELATIONSHIPS

All couples in a culturally diverse marriage need to decide how much of the alien culture they are going to assimilate into their own identity. Four types of strategies are possible to discern among culturally diverse couples.

Continental Dividers

People can choose to retain their own cultural heritage and ignore the cultural heritage of their spouses. "Continental dividers" tend to have a dichotomous view of the world and a great sense of pride in their own cultural background. These daughters- and sons-in-law are very difficult to incorporate emotionally into the family of origin because they will actively resist attempts at inclusion and socialization into the family ways and mores. They may or may not be willing to let their spouses retain their own cultural ways. Obviously, in-law relationships will suffer more when spouses want their mates to disengage from their cultural heritage.

Bridgers

A second option for spouses is to choose to give up parts of their own heritage and pick up aspects of their partners' culture in an attempt to bridge a lifestyle that encompasses both backgrounds. "Bridgers" typify the most dominant coping strategy in today's intercultural marriages. People try to adopt the rituals and values that are most important to their spouses' families. At the same time, they will resist changes that interfere with important aspects of their own culture. In-laws tend to respect "bridgers" and treat them as well-loved outsiders.

Mergers

A spouse can also choose to abdicate his or her own cultural background and adopt or assimilate as much as possible into the mate's culture. The "merging" style leads to the most parent-in-law acceptance because the child-in-law has validated the worth of the in-laws' values and lifestyle in a way more striking than their own children ever could do for them. If the culturally abandoned in-laws can accept the new lifestyle of their child, the relationship can work for both families of origin.

Cultural Orphans

Some people choose to alienate themselves from their own cultural heritage and are just as disdainful and rejecting of the cultural heritage of their spouses. These people do not want to have stereotyped symbols of either cultural background as part of their lives. They do not want to go to either set of parents for the December holidays. They want to keep both extended families at bay. Although this sounds like a maladaptive style, in reality, certain couples come from such highly dysfunctional, rejecting families that the cultural orphan strategy may be the most healthy one for them to adopt.

Of course, the cultural coping style adopted by one spouse interacts with the cultural coping style adopted by the other spouse. Some spousal combinations are more frequent and more adaptive than others. For example, it would be very rare for both adult children to merge with the other's in-law culture and relinquish their own cultural habits. On the other hand, an extremely common and adaptive pairing is when bridgers marry bridgers or mergers. Even continental dividers can have happy marriages if their spouses are seeking to distance themselves from their own parents and they are bridgers or mergers. Indeed, sometimes adult children marry culturally different spouses so that they can extricate themselves from family-of-origin attitudes, lifestyles, and rituals that are noxious to them but that they are incapable of disentangling themselves from on their own. When they marry a culturally different spouse, all the movement away from the family can be attributed to the spouse's discomfort. An authentic confrontation between the adult child and parents can be permanently avoided, and the in-law can be a permanent and often willing scapegoat.

It is important to remember that although interfaith and interracial differences can pose enormous problems to a marriage, this is not the norm. Indeed, studies have shown that it is difficult to predict marital satisfaction by knowing the degree of religiousity of each partner, their ethnic identiies, or their religious affiliations.

THE PHENOMENON OF CULTURAL CONFUSION

Sometimes, none of these strategies can work because there is cultural confusion and one or both of the in-laws are ignorant of the cultural ways of their new in-law. Nowhere is this more obvious than in the case of homosexual "marriages."

For example, consider the problems posed when a young lesbian couple come out to their respective parents. After the parents have accepted the alternative sexual orientation of their daughters, they must still deal with the fact that instead of a son-in-law, they have a daughter-in-law. For the traditional couple, mother and daughter can usually continue to spend visits talking and sharing, whereas the young husband finds different activities with which to busy himself. The young lesbian couple arrives home with two women eager to talk and share with the mother. Very often, the daughter-in-law is not interested, at that time, in watching TV or playing tennis. Like her mate, she is often most eager for social acceptance and interaction with the mother (Berg-Cross, 1988).

Also, there are many types of helping behaviors that a mother-in-law would accept from a son-in-law but feel very awkward accepting from her daughter-in-law. On the positive side, the opportunity for shared rituals, intimacy, and acceptance is probably much higher among lesbian couples than among heterosexual couples.

Although all of these interrelationships are due to stereotyped conditioning of sex and gender roles, the fact is that such role behaviors still govern most everyday interactions. Yet homophobia, more than gender roles, is the biggest roadblock to good in-law relationships among homosexual couples. Serovich, Price, and Chapman (1991) found that in-laws' attitudes toward homosexuality and their socioeconomic status were the best predictors of acceptance of the homosexual daughter- or son-in-law. Parent-in-laws who were open to the idea of homosexual unions were more educated, better off financially, and more willing to embrace the child's same-sex partner than parent-in-laws who were ambivalent or rejecting of homosexual unions, less educated, and of more limited financial means. Perhaps, higher socioeconomic status serves as a cushion against any expected social scorn resulting from their child's lifestyle or perhaps the cultural taboos against homosexuality are less prevalent among educated and financially secure communities.

Poor in-law relationships and strained adult child-parent relationships are exceedingly common in gay male relationships. It often takes parents and in-laws years to accept the child's partner as "part of the family" and in many cases, this will never occur. Gay men and women have developed a variety of boundary setting, and coping mechanisms that protect their relationship from the poison arrows and antipathy of the parent generation (LaSala, 1998). It may mean that when an invitation to Christmas Eve dinner is made, the gay man tells his mother that he already has plans, rather than argue with her about why his partner would not be invited or welcome. It may mean that once or twice a year, each partner makes private visits to the parents, accepting that his parents will never really know their son or accept him as an adult. One of the biggest emotional tasks about "coming out" is facing the potential lifetime of rejection and disdain from one's parents and family of origin. We can only hope that the next generation of parents will more actively embrace their own children as well as their children's chosen partners so each may reap the joys of an accepting, supportive family.

The good news is that when in-law relationships are positive and strong, they can withstand enormous adversity—even the end of the marriage! Duran-Aydintug (1993) found that women and men who had developed strong, independent relationships with their in-laws were able to maintain those relationships, albeit at a less intense level, after the adult children's divorce. In solid in-law relationships, the divorced spouse was also able to ask for and receive support from the former in-law. Serovich, Price, and Chapman (1991) reported similar findings, suggesting that although frequency of contact with in-laws decreased after divorce, the relationship for some was still a source of support, especially for female in-laws with children.

The following three chapters explore at a more clinical level how jobs, parenting, and in-law relationships affect the health and well-being of a marriage.

REFERENCES

Berg-Cross, L. (1988). Lesbians, family process and individuation. *Journal of College Student Psychotherapy, 3,* 97-112.

Berg-Cross, L. and Cohen, M. (1993). "Diversity and the in-law relationship." Paper presented at the American Psychological Association, Toronto, Canada, August 20-24.

Borum, R. and Philpot, C. (1993). Therapy with law enforcement couples: Clinical management of the "high-risk lifestyle." *American Journal of Family Therapy, 21*(2), 122-135.

Davidson, J. (1992). Theories about black-white intermarriage: A clinical perspective. *Journal of Multicultural Counseling and Development, 20*(4), 150-157.

Duran-Aydintug, C. (1993). Relationships with former in-laws: Normative guidelines and actual behavior. *Journal of Divorce and Remarriage, 19*(3-4), 69-81.

Elkind, D. (1994). *Ties that stress: The new family imbalance.* Cambridge, MA: Harvard University Press.

Friedman, E. (1985). *Generation to generation: Family process in church and synagogue.* New York: Guilford.

Greenstein, D., Carlson, J., and Howell, C. (1993). Counseling with interfaith couples. *Individual Psychology Journal of Adlerian Theory, Research, and Practice, 49*(3-4), 428-437.

Hurvitz, N. and Straus, R. (1991). *Marriage and family therapy: A sociocognitive approach.* Binghamton, New York: The Haworth Press.

LaSala, M. (1998). Coupled gay men, parents, and in-laws: Intergenerational disapproval and the need for a thick skin. *Families in Society, 79*(6), 585-595.

Petsonk, J. and Remsen, R. (1994). *The intermarriage book.* New York: William Morrow.

Serovich, J., Price, S., and Chapman, S. (1991). Former in-laws as sources of support. *Journal of Divorce and Remarriage, 17*(1-2), 17-25.

Sung, B. (1990). Chinese American intermarriage. 12th International Congress of Anthropological and Ethnological Sciences, Zagreb, Yugoslavia, 1988. *Journal of Comparative Family Studies, 21*(3), 337-352.

Chapter 4

Parenting and the Couple Relationship

The value of marriage is not that adults produce children, but that children produce adults.

Peter De Vries

THE TASK OF PARENTING

If the marital road is marked by a number of forked pathways, none is more divergent than the decision to have children. Once children enter a couple's life, their own relationship is forever changed. Commonsense dictates that the arrival of children puts enormous stresses on the marital relationship. Still, couples everywhere are shocked to find that once children arrive, the household division of labor drifts to a more traditional arrangement and the couple's leisure time and activities are drastically reduced, if they don't disappear altogether. Conflicts increase and marital satisfaction decreases in the child-rearing years (Belsky and Rovine, 1990; Lewis, 1988a, 1988b).

For the segment of the population with two parents working outside the home, children create chronic role conflicts and logistical nightmares on a daily basis (Clarke and Alison, 1989). Such parents can no longer be confident about which child care person will care for their children on any one day, who their doctor will be from one illness to the next, or what is happening to their children in their absence. They must trust a system that is not trustworthy. They feel guilty and trapped. In addition, increased travel demands made by many jobs make scheduling nonwork hours disjointed and stressful. Some spouses constantly shift between being a single parent (when their spouse is away on business) and being a coparent. Once an area of conflict reserved for families in the armed services, increasing job responsibilities are now linked with increased travel for many different

169

types of Americans: from the district managers of McDonald's to the systems analyst to the small-business owner trying to expand.

Cowan and Cowan (1992) studied 100 partners as they made the transition to parents. Among their most significant findings was the conclusion that the couples who have the most trouble adjusting to being parents and dealing with the new family configuration had the most ambivalence and conflict with each other before the children. This is no great surprise, but it is comforting to empirically confirm that a strong marital relationship before children is the single best predictor of a strong marital relationship after the children arrive. Another compelling finding was that professionally led groups for expectant parents significantly reduced the risk of divorce after the children arrived. Thus, marital strength can be pruned and fertilized before the major stressors of parenthood descend, protecting the couple and allowing them to work more effectively together. This finding also highlights the critical preventive role of family life education. One can learn to be a better parent and a better spouse. Skills and insights, such as those presented in this text, really can have a significant, positive influence on children and marital relationships.

Children influence the marital union in three different ways. First, the parental role is often a source of conflict between spouses. Husbands and wives often have different values and different theories of child rearing. Conflicts in the parenting role spill over into the spousal relationship just as conflicts in the spousal role spill over into the parenting role. Second, children affect parents. The new interactional approach in family psychology is demonstrating that children help to shape the personality and behavioral style of parents just as much as parents affect children. Third, the family system influences the willingness of couples to remain emotionally open and cooperative with each other. Each of these three influences will be discussed, in turn, beginning with the most well-known phenomenon of parental conflict over child-rearing strategies.

Four Classic Parenting Styles

Stereotypes suggest enormous differences in parenting practices associated with different socioeconomic statuses. There is also a popular belief that large variations exist between the various cultural groups. However, recent studies from the National Survey of Families and Households controlled for socioeconomic status (SES) differences and examined parenting practices among Caucasian, African-American, Hispanic, and Asian-American parents. Although ethnic parents placed a stronger emphasis on having their children exercise self-control and succeed in school, covariate analyses indicated more similarities than differences between and among the four parenting groups (Julian, McKenry, and McKelvey, 1994). In fact, no more than 4 percent of the total variance could be attributed to cultural group membership for any one parenting practice or parenting attitude. It appears that the parenting differences between husbands and wives is as great, if not greater, than any other cultural group difference.

Four basic parenting styles occur within all ethnic groups and social classes: (1) the authoritative; (2) the authoritarian; (3) the permissive; and (4) the uninvolved. These four groups differ in the degree of nurturance and love that parents express toward their children (high or low) as well as the degree of control they exert over their children's behavior and choices (high or low). Couples have conflicts over which parenting style to use in different situations with different children at different ages as well as the particulars about how to implement any one style. Both husband and wife can be distraught about spousal expectations for them as a parent, about how their own needs to parent are being thwarted by the mate, or by an inability to negotiate flexible parenting roles. A brief discussion of each parenting style will highlight potential conflict areas for parents who adopt each style.

Authoritative parents are high on nurturance and high on control. Although they are very responsive and child centered, they do have demanding standards that they make sure children live up to. The authoritative parenting style respects the individuality and rights of even the littlest person. At the same time, developmental limitations are acknowledged and the roles of the parent as guardian and teacher are stressed. In this type of parenting, children are treated in a democratic fashion in a number of important areas, but parents still retain the right to direct or restrict the child's activities if they appear particularly dangerous or foolish.

Baumrind has consistently found that the authoritative parent produces the most successful children. That is, children whose parents use an authoritative parenting style tend to be friendly with peers, cooperative with adults, independent, energetic, and achievement oriented. They show a high degree of self-control and inner direction (Baumrind, 1967, 1968). There is even longitudinal evidence that authoritative parents are very successful in protecting their adolescents from getting into problems with drugs, and in generating competence (Baumrind, 1991).

It has also become increasingly clear that individuals who have a good theoretical and applied grasp of developmental milestones and developmental limitations lean toward an authoritative style of parenting. It is as though knowing what a child is capable of at various stages allows the parent to lovingly but firmly enforce limitations and standards of behavior appropriate to the child. The child responds to this protection by consolidating the social learning required of one stage before taking on new and more complicated social tasks. Parenting programs that stress what children at each stage understand and need for positive development have been shown to reduce the incidence of child abuse as well as increase children's learning potential and social adjustment (Grotberg, 1992). Parenting does not come naturally to everyone. Luckily, virtually all men and women can learn the skills necessary to be a "good enough mother" (Winnicott, 1965, p. 42).

Authoritarian parents are high on control and low in nurturance. They are both demanding and rejecting. Authoritarian parents feel that there should be rigid boundaries between parents and children: Children are to be seen, but not heard; a parent's job is to tell the child what to do, the child's job is to do it. Many of these parents believe that if you spare the rod, you will spoil the child. The authoritarian parent believes that children have qualitatively different rights and obligations than adults. Their style of governing the family is totalitarian (Baumrind, 1968, 1971).

Children of authoritarian parents are the true unhappy campers of childhood. Boys act out their frustrations by becoming aggressive; the girls act out their frustrations by becoming more dependent. Both sexes have lowered self-esteem, poor peer relations, and lowered school achievement in adolescence (Baumrind, 1968; Buri, 1988).

Permissive parents are moderately nurturant and low in control. They believe that children will naturally end up doing the right thing if left to their own devices. Children create their own bedtimes, their own diets, their own ways of addressing parents and responding to their requests. Parents make few demands of their children and more or less give them unconditional love and positive regard. There is no "right" answer for the permissive parent. They believe that children learn best by learning for themselves. Their style of governing is exceedingly democratic and sometimes verges on anarchy.

Children raised by permissive parents also have trouble learning to control themselves. They are prone to tantrums and aggressive behaviors. Despite their "freedom," they are less self-reliant than children who had been raised by authoritative parents. This suggests that to be a confident, autonomous adult, a child requires much monitored, guarded practice with a watchful parent (Baumrind, 1968).

Uninvolved parents are both low on nurturance and low on control. They are parent centered but do not enforce any standards or controls in regard to the children. They appear uncommitted to their parental role and are emotionally detached from their children. They rarely converse with their children and are not familiar with many of the children's friends. This estrangement has profound effects on children: They suffer from poor self-esteem, heightened aggression, and poor impulse control. The earlier the neglect, the more severe the damage to the child. One-year-old babies who were neglected by their parents were far more likely to be classified as anxiously attached than were abused infants (Egeland and Sroufe, 1981).

Parenting highlights the differences in personality and attitudes between a couple. One parent may have a permissive style, whereas the other has a more authoritarian style. When parenting styles conflict, arguments over what is the best way to handle a daily child crisis can fuel an argument that spans many weeks. Partly, this is because parents feel as though small decisions can have a major influence. There are few "unimportant" decisions in the life of a parent. Consider the simple decision of whether to give a child an allowance.

Parents often have conflicts over whether to give children an allowance, and if so, how much and under what conditions. Most experts seem to concur that children should not be paid for doing routine household tasks that are intrinsically helpful to having the family function effectively. When there are special jobs that the parents would hire outside help for (e.g., painting the outside of the house), paying children for their contribution is appropriate. Most Americans do not listen to the experts on this topic.

A group of researchers at the University of Minnesota surveyed 856 local high school students to assess the range of allowance practices and if they were related to intrinsic or extrinsic work values (Mortimer et al., 1994). Of the ninth graders surveyed, 74 percent had at one point or another received an allowance; 44 percent were currently receiving an allowance. The average age for starting an allowance was eight years old, and the mean allowance rate was $8.86. Of the students, 80 percent reported that they had to do household work to get the allowance. Although wealthier parents were more likely to give their children an allowance, the amount remained stable whether you were looking at the wealthiest children studied or the poorest children studied. This suggests that allowance stipends are not related to the resources of the parents in any systematic manner but are more related to the parent's philosophy of child rearing. Children who got an allowance thought that work was less enjoyable and that the extrinsic rewards of work may not be worth the effort. Another interesting finding was that girls were routinely given an allowance, but it was not contingent on doing specific household chores as often as the boys' allowances were tied to specific work assignments. This is because girls are supposed to clean "out of love" (see Chapter 5). Boys received an allowance based on their performance, girls received an allowance based on the emotional relationship between parent and child. The effect of this arrangement is quite likely to make girls more dependent and boys more independent.

Thus, parents' decisions about giving allowances affected different children in different ways. Many times, giving allowances did not have the effect parents had intended. Unfortunately, most parenting decisions are like this; there are so many variables, interacting in complicated ways. Although parents know that their decisions will have a significant influence, it is extremely difficult to predict the effects of any one decision. This leads to arguments without end because it is nearly impossible to prove that any well-meaning parenting strategy is "right" or "wrong," "helpful" or "hurtful" beforehand.

Parents can explore how many of their values are conflictual by taking Self-Exploration 1: Comparing Parenting Values (see page 209).

CASE STUDY 1:
SPOUSAL STRESS RELATED
TO PARENTING PHILOSOPHIES

Claire and George were the all-American couple. Good-looking professionals from distinguished Mormon families, they had an excellent rapport with each other and with their extended families. They were childhood sweethearts who went through college together and got married while George was in medical school. They had two children (a boy and a girl), a big house in the suburbs, significant community involvement, and a deep and trusting marriage.

When they were forty, an unplanned pregnancy occurred, and Claire gave birth to a little boy with Down's syndrome. The family went through the usual stages of shock and anger but quickly acclimated. Tommy was soon the joy of the entire family. Claire had heard that plastic surgery could alter many of Tommy's typical Down's features; the slanted eyes could be made more Caucasian-looking and the broad nose sculpted. George was very hesitant about such a procedure, feeling it was simply denying the limitations Tommy would always have, regardless of how he looked. But because there was evidence of increased peer acceptance after such operations, George agreed. This was the first of many decisions which Claire and George fought about during the next fifteen years. Claire was always pushing Tommy to do what all the other kids were doing. George was more invested in protecting Tommy from frustration and socially embarrassing situations. Whether it was the type of summer camp, the structure of the school setting, or having responsibilities around the house, George and Claire argued and stewed over their decisions.

(continued)

(continued)

When they came for treatment, they could not remember a single time that Tommy's future had been decided without a fight. They both had a highly authoritative style of parenting their other two children. The rarely disagreed, and were able to support each other's decisions. Their disagreements always concerned Tommy.

They were referred for therapy by Tommy's resource teacher who thought they needed help to decide the best high school placement for him. It soon became clear that fighting about Tommy had taken its toll. They tried to put off decisions because they knew discussion would not be effective in swaying the other's opinion. Their basic philosophical differences were well understood. Each could point to numerous incidents over the years when their own philosophy turned out to be correct and the other's faulty.

After spending a few weeks recounting the various choice points, the therapist made a big chart summarizing what had been discussed so far. It looked as follows:

The following ideas were helpful for Tommy:

- Have the operation (Claire's idea)
- Share a room with his sister (George's idea)
- Start with the specialized language teacher (George's idea)
- Go to sleep-away camp with his siblings (Claire's idea)
- Learn to ride his bike (Claire's idea)

These ideas created trauma for Tommy:

- Being taunted by the other children in the mainstreamed elementary school (Claire's idea to mainstream him)
- Being given books he couldn't read (Claire's idea)
- Being on the regular soccer team from the neighborhood (Claire's idea)
- Getting Ds on his report card (due to Claire's idea to mainstream him)
- Having a tutor during his lunch hour at school (George's idea)
- Not being allowed to go to girl-boy parties (George's idea)
- Having to carry a cellular phone in case he needed help (George's idea)

After examining the list, it became abundantly clear that sometimes Claire had made the right choice for Tommy, and sometimes she had made bad choices. The same was true for George. Many of their decisions had both positive and negative effects on Tommy. Obviously, neither had a parenting strategy that was surefire. When the conversation shifted from finding the right strategy (which was impossible and frustrating) to trying hard to make the right choice in any one particular situation, George and Claire felt very relieved. They were pushed to explore options that did not automatically follow from either of their general strategies. They realized that whatever school decision was made this year might have to be revised next year. They decided to widen their decision making to include Tommy and his two siblings. Most of all, they made a pact that they would make a joint decision, and, in fact, they did just that.

(continued)

(continued)

Improved communication was facilitated by having the rest of the family contribute their ideas, by setting up a series of four "thinking" sessions in which ideas could be explored but no decisions made, and by encouraging both parents to learn from each conversation and shift their opinions based on new information. They started each session by saying, "I'm looking for a good solution and hope you can give me some new ways of looking at our options." They ended each session by saying, "I'm going to think about all that you've said. I'm going to try to improve on my position. Thank you for trying to explain yourself." Although initially these statements, which were written on index cards and given to the couple, were seen as very artificial, both felt it helped create a positive frame for the conversations.

George and Claire continued to come in once or twice a year to focus on their concerns for Tommy and how they were dealing with him as a couple. To date, Tommy obtained a full-time job in the special needs preschool he attended as a child. His parents are seeking group living arrangements for him in the near future.

THERAPEUTIC INTERVENTION 1: ASSESSING PARENTING STYLE

Parents can use many universal interventions to remediate problem behaviors in their children, such as modeling, reinforcement, time-out, and systematic problem solving. However, each parent needs to be approached and instructed in these techniques in a unique way, depending on his or her parenting style. The therapist needs to present style-specific rationales for each procedure. That is, permissive parents will be more motivated to change if they believe it will help the child learn to be more flexible; authoritarian parents will be motivated toward greater change if they believe the child will show increased compliancy.

When a couple desires help with a child problem, the therapist should first assess the parenting style of each parent. Each parent should be asked, "On a scale of 1 to 100, how loving and affectionate have you been to (child's name) over the past few weeks? How much time do you have to spend restricting him or her from doing what he or she wants to do or ordering the child to do things that he or she doesn't want to do (measuring control)?" On this scale, 50 represents how each parent thinks the average parent would act toward the average child. Parents who score high on both affection and control are authoritative; parents who score high on affection and low on control are permissive; parents who score low on affection and high on control are authoritarian; and parents who score low on both affection and control are neglectful. A parent who says that he or she would score an 80 on love and a 80 on restrictiveness is likely to be an

(continued)

(continued)

authoritative parent who will respond well to parenting advice and learning appropriate developmental expectations. A parent who scores 20 on love and 20 on restrictiveness is likely an uninvolved parent who may need intensive reparenting himself or herself as well as a series of parent-child bonding experiences before the misbehavior is addressed. Although the validity of self-report is questionable in assessing parenting styles, therapists are still wise to incorporate such quickie verbal assessments as a way of confirming their clinical hunches.

When the therapist is sensitive to the style used by each parent, she or he can sensitively combine an analysis of what is appropriate for a child at a certain age with a behavioral analysis of what can be done to teach the child the age-appropriate behavior. This usually leads to a successful intervention and gets the parents on track.

Gender Differences in Parenting

> When you are a mother, you are never really alone in your thoughts. You are connected to your child and to all those who touch their lives. A mother always has to think twice; once for herself and once for her child.
>
> Sophia Loren

There are differences in parenting based on gender. Men play more with the children than do mothers; mothers socialize the children and talk to them about interpersonal issues much more than fathers do (Lamb, 1977a, 1977b; McBride and Mills, 1993). Mothers most often try to get the children to listen and obey. When disciplining, mothers tend to use guilt-induction strategies, and fathers tend to use high-power, assertive strategies (Stafford and Bayer, 1993). Couples need to acknowledge that they will differ in their interaction styles with the children. This diversity is probably critical for the children and is unavoidable due to human nature.

As discussed in Chapter 5, moms still do the large proportion of daily hands-on care for children (Crouter and Crowley, 1990). However, fathers are getting more involved in the home as well as in the community. Research has shown that family life is improved when the fathers are more equal caretakers, and the psychological adjustment and social competence of the child is improved when the father takes part in community child care activities such as the Head Start program (Levine, 1993). Overall, though, regardless of the social class, job status, or education of the parents, moms do more than dads.

Taffel (1993) believes that the dominant child-rearing paradigm of "Mom is responsible—Dad helps out" is the central factor underlying ordinary parental disagreement in most of today's two-parent families. Taffel argues that women contribute to this quandary as much as men. Women find it difficult to give up their endless list of chores due to three factors: (1) many women believe it is much easier and less stressful just to get the job done themselves; (2) others believe that the caretaking role is primarily a feminine role; and (3) if the children do not turn out "right," society will blame the mother. Hence, she is much more invested in having maximal input because she senses her ultimate responsibility.

Taffel's suggestions for shared parenting require men to develop and express their nurturant side. Many everyday people as well as gender psychologists question whether this nurturant tendency exists in men to an equal degree as in women (whether due to genetics, socialization, or some combination of both). Taffel's shared parenting assumes that men and women are best off when each can develop similar sets of androgynous behaviors and attitudes. The ideal here is for feminine and masculine characteristics to exist side by side in each individual. Both men and women should learn to enjoy and engage in activities and ways of thinking that normally typify one of the genders. If all parents were "monoandrogynists" and expressed both male and female attitudes and behaviors, parenting could be truly a shared activity (Trebilcot, 1993).

In contrast to this monoandrogynism, radical social theorists have long advocated an ideal of polyandrogynism, which advocates no single ideal of behaviors and attitudes that all people must ascribe to but, rather, a variety of options, including pure femininity and masculinity as well as any combination of the two (Safilios-Rothschild, 1974). In this model, it is up to each couple to explore and find the optimum ways of expressing their unique potentials, needs, and abilities as parents. Here, the "endless list" that Taffel (1993) states women are unfairly left composing and executing is a list that could be the primary responsibility of the father or the mother or could be shared. What is important is that each partner feels recognized and appreciated for his or her contribution and that each partner contributes all that he or she is able to contribute (Belsky, 1993).

Indeed, important cultural differences exist in the United States in terms of male contributions to child care. For example, Hossain and Roopnarine (1993) found that although dual-earner African-American couples revealed gender-differentiated patterns of involvement in child care and household work, fathers were far more involved than was typically reported and that the involvement was present to the same extent whether the wife was employed full-time or part-time. This continues a long line of research that has documented that African-American men have much broader role genders than other male groups in America.

Self-Exploration 2 ("Who Takes Responsibility for the Children?") will help couples explore how their own endless list is shared (see p. 210).

THERAPEUTIC INTERVENTION 2:
THE SIX-STEP PROGRAM
TO EQUALIZE CHILD RESPONSIBILITIES

Taffel (1993) proposes that mastering the following six goals helps parents learn to divide their responsibilities more equitably.

1. For several days, each couple keeps a list of who does what with and for the children. Denial is reduced and insight increases with a valid measure of daily contributions. Of course, the consciousness-raising associated with self-monitoring will provoke changes in itself, particularly if the chore baseline of the monitoring spouse is very low.

2. Mothers and fathers need to learn that neither of them is solely responsible for how their children turn out. Parents need to be aware of the effect that children have on them as well as the effects that they have on their children. Having parents discuss their worst fears over how they have already influenced their children will help ground the conversation in particulars relevant to that family. Historically, the psychological literature has unmercifully blamed mothers for the ills of their children—from schizophrenia to criminality. More education about the role of genetics and wider social influences would help take parents, particularly mothers, off an endless "guilt trip" over unsuccessful children.

3. Mothers need to learn to ask for help—consistently, assuredly, and with a spirit of comradeship. Most feminist therapists have a hard time with this recommendation. If parenting is a partnership, one partner should not be relegated to pleading with the other to do his or her fair share (A. Boscov, personal communication, September 17, 1995). Knowing when something needs to be done and initiating the project are just as critical as actually doing the project. If there is nothing in the refrigerator for dinner, noting that fact, planning what to buy, and going to the supermarket are essential preparatory behaviors. If the wife comes home and says, "Can you cook dinner?", the request is meaningless if the groundwork has not been done. Women often feel that for dinner to appear they would need to get up in the morning and say, "Can you check if there is anything in the refrigerator for dinner?" "Can you figure out what to cook?" "Can you go to the supermarket and buy the necessary ingredients?" and "Oh, by the way, can you cook dinner tonight?" In short, asking for help is not as easy as it sounds.

(continued)

(continued)

4. Mothers must learn not to criticize fathers once they have asked for and received help. Better to appreciate a lopsided good effort (poorly folded clothes or a half-clean floor) than punish it as being only a halfhearted attempt. Poor-quality chores that are the result of resistance and passive-aggressiveness instead of incompetence put the wife in a double bind. She will find resentment and anger building if she does not criticize; she knows that the job could be done well. However, if she does vent her disapproval, the husband will act as though she is totally unappreciative unless everything is done her way. The answer, for most couples, is to develop joint standards for daily chores.

5. Neither the father nor the mother should get into the habit of congratulating the father for his participation. It is not a grand achievement. It is the only responsible and ethical way to maintain a family in today's world. Abundant wifely thank-yous imply that the husband is graciously helping the wife with her chores.

6. Moms should travel more. Instead of cooking everything a week ahead and arranging every bit of child care before leaving, the husband should be responsible for everything from the word "good-bye." Whether she is going to visit her relatives, on a business trip, or off on a carefree weekend with some friends, the mother who learns that she can successfully delegate will be better able to loosen her control strings on a regular basis.

The Effects of Parental Conflict on Children

There is a commonsense adage that one should not fight in front of the children. It is true. Studies have long confirmed that marital discord is associated with child maladjustment. More refined investigations have pinpointed children's exposure to overt intraparental conflicts as one of the most deleterious risk factors for child problems (David et al., 1996; Grych and Fincham, 1990). The more frequent the arguments and the more intense they are, the more psychologically damaging the arguments are for a child (Fincham, 1994; Jouriles, Bourg, and Farris, 1991).

There are a variety of explanations for how marital conflicts mediate child psychopathology. The most obvious explanation is that hearing parents argue directly threatens the security and identity of the child. Witnessing the heated, hurtful exchanges of primary love figures is in itself distressing and leads one to fear similar anger or abandonment.

We all intuitively know that children understand the many nuances and emotional implications of parental arguments. So it is not surprising that research has demonstrated that children are less upset if they can see that their parents have "made up" and are happy with each other after an argument than if they sense that the animosity is still lingering between the parents. Children do not have to know how the situation was resolved; they just need to know that their parents are happy again. When the parental situation remains tense, emotional insecurity, anxiety, or anger are the inevitable reactions of most children (Davies, Myers, and Cummings, 1996).

Another leading theory is that conflict in the marital relationship adversely affects the consistency and quality of parenting that the child receives. When parents are unhappy with each other, they are more likely to be erratic or irrational with their children, who are easily used as scapegoats. Couples in distressed marriages do, in fact, seem more prone to use anxiety-guilt inductions as a means of discipline. Also, the more parents are verbally and physically aggressive with each other, the more likely they are to be aggressive with their children. The constant bickering of conflict-ridden couples is so emotionally draining that parents quickly become unable to recognize and fully respond to their children's emotional needs (Fincham, Grych, and Osborne, 1994).

Children are less likely to obey their parents when the parents are experiencing significant marital conflict. Perhaps this is because distressed couples argue more about parenting strategies and are less consistent in how they respond to the children. This inconsistency provokes anxiety and confusion in the children. Unsure of what is really required and having their coping resources compromised by the stress of parental arguments, they disobey or are unable to successfully carry out their parents' requests (Webster-Stratton, 1989). An important longitudinal study by Belsky and colleagues (1991) found that fathers who reported feeling less love for their wives over the course of the marriage had children who were more disobedient. The tension is returned by the fathers in distressed marriages; they are much more upset by a child's disobedience than fathers in happy marriages (Easterbrooks and Emde, 1988).

Not surprisingly, boys and girls tend to be affected by parental arguing in different ways. Girls who react adversely to parental problems are more likely to internalize the conflicts and feel that somehow they are responsible or to blame. They feel that they should be able to make the parents get along. Boys, on the other hand, are more likely to become aggressive and externalize the problems. Boys with good coping skills are buffered from the adverse effects of the parents' arguing; girls are affected regardless of the level of their coping skills. This may be because of the personal responsibility that females feel for maintaining positive social relations (Cummings, Davies, and Simpson, 1994).

Boys and girls are also differentially affected by each gender's ability to offer a quality parent-child relationship. Cowan and colleagues (1996), study-

ing the behavior of kindergarten children, found that when fathers had unresolved issues with their family of origin and were experiencing marital
strife, children became more externalizing in the classroom. They were more
frequently reported by the teachers as off-task, disobeying, breaking rules,
arguing, lying, being uncooperative, getting in fights, and unable to sit still.
This was in marked contrast to children whose fathers had a clear, detailed,
consistent, and coherent relationship with each of his own parents (even if it
was negative). Those children were low on externalizing and were seen as
cooperative and nonaggressive in the classroom. On the other hand, internalizing behaviors were associated with mothers who had unresolved issues
with their families of origin. That is, the teachers reported that children were
more sad, shy, nervous, and preferred solitary activities. The children whose
mothers had a secure relationship with their own parents were described as
gregarious, cheerful, and relaxed. The results of this study are actually quite
complex, with mother variables also predicting some externalizing behavior
in the children (39 percent of the variance compared to father's 69 percent)
and father variables also predicting some internalizing behavior in the children (41 percent of the variance compared to mother's 60 percent). Nonetheless, the gender differences are strong and thought provoking.

Temperament also affects how children will respond to parental conflict.
Toddlers with more difficult temperaments are far more reactive to parental
arguments than more even-tempered toddlers (Easterbrooks, Cummings,
and Emde, 1994).

Children are buffered from the devastating effects of parental strife when
they feel that they have a close and stable relationship with each of their
parents. Male or female, the child who is secure that he or she has a loving,
secure relationship with each parent that will not be undermined by parents
vying for a primary emotional allegiance is given the best odds of emotional
health.

THE BIDIRECTIONAL APPROACH:
HOW CHILDREN INFLUENCE PARENTS

> For years, my husband and I have advocated separate vacations. But
> the kids keep finding us.
>
> Erma Bombeck

Children play a large role in determining how their parents will treat
them. Parents do not directly project all of their child-rearing theories,
personal psychopathologies, and idealizations onto a tabula rasa child. Each
child provides a powerful stimulus that prompts different types of parental

responses. A number of very clever studies have been devised to empirically prove this point. In one set of studies, ten-year-olds were trained to exhibit either oppositional or socially withdrawn behavior while playing a board game with a range of different mothers. Results showed that mothers adapted to the type of child they were interacting with at that moment, becoming stricter with the more oppositional child. Other experiments have dressed toddlers in unisex snowsuits and given them names that indicate different genders. Adults interact with the child differently, depending on the presumed sex of the toddler.

Similarly, studies have monitored maternal interactions before and after their hyperactive children are given stimulant medications. Among the children who are drug responders and whose behavior changes, the parental behaviors change just as much. Among the nonresponders, no change is evident in parent or child. Indeed, when a mother does not change her own behavior in response to her medicated child, she may be in need of pharmacological help to be a more appropriate mother. This was clinically demonstrated at the Western Psychiatric Institute and Clinic when, using a double-blind procedure, they demonstrated that a mother was much better able to monitor and manage her son who had been diagnosed with attention-deficit-hyperactivity disorder (ADHD) after her own ADHD was diagnosed and she was properly medicated (Evans, Vallano, and Pelham, 1994). Thus, it is normal for parents to change in response to changes in children; failure to do so suggests serious personal problems.

Parental Anger and Discipline Strategies

Many childhood behaviors act as triggers and provoke anger in parents. But not all parents respond with the same degree of intensity to the same provoking behaviors. The following ten child behaviors are most likely to provoke parental anger:

1. Disobedience
2. Seeing the child make the same mistakes that the parent made
3. Sibling rivalry
4. Intrusion on parental privacy
5. Being tired or rushed and having demands made by the child
6. Acting immature
7. Rejecting the parent or trying to avoid him or her
8. Intense nature—either in activity or affect
9. Being jealous of how good the child has it compared to the parent
10. Acting in an embarrassing manner in public

Parents differ about how to discipline children because each reacts to different triggers. Different situations can provoke very different reactions: Behavior that one parent views as cute can be viewed by the other as monstrous. By examining parental differences in anger across different situations, the therapist can predict the degree of spousal conflict regarding parenting.

However, even when parents are angered by the same types of situations, their methods of handling the anger may vary dramatically and be a source of major conflict. Parents have different styles of dealing with child anger, ranging from physical punishment to verbal punishment to avoidance to restriction of privileges to verbal explanation. Many arguments between spouses focus on whether physical or verbal punishment should be used to discipline children.

When there are two parents in the home, the extent of parental punishment is often underestimated when only one parent is queried. Perhaps, this is because parents focus on defining either themselves or the other as the primary disciplinarian and are unable to see the cumulative impact of shared disciplining. In cases in which only one parent is the disciplinarian, research indicates that, at least in certain segments of America, a significant correlation exists between mother's and father's use of physical punishment. The more the father uses physical punishment as a disciplinary strategy, the more likely the mother will also use that strategy. Parents adopt similar punishing strategies, even though one parent may be more frequent and intense in the use of that strategy than the other. This is important for clinicians to be aware of since the impact of physical punishment on the child may be much greater than one would get on an initial parent report (Nobes and Smith, 1997).

Parents whose children are aggressive or domineering with peers often benefit from exploring their individual and joint punishment styles. It is a well-documented fact that the more children receive physical punishments from their parents, the more likely they are to bully their friends (Nobes et al., 1999). By weighing the accumulated punishments from mother, father, and any other caretakers, the total impact of modeled aggression becomes more understandable. Each parent realizes that he or she is not the only one teaching that violence is the way to get what one wants. Each parent needs to stem the tide and teach alternative methods of eliciting good behavior from their children.

Cultural attitudes toward physical punishment as a form of discipline vary widely, but there are many parental groups in America who believe that it is their responsibility to use corporeal punishment to teach their children long-term values of correct and incorrect behavior. Yet, cultural stereotypes are most often just that—overgeneralized. For example, the stereotype that African-American parents prefer physical punishment is being refuted by the data. Similar to many other American groups, African Americans may prefer an authoritative style where physical punishment is most likely to occur when a child has directly challenged the authority of the parent. American-Caribbean parents, on the other hand, may be more likely to endorse physical punishment as a generally appropriate disciplinary strategy (Bradley, 1998).

The consensus among family therapists is that physical punishments must be a target of intervention if: the child is experiencing repeated physical trauma, the parent is acting out of anger in an impulsive manner, or because the parents are unskilled in the wide range of nonpunitive parenting strategies. For many therapists, though, all physical punishment is abusive of children and therefore intolerable.

Most animal model studies concur that when punishment is sufficiently intense, a targeted behavior can be completely suppressed. Unfortunately, along with the infliction of intense punishment comes extreme fear and hatred of the person who inflicted the punishment. The benefits achieved from physical punishment are virtually never worth the cost. Many parents profess that not all physical punishment is the same and an attentional slap is a far cry from a brutal beating. The idea that lower levels of pain infliction are appropriate for children is contraindicated by the fact that mild punishments often need to be escalated to maintain their effectiveness. There is also the moral argument that it is inappropriate to deliberately inflict pain on another person.

Physical punishment causes psychological distress in children. The greater the punishment and the more frequent, the more severe the reaction. Even in cases of moderate physical abuse, children may develop various psychopathologies and show increased aggression toward themselves, peers, and siblings and later to their own spouses and children.

Parents who are not educated in child development become more easily aggravated and baffled. As parents learn about different ages and stages, they become sensitive to the changing needs and limitations of their children and are less likely to behave in an abusive manner. Yet ignorance is not the only reason for abuse. Parents also abuse children because they are the quintessential, helpless victims—the easy, powerless scapegoats that adults use to vent all their frustrations.

Getting Them to Listen: An Interactive Analysis of Compliancy and Preemptive Distraction

One of the primary sources of arguments between couples comes from the oppositional behavior of children. Fathers blame mothers' child-rearing strategies for the noncompliance; mothers blame fathers' strategies. All too infrequently do both parents appreciate and commiserate over the child's personal contribution to the ongoing power struggle! Oppositional behavior is considered normal during the "terrible twos." After that, we have a myth that a "good" parent can create a compliant child. This simply is not true. Children refuse to obey their parents due to their own legitimate needs, personality styles, needs to practice and perfect negotiation strategies, and the judged validity of the parent's request (Stafford and Bayer, 1993).

Parents are not great role models for compliancy. Children respond to parental requests and demands with a far greater frequency than adults respond to children's requests and demands (Stafford and Bayer, 1993). Although many parents still believe that their job is to make the demands and the child's job is to obey them, this authoritarian parenting strategy tends to meet with frustration and resentment over the long haul.

When there is a reciprocity in responding to requests, both parent and child end up having a better time. This has been demonstrated in the lab, during mother-daughter tea parties. When a mother responded positively to her child's play requests, the child responded to the mother's play requests. But when the mother was unwilling to yield to her daughter's suggestions, the tea parties fell apart and were more likely to end in frustration or tears (Rocissano, Slade, and Lynch, 1987).

Other parenting strategies, besides reciprocity, tend to increase compliance. But these strategies are all geared toward tuning in and working with the unique child in front of the parent, understanding his or her age, temperament, needs, and frustration levels. The parents who have the least problems with getting their children to behave are those who put an enormous amount of work and energy into "preemptive distraction" (Holden and West, 1989). If they want the children to go to bed at 8:30 p.m., they make sure the TV and other entertaining pastimes are put away at 8:00 p.m. If they want the child to do his or her homework after school, they are there to make sure it gets done (or have a parent substitute on the scene to guide the work). In this way, parents are never at rest. They are rarely able to attend to each other with undivided attention. Mostly, women take on the job of environmental engineer. Then their husbands feel that they are being ignored, neglected, and minimized as they unsuccessfully try to interact with their wives at home. In some way, they are being marginalized, because part of the wife's attention is frequently diverted from the spouse and is busy scanning and organizing the environment. Husbands who do environmental engineering are perceived similarly by their wives.

With all the competing demands for attention, it is not surprising that parents act differently when they are alone with children than when they are interacting with their children in front of the spouse. Despite general feelings of spousal neglect, parents do interact more with each other and reduce the amount of direct interaction they have with the child when all three are present, compared with when either one is alone with the child. When they do interact with the child, the nature of the interaction changes. Lytton (1980) found that mothers provided more positive verbalizations to children when the fathers were present. Mothers also decreased their demands on the child when the father was present. In short, mothers emphasized the nurturing role when their husbands were present. However, having both mother and father in the room increased the likelihood that children would listen to a command from the mother, when it occurred.

The Child's Self-Esteem and Success Influence the Parent

Although there is evidence that parents can have a fortifying or devastating effect on children's self-esteem, the child's self-esteem level can help shape how parents respond to him or her (Felson and Zielinski, 1989; Rosenberg, 1965). For example, children with low self-esteem tend to be defensive or depressed, and/or to engage in defiant behaviors. Such behaviors tend to provoke negative or punitive responses from parents instead of positive ones. People who criticize a parent for constantly screaming or controlling a child often are shocked to find their own behavior following suit when they are asked to stand in and watch the child for any significant period of time. Bartle, Anderson, and Sabatelli (1989) have documented how children with high self-esteem are easier to parent, and this reduced parenting strain lessens the spillover and stress on the spousal relationship.

Parents invest so much time and energy in their children that it is not surprising that the success or failure of the child during any particular period has a direct effect on how successful or failure-ridden the parent feels. Most parents can remember with great personal pride the school and sports accomplishments of their children. When the offspring are young, endearing, and full of possibilities, parents are buoyed daily by the clever remark, the precocious observation, or the mastery of a skill. But as children enter adolescence and start marching to their own tunes, they experience more visible failures, interpersonal conflicts, and personal angst. The parent's misery follows in their child's footsteps. As mothers struggle with difficult teenagers, their self-esteem plummets and they question all of their parenting history. On the other hand, if one's teenagers are engaging and productive, capable of expressing closeness and appreciation, then the parent's self-esteem is enhanced (Demo, Small, and Savin-Williams, 1987).

Genetic Boundaries of Bidirectionality

Although there are strong bidirectional influences between parent and child, biologically determined limitations have an influence. Most couples struggle with deciding which of their children's traits they can influence and to which they must simply stand witness. As science provides more details, parents may stop ideologically blaming themselves, their spouses, or both for having children who need to struggle with inevitable human frailties and problems.

The role of genetics is being understood in greater detail every year, and with this understanding comes a more rational, limited view of how parents really can influence or shape their children. Parents can and do teach general values, but children live out those values according to their own scripts. For example, a parent may teach the value of "honesty" and then be horrified to find the child refusing to apply to college because he or she "honestly" does not want to be in school.

Many genetically determined predispositions interact with the environment to shape one's destiny. A variety of inborn temperamental qualities, such as social withdrawal, negative mood, and inflexibility have been observed in children who subsequently have behavior problems or substance abuse problems in adolescence. In fact, one study found that the more deviant their biologically based temperament, the more severe their drug use (Glantz, 1992). The most damaging inborn temperamental qualities, however, appear to be those related to affect. Those children who from their earliest days are characterized by a bad mood, low threshold for emotional arousal (upset), low soothability, and social withdrawal appear most at risk for later maladjustment. These temperamental qualities appear in the earliest days of life and are fairly stable. Most developmental psychologists believe that the data indicate that parents cannot provoke these traits in their children—they are genetic givens.

Parent temperament seems to have a strong interacting effect with a child's temperament. Blackson and colleagues (1994) conducted a series of studies in the effort to understand what factors determine child behavior problems among predominantly Caucasian families with a substance-abusing father. It is well-known that a substance-abusing father puts a child at risk for problems; however, some children appear remarkably resistant to such stressors and others remarkably vulnerable. What makes one child resilient and the other vulnerable? Blackson and colleagues found that the interaction of father and son temperament could explain the situations in which a substance-abusing father had a toxic effect. In those situations in which the father and son had difficult temperaments, the most destructive family interactions and behavior problems in the child were found. In these studies, temperament was measured by means of self-report and interviews. The three major dimensions measured were how much the son and father used approach versus withdrawal in novel or stressful situations, how flexible or rigid they were in their problem-solving styles, and if they were positive or negative mood types. The group of father-sons who were most withdrawn, rigid, and negative in mood had sons who showed more externalizing and internalizing coping responses and were judged by the mothers as more depressed, uncommunicative, obsessive-compulsive, with somatic complaints and social withdrawal. That is, the combined difficult temperaments of the father and the son predicted the behavioral problems of the son. When two difficult temperaments must interact with each other, tensions and conflicts are inevitable. When the stressor of a substance-abusing father is added, the temperament of the two males is a key factor in determining which children will succumb to clinically identifiable problems. It seems as though a son with a difficult temperament can be helped or buffered through adolescence if his father models more adaptive traits and can good-naturedly reach out to his son.

Rather than being a fatalistic study, these findings point toward powerful preventive interactions. Parents who have difficult temperaments need the most guidance on how to react to their children's emotional lability. They need to learn how not to escalate problems. Without intervention, these sons will prematurely disengage from the parental sphere of influence and will be susceptible to deviant peer influences or social withdrawal. If the mother can cultivate a positive relationship with her son, she may provide the needed buffer for the child. This viewpoint stresses the adaptive nature of parent-child allegiances as well as the negative effects of such relationships.

Besides temperament, another biological factor that greatly determines how our children turn out is their rate of maturation. It has been repeatedly shown that early maturing boys are at a strong social advantage. They are seen as smarter and more competent. They are more likely to be leaders in adolescence and in adulthood. Their parents and teachers have greater maturity expectations for them, and they are given more independent responsibilities at an earlier age. This early training in competency gives the early maturing boys an even greater advantage. Early maturing girls, on the other hand, are often at a social disadvantage. They are unable to easily relate to their less mature girlfriends and are ostracized by the very immature boys in their age group. In addition, all children go through dramatic changes in their interactions with their parents as they go through the various stages.

Puberty, in particular, is a trying time for parents and adolescents. The puberapex, defined as the six-month period in which boys show the greatest growth, is associated with dramatic changes in the mother-son relationship. Before the puberapex, boys will cuddle, cry on their mother's lap, and seek her out for comfort and advice. After the puberapex, American boys start to distance themselves from their mothers. Many begin to take a superior attitude, and they avoid physical contact. They begin to seek out a new rapprochement with fathers. Mothers often go through a roller coaster of emotions: They are proud, hurt, and angry. Often, they are unaware of what is happening and just know that things are different.

CASE STUDY 2: THE EFFECTS OF TEENAGE DRUG ABUSE ON PARENTS

The Winstons were a hardworking blue-collar couple: Marie worked as a waitress at the local Holiday Inn, and Johnny was a plumber. They had three children and always felt that they were a typical, tight-knit family. The eldest son, Kevin, was a funny, energetic child, but he started to withdraw from the family at around age twelve. He pierced his ear, listened to heavy rock music, stayed out too late, and was uninterested in school. His parents thought it was a phase, but by the time he was fourteen it was clear that he was heavily into drugs and alcohol.

Marie's father had been an alcoholic, and she was determined that Kevin would get treatment and get it early. Although Johnny knew lots of families who had drug problems, he had grown up a practicing Buddhist and had never been personally confronted with drug abuse. He was stunned by the realization that his son had taken all kinds of dangerous pills and drugs, including cocaine and heroin. He and Marie put Kevin in a thirty-day treatment program, and they were heavily involved in the parents' group and family counseling. They felt more and more alienated from Kevin during treatment, because he thought it was all a bunch of hype and he wasn't in any real danger. Neither Marie nor Johnny could sleep at night, and they found it difficult to attend to the other children. Marie missed so much work during that month that she was fired. Money quickly became a big problem, but Marie felt she couldn't work and watch Kevin at the same time. When Kevin came out of the treatment center, he went right back to his old ways, so his parents put him in a long-term treatment facility. He ran away from that program within two weeks and started living on the street. Marie and Johnny spent all their free time frantically looking for him and pleading with him to come home. Marie was emotionally unable to find another job, and they had to keep dipping into savings to cover their monthly expenses.

(continued)

(continued)

Over the next year, Marie and Johnny grew more and more distant. The worse Kevin's problems became, the more alienated they felt from each other. They couldn't go out because of the money crunch, and they didn't enjoy spending time with each other. From the time they found out Kevin was a user until they dealt with the issue in therapy, they had not had sex—a period of fifteen months. Many of the family programs they entered tried to get them to see how the family had dysfunctional, unclear communications which had enabled Kevin. Neither of them felt comfortable with these interpretations. They believed that they had a warm and loving home. Kevin was the way he was for unknown reasons, but they wanted to help him. They felt that their marriage was being destroyed in the process and that they needed help with the problem.

Treatment focused on getting Marie and Johnny to reinforce the traditional strengths in the family. They were encouraged to share with each other their grief and anger at Kevin. The need to forfeit pleasure while Kevin was still in trouble was explored repeatedly. Both felt sex was just inappropriate, because it meant they were going to go on enjoying life while their firstborn son was busy destroying his own. They felt the abstinence was also a way of repenting for any mistakes they had made in their parenting. They missed the intimacy and knew they were drifting apart emotionally because of it. After they decided to become sexually intimate, they celebrated by taking all the children out for dinner to "declare" that the trauma was over for the family. They were going on with their lives, supporting Kevin in his treatment but not absorbing all of his pain as their own and all of his disappointments as their disappointments. Kevin was at the dinner and, in an emotional speech, applauded his parents for showing him that they can move on and not stay buried in the problem.

Shortly after the couple resumed sex, they started planning trips to visit relatives and friends. They began to talk to neighbors and co-workers about Kevin's recovery process. They began to laugh. Slowly but surely, they entered the world of recovering parents, battered with blame and shame but resilient in spirit and resourceful.

If children's behaviors are, in large part, genetically funneled into particular behavioral grooves, it should come as no surprise that some parental behaviors are also independent of the shaping efforts of children. Perusse and colleagues (1994) assessed the child-rearing practices of 1,117 pairs of adult twins, concordant for having had children, and found that the caring behaviors of mothers were strongly linked to genetics as were the overprotective behaviors of fathers and mothers.

INFLUENCE OF FAMILY DYNAMICS
ON MARITAL RELATIONSHIPS

Before I got married, I had six theories about bringing up children; now I have six children and no theories.

Lord Rochester

With the addition of children, couples shift from living in an intimate, dyadic world to a complicated, multiperson living situation. The laws of group dynamics come to override individual sentiments and couple concerns. Couples drift apart because the waves of family concerns are more forceful and compelling than individual needs and desires. Although it is true that isolated parents can have a predictable influence on isolated children and isolated children a predictable influence on isolated parents, they are both profoundly affected by the greater wholeness of the family.

The baffling power of family systems has been the major focus of family psychologists for the last fifty years. There are dozens of empirically validated models of family systems. I have chosen to describe a modified version of the Beavers model (Beavers and Hampson, 1990) because it has direct clinical applications for understanding and treating couple dysfunctions and covers most of the basic concepts used in family systems analyses (Berg-Cross, 1988).

The two most important characteristics of family systems are how competent the family is, as a whole, in responding to problems and crises (family competency), and how closely knit, emotionally, the family members are to one another (family closeness). There are four major components of family competency (family structure, myths, autonomy, and family affect), each affecting the couple's relationship as well as other family subsystems. Each component will be discussed first, followed by a description of the two types of family closeness (centripetal families and centrifugal families)

Family Competence

Family Structure

The family structure can be exposed as clearly as the beams of a home by examining five structural skeletons of family life:

1. How power is distributed or concentrated within the family
2. Parent-child coalitions and triangles

3. Family myths
4. How emotionally autonomous or fused family members are
5. The range of affect that family members feel free to express

Together, these engineering blueprints combine to create a picture of family structure, as unique to each family as a fingerprint.

Power in the Family

Family power is exercised, in large part, by controlling the flow and direction of family conversations. Satisfied couples feel comfortable with the power distribution; distressed couples do not. So if the wife is the only family member who talks to the daughter and she cuts off other family members from directly speaking to the teenager, she would be very powerful in the family system. Her powerful position would make the father less powerful. All of their dyadic interactions would be colored by the fact that the mother dominated their child. If the father were thankful that the mother was taking on the responsibility of communicating with their daughter, the relationship would be strengthened. More often, a father is resentful about being marginalized and excluded. Thus, the mother's and the father's style of relating to daughter would influence the couple dyad. Their interactions would be colored and shadowed by their conversations with other family members.

Like controlling communication, controlling decision making is a very basic mode of distributing power in the family. One of the most effective ways for families to make decisions is to make sure that everyone's diverse viewpoints are understood and to be willing to subordinate these, if necessary, to a common purpose (Swanson, 1993). Like a sports team, the differentiated roles and individual styles in a family need to be coordinated by a "master plan" that is more important than the contributions of any one player.

Swanson (1993) assessed the extent to which couples honor and embody diverse points of view or subordinate differences in members' outlooks to a common purpose. He found that personality helps determine a family's decision-making style. Families are more likely to have the father be the family chief if the father is "an able and energetic person who is open to many points of view. The more helpful he [is] in personal relations and group activities, and capable of being decisive, the more likely power to make decisions was vested in him" (Swanson, p. 245). The decision-making power of other family members is mediated by the mother's personality. If she is assertive, she and her children are heard and valued in decision making. Swanson's study was limited in the number of couples studied and the diversity of their backgrounds. Although the specific personality factors that predict inclusion in decision making may vary across cultural groups, the basic finding that personality mediates decision-making styles among couples is apt to be a robust finding.

Thus, the therapist needs to be sensitive to the fact that the decision-making style of families is probably rooted in deep personality dispositions. This explains why many quick-fix, formulaic solutions do not work in marital therapy. The therapist needs to work within the personality styles of each spouse to shape agreeable new modes of decision making that feel natural and that "fit." Difficult personalities are not going to be transformed overnight, and there is no "one size fits all" for adaptive decision making.

When husband and wife have conflicting personality styles (e.g., the wife wants to give her opinion and the husband wants to be the authority), the family decision-making model seems to be determined by the power structure that was inherited on the day of the marriage. Spouses who come from a higher social status (more educated, richer, more refined, etc.) are able to have their preferred style dominate because they came into the marriage with more power and prestige. This finding explains why men who marry beautiful women often follow the woman's preferred decision-making style and women who marry successful men follow the man's preferred decision-making style.

In chaotic families, where no one can maintain any power, the parents are trying to hold their marriage together while living in a family blender that cannot be turned off. No one knows how to make a family decision, and there are no comfortable rules that explain who talks to whom in the family about which issues. The ideal, for most families in mainstream, homogenized America, is to have an egalitarian power structure where various members play a powerful role at different times under different circumstances.

In summary, as soon as children enter the scene, life becomes a series of communication problems and day-to-day decisions. The constant demands of children soon make the negotiation style of the parents exaggerated and ritualized. Successful partners have learned to be very efficient in their power allocation and flexible in shifting power according to the developmental needs and crises that arise in the family. Successful couples agree about who will initiate which type of solution for which type of problem. Troubled partners are very inefficient in this domain. For a distraught couple, if the mother talked to the schoolteacher last week, there is still no understanding of who will respond to the teacher's call this week. Such couples have no set routines to engage in job sharing (in which case the father should call) or delegation of tasks (in which case the mother should follow up). Among troubled partners, every problem is solved in a very inefficient, tension-generating manner. Therapists need to link these inefficient, destructive methods of handling daily living to the underlying tension in power allocation between the couple.

THERAPEUTIC INTERVENTION 3:
ASSESSING FAMILY DECISION-MAKING STYLES

Therapists need to understand what type of decision making a couple engages in and facilitate their exploration of the following issues:

1. On what basis has the authority been vested in one person, or what was the process by which the couple came to decide things in a democratic manner?
2. Does the style of decision making work for the family unit as a whole? Is it good for the couple? Is it working for the children?
3. What would be the preferred decision-making style of the husband? Of the wife? Of the children?
4. How has the decision-making style of the families of origin affected the type of decision-making style exhibited in the nuclear family?

Parent-Child Coalitions and Triangles

Childless couples are often stuck with each other and need to resolve their disagreements if they want to have anyone pleasant to interact with when they are in the house. Once children arrive, it is very tempting not to work through couple issues and use other people in the house for support, entertainment, or for venting one's anger. Children can be triangulated into parental conflict in three ways: (1) the detouring triangle, (2) the parent-child coalition, and (3) the split-loyalties triangle.

The detouring triangle is the most discussed triangular relationship. This pattern occurs when the parents inadvertently reinforce or exacerbate problem behavior in one or more of the children because dealing with the child allows the parents to detour from or avoid their own marital problems. It is so much easier to avoid talking about the unequal division of power or the emotional neglect one feels when one can spend the time worrying about the children. For example, one parent may notice a slight lisp or stutter and begin to correct the child frequently. The other spouse can become involved either by joining in on the concern or by battling with the spouse about the significance of the problem. Either way, the conflict, on the surface, is diverted from couple concerns onto child concerns. However, because the couple conflict is never resolved, tensions continue and usually worsen.

In detouring, both parents may be unaware of their own problems or conflicts. They may be unconsciously deflecting their conflicts with each other onto the child and adamantly deny that anything is wrong with their relationship. A classic example is the couple who harass their adolescent daughter about her alleged promiscuity instead of dealing with their own sexual problems and frustrations.

Sometimes, the expressions of detoured conflict become focused on religious and ethnic issues. When a historically triangulated child leaves home to marry, the parental relationship becomes unhinged. The historically triangulated child has been the focus of the excess emotion in the parents' relationship. His or her departure leaves a vacuum in the parental relationship, with threatening, unresolved hurts orbiting and ready for entry. Rather than focus on the long-avoided couple issues, the parents jump on the differentness of the prospective in-law. After working with hundreds of Christian-Jewish intermarriages, Friedman (1985) found that

> it was impossible to predict how parents might react (to an interfaith marriage) based on information such as their section of the United States, their degree of Jewish education or synagogue attendance, the amounts they gave to the United Jewish Appeal or their trips to Israel. A history of cultural commitment simply was not sufficient to create the reaction. Rather, it was the child who had been triangulated, often the first born, who was at risk for parental harassment and rejection. The adult children often would understand that they had been singled out for a differential reaction from their siblings and say things like, "My brother could get away with this and it wouldn't mean anything." Ironically, it is the children who are most triangulated with the parents that are most likely to intermarry as a way of proving their individuality and separateness from a suffocating, critical family. (p. 58)

Not surprisingly, children who are detoured due to parental conflicts internalize much of the tension by experiencing anxiety and socially withdrawing (Kerig, 1995).

Parent-child coalitions occur when one child and one parent form a close, rigid alliance against the remaining parent. The primary family dyad becomes parent-child instead of parent-parent. Research has consistently shown that the most distressed families that come into mental health clinics and the most psychologically distressed adolescents come from families in which strong parent-child coalitions are evident (Madonna, Van Scoyk, and Jones, 1991).

These families report more interpersonal conflict and more negative affect in the family (Kerig, 1995). Some of these projects have actually coded the number of supportive statements made between spouses and compared them with the number of supportive statements made between parent and child. When parents are making more supportive statements to each other than to their children, the whole family seems stronger and healthier (Whittaker and Bry, 1991).

The concept of split loyalties refers to a pattern in which the child is caught between two parents, each of whom wants the child to side with him or her against the other parent. The child is in a chronic no-win situation. An expression of care or concern for one parent cannot be voiced without betraying the other. Most children become frozen when they are put into this situation. Usually, they leave the family as soon as possible.

In very distant and untrusting families, it is often difficult to find any dyad that has a truly strong alliance. Sometimes, the triangles in these families involve pets instead of family members. The function of pets in family triangles is easy to understand once we concede that all human beings need to be in a caring relationship. If two family members are very angry with each other and one or both of them are unable to positively reach out and engage another family member in a triangle, they can alternatively seek out the comfort of a pet. Sometimes the pet is the focus of a split alliance in which both parents and siblings try to turn the animal into their own intense personal ally and create a lot of distance between the pet and the rest of the family.

In short, chronic, static, triangular relationships disturb couple relationships because they defensively prevent the couple from openly dealing with their own hurtful or angry feelings toward each other.

Family Myths

A myth is a family story that has a powerful effect on shaping each family member's understanding of family history and future options. Couples who create family myths are then destined to have themselves and their children molded by the fantasy. Many family myths transmit life goals and core values, and help shape the family's psychological identity. Myths serve a cohesive function, cementing one generation to the other. Each couple has myths from their families of origin that they, consciously or unconsciously, want to perpetuate, as well as myths they have developed over the course of the marriage (e.g., "Our family is the kind that always has room for one more").

Our social life, particularly within the family, still remains a mystery to us, calling for stories of explanation. The most popular myths are "Prometheus" myths, stories that recount the creation of the nuclear and extended family: How Mom and Dad met, the circumstances surrounding the birth of each child, and how Grandma lived her last years. When the Prometheus myths are negative or filled with tragedy, a sense of doom can hang over the whole family. When they are conservative and proper, the message is to keep the family following a straight line.

One of the most vivid cultural portrayals of the positive and negative effects of myths occurs in Edward Albee's *Who's Afraid of Virginia Woolf?* The play revolves around a childless couple who have developed a mythical son who bonds them together. When the husband, in a fit of destructive anger, announces that the mythical son is dead, it pushes the couple into a crisis in which they either have to grow and change their relationship or have it disintegrate (Caprioli, 1987).

Family myths have developed for the internal vitality of the family and often are not shared by outsiders in the network or community. For example, a family myth that "we are all math wizards" might not be shared by the sixth-grade teacher who has Johnny fumbling with his fractions each day. When the family myths are not congruent with outsiders' evaluations of the family, the family is put under enormous strain and shame. Because so many of us have family myths that contains stories of athletic prowess and victory, this explains, in good part, why parents go berserk during the sports events of their children and feel embarrassed or humiliated when the child's team fails or the child fumbles.

Couples argue over which family myths are most important to maintain and which should be changed. Indeed, many of the arguments about how to parent the children are really arguments over which family fantasy will prevail. The husband may want to enact a myth that the children are orderly and obedient; the wife a myth that the children are relaxed and carefree. Specific problems in parenting will never be successfully resolved unless the guiding mythologies are described and revised.

Autonomy

Autonomy in a family refers to the freedom of family members to be who they want to be, say what they want to say, and do what they want to do. Satisfied Western couples tend to report fairly high autonomy in the relationship. Yet in any group setting, autonomy is compromised to achieve higher group goals. The only way autonomy continues to blossom for each family member is if the power is fairly equitably distributed and there is a constant open flow of communication.

Even in a didactic relationship, couples have extreme difficulty learning to communicate clearly, expressing their own thoughts and feelings in a way that mates can understand. The introduction of children only confounds this already difficult task. Time constraints, environmental restraints, and conversational demands of children all impede effective couple communication.

Conversation is restricted because parents do not feel free to communicate openly around the children. This leads to "holding in" many thoughts and feelings. Couples wait until they can discuss the issue in private, and that time never becomes available. So much effort is spent on the "family way of communicating" that the spouses begin to wonder what happened to them and to their own personalies.

When listening to a family interact, autonomy is reflected in the degree to which family members are allowed and encouraged to speak clearly and directly, expressing their own thoughts and feelings. Highly autonomous families have found ways to let each person contribute his or her point of view and still be part of the family.

At the other extreme, there are highly dysfunctional families in which honest expression of feelings is a family act of treason. In these families, there is a bland acquiescence to what is the "appropriate" thing to say. Listening in on their conversation, it is difficult to pinpoint each person's viewpoint. Family members, in the extreme, will never ask for a clarification of one another's position (even though it is clearly muddled). Some strained semblance of family harmony is being bought at the expense of individual expression.

Therapists who see only the couple as a unit, without the children, may find it difficult to assess autonomy in the family. Within the dyad, however, autonomy issues can be explored by itemizing how many topics that lead to arguments or tension are kept to oneself. The more topics that are off-limits, the more compromised the autonomy of each spouse.

Family Affect

Just as children restrict the range of communication, they may greatly hamper the range of positive affect shown in the family and increase the propensity of parents to show negative affect to each other. The evolution of children ensures that they get more than their share of positive attention. Yet there appears to be additional restrictions on adult affect due to the range and intensity of the affect expressed by the children. With so much emotion expressed by children, parental emotion can narrow as a defensive strategy or explode in response to the annoyance of children's high-intensity affects.

Competent families usually show a wide range of emotions, in both the children and the adults. Distressed families allow relatively few types of emotion to be expressed. The least competent families have a singular sense of anger and despair hanging over them; it seems futile to try to emotionally clarify their feelings so they withdraw, shout, or have a bland cheerfulness that fences off the potential expression of any challenging feelings.

Within the world of negative emotions, the strong emotions of anger and contempt are much more deleterious to a strong parent-adolescent relationship than the weaker negative emotions of sadness, anxiety/tension, and petulance (Capaldi, Forgatch, and Crosby, 1994). Parsimony would dictate that this may also be the case with spouses. Within the world of positive emotions, some are more important than others, also. For example, Kelly (1992) found the higher-functioning stepfamilies were the ones that could tolerate the need for special dyadic relationships, particularly the need to continue a special tie between the biological parent and the child. This willingness to embrace a strong biological parent-child tie that excluded oneself was the most important positive emotional predisposition in protecting second marriages.

CASE STUDY 3: A DEMONSTRATION OF FAMILY COMPETENCY AND COHESIVENESS

Paul and Nita, married for twenty-three years, were partners in Nita's family's florist business. Paul was in charge of buying and distributing the flowers for all eight stores in the Washington, DC, area. Nita worked exclusively with the area churches. It was an amazingly busy and prosperous family business; all five of Nita's brothers and sisters were employed in the business, as well as three of their spouses. All of the siblings lived within ten miles of the parents. The family myth was that Nita's parents would always be essential for everyone's financial well-being and that the reason the family business was so successful was that the siblings were extraordinarily close and supportive of one another.

Although the relatives would go weeks without seeing one another socially, they were in constant interaction over the course of the work week.The status of each person's job seemed to be directly related to the status that particular child or in-law held with the parents, who were the sole owners. Paul and Nita, who shared power within their marriage and on the job, felt they held "middling" jobs (in terms of status). They were free to voice their opinions at all times but were never given the opportunity to make decisions. Yet all the new growth and profits could be attributed to Paul's innovative buying strategies and Nita's intensive contacts and com-

(continued)

(continued)

mitment to the area churches. They wanted to be given more power over the long-term decision making in the company. Paul felt very strongly that the owner/parents had to pick a successor for the leadership of the business. Nita knew this would lead to a horrible schism in the family because each of the five children wanted to be given a controlling interest. In an effort to avoid acrimony, everyone avoided the issue but Paul. He tried to convince Nita that this was the proper thing to do, but Nita fought him for making waves.

Paul and Nita had two sons: Ralph, fourteen, and Richard, seventeen. Richard started working with his father when he was twelve. Ralph started with his mother at the same age. During the Christmas holidays, one of the employees found Richard stealing money (over $100) out of the cash register. The first time, she did not say anything. The second time, she felt compelled to point the finger, because she knew that someone else would be wrongly blamed for the theft. Richard's theft was met with swift and brutal punishment. Nita's father made him pay back double what he stole and forbade him to ever come into the store again. Paul was told that he was responsible for making Richard think the business belonged to his own nuclear family (Richard had stated it was simply like taking money out of the money jar at home because it belonged to them anyway) and that the truth was they were simply employees.

Paul and Nita sought a consultation to see how to handle the situation. The grandfather was a stubborn person and would not renege and have a thief in his store. The parents wanted to punish Richard, but they also wanted to defend him. They were furious at him for shaming them in front of the rest of the family but even more furious that the rest of the family was so unwilling to be compassionate to one of their own kin. Paul wanted Nita to make a clean break with him from her family over this issue and start their own competing business. Nita could not bear to betray her family.

First, Paul and Nita explored their position in and problems with the family business. An effort was made to discern what was in the best interests of the company, of their nuclear family, and of the extended family. This analysis concluded that the business and extended family could prosper without them and that they could certainly prosper more on their own than they were being allowed to under the current structure. Nita acknowledged that she was unsure of how to relate to her family outside of the business but that she would prefer that type of conventional relationship.

Both felt that Richard had made a stupid mistake. They did not feel that he was a bad kid, and he had been upset and shaken since the day he had been caught. He had started attending Sunday mass again and begged his parents to forgive him. They did not want this situation to erode their marriage and came to realize that tensions would remain high if Richard could not be accepted and forgiven. Over the course of four sessions, they

(continued)

(continued)

decided to become an independent competitor. They applied for a small business loan and held a meeting with Nita's clan to explain their decision and ask for the family's support.

Several more sessions were spent with the parents and Richard. He resented having to work in the family business. He was much more interested in getting involved with the fire department as a volunteer and thought that after graduation he might want to join up as a professional firefighter. His parents were surprised at this announcement but immediately gave him their full support. Although Richard saw no connection between his acting-out behavior and his hidden resentments about having to work in the business, his parents were relieved that this might explain what had happened.

By the next Christmas, I got a note saying that the new floral shop had been opened for two months and was prospering. One of the nephews had come to work in the shop. Members of the extended family were relieved by Paul and Nita's decision because it allowed some people to move up in status and left fewer people to fight over control.

Family Closeness

Couples without children vary dramatically over how fused or individuated they are as a couple. The most enmeshed couples make all their decisions jointly, spend all of their leisure time together, and have a sense of deep incompleteness when they are not together. Highly individuated couples sometimes spend a good portion of the year working on different continents, have circles of friends unknown to the spouse, and feel a great deal of autonomy in their decision making over a wide range of issues.

With children, fusion and differentiation take on new, complicated patterns that include the entire family. Although families exist along a continuum of closeness, studying the most extreme types heightens sensitivity to such inclinations in more typical families. Thus, in the following discussion of centrifugal and centripetal families, we should understand that most families present a mixture of these styles across situations and across the family life cycle.

The centrifugal (disengaged) family is at the extreme of valuing individual autonomy over closeness. Family is merely an address for these biologically related individuals. These families greatly discourage or ignore the dependency needs of both the children and the adults. Typical of extreme centrifugal families are children who are latchkey by first grade and spouses who go to the hospital for major surgery unaccompanied by a family member. Such families do not hide disagreements and are openly confrontational. Members do not live in proximity to each other even when they are in the house at the same time. One stays in the bedroom, another in the basement, and another at the dining room table. Adrift in a random flotilla, they see no need to be concerned with appearances and social approval. They see no need to even pretend to have interest in one another. They avoid eye contact when they are speaking to one another, engage in name-calling, and act disrespectfully to one another. Angry and hostile behavior is not only allowed but sometimes subtly encouraged. It is easy to express hatred and resentment in these families. It is very difficult to express love and caring.

Beavers and Hampson (1990) describe the extreme centrifugal family as

> lacking an effective parental coalition; in fact, the parents are habitually bucking for control of the children, blaming each other for family problems, and attempting to line up allies (sometimes through illicit alliances) in their offspring. The children receive minimal nurturance; discipline is sporadic criticism, attack and ridicule (interspersed with ignoring for more appropriate behaviors). Hence children develop a sense of cynicism about themselves, their relationships (playing one parent off against the other), and about consistency and depth of trust in other people. (p. 45)

An extreme centrifugal family, by definition, has severe marital problems. Spouses in this type of family easily become overly involved in their jobs, have affairs, and spend inordinate amounts of time with friends or in community activities. Scattered across different social classes and ethnic groups, the marital distress is uniform. Something very wrong has traumatized the entire family, and the marital dyad is nothing more than another ruptured family system.

The extreme centripetal (or enmeshed) family is diametrically the opposite in emotional style. For the extremely enmeshed family, dependency needs are encouraged. Family members constantly try to do things for one another and to anticipate one another's needs. When adult conflicts occur, they are hidden and denied. Family life is critically important, and both parents are invested in denying any conflicts that would put the spotlight on problem areas instead of on family harmony and mutuality. Enmeshed families stay physically close to one another, and usually engage in a great deal of touching and hugging. They eat together and watch TV together. There are still "family outings" among the centripetal types. They are very concerned with making a good impression on others and want their children, as well as the adults, to be well behaved in public. Politeness, good grooming, and highly developed social skills are stressed.

Beavers and Hampson (1990) state

> that the "golden years" of highly centripetal families are the young child bearing and child rearing years. Husbands are "husbands" and

wives are "wives." The family stopwatch is set at about the time of birth of the second child. The centripetal family is set more in the context of the middle and upper classes. In the extreme, control is maintained by dependency, guilt manipulation and looking to authority; the father's authority is unchallenged overtly, and overt defiance is minimal. Instead, members internalize their feelings such that disappointment is seldom expressed; depression and anxiety are the predominant negative feelings. (p. 43)

Couple satisfaction shows far more variation among extremely enmeshed families. Some enmeshed husbands and wives are truly satisfied with the marital dyad; others are bitter and angry but cannot express it. With such a strong need to preserve social presentability, most of the enmeshed couples (happy and unhappy) appear as the picture of marital bliss: kissing each other good-bye, holding hands, and calling each other at work just to check in. Because they are unable to openly discuss conflict (and conflicts abound in every family), the anxiety in the system can easily become unbearable. Then one of the children may begin presenting symptoms (e.g., not obeying parents, taking drugs), or one of the parents may become consumed with anxiety, depression, or hypochondriacal complaints. Families who appear to have it all, but who have symptomatic children or adults, are usually classic centripetal families.

Interestingly, comparisons of European-American, African-American, and Mexican-American families in which one child was developmentally disabled revealed that the ethnic groups did not differ in competence or health; rather, ethnic differences were most likely to be found in the style of closeness characterizing the family interaction. Perhaps this means that a universal need exists for families to show a significant amount of efficient problem solving and positive family identity for them to prosper as a family (Hampson, Beavers, and Hulgus, 1990). Closeness may be more easily shaped by cultural and class factors.

The complicated culture of stepfamilies predisposes them to a centrifugal style and creates roadblocks toward closeness. This relative lack of closeness may explain the consistent empirical evidence that children in stepfamilies exhibit more adjustment problems than do children in original, two-parent families and the same number of adjustment problems as children in single-parent families (Hanson, McLanahan, and Thomson, 1996). Hanson and colleagues concluded that stepchildren are exposed to an equivalent amount of intrahousehold conflict as children from original, two-parent families and an equivalent amount of interhousehold conflict as children in single-parent households. However, the combined burden of dealing with greater overall conflict from two different sources creates decreased feelings of cohesiveness and closeness which are disruptive to healthy developmental processes.

When a family is blended, the stepparents need to find ways to reduce conflict and create closeness with the new stepchildren while allowing the children to maintain their allegiance, conflict free, to previously existing parent-child bonds. Creating a sense of belonging to the new family unit is usually the core therapeutic task when working with stepfamilies. To facilitate the development of family closeness, the therapist can take these steps (Cissna, Cox, and Bochner, 1990; Visher and Visher, 1990, 1991):

1. Validate and normalize the stepfamily, giving it recognition and respectability.
2. Identify the differences in family structure between first-marriage families and stepfamilies so that the difficulties become understandable and surmountable.
3. Find ways for the new couple to continually nourish their bonds.
4. Forge a workable parenting coalition between the various households.
5. Help establish the credibility of the stepparent as an authority in relationship to the stepchildren.

Reducing conflict and increasing closeness clearly help minimize the trauma of creating stepfamilies. Hanson, McLanahan, and Thomson (1996) demonstrated that when children in stepfamilies experience little or no conflict, they do as well as the average child in an original, two-parent household with respect to aggressiveness, acting out, shyness, and overall quality of life. Even without the conflict, though, theysuffered in school performance and initiative.

DEVELOPMENTAL TASKS FOR COUPLES DURING THE FAMILY LIFE SPAN

Although family competency and closeness always influence the marital relationship, the challenges to and nature of these global family dynamics are determined by the different psychological tasks that face each marriage in the course of its development. Wallerstein and Blakeslee (1995) have discerned nine distinct tasks that couples face at different points in their history:

1. They must separate emotionally from the family of one's childhood so as to invest fully in the marriage and, at the same time, redefine the lines of connection with both families of origin.

2. They must build togetherness by creating the intimacy that supports it while carving out each partner's autonomy. These issues are central throughout the marriage but loom especially large at the outset, at midlife, and at retirement.
3. They must embrace the daunting roles of parents and absorb the impact of Her Majesty the Baby's dramatic entrance. At the same time, the couple must work to protect their own privacy.
4. They must confront and master the inevitable crises of life, maintaining the strength of the bond in the face of adversity.
5. They need to create a safe haven for the expression of differences, anger, and conflict.
6. They need to establish a rich and pleasurable sexual relationship and protect it from the incursions of the workplace and family obligations.
7. They should use laughter and humor to keep things in perspective and to avoid boredom by sharing fun, interests, and friends.
8. They must learn to provide nurturance and comfort to each other, satisfying each partner's needs for dependency and offering continuing encouragement and support.
9. They need to keep alive the early romantic, idealized images of falling in love while facing the sober realities of the changes wrought by time. (pp. 27-28)

Although these tasks are stated in a rather idealized way, one can see how each task requires family competency and closeness for success.

A moment's reflection on this chapter should persuade therapists that when couples are in therapy, it is vital to understand the dynamics of their family system. The marital dyad is not totally orthogonal to the parenting dyad or the total family group.

THERAPEUTIC INTERVENTION 4: EXPLORING CENTRIPETAL AND CENTRIFUGAL FAMILY STYLES

Beavers and Hampson (1990) assess family type by having the entire family come and engage in a ten-minute family discussion that is observed and videotaped. The task is "Discuss together what you would like to see changed in your family." Analyzing the videotape and rating the family on the various family competency and style dimensions, the therapist categorizes the family according to competence (severely dysfunctional, borderline, midrange, adequate, optimal) and style (centripetal, centrifugal, or mixed).

(continued)

(continued)

Therapists who are unable to obtain a ten-minute conversation sample can get a good idea of the family style by asking the following three questions and having each family member rate the family on a scale of 1 to 100, in which 1 means that the described interactions and sentiments never happen or do not apply, and 100 means the described interactions unfailingly happen or always apply.

1. How typical is it for the family to get into an out-and-out argument and for you to really let everyone know what you are feeling?
2. How typical is it to have privacy in this family—have your own friends; your own schedule for eating, sleeping, and recreation; and your own physical space?
3. How typical is it for the family to embarrass one another in the neighborhood, the school, or the community?

The lower the score, the more centripetal the family; the higher the score, the more centrifugal.

Therapists rarely see mixed family types (they tend to be very healthy), and they see centripetal and centrifugal families only when their competency levels have become severely stressed.

Centripetal families always want to stay in control, so therapists must help the family save face by taking the role of an exploratory consultant and reframing the problem so that the family can mobilize its own resources for change. The problems can often be reframed to express how the family's well-meaning attempts to solve the problem are really just the thing that is exacerbating it. These families also have trouble expressing emotion, so they need guidance in expressing a variety of opposite and intense feelings. This can be done by rephrasing a very polite explanation of the problem by a family member. For example, if an adolescent daughter says, "My dad just worries so much about me; he can't be relaxed if I go out on a date," the therapist can say, "You clearly are sensitive to how much your father cares about you, but I imagine you feel pretty resentful and angry that you can't date like the other girls your age."

It is best to relabel severely dysfunctional centrifugal families as desperately attempting to deal with their own grief, fears, and neediness. A father who does not call when he is out of town traveling exhibits a defensive sign of his own anxieties about acknowledging how much he needs and loves his family. The daughter's refusal to help paint the living room is due to feelings of inadequacy and that she may not be able to do the job well enough or fast enough to please the others. These interpretations, if accepted by the family, open new models of understanding family interaction. If an interpretation is rejected, it is often rejected with such a vehemence that family members change just to avoid having that type of interpretation tied to their behavior. The therapist needs to look for ways for the centrifugal family to find psychological satisfactions in the family unity. Finding ways of enjoying home time and making family members interdependent are helpful therapy goals.

LEARNING AIDS

Therapeutic Dialogue (Parenting)

1. How would you describe your parenting style and the parenting style of your spouse: authoritative, authoritarian, permissive, or uninvolved? Explain your answer.
2. What are the parenting styles among your friends and family that you admire most? That bug you most? Explain your answer.
3. How can you change your ideal model of appropriate parenting styles to make it more attainable?
4. What gender differences, if any, exist in how you and your spouse deal with the children? Are there any stereotypic male behaviors or female behaviors involved in your parenting styles?
5. What are the gender differences you see among your friends and family in terms of parenting behaviors?
6. How can you change your model of ideal parenting styles to make it more attainable?
7. Ideally, how much arguing and conflict should spouses do in front of children of different ages?
8. How much arguing and conflict do you do with your spouse in front of the children?
9. How much arguing and conflict did your parents do in front of you as a child?
10. Among your friends and family, how much do various couples argue or air their conflicts in front of you?
11. How can you change your model of the ideal amount of honest disagreement to show in front of the children to make it more attainable?
12. What is the ideal power distribution in your family? What are the ideal myths that would guide your family's behavior?
13. What is most distressing about your current family structure in terms of power distribution? What are the most destructive myths guiding the family?
14. What are the most inspiring and depressing family structures you see among your friends and family in terms of power distribution and myths?
15. How can you change your ideal model for your family structure to make it more attainable?
16. What is the ideal amount of closeness and separateness that should exist within your family?

17. What parts of your family life are too close and suffocating for you? What parts of your family life are too separate and alienated for you?
18. Among friends and family, describe how close or separate their family units function.
19. How can you change your ideal model of closeness and separateness to make it more attainable?

Self-Exploration 1: Comparing Parenting Values

Rate how important each of the following child behaviors and activities are to you:

1	2	3	4	5	6	7
Not at all important			Moderate			Very important

Following family rules
Doing well at school
Being independent
Being kind and considerate
Controlling temper
Doing what parents ask
Carrying out responsibilities
Doing well in creative activities
Keeping busy by themselves
Getting along with other children
Doing well in athletics
Trying new things

Rank your answers and then compare them with your partner's ranked answers. The goal is to understand each parent's values. Do the differences in values explain any of the different parenting strategies employed in each area? When one activity is ranked high by one parent and very low by another, it is a likely source of conflict. Try to figure out how to support your spouse in furthering the values important to him or her.

Self-Exploration 2: Who Takes Responsibility for the Children?

The following "Who Feels Responsible for the Kids" Quiz is from Dr. Ron Taffel, *Why Parents Disagree,* Copyright 1994 by Dr. Ronald Taffel. Used by permission of William Morrow and Company, Inc.

1. Who first notices the signs that one of your kids is getting sick?
2. Who informs the school that your child won't be coming to school due to illness?
3. Who attended the last parenting workshop in your school, church, or community center? If both of you attended, whose idea was it to go?
4. Who first heard about and actually bought the last book on any aspect of child rearing?
5. If you've ever consulted a mental health professional about your kids, who initiated the contact?
6. Who searched for and interviewed prospective pediatricians? Baby-sitters? Who found out which doctors and baby-sitters other parents in your neighborhood use?
7. Who bought the last small "thinking of you" present when your child seemed to be blue?
8. Who thought to call the parents of the friend with whom your child had a bad rift? Who actually made the call?
9. Who thought to call the parents of your daughter's playmates after she came down with the chicken pox or some other communicable disease?
10. Whose mood is most affected when your child has trouble with friends or at school?
11. Who calls your son's classmate when he's ill to make sure he gets the homework assignment?
12. Who usually tries to talk to your child when he or she is feeling sad?
13. Who plans and organizes birthday parties and other special events for the kids?
14. Who first researches nursery schools, camps, and afterschool activities?
15. Who usually makes weekend plans for the family?
16. Who coordinates car pooling for ferrying kids between activities?
17. Who remembers to bring juice, wipes, and other essentials to the playground, on a day trip, or a vacation?
18. Who first notices that your supply of "kid foods"—Cheerios, mini waffles, macaroni and cheese—is running low?

19. Who first notices that shoes are too tight, pants are too short, and sweaters too frayed?
20. Whose date book contains the dates of the school concert, Little League sign-up, and other kids' birthday parties?

If a discrepancy is evident between the spouse's responsibility scores, chances are the couple is caught up in constant animosity over the distribution of chores and fairness in the marriage.

Sample Workshop Flowchart Intended for Groups of Four or Five Couples Working on the Parent Role

I. Psychoeducational Strategies
   A. The task of parenting
      1. Four classic parenting styles
      2. Gender differences in parenting
      3. Effects of parental conflict on children
      4. Cultural influence of parenting on children's development
   B. The bidirectional approach: How children influence parents
   C. Influence of family dynamics on marital relationships
      1. Competence
         a. Family structure: power, coalitions, closeness
         b. Myths
         c. Autonomy
         d. Family affect
      2. Family closeness
         a. Centripetal
         b. Centrifugal

II. Self-Explorations (Done by couples in private and shared before rejoining the group)
   A. Comparing parenting values
   B. Who takes responsibility for the children?

III. Therapeutic Dialogue (Done by couples in private and shared before rejoining the group)
   (Proceeding in the order presented, both partners respond to each question before going on to discuss the next question)
   In the group, the therapist explores with couples how relationship goals can be achieved by modifying overly ambitious, pie-in-the-sky expectations. Using information about their current situation and the realities seen among friends and family, couples fine-tune expectations so that they are achievable and motivate rather than discourage attempts at change.

IV. Therapeutic Interventions
   Work with a couple in front of the group and apply one or more of the
   therapeutic interventions. Share the rationale during demonstrations.
   Let the group discuss additional interventions.
   A. Assessing parenting style
   B. The six-step program to equalize child care responsibilities
   C. Assessing family decision-making styles
   D. Exploring centripetal and centrifugal family styles

V. Finding the Motivation and Time to Make the Changes
   Group discussion

Bibliotherapy

Belsky, J. and Kelly, J. (1994). *Transition to parenthood: How a first child
   changes a marriage: Which couples grow apart and why.* New York:
   Delacorte.
Bornstein, M. (Ed.). (1995). *Handbook of parenting* (4 vols.). Hillsdale, NJ:
   Lawrence Erlbaum.
Elkind, D. (1994). *Understanding your child from birth to sixteen.* Need-
   ham, MA: Allyn & Bacon.
Fishel, E. (1994). *I swore I'd never do that: Recognizing family patterns
   and making wise parenting choices.* Berkeley, CA: Conari.
Price, S. and Price, T. (1994). *The working parent's help book: Practical
   advice for dealing with the day to day challenge of kids.* Princeton, NJ:
   Peterson's Guide.
Taffel, R. and Isrealoff, R. (1994). *Why parents disagree: How men and
   women parent differently and how we can work together.* New York:
   Morrow.
Visher, E. and Visher, J. (1996). *Therapy with stepfamilies.* New York: Brun-
   ner/Mazel.

Videotherapy

National Lampoon's European Vacation. (1985). Directed by Amy Heck-
   erling. Parents trying desperately to have a once-in-a-lifetime European
   vacation with their children.
National Lampoon's Vacation. (1983). Directed by Harold Ramis. The
   trials and tribulations of having fun on a family vacation.
Parenthood. (1989). Directed by Ron Howard. Multigenerational perspective on the trials and tribulations of parenthood.

Professional Development Questions
(Children, Parenting, and the Spousal Relationship)

1. Do you believe that children can have a profound influence on the couple relationship? Using evidence from the chapter and your own experience, support your belief.

2. Do you think it is possible for a family unit to be very close to one another and the couple to feel distant from each other? How can you explain this phenomenon?

3. Do you believe that there are cultural differences in how power (e.g., decision making) is distributed in different social classes and ethnic, racial, or religious groups? What is the basis for your beliefs? How could you scientifically test your hypothesis?

4. When a couple comes to therapy, what aspects of their parenting and family life would be important to explore and why?

REFERENCES

Bartle, S. E., Anderson, S. A., and Sabatelli, R. M. (1989). A model of parenting style, adolescent individuation, and adolescent self-esteem: Preliminary findings. *Journal of Adolescent Research, 4*(3), 283-298.

Baumrind, D. (1967). Child care practice anteceding three patterns of preschool behavior. *Genetic Psychological Monographs, 75*(1), 43-83.

Baumrind, D. (1968). Authoritarian vs. authoritative control. *Adolescence, 3*(11), 255-272.

Baumrind, D. (1971). Current patterns of parental authority. *Developmental Psychological Monographs, 4*(1, Pt. 2): 1-103.

Baumrind, D. (1991). The influence of parenting style on adolescent competence and substance use. *Journal of Early Adolescence, 11*(1), 56-95.

Beavers, W. R. and Hampson, R. B. (1990). *Successful families: Assessment and intervention.* New York: Norton.

Belsky, J. (1993). Promoting father involvement: An analysis and critique: Comment on Silverstein (1993). *Journal of Family Psychology, 7*(3), 287-292.

Belsky, J. and Rovine, M. (1990). Patterns of marital change across the transition to parenthood: Pregnancy to three years post partum. *Journal of Marriage and the Family, 52*(1), 5-19.

Belsky, J., Youngblade, L., Rovine, M., and Volling, B. (1991). Patterns of marital change and parent-child interaction. *Journal of Marriage and Family, 53*(2), 487-498.

Berg-Cross, L. (1988). *Basic concepts in family therapy.* Binghamton, New York: The Haworth Press.

Blackson, T., Tarter, R., Martin, C., and Moss, H. (1994). Temperament-induced father-son family dysfunction: Etiological implications for child behavior problems and substance abuse. *American Orthopsychiatric Association, 64*(2), 280-292.

Bradley, C. (1998). Child rearing in African-American families: A study of the disciplinary practices of African-American parents. *Journal of Multicultural Counseling and Development, 26*(4), 273-281.

Buri, J. (1988). The nature of humankind, authoritarianism, and self-esteem. *Journal of Psychology and Christianity, 7*(1), 32-38.

Capaldi, D. M., Forgatch, M. S., and Crosby, L. (1994). Affective expression in family problem-solving discussions with adolescent boys. *Journal of Adolescent Research, 9*(1), 28-49.

Caprioli, V. (1987). Teatro e psicologia (Theater and psychology). *Giornale Storico di Psicologia Dinamica, 11*(22), 31-39.

Cissna, K., Cox, D., and Bochner, A. (1990). The dialectic of marital and parental relationships within the stepfamily. *Communication Monographs, 57*(1), 44-61.

Clarke, S. and Alison, K. (1989). Infant day care: Maligned or malignant? *American Psychologist, 44*(2), 266-273.

Cowan, C. and Cowan, P. (1992). *When partners become parents: The big life change for couples.* New York: Basic Books.

Cowan, P., Cohn, D., Cowan, C., and Pearson, J. L. (1996). Parents' attachment histories and children's externalizing and internalizing behaviors: Exploring family systems models of linkages. *Journal of Consulting and Clinical Psychology, 64*(1), 53-63.

Crouter, A. C., and Crowley, M. S. (1990). School-age children's time alone with fathers in single- and dual-earner families: Implications for the father-child relationship. *Journal of Early Adolescence, 10*(3), 296-312.

Cummings, E., Davies, P., and Simpson, K. (1994). Marital conflict, gender, and children's appraisals and coping efficacy as mediators of child adjustment. *Journal of Family Psychology, 8*(2), 141-150.

David, C., Steele, R., Forehand, R., and Armistead, L. (1996). The role of family conflict and marital conflict in adolescent functioning. *Journal of Family Violence, 11*(1), 81-91.

Davies, P. T., Myers, R. L., and Cummings, E. M. (1996). Responses of children and adolescents to marital conflict scenarios as a function of the emotionality of conflict endings. *Merrill-Palmer Quarterly, 42*(1), 1-21.

Demo, D. H., Small, S. A., and Savin-Williams, R. C. (1987). Family relations and the self-esteem of adolescents and their parents. *Journal of Marriage and the Family, 49*(4), 705-715.

Easterbrooks, M., Cummings, E., and Emde, R. (1994). Young children's responses to constructive marital disputes. *Journal of Family Psychology, 8*(2), 160-170.

Easterbrooks, M. A., and Emde, R. N. (1988). Marital and parent-child relationships: The role of affect in the family system. In R. A. Hinde and J. Stevenson-

Hinde (Eds.), *Relationships within families: Mutual influences* (pp. 83-103). New York: Oxford University Press.

Egeland, B. and Sroufe, L. A. (1981). Attachment and early maltreatment. *Child Development, 52*(1), 44-52.

Evans, S., Vallano, G., and Pelham, W. (1994). Treatment of parenting behavior with a psychostimulant: A case study of an adult with attention deficit hyperactivity disorder. *Journal of Child and Adolescent Psychopharmacology, 4*(1), 63-69.

Felson, R. B., and Zielinski, M. A. (1989). Children's self-esteem and parental support. *Journal of Marriage and the Family, 51*(3), 727-735.

Fincham, F. (1994). Understanding the association between marital conflict and child adjustment: Overview. *Journal of Family Psychology, 8*(2), 123-127.

Fincham, F., Grych, J., and Osborne, L. (1994). Does marital conflict cause child maladjustment? Directions and challenges for longitudinal research. *Journal of Family Psychology, 8*(2), 128-141.

Friedman, E. (1985). *Generation to generation: Family process in church and synagogue.* New York: Guilford.

Glantz, M. (1992). A developmental psychopathology model of drug abuse vulnerability. In M. Glantz and R. Pickins (Eds.), *Vulnerability to drug abuse* (pp. 389-418). Washington, DC: American Psychological Association.

Grotberg, E. (1992). *A guide to promoting resiliency in children: Strengthening the human spirit.* Birmingham, AL: Civitan International Research Center.

Grych, J. H. and Fincham, R. D. (1990). Marital conflict and children's adjustment. A cognitive/contextual framework. *Psychological Bulletin, 108*(2), 267-290.

Hampson, R. B., Beavers, W. R., and Hulgus, Y. (1990). Cross-ethnic family differences: Interactional assessment of white, black, and Mexican-American families. *Journal of Marital and Family Therapy, 16*(3), 307-319.

Hanson, T. L., McLanahan, S. S., and Thomson, E. (1996). Double jeopardy: Parental conflict and stepfamily outcomes for children. *Journal of Marriage and the Family, 58*(1), 141-154.

Holden, G. W. and West, M. J. (1989). Proximate regulation by mothers: A demonstration of how differing styles affect young children's behavior. *Child Development, 60*(1), 64-69.

Hossain, Z. and Roopnarine, J. (1993). Division of household labor and child care in dual-earner African-American families with infants. *Sex Roles, 29*(9-10), 571-583.

Jouriles, E. N., Bourg, W. J., and Farris, A. M. (1991). Marital adjustment and child conduct problems: A comparison of the correlation across subsamples. *Journal of Consulting and Clinical Psychology, 59*(2), 354-357.

Julian, T., McKenry, P., and McKelvey, M. (1994). Cultural variations in parenting: Perceptions of Caucasian, African-American, Hispanic, and Asian-American parents. *Family Relations, 43*(1), 30-37.

Kelly, P. (1992). Healthy stepfamily functioning. *Families in Society, 73*(10), 579-587.

Kerig, P. (1995). Triangles in the family circle: Effects of family structure on marriage, parenting, and child adjustment. *Journal of Family Psychology, 9*(1), 28-43.

Lamb, M. E. (1977a). The development of mother-infant and father-infant attachment in the first year of life. *Child Development, 48*(1), 167-181.

Lamb, M. E. (1977b). The development of mother-infant and father-infant attachment in the second year of life. *Developmental Psychology, 13*(6), 637-648.

Levine, J. (1993). Involving fathers in Head Start. A framework for public policy and program development. *Families in Society, 74*(1), 4-21.

Lewis, M. (1988a). The transition to parenthood: I. *Family Process, 27*(2), 149-165.

Lewis, M. (1988b). The transition to parenthood: II. *Family Process, 27*(3), 273-278.

Lytton, H. (1980). *Parent-child interaction: The socialization process observed in twin and singleton families.* New York: Plenum.

Madonna, P., Van Scoyk, S., and Jones, D. (1991). Family interactions with incest and nonincest families. *American Journal of Psychiatry, 148*(1), 46-49.

McBride, B. and Mills, G. (1993). A comparison of mother and father involvement with their preschool-age children. *Early Childhood Research Quarterly, 8*(4), 457-477.

Mortimer, J., Dennehy, K., Lee, C., and Finch, M. (1994). Economic socialization in the American family: The prevalence, distribution and consequences of allowance arrangements. *Family Relations, 43*(1), 28-29.

Nobes, G. and Smith, G. (1997). Physical punishment of children in two-parent families. *Clinical Child Psychology and Psychiatry, 2*(2): 271-281.

Nobes, G., Smith, M., Upton, P., and Heverin, A. (1999). Physical punishment by mothers and fathers in British homes. *Journal of Interpersonal Violence, 14*(8), 887-902.

Perusse, D., Neale, M., Heath, A., and Eaves, L. (1994). Human parental behavior: Evidence for genetic influence and potential implication for gene-culture transmission. *Behavior Genetics, 24*(4), 327-335.

Rocissano, L., Slade, A., and Lynch, C. (1987). Dyadic synchrony and toddler compliance. *Developmental Psychology, 23*(5), 698-704.

Rosenberg, M. (1965). *Society and the adolescent self-image.* Princeton, NJ: Princeton University Press.

Safilios-Rothschild, C. (1974). *Women and social policy.* Englewood Cliffs, NJ: Prentice-Hall.

Stafford, L. and Bayer, B. (1993). *Interaction between parents and children.* Newbury Park, CA: Sage.

Swanson, G. E. (1993). The structure of family decision making: Personal and societal sources and some consequences for children. In P. Cowan, D. Field, D. Hansen, A. Skolnick, and G. Swanson (Eds.), *Family, self, and society* (pp. 235-263). Hillsdale, NJ: Lawrence Erlbaum.

Taffel, R. (1994). *Why parents disagree. How women and men parent differently and how we can work together.* New York: William Morrow.

Trebilcot, J. (1993). Two forms of androgynism. In C. Sommers and F. Sommers (Eds.), *Vice and virtue in everyday life.* Orlando, FL: Harcourt, Brace, Jovanovich.

Visher, E. and Visher, J. (1990). Dynamics of successful stepfamilies. *Journal of Divorce and Remarriage, 14*(1), 3-12.

Visher, J. and Visher, E. (1991). Therapy with stepfamily couples. *Psychiatric Annals, 21*(8), 462-465.

Wallerstein, J. and Blakeslee, S. (1995). *The good marriage.* Boston: Houghton Mifflin.

Webster-Stratton, C. (1989). The relationship of marital support, conflict and divorce to parent perceptions, behaviors and childhood conduct problems. *Journal of Marriage and Family Therapy, 51*(2), 417-430.

Whittaker, S. and Bry, B. (1991). Overt and covert parental conflict and adolescent problems: Observed marital interaction in clinic and nonclinic families. *Adolescence, 26*(104), 865-876.

Winnicott, D. W. (1965). *The maturational processes and the facilitating environment.* New York: International Universities Press.

Chapter 5

Effects of Housework and Employment on Couple Relationships

Life requires that most us engage in a number of self-sustaining activities each day, many of which are not of our own choosing. There are jobs to be done at home and the necessity of employment to make money. Both activities influence the marital relationship, and each will be discussed in this chapter.

HOUSEWORK AND THE COUPLE RELATIONSHIP

There are at least five different types of work that need to be done within the family: housework, child care and spousal care tasks, transactional matters, household management (setting priorities, assigning tasks, quality control, etc.), and emotion work. Marital satisfaction involves successfully delegating and executing the work within each area.

Sharing of Housework

Housework is an unpopular activity among men and women. Compared to most paid jobs, it is more routine and provides less intrinsic motivation and many fewer extrinsic symbolic rewards (Bird and Ross, 1993). Yet housework has traditionally been, and continues to be, predominantly "women's work." With changing gender definitions, men have begun to do more and more housework. Today, most women in their thirties can look back at the time when they were first married or cohabiting with their present husbands and recall a more peaceful, equitable division of labor. Women are befuddled and angry that somehow, without their conscious acquiescence, they became the primary houseworkers and their husbands do not seem to mind. How did this happen?

In comparison, men are more likely to clean, cook, shop, and do the laundry in the early years of a marriage, than in subsequent years as the marriage progresses. As children arrive, and the demands of life increase, the overwhelming majority of married couples fall into a female-dominated housework world. It often takes years or decades of struggle, fighting, and negotiation to bring the husband around to the point of even sensing the unfairness of it all. When husbands share housework more equally, regardless of the stage of the marriage, wives benefit (Hochschild and Machung, 1989).

Shelton and John (1993) compared the time that cohabiting men and women spent doing housework in relation to married men and women. Keep in mind that there is a built-in bias for the cohabiting men to do more housework because they tend to be younger, to be more likely unemployed, and to have more liberal sex-role attitudes than their married counterparts. Still, they found that married men spent nineteeen hours a week doing housework and cohabiting men spent twenty hours a week. This was not a significant difference, although other research has confirmed that cohabiting men work more around the house than their married counterparts. The results on the women are far more revealing. The married women spent forty hours a week doing housework and the cohabiting women only thirty-four hours a week. The married women did significantly more work than their husbands (twice as much), but they also did significantly more than their cohabiting sisters. Thus, what happens during marriage is not so much that the men do so much less (although they do decline in what they do) as that the women increase their workload after marriage.

The presence of children probably adds the greatest number of housework hours for married women, but being married may also have certain psychological effects regarding how a woman is motivated to organize her home. This increased workload on women is critical for therapists to realize because it allows them to decenter from the "equity" discussion and work with women regarding how they feel pressured to do more work now than earlier in their lives. For some women, this obviously will not be true. But for those who can chart the difference in their own behavior, who see that more needs to be done, changes in expectations and negotiation become much less charged. It is not that the man is doing less but that the woman is doing more and perceives that more needs to be done. Men exposed to this argument may be able to rationally discuss the increasing demands in a nonthreatening way.

Overall, the typical American woman does 70 percent of the total housework chores (in terms of time). Nearly 10 percent of women state that they do 100 percent of the housework, whereas virtually no women (less than 1 percent) say they do 25 percent or less of the housework (Mederer, 1993). The only housework men are more likely to do than women is to take care of the car and do the snow removal and lawn care. These activities occur far less frequently than chores such as food preparation and home cleaning.

Obviously, each couple's arrangements are unique, but it is surprising how much of the variation is determined by such factors as education, income, gender attitudes, and age of children. For example, women who are more educated and make more money do significantly less housework than other women, and their husbands do significantly more housework than other men. The younger the children, the more management work the woman does, in absolute terms and relative to the husband. Perhaps, this is why women with young children are so angered by the unfair division of labor (Mederer, 1993).

Continuing along these lines, Pittman and Blanchard (1996) found that the longer women wait to get married, the less housework they reported doing. Partly this was because these women ended up having fewer children (and thus less work), but partly it was because older women had a history of continuous employment and continued their careers after marriage. Continuous employment for women was associated with increasing levels of housework from men. Indeed, continuity of work history may be more important than either spouse's occupational status or income when predicting husband's contributions.

Equity of household chores is a big issue for all couples, but it becomes the dominant clinical issue for many women who are employed full-time outside the home and continue doing the lion's share of household chores. Unless the woman is exceedingly traditional in her views of gender or employed part-time, the husband's lowered contribution to housework becomes equated with exploitation and nonsupport for the wife (Pina and Bengtson, 1993). It is not simply the housework that is remaining undone —a passive act without human consequences. Not doing housework is viewed, by the wife, as an active attempt at exploitation and inconsiderateness. It is not helping the wife. It is using the wife. Women with recalcitrant, antihousework spouses need to work hard to disengage their own feelings of abandonment and neglect from their partners' negative feelings that focus on the housework. Wives view housework symbolically. Cooking the dinner and washing the floor means "I am taking care of someone." Having these chores done by the spouse means "I am being taken care of " (Hochschild and Machung, 1989). Within this context, the physical stress of additional chores is compounded by the emotional stress of feeling neglected and used.

Inequality in the division of labor is often more stressful than the actual amount of work that is done. In examining a wide variety of chores, a large study of over 1,180 adults, ages eighteen to sixty-five, revealed that inequality in the division of labor had a greater impact on a spouse's distress level than the actual workload. If the wife was only doing three hours a week of housework but the husband was doing three minutes, those three hours created a lot of stress, dysphoria, and anger. This same study found that men, on the average, reported performing 42.3 percent of the housework in their homes, while women, on the average, reported doing 68.1 percent. When women were working full-time outside the home, doing more than 46 percent of the household chores resulted in increasing levels of depression (Bird, 1999). Clearly, the average woman is performing household chores to the extent that it causes a negative impact on her psychological health. This is not to say that the actual amount of work done is irrelevant; just that the impact of multiple chores is not as strong as the inequality context in which those chores are completed.

When women become overburdened with housework, the first release valve is eating out. Going out to eat benefits everyone in the family (it is enjoyable, a change of pace, more relaxed, etc.). Although it does not save time, it does save the energy of planning, orchestrating, cooking, and cleaning up. Most dual wage earners eat out once a week or more. On the other hand, getting paid housekeeping help is most often resorted to only after the wife's income can free her from those responsibilities (Bird and Ross, 1993; Oropesa, 1993).

Developmental differences in men's and women's household participation are related to age and time availability. Coltrane and Ishi-Kuntz (1992) demonstrated that men who become fathers after the age of twenty-eight do significantly more housework than men who become fathers before that age. If these older fathers had a liberal gender ideology and time available, they did a great deal of housework. The explanation for this finding is that when couples delay the transition to parenthood, the men are more secure in their jobs and can arrange their work schedules easier. They are also more mature and have spent a longer period of time negotiating household tasks with their wife.

After the age of fifty, as children leave home, men have another surge of household participation. Older women typically continue to have primary responsibility, but the men do more chores when they retire. Unfortunately, the increased involvement is not as great as women expect or hope for. Women, when they retire, also increase their involvement in housework, but much more so than the men. This is true despite the fact that the majority of women continue to perceive housework as repetitive, menial, low status, and isolating. There are also a fair number of cases in which women resent men intruding into their household activities after years of neglect. They seem to be saying, "I did it in all the hard years without you. I certainly don't need your help now" (Ward, 1993). Still, most older women are the happiest when they perceive household work and responsibilities as equitably shared. Indeed, evidence supports that, particularly after retirement, marital happiness is ever more related to joint decision making, sharing, and expressive equity within the relationship than in the early years of marriage.

When working with couples concerning the issue of housework, the social norms of female oppression are hard to avoid. For example, rarely do sessions focus on whether to involve the wife at all in housework. Rather, it is a "given" that wives are to provide domestic services to prove that they care for their families. The negotiating chip is how much men can or should "contribute." Women are made to feel that their acts should be without effort because that is how they show they care. Zvonkovic and colleagues (1996) have even found that when both couples think they are deciding together how to allocate chores, an objective assessment reveals that husbands most often get their way. Therapy needs to help women see that caring is effortful for all people and that it is not a character defect to want help caring for those in the family.

Understanding the particular ideologies each partner has concerning family work roles and sex-role attitudes can help the therapist pinpoint how much conflict exists in their current lifestyle. For most couples, housework creates burdens when they have discrepant expectations about who "should" be doing various chores. A wife or husband who has very nontraditional sex-role attitudes but a traditional work role in which she does the homemaking and he does the money making will feel angry about the housework allocation. Conversely, when spouses have traditional sex-role attitudes and find themselves in a full-fledged, two-earner, split child care arrangement, frustration and resentment are common in both spouses (Crouter and McHale, 1992; Pina and Bengtson, 1993).

Sharing of Child Care

Parent involvement can be looked at through three different lenses according to Lamb and colleagues (1985, 1987): (1) the amount of time that the parent spends in direct interaction with the children; (2) the total amount of time that the parent is accessible to the children (although not engaged in direct interaction, usually this means time spent in the home each day); and (3) parental responsibility for the children (e.g., taking charge and making sure that certain activities are carried out). On all three dimensions, across hundreds of studies, mothers are more involved with their children than are fathers.

In the beginning, mothers seem destined to spend more time with their infants. Those who breast-feed are biologically tied to the child in a way that excludes the father. Even among those who do not breast-feed, mothers appear to be the ones motivated to take primary responsibility for the newborns. Cross-cultural comparisons confirm that this motivation is, in part, the result of traditional socialization patterns and can be significantly altered with appropriate societal incentives (Hyde, Essex, and Horton, 1993). For example, in Sweden, where paternal leave has been a national policy since 1974, fathers have increased their participation every year. In 1974, only 4 percent of the fathers participated in the Swedish plan and in 1994, nearly half of all fathers participated. The Swedish fathers take off, on the average, fifty-three days to care for the child. Mothers take off 225 days (six months). Interestingly, though, the most common pattern is for the wife to take the first six months and then for the father to take a month or two. Once the child is crawling, father participation increases.

In the United States, paternity leave is still being developed, but the popular culture supports most fathers' taking some leave from work when a baby arrives. Numerous surveys suggest that the average American father takes off one week when a baby is born. Most often, he is using vacation time and sick days (Hyde, Essex, and Horton, 1993).

Although fathers do become more active in the toddler phase, both fathers and mothers spend the most nurturing and caretaking time with infants and toddlers. As children get older, parents spend less and less time actually interacting with their children: School-age children have significantly less parental involvement than preschoolers, and adolescents have significantly less parental involvement than children. No empirical evidence suggests that fathers spend more time with their children as they get older. Yet in survey after survey, fathers report desiring more involvement with their children.

As children get older, lots of arguments between couples arise because the wife perceives that the husband is not adequately involved with the care and raising of the children. Normative data are important here to build a community model of what it is like in the real world. Deutsch, Lozy, and Saxon (1993) reported on 268 dual-career couples living in western Massachusetts and northern Connecticut. They asked the percentage that each spouse contributed to specific child care tasks. Mothers and fathers showed surprising agreement on how the tasks were divided, although men consistently and significantly saw themselves as doing more than their wives were giving them credit for. There were no chores that the "average" man did more than 50 percent of the time. The fathers were most likely to equitably share child care tasks such as "helping the children to learn," "playing with them," "disciplining them," "supervising them," "worrying," "giving attention," and "setting limits." They were least frequently involved in child care activities such as "buying clothes," "arranging the social life," and "arranging child care."

Contrary to perceptions about specific tasks, wives thought their husbands contributed a greater percentage of parental time and a greater percentage of the total child care than did the husbands themselves. That is, wives were generous in their total evaluation percent—the total was more than the perceived sum of the parts.

Child care has turned topsy-turvy since women have entered the workforce. What was once the sole, indisputable domain of women has become the focus of shared parental concern along with the domain of paid child assistants, be they nannies or day care workers. Arguments rage and research projects fly off the press trying to prove that absence of maternal care is detrimental or stimulating for children. The most interesting research is the type that asks, "For this particular type of parent, with this particular type of child, doing this particular type of work, in this particular type of family, what are the effects of maternal employment?" For some mothers, working probably benefits their children in a number of positive ways: The child care arrangements may place the child in a safer environment or in a more intellectually stimulating environment or in an emotionally more supportive environment. For other families, the mother is clearly the person who can offer the child the most emotionally supportive, intellectually interesting, and safest environment. Helping parents decide how much child care and what types of child care are good for their situation involves helping them appraise what assets they have to give their child and what assets the paid or alternate child care workers provide.

Greenstein (1993) did a provocative study on this topic, studying the parents of four- and five-year-olds. He found that the higher the income of the family, the less beneficial the effects the child received from child care. Parents in the highest income group had children with many more behavioral problems if they worked full-time since the child was born than if they stayed home full-time. Parents in the lowest income group had just as many problems with their children if they stayed home all the time or worked all the time. According to Greenstein, this finding is because the higher-income families had potentially more emotional support and intellectual stimulation to offer their child. The care that they bought was not as good as the care they could have offered themselves.

Olds and colleagues (1993) have proposed that perhaps the most equitable child care arrangements are likely to occur when the wife is working part-time and the husband full-time. The wife feels justified in asking for help with child care in this situation. After all, she does have obligations in the work world and she is doing the lion's share of child care anyhow. The full-time working mother has delegated so much of her child care to nonparents that she is usually very ambivalent about delegating any of the after-hours care to anyone but herself.

Olds's data are convincing: Men do 5.8 hours of solo child care when they have a part-time working spouse and only 3 hours of solo child care when both spouses are working. (Spouses of full-time homemakers logged in at a low 1.5 hours of solo child care.) Large national surveys conducted by magazines such as *Parents* (Groller, 1990), found that 62 percent of women stated that they would prefer working part-time, 25 percent would prefer to be full-time homemakers, and 8 percent would prefer full-time work. Despite the fact that 39 percent reported working full-time, part-time work obviously is preferred by most women with families.

There are also strong gender differences in how mothers and fathers act and interact when they are alone, in charge of a child. Researchers have affirmed that dads are more playful with kids; mothers are more involved as comfort givers and caretakers. This may explain why mothers are significantly more likely than fathers to experience family time (with spouse present) and time with children (with spouse absent) as work and less likely to report these situations to be leisure (Shaw, 1992).

CASE STUDY 1: HOUSEWORK HASSLES

Marty and Sarah were an African-American couple with five children. There were three-year-old male twins, and three girls, ages seven, ten, and fourteen. Both were very involved, committed parents with a strong history of sharing housework and child care. Marty was a geological engineer who had recently changed jobs so that he would not have to travel so much. Sarah was a high school teacher. They came to therapy seeking help to rearrange their priorities. They wanted to be able to meet their child care and home-keeping responsibilities without constantly bickering.

Their life was typical suburban pandemonium. The morning routine started for Marty at 6 a.m. For two hectic hours, breakfast was made, school lunches were prepared, and children were dressed.

(continued)

(continued)

Sarah left at 6:15 a.m. and was free of those responsibilities. However, after school she was overwhelmed with dance lessons, soccer lessons, visiting school friends, doctor's visits, grocery shopping, cooking dinner, and homework. Marty came home at 6:30 p.m., and they ate dinner at 7:00. As Marty cleaned the kitchen, Sarah would do the wash and continue with the homework and bathing routines. By 8:30, they usually faced a clean kitchen but a messy house. They still had paperwork for their jobs to do, bills to pay, relatives to call on the phone, and bedtime reading with the children waiting for them. When they finally could sit down and talk, they were mostly angry about all the jobs that had remained undone or were done inappropriately during the day.

We contracted for three solution-focused sessions spaced over a three-month period. In the first session, each picked the chores that were most onerous and least rewarding. Marty picked grocery shopping on the weekend and Sarah picked taking the girls to two different after-school activities on any one day. Sarah then made two important concessions. She agreed to get anything Marty wanted for the weekend on Friday when she went to the grocery store. Also, she decided to keep the girls out of soccer in the spring, dramatically reducing the transporting nightmares. During the second session, Sarah felt very overwhelmed. She wanted Marty to help the girls with their homework and to spend time on the weekend taking care of the twins so that she could have two hours to herself. Marty committed himself to helping his eldest daughter with all her homework and his youngest daughter whenever she needed help. However, he felt that the twins were such a burden that he also needed relief time. On Saturday and Sunday the solution was to divide the weekend into four relief periods. The older children split the morning responsibilities for watching the twins (the eldest daughter watched the twins on Saturday morning and the two younger girls watched the twins on Sunday morning) and Marty and Sarah split the afternoon responsibilities. This proved to have a dramatic effect on reducing everyone's stress level.

By the third session, Marty and Sarah wanted to focus on increasing their couple time together and finding a method of organizing their bills. They decided to go out each Wednesday evening for coffee and discuss better finance procedures. When they had conquered that task, they hoped to keep that evening for mini escapes to the village diner for un-rushed, private conversations. Five months after therapy ended, the therapist got a note from Marty saying that life was the smoothest and happiest it had been in years.

**THERAPEUTIC INTERVENTION 1:
ASSESSING STRESS OF CHILD CARE**

To explore if child care is a source of conflict, ask the following types of questions (adapted from Olds et al., 1993):

1. How did you decide on your current child care arrangements? Do you think that it is working well? How do you handle things if there is a crisis like a child getting sick? What would the ideal child care arrangements be like? How do most of your friends deal with child care?

2. What were each of your parents' working/child-care arrangements? Did you think their arrangement worked well for them as adults? For you as a child? Do you think your parents' satisfaction with their marriage changed after the children left home?

3. Are things working out the way you thought they would for this phase of your life? How so? How different is your life at this phase from the life of your friends? How so? Ideally, what would you like this phase of your life to be like?

4. How has your relationship with your spouse changed since you had children? Are these changes similar to or different from the changes you see other couples go through? Ideally, how would you have liked your relationship to have grown over the past few years?

5. How has your relationship with other people changed since you had children? Do your friends have similar experiences? Ideally, how would you like your relationships with friends to be at this time?

Transactional Work

Transactional work involves making medical appointments, bill paying, and arranging for home repairs. Most of this is considered "women's work." Popular magazines have advice and support each month for the legions of women using their lunch hour to negotiate children's doctor's appointments and when the electrician can come to the house. Transitional work is grunt work, but it is intimately tied to household management, a far more prestigious and powerful role.

Household Management

This aspect of family work is primarily mental. It is spread out over time and mixed in with other activities. Household management requires defining what needs to be done, setting the standards, and overseeing the completion. Deciding what each child should be for Halloween requires consulting the children, thinking about the budget, deciding how time and material will be allocated, and overseeing the actual creations.

Women tend to enjoy household management, primarily because it is a source of great power. The household manager shapes the family psyche and generates the plan for family productivity. However, as a rule, as women gain in education, income, and drives toward equity, they become more and more disturbed by the imbalance in household management. Thus, although women believe that the distribution of household management is unfair, it does not lead to the type of marital conflicts that come from the unequal allocation of housework (Mederer, 1993).

Many family theorists have tried to find explanations for women's willingness to take on so many of the family management tasks. Some posit that family management is highly valued because women like having the power of determining what should be done and who should do it. Others suggest that it simply takes much less negotiation and compromise to allocate household tasks than to share and allocate household management. A third reason may be that women value the efficient, harmonious running of the family team more than men. Finally, a women's gender identity may be more strongly linked with household management and kinskeeping than with housework.

Women's willingness to oversee and orchestrate the broad strokes and minutiae of family life may enhance their power base, but it gives them no "down time." Mederer (1993) aptly summarizes the dilemma when she says, "The extra power which helps keep women in charge even when they delegate and oversee, also constrains them. Inasmuch as their responsibility is invisible, it is not defined ideologically as work" (p. 143).

Emotion Work

Emotion work is the therapeutic work of making people in the family feel comfortable, loved, and understood. It is largely the work of women. It is the job of orchestrating the Sunday picnic so each person has something special to look forward to and the job of physically and temporally orchestrating events to minimize family conflicts. One reason it has been so difficult to understand women's sense of injustice about family work is that no one seriously considered this to be "work" until very recently. Traditionally, being the family's emotional caretaker was viewed as something women *were,* rather than as something *they did.* Also, supportive behaviors appear to be "spontaneous" to many male onlookers and were discounted as not requiring any effort.

Current work by Erickson (1993) and others indicates that providing emotional support may be the most important type of family work in predicting marital happiness. Erickson measured emotional support by asking 205 white working women to assess such things as how often their husbands confided their innermost thoughts and feelings, had faith in them, stuck by them in times of trouble, and initiated talking things over. The women also rated how they acted toward their husbands in these areas. Erickson found that although the husband's involvement in housework and child care did have a positive effect on marital well-being, it was minimal compared to the whopping effect that emotion work had on the wife's marital well-being. Overall, women want men who talk, listen, and understand. This is not new. What is important here is that emotional supportiveness may be more valued than participating in housework and child care.

Indeed, as automation and changing social mores have robbed the family of its many functions, the demand for intimacy within the marriage has increased proportionately. The fact that many women believe they are providing large amounts of socioemotional support for the family is misleading in judging couple wellness because (1) women desire and expect reciprocal stroking and emotional support and (2) men often do not perceive the support as available. Unfortunately, the "intimate companion" is the hardest marital role in which to achieve success, for men or women. Kitson with Holmes (1992) found that of the five marital roles they studied (e.g., helpmate, homemaker, sexual partner, leisure time companion, and someone to talk things over with), the one most likely to fall short of expectations, for both men and women, was having "someone to talk things over with." This was true for 64 percent of divorced couples who were thinking back on their marriage and for nearly 50 percent of married couples who had any expressed role problem.

Self-Exploration 1 at the end of the chapter presents a scale to assess the amount of emotion work that couples experience in their relationship.

EMPLOYMENT AND ITS EFFECTS ON THE COUPLE RELATIONSHIP

A number of different factors in the work situation affect couple interactions. Most critical, though, are the number of hours spent on the job and how flexible those are, the monetary rewards of the job, and the joys and stresses associated with the job.

Number of Hours Spent at Work

A generation ago, the average family work week was forty hours. Now, couples log a total of more than eighty hours (Freeman, Carlson, and Sperry, 1993).

It is obvious but empirically true that the more hours each spouse spends working, the more family conflict is evident and the less time spouses spend together. Time is lost in every aspect of domestic life, from household chores to recreation to conversation.

When couples work different shifts, which is a more common pattern when the children are young and in need of constant care, the marriage is strained even more. In fact, shift work increases the likelihood of divorce (White and Keith, 1990).

Income

Income affects marital happiness but not in the way expected. As the husband's income rises, so does the marital happiness of both spouses. Both feel that the husband is fulfilling his dominant provider role. However, as the wife's income rises, some studies have found that marriages become more unstable and divorce more likely (Booth et al., 1984). True, women who cannot support themselves are less hesitant to leave a bad marriage, but it may also be that men and women, in the 1980s, still had a more difficult time dealing with the loss of male supremacy related to earnings (Vannoy and Philliber, 1992).

Job Commitment and Job Stress

Many researchers have found that the overall happiness of couples is best predicted by a combination of job satisfaction and marital happiness (Zedeck et al., 1988). This is expected and validates the old Freudian notion of "love and work" (Leib und Arbeit), a dictum that Freud thought summed up all the meaningful pleasures of life. The positive "spillover" of a rewarding job and career to family life is being discovered by more and more middle-aged couples who switch careers to enhance both job satisfaction and marital satisfaction. Often, the job shift is to a lower-paying, less prestigious, less harried job. It is a case in which less is more: more freedom, more control, and more time for the family.

Five Types of Work-Family Relationships

Money, pressure, satisfaction, and a host of other variables interact to create five major different types of relationships between professional and personal life. People adopt different relationships depending on how emotionally satisfying or frustrating work is and how important they value their work relative to their family life. The current work comes from a study conducted only on men, so hunches as to how females react within this framework will be suggested (Barnett, Marshall, and Pleck, 1992). The first four relationships will be mentioned briefly, and then we will concentrate on the most prevalent, problematic relationship type (Type 5, The Spillover Relationship) in greater detail.

Relationship Type 1: The Independent Relationship

In this relationship, a person feels that work and family life exist side by side and for all practical purposes are independent of each other. The thinking here is, "It is quite possible to be successful and satisfied in my career and my home life, in one or the other, or in neither."

Between 15 percent and 20 percent of the respondents in the study felt that their two roles were quite independent of each other.

Relationship Type 2: The Conflict Relationship

Individuals caught in this relationship feel that their work life and family life are in conflict with each other and cannot be easily reconciled. Success and satisfaction in the career necessarily entail sacrifices to the home life; and having a satisfying home life entails making compromises with respect to the career.

Less than 10 percent of the men reported feeling conflicted between work and family. Again, the data for women would probably be the mirror image, with most full-time working women with young children experiencing conflict between having a satisfying career and a satisfying home life.

Relationship Type 3: The Instrumental Relationship

Here, work is primarily a means to allow the person to have a more pleasant family life. It is the means to build and maintain a satisfying and successful family and leisure lifestyle. Less than 10 percent of the men in the study felt work was merely a means to an end. Women might well experience this more than men during the child-rearing years.

When an individual has shifted jobs to avoid negative spillover, the next job often has an instrumental orientation. People do not want to fall into the same trap twice. They keep telling themselves that they are working to get a paycheck and that they can get all their needs met in their after-work hours if they do not drive themselves nuts taking the stress of work home with them. Often older workers, who feel that they have plateaued and that their job will not become any more challenging or interesting, have an instrumental relationship with the workplace.

Relationship Type 4: The Compensation Relationship

This work-family relationship is characterized by the feeling that each area has a way of making up for what is missing in the other. The less satisfying their work and career, the more these individuals look to family for fulfillment and development. Or, if the family life is less than satisfying, then they turn to work and career development.

Less than 10 percent of the men experienced emptiness in either the work or family sphere that they felt could be rectified or compensated for in the other sphere. This style is often adopted by younger people who are having a difficult time finding rewards at work but are still optimistic about their careers. They temporarily look to the family for all of their satisfaction. Ironically, if work is too satisfying and rewarding, young people, in particular, get caught up in a spiral of success that excludes the family.

Relationship Type 5: The Spillover Relationship

In this family-job relationship, work life and family life are always affecting each other. Folks in this category think, "If I am satisfied in my work, this will contribute to my family life, while if I am unsatisfied in my career, this will have a negative effect on my family life. In a similar way, satisfaction with my family life may affect my feelings about my career and work."

Over half of the managers studied and a third of their wives (describing the lifestyle of their husbands) found the spillover relationship most apt. Perhaps, not surprisingly, the spillover was unanimously one way: Men who were stressed at work ended up grumpy and taking it out on others at home. But when the men had a successful day at work, they were not in better than normal spirits at home. Beach et al. (1993) analyzed the types of social support and interpersonal stressors in the workplace that spill over into the marriage. Although workers most often see the most supportive person in their life as their spouse, the greatest source of stress was as likely to come from a co-worker as a spouse. This suggests that the work environment is particularly prone to negatively affect the marital relationship.

Although co-workers did provide social support, they were far more often a source of stress. A co-worker was, in fact, more likely than a spouse to get on one's nerves, act angry, or show dislike. In fact, co-worker stressors were four times as important in accounting for negative affect as was interpersonal support at work in buffering negative affect. No wonder the workplace becomes a real hotbed of trouble. Ultimately, it is the spouse who must provide first aid or emergency care for the narcissistic wounds routinely administered in the marketplace.

People who work in high-stress environments have more spillover than others. Particularly when the couple is already in conflict about an issue (child care, finances, or whatever), it is easy to triangulate the work situation into the relationship and focus the fighting and arguments upon how the job demands prevent a normal home life. When one spouse is overinvolved and overstressed at work, the other spouse becomes jealous. How can there be so much energy and commitment for work and none for them? This resentment polarizes the couple even further, as they see the hostility as a threat to their career or needed emotional support (Borum and Philpot, 1993).

Thus, among the people who report experiencing spillover, the most common experience is negative work-related feelings affecting the family. Feelings such as tension, anger, guilt, worry, and disappointment surround them as they walk into their homes. As most Americans know, the "fussy" hour of babies (usually 5 p.m. to 7 p.m.) now extends to all members of the family, particularly the work-weary adults.

Individuals prone to developing a spillover relationship (Type 5) or a conflict relationship (Type 2) are sometimes addicted to their work. That is, the work role is more important than any of their other roles and is given top priority at all times. Work addictions satisfy cravings for self-esteem, efficacy, purposefulness, and challenge. They can be driven by compensatory drives or childhood feelings of incompetency. Realistically though, home and family are universally important to people, but they are not always the most important, satisfying, or successful of our adult roles. Some empirical evidence supports that men are more likely to be distressed by work events and financial events, whereas women are more stressed by negative events within the family (Conger et al., 1993). This suggests that men may have more negative spillover from work to home and women more negative spillover from home to work. Clients may get some insights into how work-addicted they are by taking the Work Addiction Test (Self-Exploration 3, p. 247).

Three of the most prevalent sources of negative job spillover in today's world are job insecurity, structural job stressors, and psychological job stressors. Each will be briefly discussed to demonstrate how it affects the marital relationship.

MAJOR TYPES OF SPILLOVER

The Stress of Job Insecurity

In the 1990s, job insecurity became endemic, affecting both men and women at all occupational levels. The stress of possibly losing one's job is different from many other types of job stressors in that it is most immediately linked with the ability of families to provide material security and psychological feelings of efficacy. Also, job insecurity is difficult to "solve." When one is unemployed, one is forced to reprioritize values, move, change careers, or do whatever else is needed to find employment. When one is in fear of losing one's job, the wait-and-see period may hover over the family for months, paralyzing them from seeing beyond the needs of the immediate situation. It is well known that uncertainty is one of the most stressful of all events—and job uncertainty is one of the worst types of uncertainty.

Larson, Wilson, and Beley (1994) studied the effects of job uncertainty in a university setting that was facing severe cutbacks and firings. One hundred fifty married faculty and staff members were sampled. He found that the stress experienced by the spouses was as great as the stress experienced by the workers. Sometimes this led to strong mutual support and strengthened the marriage. The younger the faculty and staff were, the more job insecurity upset them. Perhaps, as we age we are conditioned to deal with such stressors with greater acceptance, or perhaps it is due to the larger nest egg many couples enjoy as they get older. Not surprisingly, workers who were in ill health were more stressed about possible job loss than healthy workers. Clearly, losing one's job when suffering from illness or disability greatly reduces one's ability to compete in a new job market and, more important, threatens the need to have adequate health coverage (which is still not universally accessible as of this writing). It is also well documented that the stress of job uncertainty can actually exacerbate medical conditions, much like any other psychological stressor (Rook, Dooley, and Catalano, 1991). Also, just when people should be performing best at work (to lessen the probability that they will be eliminated), job stress leads to a decreased tolerance for co-workers, frustrations in the workplace, and reduced job satisfaction. Finally, Larson, Wilson, and Beley (1994) found that the presence of a problematic marriage only makes job uncertainty more stressful for both partners. It was just one more thing going wrong for the couple.

Marital stress potentiates all job stressors, including job uncertainty. Although this discussion is limited to the effects of work on the marriage, the spillover, as mentioned previously, works both ways. When marriages are strong, job stressors and job uncertainty seem more endurable than when the marriages are fragile and need strong external supports.

The partner who is unemployed or whose job is threatened plays a major role in determining how much stress the supporting spouse will feel. If the worker has an "It's OK" attitude, then the spouse usually feels that she or he will be able to cope. The threatened spouse acts as the thermome- ter to indicate how dangerous the situation is for the couple.

When a community or organization faces layoffs, family support and intervention programs are sorely needed to prevent the occurrence of individual stress reactions and destructive marital interaction cycles.

Structural and Psychological Job Stressors

There are two other types of job stressors, each potentially having a different spillover effect on couples (Hughes, Galinsky, and Morris, 1992). First are structural job stressors. These include such factors as work hours, travel demands, weekend work, and flexibility in job scheduling. Structural job characteristics can seriously erode the time available at the home front and thus have the potential to reduce one's ability to carry out home and family responsibilities. If you are away in Seattle all week, you cannot take Johnny to his Cub Scout meeting on Wednesday evening. It is that simple.

The second type of stressors are psychological job stressors. These include the inability to control decision making related to one's job, psychological workload, how insensitive a supervisor is to family needs, and how incompetent the worker feels the supervisor is. People carry these types of stressors around inside of them. Although psychological stressors do not prevent a parent from taking Johnny to his Cub Scout meeting, they may prompt the parent to use Johnny as a convenient scapegoat or cause the parent to become quiet and withdrawn all the while they are in the car together.

Whenever either of these two types of job stressors are present, some spouses will have "spillover" and become more moody, less energetic, and interpersonally less available to their family. The spillover is not confined to any one aspect of family life. A wife frustrated at not getting a positive work review may not want to have sex or may become angry when her husband wants her to visit friends on the weekend. Work stressors seem to spill over into any and all aspects of the marital relationship. Like water, job spillover seeks the easiest route to escape.

The more harmonious the marriage, the more likely spouses are to suffer "emotional reverberations" from external events that are negatively affecting their partners. Estranged spouses seem less affected by the fortunes and tragedies in their mates' work life. Maybe the disgruntled spouses are less upset by spillover because their partners are not looking to them for support and they have cut off the desire for empathy (Rook, Dooley, and Catalano, 1991).

Karen Rook and colleagues (1991) empirically investigated whether marital tension does serve as a moderator for how work stress is transmitted to a spouse. The research group had access to 1,383 women who were part of the Los Angeles Stressor Project, a large project that looked at economic stressors and physical health. All of the women sampled considered their husbands to be the primary breadwinner and all the husbands had been employed over the previous six months. Rook and colleagues found that, overall, job stressors experienced by the husbands caused clinically identifiable psychological distress among the wives. In fact, the husband's job stress caused as strong an emotional reaction in the wife as the personal stressors in her own life. This was true, despite the fact that the women whose husbands were job stressed felt that their husbands were as supportive of them as did the women whose husbands were without job stress. Results also indicated that it was in the strongest, least conflictual marriages that the wife experienced the most stress. This supports the idea that the spouse of a distressed worker in a good marriage offers psychological support, worry, and empathy at the cost of his or her own mental health. The mechanisms by which the spouse becomes adversely affected are potentially many. It may be empathy or frustration at one's inability to make the partner feel better. It may be an inability to attend to one's own needs when the spouse needs so much time and attention or even an unconscious desire to become symptomatic to reduce the spouse's apparent dysphoria from being deviant. All of these possibilities should be explored when one spouse appears to be adversely affected by the other's job stress. Regardless of the specific factors responsible in any particular marital situation, the results strongly suggest that there is no free lunch and, as many poets have tried to teach us, caring costs and love hurts.

An additional kind of spillover occurs for working women, the kind caused by the resentment of husbands who do not support women as serious workers doing serious work. Working wives can create stress in some marriages just because the wife is working. That is, husbands who have traditional gender stereotypes and feel that wives should devote themselves to hearth and home instead of the workplace may experience stress every time work obligations interfere with the family needs. Even when the wife has a professional job and earns more than her husband, it is the husband's ideology more than the wife's ideology and her own work stressors that will predict how deleterious her career is to the marriage. If the husband believes in androgynous (flexible) gender definitions for himself and his wife, there are no negative ideological effects from the wife working. In fact, data suggest that the wife only needs to believe that the husband holds these attitudes to be emotionally buffered: whether he actually feels that way may be secondary (Vannoy and Philliber, 1992). When the husband believes that a women should act like the stereotyped traditional definition of a women and he should act within the stereotyped traditional definition of a man, women's work outside the home is associated with marital strife. Women need to feel supported by their man when they are out in the workplace if they are not to have "spillover" into the marriage (Pina and Bengtson, 1993).

Effect of Family and Work Stressors on Physical Health

Some theorists and researchers have postulated that working and family life enhance one's physical and emotional well-being, yet others have documented that work and family disorganization can lead to symptoms of fatigue, depression, and illness. Obviously, both work and family factors can have positive or negative spillover onto one's physical health.

This model of interdependence between physical health, work, and family connections has been empirically tested by the Resiliency Model of Family Adjustment and Adaptation (McCubbin et al., 1992). The subjects were 798 men and women who were part of a midwestern insurance company's health promotion program. The men's health risk was increased by work factors such as pressures, deadlines, and a management style that talked down to employees. However, McCubbin and colleagues found that men's health risk was protected if they had families that emphasized listening and hearing in its problem-solving efforts. Larson and colleagues (1994) found that men are very reactive to the negative stressors of work.

Women, on the other hand, presented a more muddled picture. Their health was protected by acknowledging the existence of work pressures but they needed to feel a sense of efficacy in the work situation. As with men, their health was associated with an open family atmosphere in which members could express themselves freely. Women were at increased health risk by being older, having families experiencing emotional problems, and having pressured, uncooperative work settings in which they could not relax. However, illness was also associated with a supportive family atmosphere, and a cooperative work atmosphere. Perhaps, inherent family and work stressors were so overwhelming for this group of women that the work and family supports were simply misguided, ineffective, or not strong enough to buffer them from the stressors associated with illness. Alternatively, some female health problems may be associated with more non-stress-related factors (e.g., genetics, nutrition) than are male health problems.

Clearly, the exact formulas for health maintenance have yet to be discovered. Although not perfect, over 85 percent of the men and women could be correctly categorized as high or low health risks based on the significant family and work variables that were assessed.

METHODS OF COPING: HOME-BASED WORK

More and more Americans are choosing to do all or some of their work at home. About 50 million Americans are engaged in some type of home-based work (Link Resources, 1996). This arrangement reduces the need for child care somewhat and increases the flexibility in the family to accomplish family tasks. However, working at home is filled with additional stressors that are not found in the workplace, particularly continuous interruptions, decreased status, and the sense that the home-based worker "really doesn't work."

Couples need to develop strategies to help the home-based worker accomplish their tasks. Therapists working with couples who have home-based work need to help them evaluate if they are working as effectively as possible, minimizing the spillover stress on the family.

THERAPEUTIC INTERVENTION 2:
GUIDELINES FOR HOME-BASED WORK

The most effective strategies for being efficient at home-based work include (Winter et al., 1993):

1. Have regular work hours when home activities are ignored or others are on call. This is the most difficult goal to accomplish. Interruptions and "emergencies" are an everyday occurrence for most home-based workers and the "workday" is usually a mixed-up, chopped-up series of mini-work units. When the "workday" is over and the work is not done, time is taken from the family to finish the work. In particular, homeworkers report that they will reduce the time spent with the family, sleep less, eat out more often, reduce housecleaning time, and cut down on social activities. In other words, they cut off aspects of their nonwork life to finish work. Far less often will individuals call in people to help them to do the housework or the home-based work. Personal resources are used instead of financial resources to cover the costs of home-based work inefficiency. This scenario is most true for women who work at home. When the man is the home-based worker and the home demands increase, women are more likely to hire outside help to compensate for the lost services. This might be due to the basic devaluation women have of their own work and the sense that it is their responsibility to do the housework. If they feel they are already doing the lion's share of the housework, lost husband services are "appropriate" to replace. Indeed, the more valued the home-based work, because it is full-time or creates a good income, the more likely that outside services will be bought, regardless if the worker is a man or a woman.
2. Maintain a separate workplace. This is critical with children. It must be a place that they are *never* allowed into during working hours unless "working" along with the parent.
3. Create boundaries between work activities and social activities. These boundaries may include not discussing work activities at the dinner table or answering business calls in the family room.

CASE STUDY 2:
A NOTE TO THE THERAPIST—
A CASE OF CHRONIC SPILLOVER

I cannot really say all this in front of Teddy, partly because he will get so defensive that it will go nowhere positive and partly because I do not want to embarrass him in front of you. So many of our problems are due to Teddy's inappropriate overcommitment to work. I know being vice president at such a large hotel chain is a constant headache, and I do appreciate the lifestyle it affords us, but it has just gone overboard. What do I mean?

The list is long, but how would any woman like to make love to someone who keeps his beeper on the pillow while making love and will actually stop in the middle of lovemaking to return an important call? When we go away for a weekend, he takes the laptop computer with him, and the first activity at any hotel is to pick up his faxes, send some faxes, and set up his "crisis corner" in the room. The kids make fun of him and think he should find a new job. He will start some activity with them but inevitably has to cut it short because he remembers some critical message that has to be immediately relayed or he is being called by one of the staff.

I have talked to Teddy about looking for a different job, but he is very insecure and says he would never get another job with this much responsibility and in this salary range. I do not think either one is worth it. When something goes wrong at work, he will have terrible stomachaches and headaches. He gets so preoccupied and withdrawn that two years ago when we planned to celebrate our anniversary at a restaurant that I had been waiting to go to, he came home two hours late because he had "forgotten" when he made the reservations that he had to give performance feedbacks that day. He had been too busy at work to call and let me know he would be late. I was furious when he came home. He was very depressed and upset at his own neurotic level of preoccupation.

My own job, as an exercise instructor, is fun and low-key. I am ready to enjoy this phase of my life, but I wanted to enjoy it with my husband. I am here alone, like a single parent. I know he loves me. I just do not know what that means in the context of our lives anymore.

THERAPEUTIC INTERVENTION 3:
METHODS OF COPING WITH WORK STRESS
SPILLOVER AND CONFLICT

The following suggestions are useful points of dialogue with couples trying to find ways to reduce spillover and conflict from their jobs.

Take a Transition Break

Most people need between thirty to ninety minutes once they get home to "unwind." Relaxation may be sought by going for a jog, reading, taking a

(continued)

(continued)

nap or bath, or simply vegging out in a chair. Some couples have resorted to picking up the kids from day care thirty minutes later than need be, to give themselves this unwinding time.

Cognitively Restructure the Nature of the Stress

Among the many philosophical attitudes that can help refocus an individual are the following:

- "It is far better to be employed here than to be unemployed."
- "This job has certain benefits that would be hard to replace, despite the problems."
- "It is worth coping with this job to be able to achieve our goals as a family."
- "I can try to make the job better by not having a negative attitude."
- "I should try to condition myself to look for good things in the workday instead of dwelling on the negative."

Redefine Family Responsibilities and Standards

Families that are having problems being productive need help. If the house is not getting cleaned, they should hire a cleaning woman. If they cannot afford to hire help, they should enlist the children and themselves in the cleaning brigade and put some funds into a "family pot" for each week that everyone does their chores. Children do far less housework these days than twenty years ago. Enormous focus has been put on having men help out women, but very little attention has been paid to getting the children involved. Parents today are hesitant about using children and hence exclude them from learning basic responsibilities of group living.

If mother or father is going berserk driving carpools, then activities should be cut back or the transportation shuffle streamlined. A time-efficiency analysis is often helpful to families to learn how to get more done in less time. For example, few people write a shopping list and dinner menu at the beginning of each week; instead they end up going to the supermarket nearly every day! This puts an enormous strain on the most chaotic part of the day. A little weekend planning can make the whole week go smoother.

Standards of what needs to be done each week may need to be modified so that the family has time to relax instead of spending all their time together trying to finish an endless list of chores.

Reevaluate Work Commitments

So many people get stuck in a job that seriously interferes with their family life and feel trapped in that situation. A women who needs to work to keep the family afloat (which is most women) may find that a forty-hour workweek is just too much. Chances are she cannot negotiate with her boss for a thirty- or twenty-hour workweek. Men are very anxious about

(continued)

(continued)

asking for increased flexibility in work hours, fearing that they will be viewed as dispensable, noncommitted workers. Both need to look, innovate, suggest, network, and try to make the hours fit the family needs and budget. Finding more family time can be done in many situations—it just needs real creativity.

For example, the author had a manager at a local McDonald's as a client. The long work hours were rigid and impossible to change. The wife felt like a single parent, and most free time was spent arguing over how they have no time together. Even though the husband's hours were inflexible, the family started visiting the husband at the store for fifteen to thirty minutes a few nights a week. The kids got to tell Dad about the day, and the couple could share their concerns. It was simple, but it worked wonders. Another case involved a couple in which the husband worked in an oil refinery with much overtime and was obviously unable to be flexible in his home time. He started calling home on his breaks: once to talk to his wife about business, once to talk to the kids about their day, and once before coming home to "sweet talk" his wife. In this case, the wife really responded. Every day she felt romanced. Her anger dissipated, and she came to realize it was her own insecurity and dependency that made her angry at her husband's work schedule. With his love being demonstrated in a way that was meaningful to her, she became determined to learn to live a full and interesting life in the hours he had to spend away. She mentally decided not to emotionally punish him for trying to do the best job possible at work.

Extend the Community of Understanding

In the old days, people got to know the folks where the spouse worked. There were dinners, parties, and picnics sprinkled throughout the year. Nowadays, people can work someplace for years and their spouses can have no contact or direct knowledge of anyone else associated with that workplace. This is strange, but this is life in today's world. It is important to encourage the extension of some friendships from the workplace to the family whenever possible. Families who form bonds with one another because their wives or husbands work at the same place share a camaraderie much like any other support group. Instead of blaming the spouse for the job-related stress, knowledge of the community allows one to externalize and put the blame on the job characteristics. Couples also learn from each other what the firm or business does that can enhance family life.

Reevaluate the "Fit" Between the Job and One's Stage of Life

Spillover can become so extreme and destructive that individuals are forced to find a new job that will not destroy their home life. Radical job change is thus one highly traumatic but effective way of dealing with chronic spillover.

(continued)

(continued)

Keep in mind that spillover often becomes the impetus for scapegoating some member of the family. When people cannot scream at the workplace, they feel entitled to scream at their children or spouses. The quick, short temper that fuels the abusive venting of family members is an unfortunate and maladaptive form of coping with spillover.

Although negative spillover is a major problem, some researchers report that men and women believe most strongly in the dramatic effects of positive spillover to the job. When parenting, the spousal relationship, and the exercise or leisure routine are all functioning optimally, people report having much more energy and interest in their jobs. They also report that they deal with the job stressors better at these times (Kirchmeyer, 1993). This would suggest that companies that act from a family values perspective really are making a strong investment in the efficient, bottom-line functioning of their firms.

The conflicts over work and family life must constantly be worked on in a strong marriage. Remember that over half of all dual-earner families report experiencing strong conflicts between their work responsibilities and family responsibilities. Nearly 35 percent of all workers report such conflicts, even if one spouse is the primary homemaker (Pleck, Staines, and Lang, 1980).

In summary, work is not simply the "social address" where one spends time during each day. Work is a tentacle of family functioning: All the nourishment and trauma received by the tentacle gets received and processed (consciously and unconsciously) in the central marital hub.

THERAPEUTIC INTERVENTION 4:
THE EFFICACY TRIPOD

Another way of helping couples visualize where their stress is coming from is to ask them to draw a tripod, with one leg symbolizing their sense of efficacy at work, one leg symbolizing their feelings of efficacy within the marital relationship, and one leg symbolizing the feelings of efficacy arising from children, friends, or extended family. The stronger their sense of efficacy, the stronger the leg of the tripod should be drawn. Once it is drawn, the tripod becomes a metaphor for how stress in one area of life can be buffered by a sense of efficacy in other areas. Stress in any one "leg" is usually buffered by the other two strong "legs." If stressed on two legs, however, the tripod will often topple over, because one leg usually cannot support the tripod. Thus, in a strong marriage, if one spouse has a bad day at work, most often the other spouse will pick up some of his or her responsibilities in the house that night without any discussion or comment.

THERAPEUTIC INTERVENTION 5 : CREATING WORK-HOME METAPHORS

Job-to-Home Transition

One easy way to approach the negative and positive influence of work on the marital relationship within the therapy hour is to ask each partner to draw a picture or list five words that characterize him or her on the job or working with colleagues. Then, ask each partner to draw a picture or list five words that characterize him or her at home with family and friends.

Analyzing the cluster of thoughts and feelings associated with each domain is a fruitful and nonthreatening way to start exploring work-family relationships.

LEARNING AIDS

Therapeutic Dialogue (Housework and Jobs)

1. In which areas are the husband and wife satisfied with the way their household chores are divided and carried out? In which areas are they dissatisfied? How do their family and friends divide home chores? How would they ideally like to divide household chores? How can the ideal division of labor be modified to make it more attainable?

2. In what areas are the husband and wife satisfied with the way their child care responsibilities are divided and carried out? In which areas are they dissatisfied? How do their family and friends divide child care responsibilities? How would they ideally like to divide child care responsibilities? How can the ideal division of child care roles be modified to make it more attainable?

3. How dissatisfied are the husband and wife with the influence that their jobs are having on the family and the marital relationship? What type of influence does work have on the families of co-workers, relatives, friends, and neighbors? Ideally, how would one like to buffer the negative effects that work has on marital relationships and family relationships, in general? How can the ideal of coping with job stress be modified so that it is more likely to be a reachable goal?

Self-Exploration 1: The Emotions Work Test

Rate your spouse on each of the activities listed below using the following scale.

1 = Never
2 = Rarely
3 = Sometimes
4 = Often
5 = Frequently
6 = Almost always
7 = Always

1. Confides innermost thoughts and feelings
2. Initiates talking things over
3. Tries to bring me out of a feeling of restlessness, boredom, or depression
4. Lets me know he or she has faith in me
5. Senses that I am disturbed about something
6. Offers me encouragement
7. Gives me compliments
8. Sticks by me in times of trouble
9. Offers me advice when I am faced with a problem
10. Acts affectionately toward me
11. Expresses concern for my well-being
12. Communicates his or her feelings about the future of our relationship
13. Is a good friend
14. Does favors for me without being asked

Note: When spouses rate each other, it is important for the therapist to stress again and again that the veracity of the behavior or attitude is not what is being assessed or tested; rather, it is the spouse's perception of that behavior or attitude. For example, many spouses will want to find fault with their spouses' ratings and argue about the extent of the emotion work they do in the marriage. Therapists may, in fact, want to explore the veracity issue at some point. However, initially, it is most important to understand what is actually being experienced by each spouse.

Source: Erickson, R. (1993). Reconceptualizing family work: The effect of emotion work on perceptions of marital equality. *Journal of Marriage and the Family, 55*(4), 888-890. Copyright 1993 by the National Council on Family Relations, 3989 Central Ave. NE, Suite 550, Minneapolis, MN 55421. Reprinted by permission.

Self-Exploration 2: The Five Work-Family Relationship Types

Ask each couple to rate how often each of the following work-family relationships has typified their life, using the following scale:

0 = Not at all
1 = Some of the time
2 = A moderate amount of the time
3 = Often
4 = All of the time

1. *The spillover relationship.* "Work life and family life always affect each other. If I am satisfied in my work, this will contribute to my family life, but if I am unsatisfied in my career, this will have a negative effect on my family life. In a similar way, satisfaction with my family life may affect feelings about my career and work."

2. *The independent relationship.* "Work and family life exist side by side and for all practical purposes are independent of each other. It is quite possible to be successful and satisfied in my career and my home life, in one or the other, or in neither."

3. *Conflict relationship.* "My work life and family life are in conflict with each other and cannot be easily reconciled. Success and satisfaction in my career will necessarily entail sacrifices in my home life; and to have a satisfying home life entails making compromises with respect to my career."

4. *The instrumental relationship.* "Work is primarily a means of allowing me to have a more pleasant family life. It is the means of building and maintaining a satisfying and successful family and leisure lifestyle."

5. *The compensation relationship.* "Each area is a way of making up for what is missing in the other. The less satisfying my work and my career are, the more I look to my family for fulfillment and development; or if my family life is less satisfying, then I turn more to my work and my career."

Instructions: Ask the couple to discuss their perceptions of how much each relationship has typified their marriage over the years. Which type of relationship was most stressful? Why?

Self-Exploration 3: The Work Addiction Test

Answer the following questions by marking an X after the word Yes, No, or Maybe. Try not to overanalyze the question. Allow yourself to answer as spontaneously as possible.

1. I think of a total commitment to work as a positive addiction.
   Yes ( ) No ( ) Maybe ( )
2. I like to be busy, doing several things at once.
   Yes ( ) No ( ) Maybe ( )
3. I work overtime a lot, but I never seem to get ahead.
   Yes ( ) No ( ) Maybe ( )
4. I have often called myself a work addict.
   Yes ( ) No ( ) Maybe ( )
5. I frequently commit to doing things involving work without thinking what it will demand of my time and energy.
   Yes ( ) No ( ) Maybe ( )
6. I feel overwhelmed a lot, as if there just is not enough time to do all that I need to do.
   Yes ( ) No ( ) Maybe ( )
7. I can become quite anxious when I am not in control.
   Yes ( ) No ( ) Maybe ( )
8. It is exciting to have many projects going at the same time.
   Yes ( ) No ( ) Maybe ( )
9. I feel extremely bored when I have nothing constructive to do.
   Yes ( ) No ( ) Maybe ( )
10. I am at the top of my profession and feel depressed a lot of the time.
    Yes ( ) No ( ) Maybe ( )
11. I am making more money than I ever dreamed possible, but I drive myself to earn more.
    Yes ( ) No ( ) Maybe ( )
12. The people closest to me are concerned about how much I work.
    Yes ( ) No ( ) Maybe ( )
13. My work achievements do not seem to make my parents proud of me, as I had imagined they would.
    Yes ( ) No ( ) Maybe ( )
14. I agree to vacations at the last minute and usually take some work with me or call the office several times.
    Yes ( ) No ( ) Maybe ( )
15. I get angry when my family or friends suggest that I work too hard or too much.
    Yes ( ) No ( ) Maybe ( )

16. I find myself failing to keep promises about cutting back on my work, or I secretly stash my work so no one will notice me working.

Yes ( ) No ( ) Maybe ( )

17. I feel alive and excited when I have a full menu of work commitments.

Yes ( ) No ( ) Maybe ( )

18. I procrastinate about work and let the pressure build until I am in a deadline crisis. Then I work energetically until the work is finished, usually just in the nick of time.

Yes ( ) No ( ) Maybe ( )

19. I consider myself a perfectionist. I'm extremely upset when I make a mistake.

Yes ( ) No ( ) Maybe ( )

20. I put far more time and thought into my work than I do into my interpersonal relationships with my spouse and children.

Yes ( ) No ( ) Maybe ( )

Evaluation: Assign the Number 3 for every "Yes" answer, the Number 2 for every "Maybe" answer, and the Number 1 for every "No" answer. Add up the numbers to get your final score. If you scored above 40 on my test, I think your work issues have become very serious.

Source: John Bradshaw, *Creating Love,* 1992, p. 360. Copyright 1992 by John Bradshaw. Used by permission of Bantam Books, a division of Random House, Inc.

Sample Workshop Flowchart Intended for Groups of Four or Five Couples Working on Homework and Job Stress

I. Psychoeducational Strategies
   A. Explain the five types of housework.
   B. Discuss the norms on the division of housework.
   C. Discuss the norms on the division of child care.
   D. Explain the five types of work-family relationships.
   E. Describe the general types of job stressors and how they can affect the marital relationship.
   F. Review methods of coping with job spillover and stress.

II. Self-Explorations (Done by couples in private and shared before rejoining the group)

A. The Emotions Work Test
B. The five work/family relationship types
C. The Work Addiction Test
D. Measuring spillover from work to home

III. Therapeutic Dialogue (Done by couples in private and shared before rejoining the group)
(Proceeding in the order presented, both partners respond to each question before going on to discuss the next question)
In the group, the therapist explores with couples how relationship goals can be achieved by modifying overly ambitious, pie-in-the-sky expectations. Using information about their current situation and the realities seen among friends and family, couples fine-tune expectations so they are achievable and motivate rather than discourage attempts at change.

IV. Therapeutic Interventions
Work with a couple in front of the group and apply one or more of the following therapeutic interventions. Share rationales during demonstrations. Let group discuss additional interventions.
A. Assessing stress of child care
B Guidelines for home-based work
C. Methods of coping with work stress spillover and conflict
D. The efficacy tripod
E. Creating work-home metaphors

V. Finding the Motivation and Time to Make the Changes
Group discussion

Bibliotherapy

Beehr, T. (1995). *Psychological stress in the workplace.* New York: Routledge.

Bravo, E. (1996). *The job-family challenge: A 9 to 5 guide.* New York: John Wiley.

Galginaitis, C. (1994). *Managing the demands of work and home.* Burr Ridge, IL: Irwin.

Groller, I. (1990). "Women and work: The results of our Readers Poll." *Parents Magazine,* June, pp. 107-114.

Gutterman, M. (1994). *Common sense for uncommon times: The power of balance in work, family, and personal life.* Palo Alto, CA: Consulting Psychologists.

Hanson, J., and Mark, P. (1993). *You know you are a workaholic when . . .* New York: Workman.

Videotherapy

Adam's Rib. (1956). Directed by George Cukor. Classic story about husband and wife lawyers on opposing sides of the same murder case.

The Way We Were (1973). Directed by Sydney Pollack. A good film for showing how careers affect marriage.

Professional Development Questions (Work)

1. What are the most common ways that work affects the marital relationship?

2. How does housework differ from other types of work? How can a therapist use this understanding to help create greater equity in the marital relationship?

3. When work pressures are adversely affecting a marriage, how can the therapist guide the couple to reassess their values and options?

4. If you were to consult with a large national corporation on developing a corporate program to strengthen family life and ease family tensions for the employees, what would be the cornerstones of your program? What would be the rationales for those cornerstones?

REFERENCES

Barnett, R., Marshall, N., and Pleck, J. (1992). Adult son-parent relationships and their associations with sons' psychological distress. *Journal of Family Issues. 13*(4), 505-525.

Beach, S. R., Martin, J. K., Blum, T. C., and Roman, P. M. (1993). Effects of marital and coworker relationships on negative affect: Testing the central role of marriage. *American Journal of Family Therapy, 21*(4), 313-323.

Bird, C. 1999. Gender, household labor, and psychological distress: The impact of the amount and division of housework. *Journal of Health and Human Behavior, 40*(1): 32-45.

Bird, C. and Ross, C. (1993). Houseworker and paid workers: Qualities of the work and effects on personal control. *Journal of Marriage and the Family, 55*(4), 913-925.

Booth, A., Johnson, D. R., White, L. K., and Edwards, J. N. (1984). Women, outside employment, and marital instability. *American Journal of Sociology, 90*(3), 567-583.

Borum, R. and Philpot, C. (1993). Therapy with law enforcement couples: Clinical management of the "high-risk lifestyle." *American Journal of Family Therapy, 21*(2), 122-135.

Bradshaw, J. (1992). *Creating love: The next great stage of growth.* New York: Bantam.

Coltrane, S. and Ishi-Kuntz, M. (1992). Men's housework: A life course perspective. *Journal of Marriage and the Family, 54*(1), 43-57.

Conger, R., Lorenz, F., Elder, G., and Simons, R. (1993). Husband and wife differences in response to undesirable life events. *Journal of Health and Social Behavior, 34*(1), 71-88.

Crouter, A. C. and McHale, S. M. (1992). You can't always get what you want: Incongruence between sex role attitudes and family work roles and its implications for marriage. *Journal of Marriage and the Family, 54*(3), 537-547.

Deutsch, F., Lozy, J., and Saxon, S. (1993). Taking credit: Couple's reports of contributions to child care. *Journal of Family Issues, 14*(3), 421-437.

Erickson, R. (1993). Reconceptualizing family work: The effect of emotion work on perceptions of marital quality. *Journal of Marriage and the Family, 55*(4), 888-890.

Freeman, C., Carlson, J., and Sperry, L. (1993). Adlerian therapy strategies with middle-income couples facing financial stress. *American Journal of Family Therapy, 21*(4), 324-330.

Greenstein, T. (1993). Maternal employment and child behavioral outcomes: A household economics analysis. *Journal of Family Issues, 14*(3), 323-354.

Groller, I. (1990). Women and work: Results of our Readers Poll. *Parents Magazine,* June, pp. 107-114.

Hochschild, A. and Machung, A. (1989). *The second shift.* New York: Viking.

Hughes, D., Galinsky, E., and Morris, A. (1992). The effects of job characteristics on marital quality: Specifying linking mechanisms. *Journal of Marriage and the Family, 54*(1), 31-42.

Hyde, J., Essex, M., and Horton, F. (1993). Fathers and parental leave. *Journal of Family Issues, 14*(4), 616-641.

Kirchmeyer, C. (1993). Nonwork to work spillover: A more balanced view of the experiences and coping of professional men and women. *Sex Roles, 28*(9/10), 531-552.

Kitson, G. C. with Holmes, W. M. (1992). *Portrait of divorce.* New York: Guilford.

Lamb, M., Pleck, J. H., Charnov, E. L., and Levine, J. (1985). Parenting behavior in humans. *American Zoologist, 25*(8), 883-894.

Lamb, M., Pleck, J. H., Charnov, E. L., and Levine, J. (1987). Biosocial perspectives of paternal behavior and involvement. In J. B. Lancaster, J. Altman, A. S. Rossi, and L. R. Sherrod (Eds.), *Parenting across the life span: Biosocial perspectives* (pp. 111-142). New York: Aldine.

Larson, J. H., Wilson, S. M., and Beley, R. (1994). The impact of job insecurity on marital and family relationships. *Family Relations, 43*(2), 138-143.

Link Resources (1996). Home-based work. <www.workathometoday.com>.

McCubbin, H. I., Thompson, A. I., Kretzschmar, H., Smith, F., Snow, P., McEwen, M., Elver, K., and McCubbin, M. (1992). Family system and work environment predictors of employee health risk: A discriminant function analysis. *The American Journal of Family Therapy, 20*(2), 123-144.

Mederer, H. (1993). Division of labor in two-earner homes: Task accomplishment versus household management as critical variables in perceptions about family work. *Journal of Marriage and the Family, 55*(1), 133-145.

Olds, J., Schwartz, R., Eisen, S., Betcher, R., and Van Niel, A. (1993). Part-time employment and marital well-being: A hypothesis and pilot study. *Family Therapy, 20*(1), 1-16.

Oropesa, R. S. (1993). Using the service economy to relieve the double burden: Female labor force participation and service purchases. *Journal of Family Issues, 14*(3), 438-473.

Pina, D. and Bengtson, V. (1993). The division of household labor and wives' happiness: Ideology, employment, and perceptions of support. *Journal of Marriage and the Family, 55*(4), 901-912.

Pittman, J. and Blanchard, D. (1996). The effects of work history and timing of marriage on the division of household labor: A life course perspective. *Journal of Marriage and the Family, 58*(1), 78-90.

Pleck, J. H., Staines, G. L., and Lang, L. (1980). Conflicts between work and family life. *Monthly Labor Review, 103*(3), 29-32.

Pratt, J. H. (1987). Methodological problems in surveying the home-based workforce. *Technological Forecasting and Social Change, 31*(1), 49-60.

Rook, K., Dooley, D., and Catalano, R. (1991). Stress transmission: The effects of husbands' job stressors on the emotional health of wives. *Journal of Marriage and the Family, 53*(1), 165-177.

Shaw, S. (1992). Dereifying family leisure: An examination of women's and men's everyday experiences and perceptions of family time. *Leisure Sciences, 14*(4), 271-286.

Shelton, B. and John, D. (1993). Does marital status make a difference? Housework among married and cohabitating men and women. *Journal of Family Issues, 14*(3), 401-420.

Vannoy, D. and Philliber, W. (1992). Wife's employment and quality of marriage. *Journal of Marriage and the Family, 54*(2), 387-398.

Ward, R. (1993). Marital happiness and household equity in later life. *Journal of Marriage and the Family, 55*(2), 427-438.

White, L. and Keith, B. (1990). The effect of shift work on the quality and stability of marital relations. *Journal of Marriage and the Family, 52*(2), 453-462.

Winter, M., Puspitawati, H., Heck, R., and Stafford, K. (1993). Time management strategies used by households with home-based work. *Journal of Family and Economic Issues, 14*(1), 69-91.

Zedeck, S., Maslach, C., Mosier, K., and Skitka, L. (1988). Affective responses to work and quality of family life: Employee and spouse perspectives. *Journal of Social Behavior and Personality, 3*(4), 135-157.

Zvonkovic, A., Greaves, K., Schmiege, C., and Hall, L. (1996). The marital construction of gender through work and family decisions: A qualitative analysis. *Journal of Marriage and the Family, 58*(1), 91-100.

Chapter 6

In-Laws and the Couple Relationship

In-law relationships affect an individual in at least two significant ways: First, the individual is forced to form intimate, familial relationships with nonblood kin whom he or she did not directly choose to make part of the "family." Rarely is this forced relationship a natural match of kindred spirits. Second, in-law relationships can have a direct or indirect influence on the spousal relationship by creating animosity and tension between spouses who have cultural and emotional allegiances with their own kin. Nonetheless, being an in-law provides constant opportunities for growth as well as problems. The challenge is to turn the latter into the former.

In-law relationships differ from most other adult relationships in three critical ways. First, we choose our spouses and most of our friends; in-laws come as a required accessory. Second, the parent-child bond is complex and in-laws enter as extra threads in an already complicated tapestry of relationships. Third, especially when people marry in their twenties, parents and adult children are struggling to separate from one another while finding comfortable ways of being interdependent. Children-in-laws usually add extra weight to the separation side of the balance, often prompting corrective closeness maneuvers on the part of the parents.

Boszormenyi-Nagy and Spark (1973) posit that one of the most prominent and primary issues that a young couple must resolve is how the respective families of origin will be included or excluded within the new family structure. The in-law problem becomes a three-way balancing problem: the loyalties to one's own family of origin, the loyalties of one's spouse to his or her family of origin, and the loyalties the couple feel toward each other.

Added to this already sticky wicket, some folks believe that their parents-in-law or children-in-law are a second-chance family. These folks attempt to work thorough issues with thein-laws that were not resolved in their own families. They want the in-law relationship to compensate for frazzled, cutoff, or inadequate relationships with friends or family members. Instead of being a fifth wheel, these in-laws are made the hub of the Ferris wheel.

IN-LAW COMBINATIONS

The Mother-in-Law/Son-in-Law Relationship

Mother-in-law jokes have been a great source of relief for men who feel oppressed by the intrusion and/or personality of their mothers-in-law. In the post-World War II period, mother-in-law/son-in-law conflicts were frequent as couples were frequently starting their married lives with the wife's family or living very close to the wife's family. The young married couple were often economically dependent on the in-laws, and the in-laws provided many other types of helping behaviors. The young men were frustrated that the mother-in-law still felt she could rule the coop and that they were unable to be masters of the house. Men are still more likely to have problems with their mothers-in-law when they have a dependent relationship with them. Particularly, men who feel that they are responsible for providing for their new family may find it difficult to accept help from the in-laws (Sussman, 1953).

The Mother-in-Law/Daughter-in-Law Relationship

Today, however, the most problematic relationship is between the wife and her mother-in-law (Christensen and Johnson, 1971; Duvall, 1954). There are three explanations for this phenomenon. First, women are the primary kinskeepers and have most of the familial power in determining the day-to-day activities of the family. They almost always plan the family rituals, cook the food, invite the relatives, buy the gifts, and otherwise create the nest. The creative act of homemaking is an individual creation, and when in-laws try to impose their own tastes and ideas, conflicts are inevitable until a way is found to incorporate the new style and needs of the new family member.

Second, the emotional attachment between mother and child is traditionally assumed to be stronger than that between father and child. The situation is changing, but today's mothers-in-law are still accustomed to traditional pairings. Wife and mother-in-law are more likely to compete for the husband/son's attention than husband and father-in-law are to compete for the wife's/daughter's attention.

Third, daughters have traditionally been more likely than their brothers to be dependent on their mothers when they marry. This dependency may lead them to exclude both their husbands and their mothers-in-laws when seeking advice and support.

Despite the expected cultural diversity found within in-law relationships, mothers-in-law are viewed similarly in cultures as diverse as Sudan, Kuwait, Egypt, the United States (Adler, Denmark, and Ahmed, 1989) and South Korea (Choi and Keith, 1991). Although there exists a general wariness about mothers-in-law, the mother-in-law/daughter-in-law ties are very complex. Often the most strained in-law relationship, it is also the relationship most likely to endure after adult children divorce, particularly when there are grandchildren (Johnson and Barer, 1987).

The Father-in-Law/Son-in-Law Relationship

Fathers-in-law and sons-in-law seem to have the best chance of having a positive or neutral relationship. Among many different American subcultures, men are still the "guests" at family rituals and spend a lot of their time together in recreational pursuits or task-oriented pursuits such as fixing cars, golfing, watching TV, and so on. They can get along with each other as though they were colleagues in the workplace. Very little personal disclosure is required, and rarely are they touching each other's turf.

The Father-in-Law/Daughter-in-Law Relationship

Similarly, fathers-in-law rarely try to be intrusive in the lives of their daughters-in-law. Why? Perhaps all men want to be liked by younger women and so try not to offend. Perhaps men do not feel the need to exert their power in the family system as much as women. Perhaps fathers are hesitant to intrude into areas where they have ceded power to their sons. The daughter-in-law is part of the son's domain, and he is the only one who can expect to exert any power over this woman (Berg-Cross and Jackson, 1986).

FACTORS AFFECTING IN-LAW RELATIONSHIPS

Regardless of the configuration, several factors seem to determine the quality of all in-law relationships. They are marital adjustment, the nature and type of family rituals, dependency on one's own parents, dependency on one's parents-in-law, problem-solving strategies used with in-laws, and interpersonal relating style (Berg-Cross and Jackson, 1986).

Marital Adjustment

Some theorists have found that a relationship exists between marital adjustment and in-law adjustment (Lager, 1977). But, clearly, the relationship is not simple or linear. One couple can increase their happiness by excluding or marginalizing the role of the in-laws, another couple will increase their happiness by enhancing interaction and interdependence with in-laws. The optimal level of interaction varies, also, for the same couple across the various family life stages. So, although most couples prefer some distance in the early years of marriage, when children arrive, they desire increased contact with parents and in-laws.

Empirical research in this area is sparse to nonexistent. There are at least two published reports that have failed to find a relationship between marital adjustment and in-law adjustment (Hoye, 1971; Jackson and Berg-Cross, 1988). Contrary to popular stereotypes, women and men may be able to separate these two family relationships so that one does not significantly affect the other. Clinicians will find distressed couples who view their spouse as "just like the rest of his/her family," but they will also find many distressed couples who cannot understand how the spouse can be so different from the loved in-laws.

Quality of Relationship with Other Family Members

The in-law relationship is greatly affected by the adult child's relationship with his or her parents. Fischer (1983) has noted that mother-daughter and mother-in-law and daughter-in-law relationships are similar in that both are intergenerational female-female bonds, bounded and defined by kinship networks. Because these two relationships are similar, and the mother-daughter relationship was present first, women may use their relationships with their mothers as models in the development of their relationships with their mothers-in-law. Women who are dependent on their mothers may look for that type of relationship with their mothers-in-law. Intuitively, it seems just as likely that they may reject help and support from their mothers-in-law because they rely only on their own mothers.

Yet the idea of transferring positive parental relationships to the in-law relationship is widespread. Womble (1966) had suggested that spouses with good parental relationships will more than likely have good in-law relationships, while unresolved parent-child tensions are sometimes transferred to the same-sex parent-in-law.

Parents-in-law bring their own limitations to the relationship. They are sometimes constrained in their repertoire and expectations because of experiences with their own in-laws. They have an image of the type of relationship that could or should exist between in-laws. Of course, all parent-in-laws try to avoid reenacting the horrors they experienced with their own in-laws. But if it was that simple, in-law relationships would be quite smooth. Whenever the new family structure is not evaluated on its own terms and old ideas of what an in-law should or should not do are guide behavior, tensions are common.

Another familial source of in-law tensions arises from the relationship between the parents and their other children. If the mother-in-law is totally involved in the lives of her two daughters, her daughter-in-law may be excluded or feel like an extra wheel. If a father has been disappointed in his own sons, he may look to his son-in-law to redeem the family expectations. The siblings may have jealousies or animosities that get played out through the in-law. Of course, once adult children divorce and remarry, in-law relationships become only more complex and continue to be a major source of conflict (Pirie and Protinsky, 1985).

Problem-Solving Strategies

Generational differences in child rearing, values, and lifestyle may very well cause conflicts among extended family members. People tend to develop characteristic ways of handling problems in specific role relationships. The four most popular strategies for dealing with in-law conflicts are to be tactfully assertive, avoidant, compliant, or defensive. For example, when a mother-in-law instructs a daughter-in-law in disciplining a child, the daughter-in-law may explain how she is going to handle it but acknowledge that the mother-in-law's children might have reacted better to her strategies (tactful assertive); listen quietly and quickly leave the house (avoidant); verbally acknowledge that the mother-in-law has a good idea even if she does not feel that way (compliant), or tell the mother-in-law that she has not been educated in child psychology and does not understand what works with her grandchild (defensive). When a child-in-law and parent-in-law are both using problem-solving styles that grate on the other, it will be much more difficult for them to have a good relationship.

Jackson and Berg-Cross (1988) found that when a daughter-in-law used compliant problem-solving strategies, she reported a very good relationship with her mother in-law. As expected, though, women reported using a tactful assertive strategy most often with both their mothers and mothers-in-law. These young women seemed to feel comfortable asserting themselves in conflict situations even though, with their mothers-in-law, they were rewarded for compliancy. Women were much more likely to be compliant with their own mothers than with their mothers-in-law. The use of a compliant strategy means taking the subservient role in the conflict. Perhaps the women felt more comfortable assuming this role with their mother due to the historical comfort with this relationship. With mothers-in-law, adult daughters sought equality (to de-identify the mother-in-law as an older person to whom one owed deference), even though compliance led to a better relationship.

Helping Behaviors

Not too long ago, parent-in-laws were a major source of support for young married people. Adult children were later the sole source of support for their elderly in-laws. As the extended family has weakened, so also have these patterns of support. Direct help still does occur—but it is to a lesser extent than in prior generations. The current national pattern is for parents to give more help to their adult children and in-laws than vice versa. The money seems to continually flow from parents to children. Services are more reciprocal. Either way, the help occurs mostly in crisis situations and for short periods of time. For example, Chang (1990) found that Taiwanese mothers-in-law were just as likely, or more likely, than their own mothers to help the mother of twins.

Goetting (1990) reviewed the in-law research and concluded that today's in-law relationships do not entail intense helping relationships and most offer minimal direct support. She did note that the parent-daughter link continues to be the strongest. The wife's parents tend to provide more assistance than the male's parents. The wife's parents also request and receive more assistance. However, unlike previous generations, grandmothers are not highly involved in child care, even though more young mothers are in need of child care than at any other time in history. Grandmothers are themselves out working or involved in active retirement pursuits. Most have no desire and feel no need to take on the child-rearing responsibilities of their grandchildren.

Goetting (1990) reports that parents help the most in the first ten years of the marriage. Financial help occurs most in the earliest years of the marriage, and then services come to predominate. One study found 79 percent of parents offered moderate financial and service help to the young couple. This included buying furniture, household equipment, and making down payments on homes or cars. Services included gardening, painting, house repair, and watching the grandchildren during vacations. Grandparents seem to offer the most help to preschool children. After this initial surge of help, parents stop providing help on a regular basis and come forth only in times of emergency. If one group is neglected by their in-laws, it is working-class males. They clearly receive the least from their parents and their in-laws at any point in the marriage.

When the parents are elderly and require home care, it is invariably the daughter or daughter-in-law who is initially called on to provide this (Globerman, 1996). Women caught between caring for their still-growing children and aging dependent parents and parents-in-law are called the sandwich generation for good reason. They are being painfully squeezed between the two forces that have given form and meaning to their life. Most elderly parents do receive help from their children when needed, but the intensity of help varies with ethnicity, geography, social class, and other limiting life situations.

Most U.S. families cannot provide long-term care for an ailing parent. When they do attempt this, it often requires over thirty hours a week. Brody and Schoonover (1986) report that when the wife is the primary caretaker of her elderly mother, the husband is really a coparticipant—providing over fourteen hours a week of direct aid to the widowed mother-in-law; nearly half of the thirty-four hours reportedly contributed by the wives. The break-down of time is interesting: The men reported the following number of hours associated with the following tasks: personal care, 2.2; housework/ laundry, 2.2; meal preparation, 2.2; using the telephone, 1.0; managing money/arranging services, 1.4; shopping, transportation, 1.5; and emotional support, 3.8. When the wives were employed, the rate of husband contribution went up to fifteen hours a week; when the wife was unemployed, the husband still contributed 12.5 hours a week.

Even in Japan, where caring for the elderly has traditionally been a revered job, women are now expressing high levels of burden as they attempt to provide long-term care for parents who are victims of stroke and dementia. Harris and Long (1993) found Japanese women reporting high degrees of stress whether caring for their own parents (which was the case for 43 percent of the group interviewed) or their in-laws (which was the case for 57 percent of the group interviewed). In the United States, caring for an in-law is perceived as far more stressful than caring for one's own parent. This is primarily due to the fact that women are motivated to care for their own parents by affection and reciprocity. They most often end up caring for in-laws by default, motivated by a sense of responsibility and decency (Globerman, 1996).

Interpersonal Styles of Relating

Individuals develop their own style of relating to others. According to Schutz (1966, 1978), interpersonal relating styles consist of three interpersonal needs: affection, inclusion, and control. These three needs vary in terms of how much they are expressed to others and how much they are desired from others. Together, they determine an individual's style of relating to other people. Interpersonal relating styles are composed, therefore, of six components: expressed inclusion of others, expressed control over others, expressed affection toward others, wanted inclusion of self by others, wanted relinquishing of control to others (dependency), and wanted affection from others.

Affection Needs

For some men and women, the quality of a relationship is directly proportional to the intensity of the emotional relationship. Intensity is expressed by frequent contact and an intermingling of values and goals. Most times, it involves a great deal of reciprocal self-disclosure, touching, and hugging. If one in-law is a private person with low intimacy needs and is trying to adapt to an in-law with high intimacy needs, feelings on both sides are likely to be hurt until a compromised style of relation is negotiated.

Inclusion Needs

The need for inclusion refers to the desire to interact and associate with others. For some people, good relationships depend on having shared good times together. They like to be included in important events and activities. Participation in these events serves as a bonding mechanism for these people. They feel that they belong and are important to the other person because they have shared an event. Other people, though, can vary considerably on this trait and may have very low inclusion needs. They prefer to be left alone without all the commotion. For example, one parent-in-law or child-in-law might feel terrible about not being included in a meeting with the caterer to decide on the final items for the wedding buffet. Others would be just as happy not being invited to go along.

Jackson and Berg-Cross (1988) found a significant negative correlation between wanted inclusion and mother-in-law adjustment. The more the young woman's style was to want others to take the initiative and include her in activities and conversation, the more likely she was to have a poor relationship with her mother-in-law. This finding suggests that the women who rely on others to initiate interactions may not achieve the level of interaction from mothers-in-law that they desire. They may interpret the absence of mothers-in-law initiated interactions as a negative reaction to them personally, and feel that they are disliked by their mothers-in-law. Thus, a mother-in-law who does not invite her daughter-in-law to participate in activities will likely find herself with a disappointed daughter-in-law if she has high wanted inclusion needs.

Jackson and Berg-Cross (1988) also found that the more a woman spoke with her mother-in-law by phone, the more positive the relationship with her mother-in-law. This finding suggests that regular contact is important in the mother-in-law/daughter-in-law relationship. The chicken-and-egg question is important to highlight here, for it is completely plausible that the reason that positive mother-in-law/daughter-in-law relationships are associated with greater telephone contact is that because they like each other, they talk to each other more. More phone contact among unfriendly in-laws might even worsen the situation.

Control Needs

Control needs refer to the need to have decision-making power over others. People vary on how important it is for them to be able to influence other people. For people high on the need for control, the urge to make decisions and guide the activity of themselves and those around them is almost irresistible. Others are relieved to delegate the burden of decision making. Obviously, it is the people low in control needs who mostly grease the wheels of group life. Yet for young couples, it is often developmentally productive to feel a strong need to shape and control the foundations of one's adult life. When a parent-in-law has high control needs, conflict with a developmentally healthy young couple is very likely. Parents-in-law need to follow a simple farming dictum: Overseed the in-laws with praise and weed out all advice and criticism.

Parents-in-law start off with most of the power. They potentially have more influence over the son or daughter-in-law than the young married person has over them. The reasons for this are fairly obvious. First, the parent generation has many emotional chips that can be played either to ease the young marital relationship or to complicate it. The power of the parents is partly societally defined and partly defined by the dynamics within any parent-child dyad.

The power of money. The most obvious type of power currency between in-laws is economic. This is the power of the purse. The one who brings home the bacon has deed to the castle. Families develop different types of expectations about how money will be used between adult children and their parents.

Many immigrant families want nothing more than for their children to be more successful than themselves and marry more successfully than themselves. They have sacrificed their homeland just to make this possible; it is their dream. If their son-in-law makes a lot of money, they are happy to make him a respected and powerful family member. They are willing to defer to him in matters of indecision. If the daughter-in-law is the big breadwinner, the in-laws are often torn between their traditional expectations that their son should be the one to succeed and the fact that the whole family is being uplifted by the daughter-in-law. All too often, both young people suffer from strained in-law relationships when the woman earns more. Her parents-in-law all too often come to feel that she does not appreciate their son and has abdicated the traditional values of hearth and home. When the son is unemployed, underemployed, or in a low-income job, the wife's salary is a reminder that their son does not have a prestigious job. For each set of parents I have met who have been grateful and overjoyed that their son is getting the financial support and backing that he needs from a successful wife, I have met a set of parents who cannot adjust to this role reversal. The woman who earns more than her husband may also find this to be a point of friction between her parents and her husband. A most common reaction of the woman's parents is that the husband is taking advantage of her—that their little girl should have been taken care of and not be in the reverse position. Using in-law expectations as an indicator, gender expectations are strong and constant as we begin the twenty-first century.

The relative income of the parents also plays a big role in defining the in-law power relationships. When parents have much more money than their children, they tend to think that this gives them the privilege of forever having power over them. Advising them, telling them where they went wrong, how they can save themselves or advance themselves are all within their privileged domain. Young married adults develop enormous resentments against these types of intrusions. Here is one power battle that usually drives the couple together against the in-laws. Neither of them wants economic currency to be as valuable in the power game as it apparently is. Both children will resent the parental power that derives from this source.

The power of dependency. When the adult child is very dependent or enmeshed with the family of origin, the parents will wield great power as in-laws. The adult child will get agitated when the mate misunderstands or berates the loved parent. He or she will feel irrational needs to defend, protect, and interpret the parent's behaviors and intentions to the spouse. The child-in-law in these situations often feels as though he or she is in competition with the parent for the love of the spouse.

It has been hypothesized that a great deal of dependency on the family of origin can poorly affect the establishment of good relations with the spouse and spouse's family of origin (Christensen and Johnson, 1971). Hoye (1971) found that the more husbands remained dependent on their fathers, the more difficulty they had in their relationships with their mothers-in-law, but no relationship was found between parent dependence and mother-in-law adjustment for the wives. Jackson and Berg-Cross (1988) found a weak but significant positive correlation between a women's dependency on in-laws and mother-in-law adjustment.

Husbands and wives, in our culture, feel that the primary emotional allegiance should be to each other. If one mate perceives that the other is emotionally more involved with the family of origin, he or she suffers all the jealousy and rage that one feels when infidelity is suspected. They may also feel guilty for having such feelings, because the rational argument is that every child is entitled to love his or her parents. How could they be so silly and spiteful?

A classic case of such dependency occurred in a young entrepreneur who was married to a successful professional woman. They had met on the East Coast and spent the first year of their married life there. When they returned to their home in the Midwest, they moved within a few miles of the wife's family. The wife was always on the phone recounting the events of the day with the mother or seeking the advice of the father on an upcoming decision. She tried to get her husband to go along with spending a good deal of the weekend with them. She so enjoyed the time that she spent with her family that she could not understand her husband's resentment of his mother- and father-in-law. The husband would get migraine headaches when he had to spend a whole day with his in-laws. He felt marginalized and infantilized with them. He felt unneeded and unimportant because whenever his wife needed comfort or advice, she felt the best and most rational resource was her parents. She did not understand her husband's resentment and felt their closeness was a cause of celebration. She saw no reason to be antagonistic and labeled her husband as "irrationally jealous" because she had a good relationship with her parents.

Actually, in today's world, it is not uncommon for a therapist (or talk show host) to see "mama's boys" who cannot develop healthy interdependent lives with their spouses because they are still dependent and spoiled by their aging mothers. It is said that we are a society that underfathers and overmothers our men. Significant numbers of bachelors who live at home or on their own have their mothers clean and/or cook for them, and consult them on decoration. When such a man marries, he continues to be very dependent on his mother. The wife feels inadequate or used in the nurturing department. The husband may be unable to open up and confide in his wife, yet he loves to sit down with his mother for hours on end and share opinions. He may seek his mother's advice on how to deal with his wife's demands as well. In terms of helping behaviors, older women who perpetuate a mama's boy relationship with their sons are classic enablers. They cook, clean, and act as real estate scouts, home health nurses, loan officers, and travel agents. They keep the dependent relationship going by rationalizing that others are jealous of the closeness and intimacy that they are able to share with their grown sons. They are just reaping the emotional rewards of having sacrificed so much for so long.

When adult children retain strong dependency needs on their family of origin, the family usually reciprocates and reinforces the dependency. Although close-knit families usually welcome a new recruit with open arms, other families are so enmeshed that they have little desire or need to know or care about the people whom their kin have married. They remain "Johnny's wife" or "Allison's husband"—never a person in their own right. This makes control attempts by the in-laws all the more objectionable, because they are being treated as "nonpersons" emotionally and are subject to the whims of the "important people" in the family of origin.

Power of family indebtedness. The intensity of positive emotion toward parents is related to the intensity of felt filial obligations (Safilios-Rothschild, 1974). The culture promotes and sanctions the idea that adult children should continue to let their parents influence certain aspects of their behavior well into their twenties (or as long as they are financially contributing to the child). First, parents may know more about the economics of setting up a first household, and buying cars and appliances. Their expertise makes them feel that they would be derelict not to let their children benefit from their years of experience. Second, even without overt pressure, adult children are still trying hard to please, appease, and live up to parental expectations. Just knowing that your parents think it is a sin to buy any camera other than a Nikon will make you squirm as your mate prepares to buy a Canon. Third, even when children are estranged or bitter toward one's parents, there are gnawing tugs and pulls to balance the ledger and make the parents proud of the type of person one has become. This desire or willingness to be influenced by one's parents becomes a major source of contention in many marriages. Sons-in-law or daughters-in-law have the illusion that they are the only or primary persons to whom the spouse should look for reassurance and guidance. To let the parents influence an adult child is to indirectly erode the power of the mate and directly question the wisdom and maturity of the mate to make independent decisions.

Power and allegiance are intermingled concepts in the family. If you allow the elder generation to influence your decisions, then you are not only acknowledging the power they have, but you are sanctioning that influence.

The first years of a marriage are sometimes centered on this power struggle between the parent-in-law and the child-in-law to see who has more influence on the child spouse. This is really the struggle of romantic love and obligations over filial love and obligations. One woman, on the brink of hysteria, pleaded with her husband during a session not to spend their vacation at the mother-in-law's lake house. She cried, "I lose my husband the minute we walk in the door. Within thirty seconds, he's her son and he stays a son till he walks out the door to go home. I'm treated like some pathetic little girlfriend who has come along to be part of the decorations." The actual interactions that make the husband turn into a son can vary dramatically. Parents have the power to pull different strings with different children. It may be remarking that it is not a good investment to buy a condo in the city compared to the suburbs that is perceived as "interfering in letting us live where we want to live," or it may be suggesting that the daughter-in-law take only one course in night school so the baby will not be in day care so much that is perceived as "wanting me to sit home and take care of her son and grandson."

Thus, the first repercussion of acknowledging the power of the family of origin on the spouse is that the illusion of fusion and oneness between the spouses is destroyed. Suddenly, they do not share the same intensity of feeling about borrowing the $2,000 for the car down payment. They begin to realize that they have different levels of investment in the parents, different interpretations of intent, and different evaluations about parental behavior. Such sharp differences make the reality of "aloneness" difficult for many young adults.

Of course, most grown children are themselves very critical of their parents and of their parents' attempts to control or influence the course of their life. Most grown children ignore parents or argue with them when they feel that their parents are overstepping their bounds of influence. However, the child's right to criticize the parent freely is rarely ceded to the spouse. It's the old "I can call them anything I like, but you better watch your words" syndrome. Despite the complaints of the spouse, the child feels the ambivalence of wanting to please the parent despite the warts that have been discovered.

**THERAPEUTIC INTERVENTION 1:
TECHNIQUES FOR IMPROVING IN-LAW RELATIONSHIPS**

What are the ways to constructively resolve power issues with the in-laws? The following guidelines can be used as stimulus points for discussions with clients.

Develop a one-to-one relationship with your in-laws. The emotional wrath directed at a controlling in-law can be diluted by having a direct relationship instead of one mediated solely by marriage. When in-laws find activities or topics that can be shared in a meaningful way, they begin to have a personal relationship instead of an appendage relationship. It is much easier to deal with a mother-in-law who is asking the young couple to come spend the entire weekend with her if the daughter-in-law knows

(continued)

(continued)

that she can enjoy a portion of the time shopping with the mother-in-law or watching Sunday football with her. Alienated in-laws will protest that they share nothing in common with their in-law. A detailed exploration will usually uncover at least a few possible bridges. The therapeutic challenge is to motivate the in-law to want to create an interdependent relationship—to choose to get to know this person who has suddenly entered his or her life.

When in-laws do not respect each other, the key is to narrowly develop goals that bring out the best of oneself in a difficult situation (e.g., "I will try to spend thirty minutes admiring my father-in-law's weed whacker"). Instead of raging at the injustice of having such in-laws, the emotional burden should be directed inward toward developing the resources needed in difficult circumstances.

Be compliant: Choose your battles carefully. It is probably true that in any in-law relationship, compliance is the road to peaceful interactions. Jackson and Berg-Cross (1988) found that compliance in the daughter-in-law was one of the best predictors of a positive mother-in-law and daughter-in-law relationship. But what are the long-term effects of compliance? If one simply goes to the in-laws and reinforces intrusive demands, will it not simply be an ever-increasing spiral? Yes and no. Clearly, some controlling people are an endless pit of demands and at no point will they decide to treat a compliant person more equitably. However, a much greater number of people are, indeed, very controlling by nature, and yet, when they find someone who is compliant, they become very endeared to that person. "How wonderful" they say, "it is to find someone who is able to appreciate how logical, efficient, and well-meaning my suggestions and viewpoints are." The more compliant an in-law, the more he or she tends to be valued and loved. Over a long period of time, compliant in-laws gain enormous power because they are loved members of the family. A slowly emerging assertiveness can be accepted more easily because the in-law has "paid his [or her] dues" and shown himself (herself) to be emotionally responsive.

Do not triangulate a spouse into the problems that the partner is having with the in-law. Whenever two people are in conflict, it is irresistible to draw a third person into the fray to gain a majority view. When couples fight, each party looks to the family of origin for vindication and support. The more emotionally fused the family of origin, the more likely they are to be triangulated into the conflict. When not fighting directly with each other, the spouses still have split loyalties—they must remain loyal to their mate and to their parents. So when a spouse talks ill of the in-laws, the mate feels a filial obligation to defend their behavior. The family of origin shadows a marriage like the rain forest shadows the plants beneath its canopy. It can nourish all that grows but also severely limits diversity and development.

Partners need to learn how to take their issues with their in-laws directly to the in-laws. So often, children-in-law want their spouses to mediate the conflicts they are having with the in-laws. They want their spouses to

(continued)

(continued)

change the in-laws' attitudes or behaviors or simply to emotionally disown their own parents. This is virtually never a successful venture. When partners learn to deal directly with the in-laws, taking up the issues that are creating the conflict, solutions become more likely.

Create clear boundaries that can change as the families change. If a mother does not want her child and child-in-law to push her toward a particular type of retirement, she has to tell them that their advice in this area is not desired at this point in time. When the boundaries are clear between the intergenerational families, both sides can learn to accept rights to privacy and independence. The trouble comes, most often, when blatantly discrepant boundaries exist between "kin" and "non-kin." When the mother is willing to accept all types of advice from her son but doesn't want to hear any input from her daughter-in-law, the mother and son become aligned in a way that reduces the daughter-in-law to a peripheral position. The daughter-in-law becomes excluded from the emotional life of the extended family, and it limits open communication between the spouses.

This is not to minimize how important it is for each adult child to have time alone with his or her parents. But when the purpose of the time together is to conduct all family business outside the awareness of the in-law, the in-law becomes estranged and angry.

Self-disclose. Partners are often afraid to self-disclose to their in-laws, but in-laws have no way of getting to know the new family member if he or she presents himself or herself only in the limited role of "Johnny's wife" or "Sue's husband." We all resent people controlling us when we do not know them or feel that they do not know us. The more people self-disclose to one another, the less important it is to maintain control over one another, and the more likely a suggestion will be interpreted as "helping" rather than "intruding."

THERAPEUTIC INTERVENTION 2:
SHARING GENOGRAMS ON INTERPERSONAL STYLES

As husbands and wives struggle to work out new ways of relating to in-laws, a genogram that allows the couple to inspect the interactions of all the in-law relationships in their family tree often provides insights into why they are "stuck" in particular modes.

Many men discover that none of the men in their family tree had carved out meaningful relationships with their in-laws. Some women are shocked to realize that all of the women, for generations, have felt they were betraying their mothers if they became too close to a mother-in-law. Sometimes one discovers a role model who was able to carve out a successful relationship in a difficult circumstance. Sharing the world of familial experiences is a broadening and deepening experience for the couple and is essential as they try to build a community model of in-law relationships.

Family Rituals and the In-Law Relationship

Family rituals are emotionally charged interactions that are repeated again and again for the pleasure and comfort that family members derive from them. Family rituals serve many of the same purposes as societal rituals, including protection, cohesiveness, communication, intergenerational transmission, identity development, understanding of unconscious phenomena, and providing a sense of continuity and stability in a constantly changing world (Bossard and Boll, 1950; Morval and Biron, 1993).

One of the most slippery tasks of married couples is to find ways to continue sharing rituals with their family of origin while developing rituals that will sustain the new nuclear family. Each family unit searches for ways to graft unique family rituals onto their traditional roots. Unfortunately, because of the emotional importance of ritual, this is easier said than done (Rosenthal and Marshall, 1988).

Several studies have shown that in the United States, families tend to organize many of their rituals around six core events: Christmas dinners, Thanksgiving dinners, birthdays, the exchange of Christmas gifts, Mother's Day, and weekly or monthly phone calls. These nodal events serve as convenient markers around which to build the rituals so important for keeping a sense of the family alive. A family's rituals set it apart from the larger society. They become its trademark, symbolizing its particular tastes and values, and helping it maintain its unique identity (Berg-Cross, Daniels, and Carr, 1992; Schvanevedlt and Lee, 1983).

One of the first and most important rituals for families is the wedding ceremony. Although the marriage is the symbolic beginning of a new life for the adult children, it is also the symbolic diminishment of the parental role. In addition, many parents are faced with the jarring realities that will now constrain the child's future life and they must give up their unbounded, grandiose expectations. Marriage is an event in which each in-law, as well as the bride and groom, needs to be symbolically acknowledged, pampered, and glorified. The wedding becomes the footbridge between the two families. The more sturdy and reliable it is, the more frequently it will be used. Families that can negotiate the different meaningful wedding rituals so that everyone feels that their emotional needs are recognized are on the way to a successful in-law relationship. It pays off, handsomely, to work out the wedding arrangements so that it is a win-win situation for everyone (Benatar, 1989).

The family of origin can have rituals that strengthen a new couple's bonds to each other, or the rituals can be very destructive to the new couple. For example, a ritual that the extended family share a beach house each year may be very destructive to some couples who need that time to regroup alone, and it can be very constructive for couples who are unable to afford a vacation any other way or who need the nurturance and company of family to relieve them of their daily pressures. Rituals can have this direct influence: strengthening or straining the relationships in a uniquely different way for each couple.

Once a ritual is in place, no one need worry about what should be done at that time, or by whom. Everyone can relax and enjoy being "us"—at once unique and part of a common culture. Rituals become a main strategy for allowing the family to relive important cohesive-building emotions, thoughts, and sentiments.

A recent study at Howard University (Berg-Cross, Daniels, and Carr 1992) indicated that ritual activity and marital satisfaction were related. Ten years after their marriage, couples who had remained married regularly shared an average of forty-two rituals. Couples who had divorced reported sharing only twenty-five rituals, on the average. The higher a husband and wife rated their marital satisfaction, the more rituals they were likely to engage in. The study also found that couples who had remained married claimed not to miss rituals they had shared with their family of origin but had lost over the years. On the other hand, couples who had divorced stated that the family-of-origin rituals they had lost during the marriage were very important to them.

This last finding hints at the destructive potential of flouting rituals that are important to a mate or the mate's family. The importance of rituals cuts two ways. Because families have so much invested in their rituals, changing or omitting any one of them—even the trivial—threatens the family's identity. It is that sense of threat—often unconscious—that sparks in-law animosities that seem out of proportion to the "trigger." In blended families, developing successful rituals becomes even more complex, for in-laws are usually even more estranged from the second or third husband or wife.

THERAPEUTIC INTERVENTION 3:
FAMILY-OF-ORIGIN SESSIONS

If in-law problems are a major focus of the couple's ongoing conflicts and there are important, unresolved issues between the adult children and their parents, family-of-origin sessions can provide a critical opportunity for change. Instead of using the daughter-in-law or son-in-law to play out old family animosities and insecurities, the adult child must confront and heal the family wounds. Family-of-origin sessions were developed by James Framo (1994) in his quest to help adult children and their parents acknowledge and deal with the developmental milestones and traumas that are part of the family's history. The sessions usually involve the entire family of

(continued)

(continued)

origin: mother, father, and siblings. Even when parents are divorced, both are asked to attend the family-of-origin session. When stepparents are historically involved, they also are asked to attend. Aunts, uncles, or cousins who lived with the client during childhood and acted as "immediate kin" are included when at all possible. The goals of the session include helping to free the family from being arrested at a specific family stage, to acknowledge mistakes, to extend forgiveness, and to grow into the current life dynamic of the family.

The sessions last anywhere from one to four hours. They usually begin by having someone in the family volunteer to provide a picture of what the family life was like when the children were growing up. Others are then asked to clarify, confirm, or expand on what has been presented. Within a short time, major themes emerge. Whether it is the family that had to deal with a chronically ill member, or the family that protected the father from confronting his alcoholism, or the mother who psychologically abused her children and spouse, the major sores open quickly and ooze. The therapist is directive, working so that each person's pain is recognized and acknowledged. The unintended nature of many hurtful events is exposed so that forgiveness can be asked for and received.

The purpose of this cathartic session is to enable the family to openly and honestly confront the future by putting aside the past. The in-law situation is saved for the last part of the session, so that the current conflict is understood in the context of the whole history of the family. Both sides can then openly express their frustrations and desires at this point. The therapist helps the family of origin find ways of effectively reaching out to include the new in-law or find ways of giving the couple the space they need to make the marriage work.

THERAPEUTIC INTERVENTION 4: AN IN-LAW ATTENDS THE COUPLE'S SESSION

When in-laws are geographically close, it is often helpful for them to come to a joint session so that the therapist can help guide a productive problem-solving conversation. These sessions must begin by each person (husband, wife, and in-laws) feeling that their point of view is being heard and acknowledged. Sometimes, this is accomplished by having each person state the best thing about their in-law relationship and the most difficult part of their in-law relationship. Other times, the participants are asked to describe what makes them angry in the relationship, how they handle the anger, and what the effect of their anger management strategy has been so far.

After everyone has expressed their view of the situation, the goal is to quickly get each person to define what he or she could do to help relieve

(continued)

(continued)

the despair of each of the other participants. The costs and rewards of this "altruistic" behavior are analyzed for each of the participants. For example, a mother-in-law who dotes on her daughter by anticipating her every need (rides to the airport, housecleaning, gifts for relatives) is perceived by her son-in-law as running their lives. The mother-in-law suggests, with a hearty laugh, that she could help relieve the despair of her son-in-law by asking for favors instead of being so nice. Everyone pursued that possibility until the mother-in-law came up with a serious list of favors she would appreciate, including making her feel that her expressions of love were valid!

It is stressed that the solutions developed in the session are only "hunches" of what may work or may not work. The goal of the session is to develop as many educated "hunches" as possible. Events following the session will determine to what extent they work. The session ends with each person being congratulated by the therapist for one of their concessions or solutions.

LEARNING AIDS

Therapeutic Dialogue (In-Laws)

1. How much discrepancy is there between how close you are to various in-laws and how close you would like to be to them? What are the different degrees of in-law closeness among other members of your family and your friends? Ideally, how close would you like to be to each of your in-laws? What is the rationale for your ideal relationship? How can you change your model of the ideal relationship to make it more attainable?

2. How much discrepancy is there between how much affection is shown between the various in-laws and how much affection you feel comfortable with? What are the different degrees of in-law affection among other members of your family and your friends? Ideally, how much affection would you like to be able to share with each of your in-laws? What is the rationale for your ideal relationship? How can you change your model of the ideal relationship to make it more attainable?

3. How much discrepancy is there between how much equity there is among the various in-laws and how much equity you would like there to be? What are the in-law power discrepancies that exist among other members of your family and your friends? Ideally, how

equitable would you like your relationship to be to each of your in-laws? What is the rationale for your ideal relationship? How can you change your model of the ideal relationship to make it more attainable?

4. What are the family rituals of your in-laws that you most enjoy and what are the ones that are most difficult for you? How much sharing of family rituals exists among the other families and friends that you know? Ideally, how would you like the two families to blend or keep their boundaries? What is the rationale for your ideal relationship? How can you change your image of the ideal relationship to make it more attainable?

5. How much help would you like from your in-laws? How much help do you think they would like from you? What are the different types of helping relationships that exist among other families and friends with whom you are familiar? Ideally, what are the boundaries that should govern helping behavior among in-laws? How can you change your ideal relationship to make it more attainable?

Self-Exploration 1: Family-of-Origin and In-Law Values and Attitudes Scale

Circle A or B, depending on which phrase or statement is more descriptive of your family. When you have finished, compare your answers with your spouse's answers. How different were your cultural backgrounds? Discuss how this has affected your ability to deal with your in-laws.

	A	B
1.	Spendthrifts	Stingy
2.	Materialistic	Nonmaterialistic
3.	Realistic	Idealistic
4.	Politically liberal	Politically conservative
5.	Outdoor types	Indoor types
6.	Traditional view of women	Progressive view of women
7.	Optimists	Pessimists
8.	Confident	Insecure
9.	Assertive	Compliant
10.	Talkers	Nontalkers
11.	Loud	Quiet
12.	Rational	Emotional
13.	Fighters	Nonfighters
14.	Individually oriented	Family-oriented
15.	Many rituals	Few rituals
16.	Independent	Interdependent

17.	Anger expressers	Anger inhibitors
18.	Rigid	Flexible
19.	Warm	Cold
20.	Cohesive	Noncohesive
21.	Clean	Cluttered
22.	Religious	Nonreligious
23.	Productive	Chaotic

Sample Workshop Flowchart Intended for Groups of Four or Five Couples Working with In-Laws

I. Psychoeducational Strategies
   A. Describe the four types of in-law combinations and general characteristics of each one.
   B. Describe the five factors affecting in-law adjustment
      1. Marital adjustment
      2. Quality of relationship with other family members
      3. Problem-solving strategies
      4. Interpersonal style of relating
      5. Family rituals
   C. Take time to go over the three interpersonal styles of relating and how the use of power affects in-law relationships.
   D. Go over constructive ways of resolving power issues with in-laws.
   E. Describe the different assimilation models used in culturally and religiously diverse in-law relationships.

II. Self-Explorations (Done by couples in private and shared before rejoining the group)
   A. The Family-of-Origin and In-Law Values and Attitude Scale

III. Therapeutic Dialogue (Done by couples in private and shared before rejoining the group)
   (Proceeding in the order presented, both partners respond to each question before going on to discuss the next question)
   In the group, the therapist explores with couples how relationship goals can be achieved by modifying overly ambitious, pie-in-the-sky expectations. Using information about their current situation and the realities seen among friends and family, couples fine-tune expectations so they are achievable and motivate rather than discourage attempts at change.

IV. Therapeutic Interventions
   Work with a couple in front of the group and apply one or more of the therapeutic interventions. Share rationale during demonstrations. Let group discuss additional interventions.

    A. Techniques for improving in-law relationships
    B. Sharing genograms on interpersonal styles
    C. Family-of-origin session
    D. In-law attends couple session

V. Finding the Motivation and Time to Make the Changes
    Group discussion

Bibliotherapy

Averick, L. (1989). *The in-law book: Coping with the strangers that you are related to.* New York: Shapolsky.
Bilofsky, P. (1992). *In-laws: Out-laws: How to make peace with his family and yours.* New York: Fawcett.
Petsonk, J., and Remsen, R. (1988). *The intermarriage handbook.* New York: William Morrow.

Videotherapy

*Father of the Bride. (*1991). Directed by Charles Shyer. Father unwilling to let go of his little girl.
Romeo and Juliet. (1968). Directed by Franco Zeffirelli. Archetypal story of how family of origin interferes with true love and its tragic consequences.
The Wedding Banquet. (1993). Directed by Ang Lee. Gay Taiwanese-American tries to fool his parents via a fake wedding.

Professional Development Questions (In-Law Relationships)

1. When in-law relationships are disturbed by differing cultural expectations, how should the therapy proceed to help the couple resolve the impasse?

2. Under what circumstances would you believe that having the in-laws attend a couple session or cross-generational session would be indicated?

3. What ethical issues might become important when one includes in-laws in the couples therapy process?

4. In premarital counseling sessions, which aspects of the in-law relationship do you believe would be most important to discuss with a

young couple (in their twenties), a career age couple (in their thirties), a second-marriage couple, and an older couple (in their sixties)?

REFERENCES

Adler, L., Denmark, F., and Ahmed, R. (1989). Attitudes toward mother-in-law and stepmother: A cross-cultural study. *Psychological Reports, 65*(3, pt. 2), 1194.

Benatar, M. (1989). "Marrying off" children as a developmental stage. *Clinical Social Work Journal, 17*(3), 223-231.

Berg-Cross, L., Daniels, C., and Carr, P. (1992). Marital rituals among divorced and married couples. *Journal of Divorce and Remarriage, 18*(1), 1-32.

Berg-Cross, L. and Jackson, J. (1986). Helping the extended family: In-law growth and development training program. *Psychotherapy in Private Practice, 4*(1), 33-50.

Bossard, J. and Boll, E. (1950). *Ritual in family living.* Philadelphia: University of Pennsylvania Press.

Boszormenyi-Nagy, I. and Spark, G. M. (1973). *Invisible loyalties.* New York: Harper & Row.

Brody, E. M. and Schoonover, C. B. (1986). Patterns of parent-care when adult daughters work and when they do not. *Gerontologist, 26*(4), 372-381.

Chang, C. (1990). Raising twin babies and problems in the family. *Acta Geneticae Medicae et Gemellogogiae (Twin Research), 39*(4), 501-505.

Choi, S. and Keith, P. (1991). Are "worlds of pain" cross-cultural? Korean working class marriages. *Journal of Comparative Family Studies, 22*(3), 293-312.

Christensen, H. T. and Johnson, K. P. (1971). *Marriage and the family* (Third edition). New York: Ronald Press.

Duvall, E. R. (1954). *In-laws: Pro and con: An original study of interpersonal relations.* New York: Association Press.

Fischer, L. R. (1983). Mothers and mothers-in-law. *Journal of Marriage and the Family, 45*(1), 187-192.

Framo, J. (1994). The family life cycle: Impressions. *Contemporary Family Therapy: An International Journal, 16*(2), 87-117.

Globerman, J. (1996). Motivations to care: Daughters and sons-in-law caring for relatives with Alzheimer's disease. *Family Relations, 45*(1), 37-45.

Goetting, A. (1990). Patterns of support among in-laws in the United States: A review of research. *Journal of Family Issues, 11*(1), 67-90.

Harris, P., and Long, S. (1993). Daughter-in-law's burden: An exploratory study of caregiving in Japan. *Journal of Cross Cultural Gerontology, 8*(2), 97-118.

Hoye, D. C. (1971). Mother-in-law adjustment of young marrieds. *Dissertation Abstracts International, 31,* 21922-A.

Jackson, J. and Berg-Cross, L. (1988). Helping the extended family: Mother-in-law and daughter-in-law relationships among Black women. *Family Relations, 37*(3), 293-297.

Johnson, C. and Barer, B. (1987). Marital instability and the changing kinship networks of grandparents. *Gerontologist, 27*(3), 330-335.

Lager, E. (1977). Parents-in-law: Failure and divorce in a second chance family. *Journal of Marriage and Family Counseling, 3*(4), 19-23.

Morval, M. and Biron, G. (1993). Family rituals and their functions. *Therapie Familiale, 14*(2), 149-167.

Pirie, C. and Protinsky, H. (1985). Family therapy with an empirical basis. *International Journal of Family Psychiatry, 6*(4), 351-361.

Rosenthal, C. and Marshall, V. (1988). Generational transmission of family ritual. Special issue: Rituals and reunions. *American Behavioral Scientist, 31*(6), 669-684.

Safilios-Rothschild, C. (1974). *Women and social policy.* Englewood Cliffs, NJ: Prentice-Hall.

Schutz, W. (1966). *The interpersonal underworld.* New York: Basic Books.

Schutz, W. (1978). *FIRO awareness scales manual.* Palo Alto, CA: Consulting Psychologists.

Schvanevedlt, J. and Lee, T. (1983). The emergence and practice of ritual in the American family. *Family Perspective, 17*(13), 21-29.

Sussman, M. B. (1953). The help pattern in the middle class family. *American Sociological Review, 20*(1), 149-154.

Womble, D. L. (1966). *Foundations for marriage and family relations.* New York: Macmillan.

PART III.

THE ADAPTABILITY CORNERSTONE: FROM ADAPTABILITY TO RIGIDITY— REDUCING CONFLICT WITH EFFECTIVE COMMUNICATION

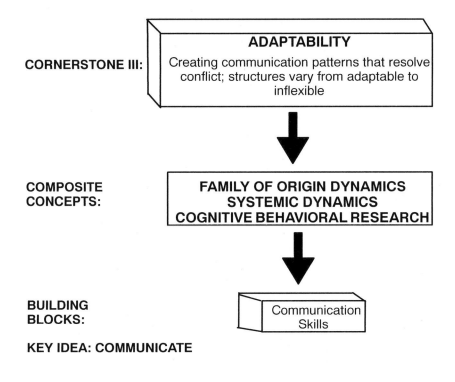

CORNERSTONE III:

ADAPTABILITY

Creating communication patterns that resolve conflict; structures vary from adaptable to inflexible

COMPOSITE CONCEPTS:

**FAMILY OF ORIGIN DYNAMICS
SYSTEMIC DYNAMICS
COGNITIVE BEHAVIORAL RESEARCH**

BUILDING BLOCKS:

Communication Skills

KEY IDEA: COMMUNICATE

THEORETICAL ORIENTATION: FAMILY SYSTEMS AND PSYCHODYNAMICS

The uneasy world of family life—where the greatest can fail and the humblest can succeed.

Melvin Chapman

The adaptability cornerstone is built on the routines that couples develop to resolve differences of opinion, unexpected crises, developmental life-stage transitions, and daily annoyances. The adaptability cornerstone contains the rules couples have developed to govern their relationship, including the distribution of power, the amount and type of intimacy, and the types of problem-solving strategies they employ. With a strong adaptability cornerstone, couples function effectively and smoothly. Productive and goal oriented, they are constantly growing and changing to meet the new demands of the relationship. Inflexibility and being stuck in the same ineffective routines typify individuals who are not strong in this area.

The most prevalent theories used by marital therapists to understand the communication problems in their clients are the family dynamic theories. Family dynamic theories focus on how developmental principles and psychological principles interact to govern relationships. Communication is an interpersonal event, and it makes sense that any attempt to understand communication patterns must be rooted in an understanding of the relationship between the client and his or her significant others. Family dynamic theories explain the interpersonal schemas that motivate couple communication, the dynamic factors that maintain functional and dysfunctional communication patterns, and the processes by which communication patterns can be changed.

The two most important family dynamic theories are psychodynamic theory and systems theory. Psychodynamic theory explains how relationships in the family of origin affect marital relationships. Systems theory explains how the couple is affected by current-day, nuclear-family relational pressures and dynamics. Each theoretical approach will be discussed in turn.

PSYCHODYNAMIC THEORIES

Psychodynamic theories explain couple conflicts by highlighting how adults continue to be affected by childhood conflicts and childhood failures in the psychosocial task of separation-individuation. When the couple's communication patterns are analyzed with a psychodynamic prism, identifying and acknowledging stylistic ways of responding to problems in the marital relationship serve as a springboard for the therapist to shift attention from the present situation to early childhood experiences that shaped partners' views of the world and taught them how to respond to intimate others. As they explore their childhood experiences with rejection, demands for perfection, and anger, they come to see that what was an adaptive or heroic attempt to cope as a child has lingered and become a handicap. This is what is meant by the term "object relations work" (Scharff and Scharff, 1991).

Indeed, Bowen (1978) and all object relations practitioners believe that successful marriages depend on each partner's ability to differentiate himself or herself from the family of origin so he or she can participate fully in their nuclear family as a unique individual. All too often, adults are emotionally fused with their family of origin into an "undifferentiated ego mass." When an adult person is still mired in a sticky, fused emotional family of childhood, the disavowed parts of the adult self continue to be repressed, rejected, or otherwise hidden from the adult partner one has chosen. The undifferentiated mate comes to the partnership crippled with emotional debt and unclear of how to balance the ledgers. The desire for pure and direct emotional interactions is distorted and stymied by the historical, unshakable need to hide who one really is and what one really feels. Routines for dealing with anger, hiding shame, asking for nurturance, and dealing with conflict are restricted to the rules of the family of origin. As we all know, many of those rules end up being far more damaging to us as adults than they ever were to us as children.

Bowen has found that when couples come in, despite the compelling nature of their ongoing conflicts, it is prudent to walk back and have them focus on their relationship with their parents instead of their relationship with their spouse. As one becomes freer to be a "whole but separate person," they return to the spouse without a hidden agenda, a covert need, or a misplaced anger. Compromise and appreciation for one's partner comes much easier when one comes in friendship and is not constantly fighting a childhood war on a distant battlefield with a stand-in enemy.

Framo (1976, 1982) has expanded on Bowen's work by having separate sessions with each spouse and his or her family of origin to work through some of the dysfunctional communication patterns in the place where they were seeded and fertilized. He summarizes the importance of early object relations work:

> The client, by having sessions with his or her family of origin, takes the problems back to where they began, thereby making available a direct route to etiological factors. Dealing with the real, external parental figures is designed to loosen the grip of the internal representatives of these figures and expose them to reality considerations and their live derivatives. Having gone backward in time, the individual can then move forward in dealing with the spouse and children in a more appropriate fashion, for their transference meaning has changed. (Framo, 1976, p. 194)

There are many secondary benefits to discussing historical childhood information in couples sessions. One practical advantage of dealing with material from childhood and the family of origin is that it helps the couple "cool down." "Talking about the events of their lives that happened before they knew each other depersonalizes the discussion and they can begin to listen to each other" (Fogarty, 1976, p. 147). Another advantage is that individuals often blame themselves for their partner's unhappiness. Learning how the partner came into the relationship with certain emotional proclivities relieves the guilty partner from shouldering the total burden for the marital problems.

A variety of therapeutic techniques allow men and women to work through their family-of-origin issues while working on their relationship. Most notable are family-of-origin sessions (à la Framo), which promote detriangulation. This technique involves the adult child talking directly to the parent outside of a therapy session about how he or she feels about being put in the middle, and developing one-on-one relationships with each of the parents as an adult (e.g., visiting the parents without the spouse, talking to the parents separately on the phone).

Marital relationships built on remediating felt childhood deprivations and winning the battles we could not win in our family of origin are doomed for failure. Such goals invariably lead to continuous frustration or arrested psychosocial development. When couples are successful in resolving these age-old problems, their relationship with their spouse improves as well as their relationship with their family of origin.

Projective Identification and Its Influence on Communication Needs

> Every theory of love, from Plato down, teaches that each individual loves in the other sex what he lacks in himself.
>
> G. Stanley Hall

Projective identification refers to the tendency of individuals to project onto the spouse all the old, forbidden impulses and desires one could not express in oneself as a child and is still fearful to express as an adult. Projective identification is an important psychodynamic process by which childhood needs influence mate selection. Initially, we want someone who complements us and expresses the parts of ourselves that have been historically thwarted, punished, or ignored. As the relationship evolves, these same traits become the major monkey wrenches preventing the authentic development of the two adults in the relationship. Let's trace how this happens.

Each of us has frustrated childhood needs that we seek to have satisfied in the marriage. Because life is difficult, almost of all of us have experienced disappointment and conflict about getting at least some of our needs met. Perhaps you wanted to dress like all the other kids in your school, but your parents made you dress in a wholesome, Amish manner. Your need to be accepted on first impressions was thwarted, and you may feel guilty about wanting to create a superficial but immediate positive impression. Or maybe you were always rewarded for being delightfully social and adept, sharing rooms with the most difficult siblings and taking up the slack caused by the irresponsibility of others. Your need for privacy and self-indulgence was never allowed to express itself. You grew up still feeling that very human need for privacy, but not feeling it was an acceptable need. Thus, the first premise for projective identification is that many people have had to historically disavow certain aspects of their personality or nature. But the need for expression still creates tension and unhappiness.

Individuals burdened with frustrated desires work out a comfortable relationship with a partner who allows them to project these frustrated desires onto them. If the husband feels guilty about superficial impressions, he will find a wife willing to accept the image of someone who wants to impress the Joneses. If the wife was the socially responsible kinskeeper, she will find a husband willing to accept the desired but feared image of someone who needs a lot of privacy. Usually the situation is a quid pro quo. In the current example, this would mean that the wife becomes caricatured as someone who only wants to acquire visible signs of success and beauty and the husband becomes caricatured as someone inaccessible who needs privacy and cannot be burdened. So the second premise for projective identification is that individuals, willingly and unwillingly, consciously and unconsciously, become what their mates most fear about themselves. No wonder so many people resent what their spouses have become. It is nothing less than their own worst nightmare.

Scarf (1987) explains projective identification as follows:

> [a] pervasive, tricky, and often destructive mental mechanism which involves one person's projecting denied and disavowed aspects of his or her inner experience onto the intimate partner and then perceiving those disavowed aspects of his or her inner experience in the intimate partner. Not only are the unwanted thoughts and feelings seen as being inside the mate, but the mate is encouraged—by means of cues and provocations—to behave as if they were there! The person can then identify vicariously with his or her partner's expression of the repudiated thoughts, feelings, and emotions.
>
> One of the best and clearest examples of the way in which projective identification operates is seen in the totally nonaggressive and never angry individual. This person, who is uniquely devoid of observable anger, can become aware of angry feelings only if they exist in someone else—in the intimate partner, most predictably. When something disturbing has happened to the never angry individual and he is experiencing angry emotions, he will be consciously out of contact with his feelings. He will not know that he is angry, but he will be wonderfully adept at triggering an explosion of hostility and anger in his spouse.
>
> The mate, who may not have been feeling angry at all before the interaction, may quickly find herself completely furious. Her anger, which may appear to be about some completely unrelated issue, is, in fact, anger that is being acted out for her spouse. She is thus, in some sense, "protecting" him from certain aspects of his inner being which he cannot consciously own and acknowledge.
>
> The never angry person can then identify with the intimate partner's expression of the suppressed rage without ever having to take personal responsibility for it—even in terms of being conscious of the fact that he was the angry person in the first place! And, fre-

quently, the feelings of anger which were so firmly repudiated within the self are just as sternly criticized in the mate. The never angry individual, in a projective identification situation, is often horrified by his spouse's hot-tempered, impulsive, uncontrolled expressions and behavior. In a similar way, the apparently never sad person may see his or her own depressed moods only as they exist in the partner. (p. 62)

When couples engage in projective identifications, the anger and resulting quarrels that they have with one another are, at the core, simply the expression of very personal, inner conflicts. From the unacknowledged inner conflict comes outrage at the spouse's behavior. If the individuals could identify their own fears and conflicts about the "problem," as reflected in their own lives, both partners could work toward resolving that problem. More frequently, the projecting partner seeks to feel better by bringing about changes and improvement in the mate. This is not destined for success because the projecting partner still has the conflict and will, unconsciously, continue to undermine efforts to effect change. That is, he or she will try to get the partner to change but, at the same time, continue to provoke or facilitate the behavior in question.

To resolve projective identifications, patients have to stop "splitting." Splitting is another psychodynamic concept that refers to the tendency of individuals to look at themselves as existing on the extremes of naturally occurring bipolar traits. Individuals start by splitting the good from the bad in an external object (a person, place, or situation) and then internalize this split perception. The multilayered nuances of reality are lost, and people become "good" and "bad," "mean" and "kind," "right" and "wrong." Splitting leads to rigid external boundaries and rigid roles within the family (Everett et al., 1989).

People then begin to judge themselves according to which side of the seesaw they have been placed. This creates frustrations, misunderstandings, and unexpressed longings. People who "always" want to help others need to acknowledge the times and situations where they do not want to help anyone or want help themselves. Those who "always" want to be humble and nonmaterialistic need to acknowledge the times and situations where they would like to luxuriate or be elegant. Only by acknowledging our own complexities can we avoid projecting all unpleasantness onto our nearest and dearest (Scarf, 1987).

Note that projective identification is rarely a conscious process. During the romance period, the similarities and attraction between the partners are stressed, and sometimes they are all that is acknowledged. Projective identification is a long-term process that occurs over many months and years of living together. It insidiously grows when the illusion of fusion begins to disappear. It potentiates the need to individuate.

Fusion-Individuation Needs Influence Couple Communication

Living with someone creates all types of multilayered communications. One learns to read the complex cues of the other on a conscious and unconscious level. One of the most pervasive unconscious filters used to decipher and encode communications to one's spouse concerns the filters of sameness and differentness.

For each partner, the struggle to be autonomous is always linked with the anger of not having someone to fuse with. Partners want their spouses to be just like them, but they want to be able to retain all of their own uniqueness and individuality. They want to be unified and separate at the same time. Sifting through different interpretative possibilities, a spouse always is asking, "Is this like me or not like me?" "Is this what I want to identify with or de-identify with?" "Is this my soulmate or an alien match?"

This basic developmental challenge—to fuse over similarities, overcoming feelings of aloneness, although still being able to differentiate and be true to one's self—occurs in all intimate dyadic relationships. The first and most important relationship in which it occurs is the infant-parent relationship. The way issues of togetherness and separateness are resolved in the family of origin provides a blueprint for how one "naturally" deals with all intimate relationships.

Most couples are not fully conscious of the fusion-individuation struggle in their family of origin or in their marriage. However, they usually have pondered the issue by asking, "Should I have married someone more similar to me? Wouldn't I have achieved greater satisfaction and happiness if I had been more 'simpatico' with my partner in terms of the basic issues?" These questions are sometimes counterbalanced with the feeling that by marrying someone with different strengths and weaknesses from one's own, at least the marriage has had the stamina to weather more crises because each person can handle different types of strains and stressors. At a deeper level, the question really is, "How much can I merge my identity with my mate and how much must I struggle to create my own identity?"

Research consistently indicates that marital happiness is associated with marrying someone similar to oneself. People tend to be happier if they marry someone of the same age, level of physical attractiveness, socioeconomic class, education, IQ, religion, personality, social attitudes, and even psychopathologies. The relationship with any one of these factors is positive but quite small. Yet, when you start packaging groups of similarities, you find that it is nicer to have a "simpatico" partner instead of a "complementary" partner. Marrying someone similar on these crucial dimensions decreases the likelihood of constant conflict over lifestyle, values, and rituals.

A number of research projects support the idea that psychologically healthy individuals tend to marry each other and that these individuals tend to have the best marriages. Kim, Martin, and Martin (1989), for instance, gave a group of couples married more than five years a personality test, the 16 PF, and found that among satisfied couples both individuals scored similarly and high on source traits such as tenderness, trusting each other, accepting others, enthusiasm, and genuineness. The lack of significant differences between this group of husbands and wives on source traits suggested that couples may have a better chance of finding their marriage to be satisfactory when they have similar healthy traits.

Surprisingly enough, most of us are pushed toward marrying someone who has a strong genotypic similarity to us. Researchers have found, by examining the polymorphic genetic markers in large samples of couples, that partners do exhibit slightly more genetic similarity than would be expected if the couples were paired randomly (Russell and Wells, 1994). No one has yet tried to predict divorce on the basis of genetic dissimilarity, but inasmuch as these traits are consistently related to marital happiness, it seems very likely that marrying someone dissimilar to you on basic traits does put you at greater risk for divorce.

Although there is no doubt that we end up much happier marrying someone similar to ourselves, many things can run amuck during the mating game, and all too many end up marrying people far too different from themselves for marital success. First, many people are initially very charmed by those who are quite different from themselves. Part of the attraction with differences is due to projective identification, as discussed above, but part of it is also due to a healthy fascination with what is new and different. When someone displays attitudes, thoughts, and behavioral styles very different from our own, we can fall in love with the person because he or she makes us more "complete." The shy male is very attracted to a dynamic, confident woman; how can he help but marvel at the ease with which she does what he finds so painfully difficult? Only after the relationship becomes "real" does he find this type of woman too domineering and too intrusive of his privacy.

Growth in Marriage: From Fusion to Individuation to Integrated

Thus, marital attraction is a complex and contradictory process. Besides the projected identification differences that exist in couples, there are true differences in temperament, background, values, and talents. Once a couple has lived together for a few years, the fusion that was so sought after is developmentally replaced by a need to individuate and define oneself. When couples start to individuate, the complementary characteristics that once were admired or tolerated start to drive people nuts. Instead of appreciating how neat a husband keeps his car, it infuriates the wife that he is so uptight about crumbs.

Phoebe Prosky (1991) states that couples know when they are in this individuation stage because they start asking,

> "Where is the partner I married?" The partners become frightened by the disintegration of the similarities that they felt initially, and commonly make frantic attempts to reinstate the former perception of merged bliss. These efforts create a very difficult but powerful learning situation, but one which is mostly outside of awareness. This lack of understanding of the process in which they are involved compounds the pain. Their fights are rarely about what they seem to be about; rather, they are superficial manifestations of the ongoing struggle. (p. 132)

This analysis explains why a number of marriages seem to become polarized after many years. Over time, instead of seeing the similarities, many couples highlight only the differences. Communicating differences becomes more important than reaffirming similarities. The need to de-identify or individuate as a person is probably the main psychological force motivating this change in perception. Fusion is frustrating and unobtainable, so successful autonomy becomes critical. The shift in focus prompts changes in communication.

L'Abate (1990) lists the following eighteen traits on which couples tend to polarize, all of which greatly affect communication patterns:

1. The expressive spouse versus the inexpressive spouse
2. The hyperactive spouse versus the passive spouse
3. The overly dependent spouse versus the overly independent spouse
4. The perfectionist spouse versus the sloppy spouse
5. The reflective spouse versus the impulsive spouse
6. The leader spouse versus the follower spouse
7. The driven spouse versus the lackadaisical spouse
8. The spouse who manipulates others to meet personal needs versus the spouse who denies needing anything from others
9. The rigid spouse versus the pushover spouse
10. The mainly giving spouse versus the mainly taking spouse
11. The spoiled spouse versus the neglected spouse

12. The self-indulging spouse versus the self-debasing spouse
13. The obedient spouse versus the rebellious spouse
14. The critical of others spouse versus the critical of self spouse
15. The showing feeling spouse versus the hiding feelings spouse
16. The gullible spouse versus the conniving spouse
17. The dominant spouse versus the submissive spouse
18. The denying of all problems spouse versus the finder of all problems spouse.

Whenever there is conflict in the marriage, each person has the opportunity to explore his or her own contributions to the conflict as well as the mate's contributions. The mature identification and recognition of true differences and projective identifications empowers people to take personal responsibility for improving the marital relationship. When people focus on what is the matter with the partner, they are still in the fusion stage—they see their partner through their own limited, narcissistic lens. Fused partners think, "If she (he) understood me, loved me, and wanted to make me complete (make up for my limitations), then she (he) would do X or would not do Y." When spouses start focusing on what is the matter with themselves, they are on the road to personal and marital maturity. They ask themselves, "What is this intense anger all about? What is each partner's responsibility in making this situation resolvable? How can I act differently in the future? What are new options and new strategies that I can try?" They begin to think, "How can I grow and change to make myself more complete and the relationship more satisfying for both of us?"

Many couples maintain a complementary/polarized relationship throughout the marriage. Sometimes this is satisfactory. However, there seem to be at least four costs associated with the "institutionalization of differences." First, frustration and anger become visible benchmarks of the relationship. The areas of friction are commonly acknowledged, and repetitive, stereotyped arguments can go on for years. For example, the driven spouse can forever criticize the laid-back spouse, using the same attack words and receiving the same counterattacks. Second, in a complementary relationship, the roles become caricatured over time, and each spouse's traits become grossly exaggerated because they never practice the mate's polar performance repertoire. Again, the driven spouse never has the luxury of relaxing, and the relaxed spouse never has the luxury of experiencing an intense flow of work in a meaningful way. Third, couples become very dependent on each other in these types of marriages. This is only risky when the mates are not too dependable and become unwilling or irresponsible in carrying out their customary, compensatory behaviors for their spouses. The fourth and most dangerous aspect of such relationships is that each partner has to live in constant fear of being left.

After many years, married couples on a healthy developmental trajectory begin to see each other in complex and interdependent ways. Gone is the need to stress the similarities and oneness. Gone also is the need to see only the differences. How do couples make the transformation? To resolve projective identifications, each spouse must undergo an individuation process and be open to a dialectical understanding of the relationship. That is, they must gain a strong sense of themselves and of their spouses as separate, independent people. People mature as they come to understand their mates in a unified, nonpolarized manner and recognize and accept the complex and interrelated nature of spousal interactions. Let's explain how this occurs.

Happy older marriages tend to cultivate and stress the expression of all potentials in each of the partners. A wife can count on her husband to support her need to be thrifty in one area of life and a spendthrift in another area; a husband looks to his wife for support when he decides to learn to knit as well as when he decides to run for county sheriff. Neither spouse has a need to create black-and-white caricatures of each other.

When couples successfully individuate from each other, they stop complementing each other's deficit areas and develop the parts of themselves that have been stunted or squelched. Stressed marriages become more and more polarized over time and emotionally charged around these differences. The spouses become salt-and-pepper couples with little in common other than that they are a societally sanctioned pair.

This developmental process of couples can be thought of as a recapitulation of the parent-child relationship. The working out of a relationship with one's parent logically serves as the developmental template used in working out a relationship with one's mate. Both require an initial ability and emphasis on establishing contact, comfort, and intimacy. Over time, this has to give way to individual growth and independence. Eventually a balance of interdependence must be achieved.

SYSTEMS THEORIES AND COUPLE COMMUNICATION

A person remains immature, whatever his age, as long as he thinks of himself as an exception to the human race.

Harry A. Overstreet

Systems theory postulates that unhappy marriages are caused by problems that lie neither in the wife nor in the husband. The problems lie outside of each of them but are deeply embedded within the psychic boundaries of "the relationship." The relationship refers to historical and current transactional patterns and the communication code that is used between husband and wife. It is a description of how each partner is influencing and is influenced by the repetitive verbal and nonverbal patterns of daily life. These patterns can create marital satisfaction or marital distress.

In systems theory, there is no reason to try and figure out which spouse is causing the problems. The problems are interactional; the husband's actions are affecting the wife's reactions, which are affecting the husband's reactions, which affect the wife's actions. Either partner has the potential to create crisis in the relationship and cause changes to start reverberating throughout the marital system.

Systems theory is distinguished by two organizing principles: homeostasis and relationship structure (dysfunctional transactional patterns and the related power struggles that define the relationship).

Homeostasis

Homeostasis is a biological phenomenon that describes the tendency of all living organisms to maintain a predictable, steady state and to return to that or a similar state when it has been disturbed. The most obvious example of homeostasis occurs in temperature regulation. We keep our bodies at around 98.6 degrees Fahrenheit, but in times of crisis (infection), our temperature rises to enhance the production of white blood cells and to destroy infectious agents. Once the infection has been destroyed, our temperature returns to normal.

In marriage, there are also steady, predictable routines. During a crisis, couples may be able to shift their routines but not for long and not without great stress. As soon as possible, they want to return to the status quo. Even when the status quo is not very satisfying, the return to routine is most compelling.

We all know that in a relationship, it is easier to be miserable than to continually work on changing the relationship. This phenomenon is what couples therapists call "homeostasis." Homeostasis is the conservative tendency for couples to continue functional as well as dysfunctional ways of relating. Having worked out some kind of balance or equilibrium, couples actively resist upsetting that equilibrium. Distressed partners can create a new level of homeostasis, but it takes an enormous amount of time, effort, and blocked pathways to the original steady state (Jackson, 1968).

What often happens when there is a crisis (e.g., a long visit from an in-law) or developmental pressure for change (e.g., spouses who thought they wanted full-time work find the demands of child care create the need for a part-time job), is that one partner will try to change and meet the new demands, whereas the other partner will redouble efforts to cling to the old ways. It is not always immediately apparent which couple is resisting change in which areas. Couples therapists have to shake the system up within the therapy session, sometimes, to observe the areas in which the husband and/or wife are resisting needed changes. Their resistance is rooted in the need for homeostasis in the relationship. Keep in mind that homeostasis also serves to maintain positive interactions that allow the couple to function more effectively.

Viewing marriages as a closed system, the most distinguishing feature is how they display constant random disorder until a state of equilibrium is found. When one person in the family changes, other family members may deny or distort the changes in an effort to recapture a comfortable state of equilibrium. When everyone must face the change (e.g., a wedding), a series of changes (positive and negative) will ensue until a new level of homeostasis is achieved (von Bertalanffy, 1968).

Many theorists are beginning to challenge the homeostasis concept. They maintain that families are open systems, intrinsically capable of responding to outside agents and changing. New models that stress the inevitable motion in a marriage between permanence and change are being integrated with internal growth models to better explain dysfunctional relationships (Moyer, 1994).

Dysfunctional Transactional Patterns

If a homeostatic analysis tells the therapist who is trying to change and who is resisting change, delineating the dysfunctional transactional patterns describes how those attempts are enacted in the repetitive, ongoing communication between the couple. There are many well-known patterns that are seen in the therapy room. The most common types include (1) mutual withdrawal, in which the communication is characterized by suppressed resentment and nonengagement; (2) mutual accusation, in which the communication is characterized by recurring, escalating arguments that are filled with blame and disdain for each other; and (3) demanding-withdrawn couples, in which communication is characterized by one of the partner's repeatedly making open gestures to resolve an issue or to express rage, anger, and disappointment, whereas the other partner simply tries to avoid discussing the issue (Wile, 1981).

Most dysfunctional communication patterns share several common features. First, underlying most dysfunctional transactional patterns is the belief that the same old argument is really a battle for "the truth." If the husband is always joking and the wife is always doomsaying, the husband must continue joking to prove the truth that "life should be taken lightly." The wife is just as motivated to continue doomsaying at every turn to prove her truth that "life is to be taken seriously." Therapists need to validate each partner's experience and dispel the illusion of an absolute truth. Only when the couple can see their viewpoints as part of an interconnected reality is there the opportunity that each can let go of the global battle plan and deal with the conflict for what it is.

Second, most dysfunctional transactional patterns are also characterized by a rigid "intimacy dance," in which moves toward closeness in one partner are immediately countered by distancing moves in the other (this is another way of saying that there are attempts to create homeostasis). When the wife says, "Let's get rid of the kids for the afternoon and make love," she is making a move toward intimacy. When the husband replies, "I was planning on going out to play golf," he is moving to distance the relationship. Later that night, he may whisper some wildly sweet and desirous words in his wife's ear only to have her make a distancing move, claiming total exhaustion and belittling him for playing golf while she was babysitting all day.

Successful marital communication requires a very vulnerable and open style of self-disclosure. When spouses do not trust each other and fear rejection and deep narcissistic wounds, they will dance around emotional schisms they have in their marriage, stepping any which way to maintain the distance they have created between each other to feel psychologically safe.

Third, dysfunctional transactional patterns are most amenable to change during times of severe crisis or upheaval. It is when the couple is forced by external pressures, illness, job changes, birth of children, and teenagers to reorganize their routines, that communication patterns are loosened and most responsive to maturing to a higher, deeper level. For example, shifts from part-time to full-time work, caring for elderly relatives, and geographical moves all create the need for massive changes in family ritual and structure. Many couples find that along with the new pressures come new opportunities to interact and communicate in a fuller, less rigid manner. Once change is acknowledged as inevitable, by each spouse, positive changes flower with more vigor than negative ones.

Power

The structure of the relationship is determined by exploring how power is distributed in the relationship. Within the marital relationship, power refers to the ability to influence the emotions, behaviors, and decision-making style of the couple. This influence is primarily exerted through the communication style of the couple. Both the words they use and when they use them determine how they will function. Haley (1984) succinctly tied marital power to couple communications when he wrote, "The major conflicts in a marriage center on the problem of who is to tell whom what to do under what circumstances."

When power is equitably distributed in marriages, the marriages tend to thrive. Equity is defined by each couple differently according to their needs and desires. For one couple, it is important that they have equal power in determining how they spend their money, how they spend their weekends, and where they live. For another couple, equity is achieved by the wife's having more power in determining how the money is spent and the husband's having more power in determining where they live. For a third couple, equity would be achieved by the husband's controlling more of the decision areas in the early years of the marriage and the wife's controlling more of the decision areas in the later years of marriage.

When one partner is consistently perceived as controlling the other, marital dissatisfaction is almost inevitable in our culture. The powerful partner adopts a confrontational communication style and the powerless partner adopts an avoidant communication style. At the extreme, a powerless partner does not even try to initiate influence attempts (e.g., telling the spouse what movie he or she would like to see, where he or she would like to go on vacation) because of the anticipatory fear of rejection and spousal anger it could provoke. This "chilling effect" only accelerates the downward spiral of the relationship satisfaction (Cahn, 1992).

During the early years of the marriage, couples have many arguments and struggles trying to develop the rules that will determine who will have what type of control in which type of situation. Still, the power relationships in a marriage may vary at different points in the marital life cycle. Also, the power one has at work and in the community can interact in complex ways with the desired level of control one needs in the marital relationship.

Of course, power is central to understanding the most devastating problem between couples: marital abuse. The relationship, though, is complex, and researchers are still trying to spell out the relationships. A number of studies seem to suggest that there are two types of physical abusers in marriage. The first type are real "control freaks." They want to control their spouse and will use physical, psychological, or verbal abuse to achieve their goals. They are offensively abusive. The second type do not feel powerful and do not want power. Instead they feel inept and strike out due to strong feelings of dependency, anxiety, and helplessness. They are defensively abusive. Their outbursts are misguided cathartic responses (Prince and Arias, 1994).

Systems theory has many other important concepts that affect the marital relationship, and some of the most salient ones are discussed in the chapter on parenting. Although most of the theoretical presentations are confined to the cornerstone introductions, the systemic concepts relevant to parenting are so vitally linked to the couple relationship that their presentation was saved for that section.

The following chapter on communication evolved from the ideas central to psychodynamic and systems theories. These theories are difficult to test and demonstrate in experimental paradigms. Thus, nearly all the research reported in this cornerstone is based on cognitive-social psychological theories. It is as though academic researchers have mined the more speculative, philosophical family theories for their ideas and translated them into a model more amenable to research. Their findings support the basic tenets of family theory even though the research models rely more on such notions as "reciprocity" and "stimulus control" than "defensive projections." Hence, although traditional family theories (psychodynamic and systemic) do not yet possess much empirical validity, their clinical validity is great and serves as creative inspiration for the studies cited in the following chapters. Family theories provide new and richer ways of viewing the couple and their problems. Building from this cornerstone, researchers and clinicians have broadened their methods of assessing couple communication problems and their repertoire of creative and effective intervention methods.

REFERENCES

Bowen, M. (1978). *Family therapy in clinical practice.* New York: Jason Aronson.

Cahn, D. (1992). *Conflict in intimate relationships.* New York: Guilford.

Everett, C. A., Halperin, S., Volgy, S., and Wissler, A. (1989). *Treating the borderline family: A systemic approach.* Boston: Allyn & Bacon.

Fogarty, T. F. (1976). Marital crisis. In P. J. Guerin (Ed.), *Family therapy: Theory and practice* (pp. 144-153). New York: Wiley.

Framo, J. L. (1976). Family of origin as a therapeutic resource for adults in marital and family therapy: You can and should go home again. *Family Process, 15*(12), 193-210.

Framo, J. L. (1982). *Explorations in marital and family therapy.* New York: Springer.

Haley, J. (1984). Marriage of family therapy. *American Journal of Family Therapy, 12*(2), 3-14.

Jackson, D. (1968). The question of family homeostasis. In D. Jackson (Ed.), *Community, family, and marriage* (pp. 1-11). Palo Alto, CA: Science and Behavior Books.

Kim, A., Martin, D., and Martin, M. (1989). Effects of personality on marital satisfaction: Identification of source traits and their role in marital stability. *Family Therapy, 16*(3), 243-248.

L'Abate, L. (1990). *Building family competence: Primary and secondary prevention strategies.* Newbury Park, CA: Sage.

Moyer, A. (1994). Cybernetic theory does not explain family and couple process: Systems theory and dialectical metatheory. *American Journal of Family Therapy, 22*(3), 273-281.

Prince, J. E. and Arias, I. (1994). The role of perceived control and the desirability of control among abusive and nonabusive husbands. *American Journal of Family Therapy, 22*(2), 126-134.

Prosky, P. (1991). Marital life. *Family Therapy, 18*(2), 129-143.

Russell, R. and Wells, P. (1994). Human assortive mating: Questions concerning genetic similarity theory. *Animal Behavior, 47*(2), 463-464.

Scarf, M. (1987). *Intimate partners: Patterns in love and marriage.* New York: Random House.

Scharff, D. and Scharff, J. (1991). *Object relations couple therapy.* Northvale, NJ: Jason Aronson.

von Bertalanffy, L. (1968). *General systems theory.* New York: Braziller.

Wile, D. (1981). *Couples therapy: A nontraditional approach.* New York: John Wiley.

Chapter 7

Communication

A happy marriage is a long conversation which always seems too short.

André, Maurois

WHAT DO COUPLES COMMUNICATE ABOUT?

One of the biggest reasons for communication problems is that today's couples have too little time to communicate and there are too many important and intimate topics that need discussion. Gone are the days of sitting leisurely on the screened porch after dinner for conversation and dessert. With all the bustle and go of modern life, a large amount of conversation involves logistical discussions of how the household responsibilities are to be divided and how to coordinate for community and extended-family obligations. Much of this conversation is pressured, asking one spouse to do what the other cannot do. The goal of the conversation is to keep up the family productivity. Sometimes, when the negotiations are quick or a spouse volunteers to do some task, these conversations are enjoyable. Most often, they are viewed with the same satisfaction and enthusiasm that a car driver feels pulling into a gas station to get directions.

The Minimum Daily Requirement: The Debriefing Conversation

Today, the most intimate and emotionally bonding type of conversation that occurs with any frequency is the "debriefing" conversation. In a debriefing conversation, each partner talks about what happened during his or her day. Many marital counselors begin the communication change process by having their clients take the time to get reacquainted and talk to each other about the trials, tribulations, and joys of their workday. Vangelisti and Banski (1993) interviewed 709 demographically diverse couples to assess the effect this type of marital debriefing had on marital satisfaction. They found that those that debriefed each other were happier with the relationship. They also found that women made a big distinction between listening and talking during debriefing conversations. They were looking for equity in both listening time and talking time. Men were more likely to view conversation as an event in itself, and were not sensitive to having equal amounts of talk time and listening time.

The content of men's and women's debriefing conversations are likely to vary. Women like to tell all about the emotional, relational issues of the day and use much more detail than men. Men prefer to talk about abstract, philosophical subjects. For example, Mary and John are colleagues at the same computer-programming firm. When Mary goes home, she talks about how difficult it is to get John to cooperate and the hundreds of little things that he does during the day to upset her. John is more likely to go home and tell his spouse how frustrating it is that the coding is not working out right and that 1,000 lines of code had to be changed.

Shared debriefing time can be more difficult when the spouses are employed in vastly different types of jobs. One spouse may feel that the other would not understand the pressures and nature of his or her workplace or may be uninterested in the minutiae of the daily routine. One husband in therapy said that he knew his wife was hungry to have someone over five years old to talk to when he got home, but that he puts in an exhausting day and has no tolerance or desire to hear about the mishaps that occur with day care: from the scrape of a knee to the spilled bottle of glue. The wife agreed such events may not be the most interesting, but they were the events of her life and should be valued by her husband for that reason alone. The goal in such situations is to get the couple to appreciate the common personal challenges and frustrations that they face. Losing a contract bid poses the same emotional challenges as having a parent withdraw a child from day care. Shifting the focus from content to emotional rewards and stressors, puts all work experiences on a more equal ground. When the jobs are very unique, understanding may be harder to come by but it is just as vital. A female surgeon once told me that she and her partner kept interest in sharing work experiences by spending one day each year shadowing each other. The partner got to observe her doing surgery from the viewing room and she got to help out in his cabinet-making shop. These experiences linked their different worlds and provided them with an open-door atmosphere for their debriefing conversations.

Debriefing conversations are one of the easiest ways for couples to reaffirm on a daily basis that they care for each other and are interested in what is going on in each other's lives. It also serves as a wonderful transition vehicle to shift roles from worker and colleague to lover and friend. Obviously, the time needed for a debriefing conversation could last anywhere from a minute to over an hour. However, most such conversations are fifteen to thirty minutes in length.

Communication Styles Among Couples

The content of couple arguments is as important as the style of or reason for their arguments. The areas of marital conflict are actually quite limited and reflected in the various chapters of this book.

Lavee and Olson (1993) have developed a computerized marriage-assessment tool (ENRICH) that evaluates couples' relationships in nine of the most common problem and conflict areas. These nine conflict areas, when assessed, give a potent picture of the content of marital arguments and the dynamics affecting the silence between couples. They include personality issues, communication failures, unsuccessful conflict resolution, financial management problems, arguments about leisure activities, unsatisfying sexual relations, children and parenting issues, conflicting loyalties to family and friends, and differing religious orientations.

Olson gave his ENRICH questionnaire to a national sample of 8,385 couples who had been married an average of ten years and had two to three children. Eighty percent of the couples were in their first marriage. The couples were predominantly Protestant (80 percent) and Caucasian (93 percent). When the responses of all these couples were analyzed, it appeared that there were seven distinct marital types. Although there are limitations to the generalizability of the findings, the seven marital types that emerged from the data provide an important window into the types of marriages that exist in the United States today. Obviously, each marital type is distinguished by a distinct profile that highlights troublesome and restorative aspects of the marriage. Different marital types are characterized by different communication needs, have different types of conversations, and argue about different topics.

Type 1, the Devitalized couple, was found in 40.5 percent of the respondents. These were couples who reported problems and strife in each of the areas. Needless to say, these couples reported being fairly unhappy in their marriages, and over 60 percent had considered divorce.

Type 2, the Financially Focused couple, was typified by 10.7 percent of the respondents. These couples responded just like the Devitalized couples except that they were in fairly strong agreement about financial issues. These were couples who had an economically agreeable arrangement, with little else going for it. Many of these couples devoted themselves to their careers instead of to the relationship. It is the classic "marriage of convenience."

Type 3, the Conflicted couple, is distressed over the intimate aspects of their relationship; these couples are low on personality, communication, conflict resolution, and finances. However, they interface well with the rest of the community and in the more visible aspects of their relationship. They score high on leisure, children, family, and religion. They have a moderately high score on sex. Of the couples interviewed, 13.7 percent fell into this category. Conflicted couples have a utilitarian marriage. It may not be what they hoped for, but it allows them to feel part of the community and find joy in the rituals of family life.

Type 4, the Traditional couple, was found among 9.9 percent of the couples. Traditional couples derive much strength from their religion and their nuclear and extended families. They are couples whose happiness is embedded in a context much larger than the twosome. Although they can experience significant distress when it comes to relating intimately to each other, they tend to have moderate agreement and derive pleasure from both leisure time and their financial arrangements.

Type 5, the Balanced couple, represented 8.4 percent of the sample. Balanced couples reported strength both in the internal aspects of their relationship and the external aspects. They have difficulties within each of these areas, as well. Although Balanced couples generally report a high level of general satisfaction, both husbands and wives considered divorce (27.1 percent) more frequently than couples who were Type 4 (18.8 percent) and Type 6 (16.3 percent).

Type 6, the Harmonious couple, occurred among 7.7 percent of the sample. Harmonious couples are happy in their intimate relationship with each other but struggle with some of the external aspects of marital life (in-laws, jobs, finances).

Type 7, the Vitalized couple, represented only 9 percent of all couples. The Vitalized couples were uniformly high in all nine areas. This is another case in which the rich get richer. Couples in this category tended to be married longer, come from intact families, and be better off economically than most other couples.

If we look at these types on a continuum, it appears that Types 1, 2, and 3 are the least satisfied with their marriages and the most distressed. They need help in a variety of different areas and argue about many aspects of their life. Type 4, the Traditional couple, is at the midpoint; they have a center of strength to their relationship, but they need to develop problem-solving skills and more empathy for each other as human beings. Types 5, 6, and 7 are doing relatively well in their marriage and would need to seek treatment only if something extraordinary occurred that threw them into crisis.

Olson's seven marital types underscore the fact that there is no one model for a happy marriage. Each couple comes with its own strengths and weaknesses and needs to communicate on those particular areas that become problematic for them as a couple. The fact that even among the Vitalized couples, who report satisfaction in all areas, over a quarter of the couples have thought of divorce suggests that personal models of marital satisfaction are of the utmost importance in understanding and promoting marital stability (Lavee and Olson, 1993).

The thought has probably occurred to you that it would be useful for couples to know their marital type during the premarital stage so they could be educated about what was in store for them. In fact, there is a premarital PREPARE inventory that looks at four types of couples (vitalized, harmonious, traditional, and conflicted). Research using the premarital PREPARE indicates that the Conflicted couples were at risk even during their engagement period—they were three times as likely to cancel their marriage plans as couples in the Vitalized group (comprising 40 percent of all couples who canceled their plans). Even with the large number of premarital breakups, the Conflicted group still comprised nearly half of the separated or divorced group at followup. Traditional couples were the least likely to have separated or divorced, even though they ranked only third in reported level of marital satisfaction. Harmonious couples were twice as likely to have separated or divorced as Traditional couples. This makes sense in that Harmonious couples are cemented by satisfaction in the relationship and have nothing binding them when that falters, whereas Traditional couples are cemented by social norms and expectations (Fowers, Montel, and Olson, 1996).

Gender Differences in Communication Styles

Therapists assessing how verbally expressive each spouse is usually rely on the conversation sample that occurs within the session. Still, to avoid gender stereotypes and the bias of situationally based therapy room behavior, it is most useful to ask a few questions that directly pertain to communication style. Four simple but powerful questions are these: (1) Do you feel an inner need to talk about your feelings? (2) When you are having problems, is talking about them essential to make things right again? (3) Do you like to keep problems to yourself? (4) Do you believe that talking about problems can actually make them worse? Following up with each partner's responses can clarify the range of verbal communication each desires and uses in everyday interactions.

Very frequently, there are clear-cut differences in the overt and covert communication styles of men and women. Women value and are more sensitive to verbal and nonverbal cues than men. Men value and are more sensitive to strategic planning and activity-based decisions (Minton and Schneider, 1985). Women tend to use longer utterances than men, whereas men tend to spend more total time in conversation. Men swear more, and women use more qualifying phrases. Women are far more likely to soften the impact of controversial messages or ask questions that serve to maintain a conversation (O'Donohue and Crouch, 1996). These differences interact with the content of what is said in still mysterious ways: The net effect is that, over time, men and women get increasingly frustrated about communicating with someone whose style is different from their own.

During the courtship and honeymoon period, some of these differences are seen as endearing and some as habits that will naturally change over time as the couple learns to work together more smoothly. However, as soon as couples say, "I do," they begin, with astonishing vigor, to struggle with their discrepant communication styles. They begin to send and receive complicated messages of need and desire. They argue over when, where, and how they will communicate with each other. The first years of marriage are well known for the terrible fights and arguments that ensue as couples struggle to negotiate the communication network that will define who they are as a couple.

When husbands and wives are deciding how to communicate, women struggle to teach men their way of communicating and men struggle to have women respect their own style. Women have been socialized or are inclined to have connection or relatedness as a guidepost for molding their verbalizations. They say things so the other person knows what they are feeling and thinking. They are interested in knowing what the other person is experiencing so that they can "connect" their experiences and come to a communal decision during conflict. Men have been socialized or are inclined to have status as a guidepost molding their verbalizations. They are interested in saying things that inform the other person that they are in the know and in control. Male communications usually have a status component—a message that says that one has influence, know-how, and power. As couples struggle to devise a method to decide where to vacation or what went wrong in the bedroom, the woman looks to the man for understanding and the man offers the woman solutions and methods of handling problems in the future (Tannen, 1990).

Men get doubly frustrated because they do not like or appreciate the female model of communicating. Tannen (1990) describes the dilemma:

> If women are often frustrated because men do not respond to their troubles by offering matching troubles, men are frustrated because women do. Some men not only take no comfort in such a response, they take offense. For example, a woman told me that when her

companion talks about a personal concern—for example, his feelings about growing older—she responds, "I know how you feel, I feel the same way." To her surprise and chagrin, he gets annoyed; he feels she is trying to take something away from him by denying the uniqueness of his experience. (p. 51)

Tannen also explains male resistance to ask for directions and other types of information as rooted in this metaneed to never put himself in the inferior position.

Tannen (1990) has described the difference in male-female communication as the difference between rapport-talk and report-talk. Men are interested in talking in the public arena. In fact, contrary to stereotypes, men do talk more than women in a variety of settings, including meetings, mixed-group discussions, and in classrooms. Women talk more than men in the private realm of the social telephone call, the at-home conversation, and groups of other women. Although women want to discuss problems at home, men are interested in discussing sports with friends. This infuriates the wife and puzzles the husband. Irrational arguments are inevitable.

Men are stereotyped as avoiding verbal communication; women are stereotyped as doing and requiring little else. Although this stereotype has some elements of truth, it also masks the significant female contribution to many marital communication problems. Let us first explore the popular explanations for the etiology of male-female differences in communication style. Then, we will explore how some females sabotage male attempts to communicate.

Females, in most cultures and societies throughout the world, are faced with the issue of how to structure calm within the home. The answer that works most effectively is one that accepts the role assignment as keeper of the peace. This role assignment structures the extent, nature, and frequency of communications. As holder of the family peace, internalizing, looking the other way, and trying to emotionally and behaviorally compensate for whatever is missing leads to more periods of calm than most other strategies. Overcompensating gets reinforced. This strategy proves effective in the short term, but it leads women to denigrate men, be disappointed in them, and to feel emotionally isolated. It is the female dilemma.

Let us keep in mind that there are many situations in which avoidance of conflict situations is important in a marriage. Alberts (1990) argues that, in some situations, one's partner or oneself cannot or should not change and that some way has to be found to tolerate the differences between the two. When an issue cannot be resolved productively (e.g., the husband loves to go sailing and the wife gets violently seasick even looking at the waves), it is best to avoid discussion of the topic.

If the stereotype states that too many women are consumed with communicating family tranquility, the flip stereotype is that too many men are consumed with communicating how powerful and masculine they are (Pittman, 1991). Masculinity is still defined as being in control, strong, active, and decisive. Men who nest all their communications within the overarching goal of proving their masculinity can end up in a variety of dysfunctional patterns. Some of them devote themselves to philandering (reaffirming their masculine identity through sexual conquest), others focus on acting as contenders (using athletic, intellectual, and business games to prove their power), and still others become nerds or brutes who prove their masculinity by rejecting all emotions, feelings, and urges as feminine and irrational. For Pittman, all of these men live in fear of coming under female control because they have had no role models of men interacting successfully and interdependently with women. They grew up in a world where being a man was equated with "running away from Mama" (either physically, psychologically, or both). Words and feelings are signs of weakness. Actions and solutions are all important.

Regardless of why it occurs, it is well documented that intimate communications are far more important to most women than to most men and that women are much more adept at understanding and sending complex emotional messages. Although both men and women usually have their speech centers on the left side of the brain, women, much more than men, tend to make use of both sides of the brain in even the simplest verbal tasks. As a result, a women's appreciation of everyday speech is deepened with affective, aesthetic, and visual overtones and undertones. Indeed, that is the reason why women are so much more adept at judging emotion from speech samples than are men.

Women's increased focus on verbalizations makes them disclose more personal and intimate information, particularly when frustrated (Stein and Brodsky, 1995), than men. But men respond to the disclosures of their wives. In fact, married men disclose more to their wives than to any other person. These mutual disclosures are essential for intimacy in a marriage. Research consistently finds that there is a positive relationship between the amount of self-disclosure in both sexes and marital satisfaction. This is true regardless of age, ethnicity, or social class (Berg-Cross, Kidd, and Carr, 1990).

The calling cry of many gender therapists is that one must accept the male-female differences in expression. Most marital therapists, on the other hand, accept a model of mutual, affective language as the developmental goal of couple communication. They view the masculine action communication style as an armor. It is the same type of shell that protects a lobster or a clam. The meat inside is sweet, but you will never experience it if you do not remove the shell.

Men or women who clam up or initially deny any personal contribution to couple conflict can, when appropriately confronted, learn to respond to disagreements with healthy debate, negotiation, and insight. The emotionally assertive spouse's will to persevere until a resolution has been found and the mate's understanding expanded, are often well rewarded. Most externalizers (male or female) can come to understand their own contributions to conflict. They can understand the deep, emotional desire for their spouse to have his or her point of view acknowledged in a meaningful way.

When previously task-oriented spouses experience this richer type of process interaction, they also learn to cherish it. This is a basic humanistic assumption underlying all couple communication skills. It is assumed that both men and women who can communicate fully with their mates will retain a fascination and appreciation for each other that are immediately obvious to even casual observers.

Although the consensus is clearly to teach men how to be verbally expressive, it seems to me there is an equally compelling need to teach women how to act and make decisions. A woman who wants to communicate her desire to buy a boat for her husband can try to talk to him about how much he would like such a toy. She could also communicate her desire to give it to him by showing him a budget plan and how they can afford it or discussing the various trips one could take with a boat. These actions are much more typical of men. If women could learn to put the words of reconciliation away and speak about ideas and activities, they would be far more successful in communicating. They would be expanding their skills in the same way that men are being asked to expand their skills. Both genders need to learn from each other.

COMMUNICATION PROBLEMS

Effects of Attitude on Communication

> We do not squabble, fight or have rows. We collect grudges. We're in an arms race, storing up warheads for the domestic Armageddon.
>
> Hugh Leonard

If there is one characteristic nearly universal to dysfunctional couple communication it is the "I'm right, you're wrong," "self-justification/partner-blaming" pattern. No matter what the conflict, people tend to focus on their own good intentions, pressing external constraints, and inner emotional needs. They do not focus on these same factors when judging their mates. Instead, they focus on the behavior deficits and inferred negative intentions of the partner. Virtually all therapy approaches try to break this pattern of interaction. Systems therapists focus on the circular nature of such interactions, showing how one person's blaming begets the partner's blame and one person's self-justification is pitted against the partner's self-justification. By pointing out the endless, repetitive nature of the interaction, couples are led to see that both are wrong and both are right at the same time. The complexity of needs and limitations within each individual is substituted for the simple right-wrong snap judgments.

It is very important to help clients learn to make "situational" attributions instead of "dispositional" attributions when they are communicating with each other. Situational attributions explain the reasons for a behavior in terms of environmental stressors and pulls, and momentary states of the individual. Dispositional attributions explain the reasons of a behavior in terms of long-term, unchangeable personality dispositions. Most people tend to make situational attributions to explain their own behavior and dispositional attributions to explain the behavior of their mates. That is, people see themselves as flexible and responding to the changing conditions around them. They see their mates as more rigid. A classic example is the husband who explains that he was late because of traffic, but that his wife was late because she is such a disorganized person.

Individuals who make dispositional attributions during an argument are often trying to "punish" the other person by showing him or her the moral defects in his or her personality. People who continually make dispositional attributions about their spouses become "prisoners of their own mind" and are unmotivated to negotiate reasonable changes. They aren't able to creatively take part in change because they think change is impossible. If Mary is simply a disorganized person, no amount of conversation or negotiation is going to make her arrive on time. However, if Mary is also stuck in traffic or has too many chores to do before leaving the house, then alternative routes and routines are clearly possible in the future.

THERAPEUTIC INTERVENTION 1:
THE WILLI METHOD

A well-known analytic method of helping couples understand or empathize with the complexity of factors influencing each partner was developed in Zurich, Switzerland, by Dr. Jurg Willi and his colleagues (Willi, Frei, and Limacher, 1993). It uses the work of the great American cognitive

(continued)

(continued)

psychologist George Kelly to help crystallize the partners' differing patterns of thinking. Instead of focusing on interactions, practitioners using the Willi method focus on working with each partner, separately but in the presence of the other, to verbalize and understand the constructs that are guiding his or her behavior, exposing the rigid or ambivalent nature of the constructs, and pushing each spouse to create new ways of thinking and conceptualizing their problems. They try to cover both the dispositional factors influencing behavior and the important situational factors.

The process begins by the therapist saying, "Today, I want us to look closely at some event from the past few days. Has there been anything that you both recently experienced that troubled you both or got you both worked up?" After a conflict is elicited, the therapist tries to get the facts of the incident and reconstruct the chain of events. She or he then starts to explore what each person was thinking at each step of the incident.

Clients usually begin by telling the therapist what they were feeling, rather than thinking. The therapist can say, then, "If these feelings could talk, what would they say?" The therapist pushes on to expand on the inner voices and themes. Then, the therapist asks for evidence of the opposite thoughts also coexisting at that time. For example, a man could say that when his wife started out the door for the party, he thought she really should take better care of herself, that she did not really care to please him, given how she was dressed. She was not considerate and that was just the type of person she was. The therapist would then ask if he also had some part of him saying the opposite: that his wife really wanted to take care of herself but had some real constraints preventing her from doing that or that his wife really did want to please him but felt marginalized because he focused on her appearance all of the time.

The therapist encourages the client to verbalize all the different and competing thoughts that occurred in relation to that scenario, not only the first thought or verbalization that he chose to share. In this way, many clients are easily made aware of the complex and ambivalent thoughts that they have.

Some people are unidimensional in their thinking. They do not have highly elaborated concepts even when prodded. They can be prodded to try on new thoughts by asking them, "If you were feeling the exact opposite of the way you actually did feel, what types of thoughts might you have had as your wife walked out the door?"

The elicitation of alternative realities and multidetermined realities is the goal of these sessions. By repeating themes, expanding themes, and rewording themes, guiding philosophies are externalized for all to appreciate and/or comment on. With this method, each spouse hears the other's experience, expanded over time, without interruptions. Each comes to understand the other's viewpoint, in a way that is impossible with the usual barrage of hostile repartees, interruptions, or psychic withdrawals. By ex-

(continued)

(continued)

ploring individual construct systems, partners begin to acknowledge their own misunderstandings, and a greater bond of mutual respect emerges.

Most important, partners elaborate enough of their thinking that they get to put situational attributions into their discussion of their spouses. Dispositional attributions no longer stand out; instead, they are one of many elements that explain why the partner acted the way he or she did. Likewise, the situational attributions of the speaker are embellished, in time, with some dispositional attributions. Thus, the couple develops a common, level playing field for understanding and resolving their conflicts. Two fragile people are revealed who are trying to make a relationship work.

THERAPEUTIC INTERVENTION 2: UNDERSTANDING A SPOUSE BY EXPLORING ONE'S PERSONAL MOTIVES

Working with couples to make the transition from dispositional to situational partner attributions usually requires using more than one teaching strategy over more than one session. Another way of shifting the focus from "bad" spouse to "understandable" reactions, given the total marital situation, is to help the damning spouse explore what would cause the spouse to act the way the he or she is acting. A wife who states that her husband is a cold, closed person needs to spell out what the forces are in their home and their relationship that make him "cold." To break through the resistance that forces her to label her husband this way, it is helpful to have an extended conversation about the type of situations in which she feels most open, relaxed, and safe and the type of situations that make her emotionally withdrawn. A list of facilitative conditions can be written down on one page and a list of inhibiting conditions written on another page. When the factors influencing warmth and openness are contrasted with the factors influencing coldness, and the situation is well understood, it pays to take another member from the family of origin with whom the woman is on good terms and do the same type of analysis. Then, the same principles are applied to the husband. The client is asked to experimentally assess if these factors really would influence her husband or not. Very specific plans of intervention can be set up with clear monitoring methods. The goal of these interventions is to see, if when the appropriate conditions are met, the spouse's behavior changes in a more reasonable direction—just as it would for the wife and other family members. The important step is for the wife to try to look at her husband's noxious behavior in situational terms instead of dispositional terms.

(continued)

(continued)

This analysis does not deny that there are differences in personality and that often people act on the basis of very unkind and unflattering motives. It does assume, however, that operating only on that level of analysis will not lead to better interactions or a change in the basic motivational structure of the difficult person.

CASE STUDY 1: COMMUNICATION, RECONCILIATION, AND THE INCEST PERPETRATOR

Someone was hurt before you; wronged before you; hungry before you; frightened before you; beaten before you; humiliated before you; raped before you. Yet, someone survived.

Maya Angelou

Terry and Howard had been together for twenty-five years, although they officially got married only five years ago. They came for therapy at the insistence of Terry's thirty-year-old daughter, who wanted to confront the sexual molestation she suffered for over four years by her stepfather, Howard. Howard came into her life when she was four years old. The sexual abuse began when she was twelve and continued until she was sixteen. Her mother had become aware of the abuse when she was fourteen years old and thought that she had put an end to it. When the daughter was sixteen, she again brought it to her mother's attention, and this time, it took a few months but then it stopped for good. The family never discussed the issue until recently, although they all readily admit it has tortured their lives.

Howard is very remorseful and repentant. He says, at the time, he believed he was doing a good thing—helping his daughter learn to accept a man's touch. Now, of course, he knows that it was a terrible thing to do. At the time, though, he thought that as long as he did not penetrate and was gentle with her, he was being fatherly.

During the years that Howard was molesting her daughter, he was also physically abusive to Terry. It was not a weekly occurrence, but it happened a few times a year. Terry had the emotional scars of a battered woman. She believed that Howard was an emotional child and needed to grow up. She believed that he had demons in him that she needed to help him get rid of. At the same time, she would have fantasies that he would go out in the street and be run over. She was terrified of leaving.

It has been over a decade since Howard last hit Terry, and fourteen years since the last episode with his stepdaughter. The primary task of

(continued)

(continued)

therapy was to come up with a narrative explanation for what had happened to the family. Shana (the daughter) had recently married, and all were worried that the family would drift apart if this issue were not put to rest. She came to therapy with the goal of reconciliation. Terry was also eager for reconciliation, and if that were not possible, she was considering leaving Howard so that she would not lose Shana forever.

We began by agreeing that all behavior, even the most horrible, is motivated by many different factors. Taking responsibility for one's behavior did not preclude one from acknowledging the many different factors that helped create the situation. Howard came to the point where he could admit that his behavior was due to his feelings of powerlessness and his desire to be in charge, that he used his stepdaughter to get back at his wife for her perceived lack of emotional commitment, and that he was reliving the themes and horrors of his own childhood. He saw how he had a fantasy that being loved by a child would meet his adult needs for love. He also accepted that he must have dissociated from his behavior, for there are hundreds of episodes that Shana remembers, whereas Howard can recount perhaps eight episodes.

Each element of the family story was explored and reanalyzed. The family came to see how the uneven power distribution was the main cause of the family disaster but that secrets, insecure alliances, and multigenerational issues were also critical factors. As Terry and Howard reviewed their genograms, they both saw that generations of their families had been subject to the cycle of abuse, secrecy, and projection of self-loathing. Yet, within each diagram, there were some survivors who had broken free of the cycle. Visually seeing the choices different family members had made was very empowering for all three of them.

Instead of viewing Terry's behavior as abandonment of Shana, it was reframed so Terry was viewed as a battered woman who saw escape as impossible. She also felt economically bonded to Howard and was afraid of losing the one adult in her life who had given her love and esteem. Due to her own abuse as a child, it was also possible that Terry had an empathic dissociative reaction and could split off acknowledgment of her daughter's abuse much as she denied her own incestuous experiences for a number of years.

Terry's love and commitment to Shana were stressed as well as Howard's current commitment to protect them both. The floodgate to the family's communication of shame, rage, and self-reproach was opened as face-saving attributions were presented with attributions acknowledging the limited skills and emotional limitations of each family member during those difficult years. Instead of saying she did not know about the abuse, Terry explored how she tricked herself into believing it was not happening. Instead of being a good father, Howard explored how he exploited the only child he would ever have and one whom he had always treasured. Instead

(continued)

(continued)

of seeking blanket forgiveness, we worked for ways that the parents could safeguard Shana's future sense of security. Therapy ended with a healing ritual that formalized the new narrative and gave a new, richer vocabulary to what had been the unspeakable hell of their past.

A follow-up six months later indicated that the three continued to grow in their forgiveness and were having wonderful stress-free family times coupled with some continuing painful discussions. Note that although this approach has the potential to heal many traumatized families, it would only be appropriate for families in which all of the members had reconciliation as the primary goal of therapy. In many cases, partial cutoffs and rigid boundaries are needed for the physical and/or psychological safety of various family members.

The Anatomy of Couple Arguments

Couples communicate by their actions, expressions, and bodily language as much as by their words. In fact, the words are often the least valid communications. Couple therapists are always looking to see if the words, actions, and bodily behaviors are congruent or incongruent with one another. When they are not congruent, the therapist must experiment and see why the communication channels are interfering with one another—why there is not a straightforward truth to the interaction. Very often, it is because couples have developed complicated contracts so that each action or gesture is trying to communicate "true" feelings while at the same time fulfilling the contract. That is, a person tries to communicate a totality of experiences and very often there are subtle nuances that must be communicated through other channels (e.g., a glance that modifies everything that is being said).

All couples develop such "covert" contracts with each other that govern their communication patterns. The two most common forms of contract are the quid pro quo contract and the good faith contract. In the quid pro quo contract, the couple has an unwritten and often unconscious agreement that specifies a series of tit-for-tat transactions. It is understood that when one partner does some endearing, positive behavior, the other will reciprocate in an equally endearing, positive manner. So if the wife helps her husband by doing the lawn when he has a headache, she is also communicating the expectation that he will do the wash when she is busy with the kids. The enactment of projective identifications, discussed in the theory section earlier, is another type of quid pro quo. Sometimes, the quid pro quo is explicit, but most often it is an implicit contract (Jackson, 1965). For example, men who affectively self-disclose and discuss relationship matters for a certain period of time are often "rewarded" with sexual relations.

Lederer and Jackson (1968) define the quid pro quo as an

> unconscious effort of both partners to assure themselves that they are
> equals, that they are peers. It is a technique enabling each to preserve
> his dignity and self-esteem. Their equality may not be apparent to
> the world at large; it may be based on values meaningless to anyone
> else, yet it serves to maintain the relationship because the people
> involved perceive their behavioral balance as fair and mutually satis-
> fying. (p. 179)

Thus, the quid pro quo is an inevitable part of any intimate relationship. When the quid pro quo is broken by one person, the other retaliates by "punishing" the mate, either directly, by being openly antagonistic, but more often indirectly, by using offensive, rejecting messages to redress the imbalance. This explains the origin and maintenance of the complicated and contradictory messages unhappy couples are constantly sending each other.

Thus, it is important when learning about the deeper levels of communication that exist in a marriage for couples to make explicit the implicit contracts and modifications to those contracts that have developed over the years. Once the implicit is made explicit, open and honest negotiations for change in the contract can occur. For example, most couples send many complicated messages through the use of money. Money is a prima-ry metaphoric communication vehicle in marriage and it is used in the creation and maintenance of many quid pro quos. For example, one part-ner may protest that he or she does not have enough money to buy and maintain a boat even though the other partner always dreams about it. The protesting partner may really be punishing the mate for not doing enough chores around the house. Withholding the money is a way of communicat-ing, "I am getting even." Making such communication codes explicit allows them to be put out for examination and renegotiation.

In this context, the therapeutic task is to help couples discover which quid pro quos are destroying the relationship and which are strengthening the relationship over a significant period of time. Lederer and Jackson (1968) suggest that as couples learn to verbalize the original contract and the ongoing nasty, payback undercurrents, they can learn to verbally com-municate without "voiding" their messages with contradictory tones of voice and body postures, or undermining behaviors. Once couples can communicate clearly, they are ready to negotiate new quid pro quos. In the critical negotiating session described by Lederer and Jackson, the spouses create lists detailing their own very specific wishes, desires, and needs in the relationship. They cannot use this time to describe what they want from their mate—only what they want for themselves. Afterward, each picks at least one item in the other's "wish list" that he or she feels is realistic and that could be realized. The partners then make a new conscious contract to facilitate these changes for each other. Spelling out the hows and wheres is facilitated by the therapist and serves as a model for future negotiations.

In a good faith contract, on the other hand, each partner has an independent contract such that he or she receives rewards for changing in the desired direction, regardless of any positive or negative changes in the mate. Whenever one of the mates engages in an agreed-on valued behavior, he or she is rewarded. For example, if Philip wants Linda to pay the bills by the fifth of each month, they may agree that as long as Linda sticks to the schedule, she will keep a standing monthly appointment with her masseuse (a rare luxury that she would love to have more frequently). Note that in a good faith contract, the positive reinforcer is independent of the change in the partner's behavior, so there is no benefit to being stubborn and refusing to change until the partner also is willing to change. The rewards will come from changing one's own behavior. In addition, the rewards can come from the partner, the therapist, or the external environment (Weiss, Hops, and Patterson, 1973).

Sager (1976) combines both types of agreement in his "marriage contract" technique. Here, over the course of many sessions, couples learn to verbalize the long-standing expectations they have had about what each is obligated to do in the relationship. The expected obligations are embedded in an explicit list of benefits that the obligated partners expect to receive in the exchange. The creation of a new, more flexible contract embodies the therapeutic working out of a viable relationship. The maintenance of the contract becomes the focus of subsequent sessions and a mechanism by which communication is deepened and sharpened. Sager does not use any formal or written contract but rather systematically pursues areas that are commonly known to be part of marital contracts. For example, in his work with remarried couples, Sager explores three categories:

> The first category deals with the expectations of the remarriage and includes such items as help in dealing, caring for, and disciplining the children; companionship, love, and a relief from the world of the formally married; and the provision of an immediate, readymade family. The second category is based on psychological and biological needs that the mate is expected to fulfill. These include: relationship modifications with one's own children; ties to the former

spouse; questions regarding closeness-distance needs; power and control; inclusion-exclusion of others; how partners deal with anxiety, nurturing and affection, specific aspects of sexual needs, and cognitive styles. The third category deals with areas of complaints that couples have. Communication, life style, money, and child rearing problems often appear here. (Sager, 1976, pp. 116-117)

By exploring the assumed obligations and expectations in each of these categories, remarried couples begin to understand the additional difficulties inherent in their marital contracts.

Bodily Communications: The Power of Physiological Upset in Creating Marital Havoc

Gottman (1991) has the most detailed theory for how marital bliss dissolves into marital despair. Gottman's theory of communication failure in marriage is nested within an understanding of emotions and physiological arousal, for how we feel, emotionally and physiologically, will determine what we want to communicate, how we communicate, and what ends up being communicated. If we feel loved and secure and our body is calm and warm, the sweetest of our spirits springs forth for expression. When we are tormented or in a rage, with a knotted stomach and a splitting headache, we often become possessed by demonic phrases and behaviors.

Whenever we hear a comment, command, or query that is different from what we want to hear or expect to hear, we begin to feel upset. This is natural and unavoidable. As reality casts shadows on our dreams, our autonomic nervous system becomes aroused, and our hearts beat faster. We sweat more, and our breathing becomes more shallow. This happens if we are confronting unpleasant communications from our mothers, our bosses, neighbors, or our spouses. Along with this uncomfortable arousal, we have feelings of anxiety or anger. When we are in such an aversive state, our style of communication changes. We act differently according to how we feel and what we are thinking. Gottman (1991) hypothesized at least three important changes in a couple's communication style when they are upset.

First, upset people are unable to efficiently understand and process what is being told to them. Their hearing becomes highly filtered. They tune into only those messages that are related to clarifying their current state of distress. How many times after an argument does a second argument ensue about who said what, when they said it, and what they meant? Much of this is because the emotionally distressed person is not processing what he or she heard fully and accurately. A wife who has trouble with her in-laws can give five reasons why they cannot go to California next month to visit them, but if the husband is angry because he wants to go to see his parents, he will hear only those communications that support his theory of in-law avoidance. Rational problem solving becomes impossible because each person is working with a different set of data.

Second, when couples are angry and upset, they turn on their oldest and most primitive routines for thinking and reacting. A husband and wife who are having a fight lose their adult reasoning resources and regress to the schoolyard at recess. Their behavior is unthinking, impulsive, and hostile.

Third, evolution has designed us so that when we are upset, we seek one of two courses of action: to aggress on our enemy or to flee from him or her. These strategies are still used in extreme ways by angry spouses; they stomp out of the house, lock themselves in the basement, or psychologically and/or physically attack the person most dear to them. These reactions are hard-wired in us, meaning that they seemed to have been passed down through evolution as a way to survive enemy attacks; that is, those who fought or flew survived. Today, however, we need to evolve further if we are to continue to survive. What was once adaptive is now life-threatening. He who is our enemy is now, most often, also, our best friend. Instead of slaying the enemy and being victorious, damage to a spouse circles back to the self in numerous ways. Angry, acting-out spouses get stressed from their own out-of-control reprimands. They feel guilty and demeaned by having to act in such a noxious manner. They are stressed by the reaction of the spouse, which is most often to flee the situation but sometimes to try to slay the partner (emotionally) in the battle.

Gottman (1992) has found that chronic physiological arousal and bad feelings are fatal to a marriage. In particular, he has empirically shown that marriages deteriorate as a function of how aroused (angry and anxious) the husband gets. The husband who finds his heart pounding, his head throbbing, his hands clammy, his face reddening, and his muscles in spasm on a regular basis is likely to find it harder and harder to remember why it was that he got married in the first place. Gottman writes,

> physiological arousal, particularly in the husband, predicted the longitudinal deterioration of marital satisfaction. Couples whose hearts beat faster, whose blood flowed faster, who sweated more and moved more during marital interaction or even when they were just silent but anticipating marital conflict, had marriages that deteriorated in satisfaction over three years. Also, couples who were physiologically calmer had marriages that improved over time. This meant that using only physiological data we could predict, with over

95 percent accuracy, which couples' marriages would improve and which would deteriorate in the next three years. (p. 232)

Affective Communications: Anger Is Not Always Detrimental,
and Playing the Peacemaker Is Not Always Productive in a Marriage

Gottman (1993) was also the first to demonstrate how useful and protective it is to vent negative emotions in a marriage. But you have to vent them at the right time and in the right way. If arguing exists alongside affection, humor, empathy, and joint problem solving, the couple grows and learns how to live in a satisfying, interdependent relationship (see Magic Ratio, p. 326). Gottman found that wives who were always compromising and expressing compliance in the early years of marriage were actually more unhappy seven years down the road than the women who were fighting to negotiate a long-term, mutually satisfying set of ground rules. At all points in time, criticism, contempt, defensiveness, and withdrawal from interaction were deadly. Assertiveness, persistence, and emotional intensity were essential for successfully molding intimate relationships.

There are basically two schools of thinking about expressing negativity in marriage: those who adhere to the usefulness of a conflict-avoiding strategy and those who adhere to the virtues of conflict-engagement strategies. According to Gottman (1994), two conflict engagers (a volatile couple) are able to sustain a happy, satisfying marriage if they find a way of using loving, positive behaviors to overwhelm the effects of the negative interactions. If they can resolve the conflicts by developing general principles that guide future interactions with integrity, the relationship will prosper.

What happens with many conflict-engaging couples is that in the early stages of the marriage, the husband does not know how to constructively engage the wife when there are disagreements. Or just as likely, the wife is so toxic when she brings up problems that the husband retreats to avoid a very destructive interaction. This results in the husband stonewalling the wife, avoiding the situation as long as possible. This is very undesirable to the wife, and after many futile attempts and angry outbursts, she starts to withdraw. Later, she becomes disgusted and starts living her life in parallel, developing her own routines, her own confidants, her own special pick-me-up treats. The husband at this point, becomes fearful of the aloneness, and both are chronically defensive. Now, the marriage is pretty well destined for failure. Gottman (1993) hypothesizes that the reason men begin their stonewalling behavior is that it takes them so much longer to physiologically recover from being upset. The avoidance and stonewalling are protective mechanisms to avoid aversive feelings of hyperarousal.

Indeed, most unhappily married women complain that they cannot engage their husbands in resolving their differences; their husbands just withdraw. Unhappily married husbands complain that their wives are always on their case, never just letting things be.

Swinging in the opposite direction and always "making nice" is not necessarily a winning strategy, either. The compliancy strategy may boomerang in the long run. Instead of resolving issues, compliancy allows conflicts to silently simmer until the boiling point is reached and a destructive blowup may be unavoidable. Husbands and wives who avoid the compliancy trap and verbally confront disagreements are, sometimes, in the long run, better off. Short-term arguments can have long-term benefits, particularly in the context of a very supportive, loving relationship (Gottman, 1991).

Individuals who are overly compliant, fearful, or sad because of the conflicts in their marriage tend to become more and more unhappy over time (Gottman, 1991). The women most likely to fall into the dysfunctionally compliant role are those whose husbands are the least able to respond appropriately to their pleas for conversation and negotiation. The short-term solution of retreating solves the immediate threat or crisis, but it leads to long-term problems. Resentment brews, and isolation and loneliness expand. If the mate reacts to pleas for communication by withdrawing, a severe, long-lasting cloud cover devitalizes the marriage and casts gloom on all of its interactions.

The conflict-avoiding couple does not look to each other for companionship or intimacy. Spouses do not communicate about what happened during their workday, and they do not expect their mate to cheer them up or motivate them to reach important goals. They live peacefully, on the surface, by having clearly distinguished roles and responsibilities. They go on, day after day, agreeing to disagree. Conflict avoiders are able to sustain a marriage, albeit a hollow one. When a crisis occurs and they are no longer able to avoid the conflicts, these couples often quickly descend into the abyss of separation and divorce.

If a husband is married to a strong conflict avoider, he may find that the only way he can get his wife to understand the seriousness of his concerns and need to talk, is to shout and be aversive, bridging the distance created by the more aloof style of the wife. Indeed, Krokoff (1991) found that when both spouses are conflict avoiders, the wife's occasional show of disgust and contempt ("I just can't take this from you anymore") leads to increased marital satisfaction three years down the road. Communicating that she is fed up works much better than simply keeping all of her hostility inside of her.

Representing the old ideal of psychological health were a group of couples known as "validators." These were couples who listened to each other, respected each other, and knew how to compromise. It should not surprise anyone that although "validators" can indeed have very stable marriages, so can "volatile couples" and "avoidant couples." The mechanism by which all three types of couples achieve this stability is discussed in more detail later when we discuss how to improve marital communication.

Verbal and Behavioral Communications: The Core Communication Problems of Criticism, Contempt, Stonewalling, and Defensiveness

Much marital communication training is predicated on the idea that couples who are avoiding, screaming, and grimacing at each other are doing so out of ignorance. They do not have the proper skills to resolve the conflicts more successfully. Yet all of us intuitively know that at least some of the time in which we are inappropriate and destructive in our interactions with a loved one, it is not because we do not know better. We do. But our desire to hurt the other is temporarily more intense than our desire to be civil. We want to get the other's goat and irritate him or her. We are looking for a payback or a way to vent our extreme frustration. To the extent that one abuses a mate because she or he chooses to do so, all the skill training in the world will not help. What needs to be changed is the desire.

Analyses of marital interactions reveal that unhappily married couples believe spouses intentionally say things to hurt them. Husbands and wives feel they are unable to adequately protect themselves from the hurt their partner is inflicting on them. Few believe the attacks are due to lack of knowledge about the proper way to communicate with a loved one. Instead, most maintain it is a matter of intent. Unhappily married spouses report hearing much criticism and contempt. They react with defensiveness and/or stonewalling. For Gottman (1994), these are the four horsemen of the marital apocalypse (criticism, contempt, stonewalling, and defensiveness).

Research confirms that unhappily married individuals do intentionally give many hostile and hurtful messages. They insult their mates and psychologically give their partners "paybacks" for perceived hurts and neglects. Many people will act contemptuously via their body language, or by mocking their mate, or by using hostile humor. Instead of just complaining and specifically stating what bothers them, they will jump to global judgments and blame the spouse for whatever the problems are in the relationship. This criticism-contempt mode is prominent within distressed couples.

The reaction to criticism and contempt is to eventually tune out and withdraw. Offended partners learn to stonewall, that is, they pretend that the spouse does not exist. This can go to the extreme when spouses will not respond to direct questions or suggestions and act as though requests were never said or registered. They simply erase the spirit of the spouse from consciousness.

Some types of stonewalling are part of a more subtle behavior pattern known as "reverse vulnerability" (Lederer and Jackson, 1968). In reverse vulnerability, the spouse who appears uncaring and unresponsive "cannot feel confident about his ability to discriminate between those times when he wishes to express loving behavior and those times when he wishes to enjoy what he regards as independence, separation, or withdrawal. Consequently his attitudes and behaviors tend to be rigid" (p. 308). Reverse vulnerability is thus a defensive way to deal with fears of fusion.

In addition to stonewalling, criticism, and contempt, Gottman (1993) has analyzed the toxic nature of defensiveness in a marriage.

Basically, defensive spouses no longer want to be emotionally neglected, abused, or stonewalled and so begin to defend their virtue in the relationship by a variety of maneuvers, including denying responsibility for their role in a conflict (it is so easy to blame the partners), making excuses when it is indisputable that they have not acted in the appropriate way, and cross-complaining (every time the spouse complains, the individual comes back with a countercomplaint and does not respond to the veracity of the original complaint). Defensive strategies also include repeating oneself, again and again, and only agreeing with the partner with a "Yes, but . . . " statement that minimizes the reality of the partner's feelings and concerns. Both spouses may use all of these strategies with each other, or they may become constricted and stylized so that the husband is always defensive and critical and the wife simply stonewalls.

The most common scenario of couple distress, though, begins with a woman who thinks that her partner is trying to hurt her. The man denies this intent but realizes that the mate does feel victimized. The woman retaliates with a conscious or unconscious desire to get back at her partner with her communications. When she succeeds, she alienates her partner even more, and he starts to stonewall her or respond with overt anger. Why do women do this? Is it that the women are hypersensitive and paranoid, seeing intention and innuendo where none exist? Are they making mountains out of molehills? Or do women have superior social perception skills, understanding motivations that are hidden from their spouses? At this time, there are no definitive answers to these questions.

However, one intriguing line of thought relates both the clinging/angry/ defensive style and the avoidant style to the same basic insecure attachment pattern that is characterized by a need to avoid vulnerability and expect perfection in the other (Sinclair and McCluskey, 1996). The feeling of being "hurt" is really a feeling of being abandoned or forgotten. The need is to feel safe and to be able to count on a significant other. Tracing couple communication problems back to individual attachment styles presumably learned in infancy and childhood, Sinclair and McClusky have shown that when the couple relationship is threatened by depression, affairs, or other life crises (thus arousing an insecure attachment and fear of abandonment), women, in particular, develop a more invasive communication style. Specifically, they are more likely to try to prod until they get a reaction from their spouse, invade his emotional space, get under his skin, and crowd and follow him. Men experience the same insecure attachment but respond with rejection or anger. This pattern completes a secret systemic pact that allows both partners to avoid expressing their ambivalence and dealing with more complex issues. In this view, women are expressing an attachment need for both of the partners, and men are expressing rejection and anger for both of the partners. Until both learn to trust one another and do not triangulate third parties into their conflicts, the pattern will persist (see the chapter on depression for further discussion of the attachment styles that affect couples).

Negative Communications Have More Impact Than Positive Communications

One of the most important observations that has been made about marital interactions is that the effects of negative interactions are much more far-reaching and long-lasting than the effects of positive interactions. A kiss on the cheek is lovely, but a raised eyebrow at the wrong time can ruin the entire evening. Gottman (1993) calls this the "primacy of negative over positive affect." I call it the power of "poison over protein" (p. 10).

Consistent evidence suggests that wives are both more likely to confront conflicts in the marriage and more likely to be sensitive to the negative qualities of their interactions. If there is a key to feminine success in marriage, it is how to make one's man openly vent disagreement and anger without pushing him to the point where he becomes stubborn, withdraws, or starts whining. This knowing of "how far to push," "when to push," and "over what issues to push" is the heart and height of feminine intuition.

If a wife is unsuccessful at modulating her husband's positive engagement in the conflict, his stonewalling becomes an unbearable emotional hardship for her, and they enter the conflict engagement cycle in which stonewalling begets criticism and defensiveness, which begets stonewalling. Men who stonewall have very specific behavioral styles: They inhibit their facial action, minimize eye contact, and turn off their listening channels to the wife. Sometimes when men are doing this, they are apparently trying to calm themselves down. Other times, they are literally "stewing" in their own juices, with the heat rising every moment. Gottman is currently trying to determine what differentiates these moments. It may be that when a husband is sad and resigned about his situation, his stonewalling is a true passive-aggressive ploy, designed to punish the wife but also very arousing for the man. If the husband is really sympathetic to the problems facing the couple, stonewalling may be a necessary "time out" in which to process all the information coming in at him from the wife.

A most interesting gender phenomenon concerning withdrawal and stonewalling during marital conflict was noted by Heavey, Layne, and Christensen (1993) in a study they conducted on twenty-nine married couples who were videotaped having two discussions: one in which the husband requested a change in the wife and one in which the wife requested a change in the husband. They found that when the husband's issues were being discussed (e.g., he wanted his wife to stop nagging him in front of the neighbors), wives and husbands did not differ in terms of how much they withdrew and how demanding they were. However, when the wife's issues were being discussed (e.g., she wanted her husband to stop nagging her in front of the neighbors), the wives became much more demanding and the husbands became much more withdrawing. This pattern of wife demand/husband withdraw interaction predicted a decline in the wife's reported marital satisfaction one year after the study. If the wife withdrew and the husband was demanding, the wife actually reported an increase in marital satisfaction. This fits with the general therapist wisdom that women usually come into therapy seeking change; men usually want to maintain the status quo.

Nonverbal Ways of Expressing Couple Problems and Unhappiness

As the relationship becomes more and more dysfunctional, a variety of clinical cues can alert the therapist to the severity of the marital problem. In addition to the all-important sign of stonewalling, there are five diagnostically corrosive signs to look for in a marriage (Gottman, 1994):

1. *Flooding.* Flooding is the perception that the partner's negative emotions are unexpected ("seem to come out of nowhere"), unprovoked, intense, overwhelming, and disorganizing. The partner who feels

flooded will do anything to terminate the interaction (e.g., run away).
Women are more prone to feel flooded than men.

2. *Felt Severity.* The felt severity of marital problems is best taken as an
accurate indicator of the depth of the problem.

3. *Distancing.* If even one of the spouses prefers to work out problems
on his or her own and refuses to engage the therapeutic process, the
prognosis must be guarded.

4. *Parallel Lives.* Couples are quite turned off to the marriage when
they have arranged their lives in parallel instead of being integrated
and intertwined into a complex web of interdependencies. They have
separate friends, eat their meals independently, and don't share their
day-to-day activities with each other.

5. *Felt Isolation.* Couples who feel lonely even when they are in the
house together have a poorer prognosis.

These perceptions and interactions are all the result of chronic, unresolved
anger in one or both spouses.

CASE STUDY 2: A FAILED MARRIAGE

Paul and Leslie came to therapy too late for their marriage to be saved.
After being in therapy for eight weeks, they decided to get a divorce. Their
story is typical of how the road to disaster can be paved with good intentions.

Paul and Leslie worked at the same New York magazine. Paul was a
photojournalist and Leslie an assistant editor. Paul had been married for
fifteen years when he met Leslie, but he was very angry and disgusted
with his life and then wife. He felt that he and his first wife had emotionally
been separated for over ten years, and they had not had any sexual
relations during that time. Leslie was ten years younger than Paul and full
of excitement and energy. She thought Paul was the most talented person
she had ever met and decided to woo him big time. Paul had never had
someone pursue him, and he fell madly in love with Leslie. When their
romance became common knowledge in the workplace, the bosses began
to act very cool toward both of them, particularly toward Leslie, who was
viewed as seducing a married man. Within a few months, Leslie was laid
off for a flimsy reason. It was clear that her romance with Paul was the real
impetus.

Leslie was unemployed for six months, and during that time Paul left his
wife and moved in with Leslie. They married as soon as his divorce was
finalized. When Leslie finally landed a job in Houston, Paul was ready to

(continued)

(continued)

follow her to the ends of the earth. Unfortunately, it was very difficult for Paul to find a job in Houston commensurate with his skills. He finally found a good job in Dallas and became a commuting husband. The commute was very difficult, and Paul missed his friends and job in New York.

Leslie was now editor of a big regional magazine, but Paul was just a little fish in a little pond. Leslie socialized with Houston society all the time, and Paul was the tag-along spouse. For over two years, he unwaveringly supported his wife and her career. She got pregnant, and when the baby came, he was the one to take off two months. He had to rush home to watch the baby two nights a week, and on weekends, he took the major responsibilities for child care. The couple had very little time together and the three-times-a-day, lovey-dovey phone calls gradually dwindled to a once-a-day chore-delegating phone call. During this time, Paul would try to get Leslie to take weekends off or come home early on the nights he was home. Leslie always had extra work, meetings, socials, and obligations. They would spend what time they had together fighting over the fact that Paul was so lonely and isolated. Leslie's attitude was that Paul could not accept the responsibilities of home and family and wanted to keep on playing, as when they were single and without children.

As Paul pouted, Leslie would get angry and start a project in the house just to shield herself from the depressive gloom that was always surrounding Paul. She thought maybe he was jealous of her success, but he had always been so supportive of her career that she couldn't understand why he would shift gears and suddenly want "the little lady at home." Leslie thought Paul's complaints were unfounded and was tired of defending herself.

When their son was two years old, Leslie wanted to get pregnant again. Paul was very hesitant, but once again, Leslie got her way. When the baby was born, Paul was overwhelmed with the responsibilities of two children. He complained and grumbled and tried to be nasty. His "paybacks" involved verbal insults and trying to make Leslie feel responsible for ruining his career opportunities. At this point, both agreed, the relationship became much worse. Leslie began to stonewall Paul and just live her life independently of him.

When the second baby was six months old, Leslie was offered the senior editor job of a nationally known magazine based in Los Angeles. She eagerly accepted, feeling that Paul would have a chance to start his career again, and finally they would live all week in the same house.

In Los Angeles, Paul did find a wonderful job. But he and Leslie rarely spoke and never went out without the children. They left messages with the nanny for each other and stopped phoning. They began to alternate working different weekends, and Paul started drinking and going out with his friends. Leslie realized she felt like a single person. She and Paul did not make love for months on end. In a fit of despair, they called to make an appointment for marital therapy.

(continued)

(continued)

In therapy, Paul was an automaton. He didn't understand what had happened in the marriage but said he felt used and depleted. He was having irritable colon problems and terrible tension headaches. Leslie was full of anger and wanted Paul to shape up or ship out. Any time they were in the room together, they would try to destroy each other emotionally. Neither professed any love for the other but felt committed to the children. Homework assignments given as part of the therapy process went undone, and common goals could never be agreed on. When the idea of a separation was explored, in detail, they admitted they would be relieved and happy to have their own space. By the fifth interview, they began to discuss what type of child-sharing arrangements they would have. By the eighth session, they announced they were going to terminate the marriage and counseling. Neither wanted to work together on a more peaceful separation. As Leslie said, "At this point, the money is all going to go to the lawyers."

All of Gottman's predictors are apparent in this case study: the shift from expressing positive emotions to expressing negative emotions, making negative personality attributions, and strong physiological upset. In this case, the wife was the one who was the recipient of the contemptuous complaints and the wife was the one who initially stonewalled. Nonetheless, the trajectory to divorce was exactly the same.

METHODS FOR IMPROVING MARITAL COMMUNICATION

The Magic Ratio and Three Communication Styles

Gottman (1993) found that for a marriage to be stable, where the couples are neither talking about divorce or planning to divorce, they must master a minimum 5:1 ratio of positive to negative interactive affects. That is, there must be five smiles, laughs, compliments, or strokes for every snide look or comment!

Gottman (1993) found that this ratio holds true across the three different communication styles discussed previously. At one extreme, there are "volatile couples" whose marriages are very stable even though their communication style is marked by extremely high levels of positive and negative affect. These couples communicate many criticisms and many compliments, verbally and nonverbally. These are very expressive and involved couples whose conversation is lively, loud, and filled with humor and affection as well as corrections and attempts at persuasion. Volatile couples prize their individuality and need to have their own space, physically and psychologically. It sometimes seems as though they thrive on conflict but still are capable of being very romantic and passionate. Such marriages are marked by egalitarianism and androgyny (Fitzpatrick, 1988).

At the other extreme, there are "avoidant couples" whose marriages are also very stable even though their communication style is marked by extremely low levels of positive and negative affect. Avoidant marriages are marked by people who always try to seek a common ground when discussing conflict and minimize the importance of airing any differences. They believe that time will resolve their disagreements and that things have a way of working themselves out without talking about them (Fitzpatrick, 1988).

In between is the old psychological model of the successful couple, "the validators." The validators express intermediate levels of positive and negative affect. Many of their conversations are characterized by an easy and calm interaction, but on important issues conflict can easily emerge. Usually one spouse will validate the other's description of a problem by nodding, paying attention, and asking respectful and interested questions. Sometimes, spouses will be empathic and let their mates know that they can understand the dilemma or conflict from their perspective. This validation occurs even when the spouse does not agree with what his or her partner is saying. The general atmosphere is one in which the couple is working together to solve a mutual problem. There is some indication that validators stress "we-ness" more than individual goals. They share physical and psychological space as well as a daily schedule (Fitzpatrick, 1988).

Gottman's work is so compelling because it destroys the myth that "validating marriages" are the only ones that are stable. Volatile and avoidant marriages appear to be just as stable as long as the couple is within the magic 5:1 positive-to-negative ratio. This work is still emerging, and it is unclear if "stability" is the primary criterion of interest to couples and marriage therapists. Many would maintain that marital satisfaction or growth is more important than stability, and data are not yet in on how these three styles relate to criteria other than marital stability.

Still, therapists should encourage individuals to try and experiment with their own minimum required ratio. If a spouse does not respond favorably with a 5:1 ratio, maybe the mate is giving off negative affect he or she is not aware of or maybe the positive affective exchanges are not being recognized by the spouse. If either of these cases prevails, increase the ratio to 7:1 to take care of the individual noise and see if that improves the situation in two weeks.

Overcoming Resistance and Blaming

One of the big frustrations with insight into dysfunctional or neurotic patterns is that it doesn't necessarily create behavioral changes. One can only hope that it does create an emotional willingness, over time, to relinquish old anger and grudges that were fueling the dysfunctional communications. It may also motivate new social skill learning when that is required. Once couples learn the nature and reasons for their dysfunctional interactions, therapists need to help them on the road toward change.

So often, even after many marital sessions, people will choose specific incidents from their past interactions to justify how they are acting in the current situation. For example, a wife says that she rejected her husband's invitation to take a ride in the country because last year they fought over when to stop, where to eat, and whether the air conditioner should be on or the window open. Although the wife can justify a surly response to her husband's positive gesture, that very often is not the way that she would prefer to respond. She would prefer a here-and-now orientation, but she is neck deep in a then-and-there orientation. Communication that is viewed in a context of resentment and old grudges gets myopically focused on two destructive, overarching interpretative lenses: The first is "I'm right and you're wrong," and the other is "Don't tell me what to do." Both of these interpretive lenses sabotage the goal of most communication—to influence another person to see the world as you do. Stripping these interpretive blinders is essential for improved communication. It is also the area where therapists meet the most resistance.

Gottman's Four Suggestions for Improving Marital Communication

Given Gottman's extensive theoretical and empirical study of marriage, it is not surprising that he has come up with four essential strategies for improving a marriage (Gottman, 1994). Simply put, they are as follows:

1. *Calm down*—Gottman's work on physiological arousal teaches us that it is counterproductive to try to resolve a problem when we are upset.
2. *Speak nondefensively*—A number of the therapeutic interventions discussed in this chapter are aimed at achieving this goal.
3. *Validate your spouse*—This refers to the basic definition of communication: It is a process of speaking, listening, and letting the other person know that you understood what he or she said. Validation stresses responding to the emotional state of the spouse and can be expressed by apologizing, complimenting, acknowledging the feelings of the mate, and taking responsibility for making the other person upset or worried.
4. *Overlearn*—This strategy involves continually working on improving the marriage and trying new ways of communicating and sharing with one's spouse. It is trying to be nondefensive and validating day after day in conflict situation after conflict situation.

THERAPEUTIC INTERVENTION 3: CREATING BOUNDARIES FOR DISCUSSING CONFLICT

Couples should agree on a time when they can discuss what is bothering them. First and foremost, that should be a time when both people are well rested. Sunday mornings and Saturday afternoons are popular times. Although the setting and boundaries of such discussion times are critical for success, being rested is the first necessary ingredient. Other rules for a successful fight include (1) picking only one issue and sticking to it, (2) stating the complaint clearly, (3) showing appreciation once it is clear that the partner has understood, (4) picking options for change, (5) receiving feedback from the partner, and (6) continuing to review options and feedback until a compromise has been reached (Bach and Wyden, 1968).

THERAPEUTIC INTERVENTION 4: MODELING POSITIVE METACOMMUNICATIONS

Sometimes it is easier to show the partner a better way of communicating by role-playing with the spouse in front of the partner. The therapist takes the specific message that the partner is trying to communicate and sanitizes it of all the angry, attacking, and ridiculing metamessages. Instead, the therapist embodies a loving partner gently sharing needs, desires, and frustrations. The therapist can begin this exercise by saying:

I want to attempt to express what you have told me during the past few minutes by trading places with you and pretending to be you speaking to your husband (wife). In this process I want to make sure that I have accurately understood your feelings and thoughts. I am going to try to tell your husband (wife) all these thoughts and feelings in a way that will not make him (her) defensive. If I am successful, hopefully he or she will be better able to understand your point of view. (Snyder, 1992, p. 27)

THERAPEUTIC INTERVENTION 5: STORYTELLING FOR SYMBOLIC HEALING COMMUNICATIONS

The process of successfully telling stories to each other is, at one and the same time, the process of self-disclosure, self-discovery, and loving acceptance. Emotionally inhibited couples can often communicate more easily symbolically than literally. Conflict-ridden couples may find it easier to stroke or compliment their mate or talk about their own deficiencies first in story form. Therapists can facilitate this type of communication by having spouses make up "pretend" stories for each other. What type of stories should spouses make up for one another? It really does not matter, because the story line will emerge from forces beyond conscious direction. The only ground rule should be that the story helps the spouse understand what the storyteller is feeling. To get into the mode, try having couples share the fol-

(continued)

(continued)

lowing stories. When the storytelling spouse makes up the story, the listening spouse should be comfortably positioned to receive the story. There is no need to discuss the story. They should just enjoy the giving and receiving.

1. Create a story about your relationship with your spouse that justifies your wisdom in marrying him or her. The story can be true or fantasy, reach into the past or into the future, and be simple or complex.
2. Create a story about your relationship with your spouse that justifies your worse fears about your husband or wife.
3. Create a story in which you and your spouse live happily ever after. Describe what you did to create the ultimate happy ending.
4. Create a story about a day when you and your spouse switch bodies, like in the movie. Go through the entire day's events and describe your adventures.
5. Create a story about you and your mate as children, going off to have an adventure together.
6. Create a story about your children being the parents and you and your spouse being the children.
7. Create a story about your spouse being the only person of his or her sex left on the planet.
8. Create a story about being on trial to prove the good you brought to the relationship. Tell another story about what you would tell the judge if you had to prove the good your mate brought into the relationship.
9. Create a story in which you take your spouse on a trip to see the ghosts of anniversaries past and the anniversaries in the future. (Howard, 1991)

Packaged Programs

The most popular packaged programs for learning how to communicate on a more intimate level include Relationship Enhancement Therapy (Guerney, 1977), the object-relations-oriented Imago Course (Hendrix, 1988), the eclectic PAIRS Communication Training (Turner and Gordon, 1995), and the Centering Program of Hendricks and Hendricks (1993). All of these programs are structured over the course of several weeks and usually are run by professional leaders working with groups of couples.

In Relationship Enhancement Therapy, the first widely validated communications program, couples are taught to clearly express their feelings and thoughts and to accept the expression of others. By practicing a series of structured exercises, couples learn how to critique and facilitate their own communication skills, changing their style of expression and learning how to reach constructive solutions of conflicts.

This skills-based approach is very different from the affective Imago Course in which marital patterns are traced back to childhood blueprints and the pain of the past is dealt with as well as current needs and frustrations (Hendrix, 1988). Couples become conscious of their "imago," a composite of all the people who influenced them at an early age (parents, siblings, relatives, friends, teachers, etc.). They then explore how these imagoes selectively guide their perception of the strengths and weaknesses in their partner. Imago exercises probe for personal feelings, connections with the past, and basic interpersonal styles. Most of the exercises are emotionally arousing, revealing, and difficult for couples. For example, in one exercise participants write down all the positive traits that characterized the people who influenced them as a child and then write down all the negative traits that characterized those people. Next, they write down all the positive and negative traits they see in their partner. When the historical list is compared with the current list for the spouse, the participants can see how their reactions to specific positive and negative traits are carryovers from their reactions as a child.

The PAIRS Communication Training is partly based on object relations theory, partly on the humanistic techniques of Virginia Satir, and partly on behavioral skill learning approaches. The founders, Turner and Gordon (1995), describe the 120-hour course as follows:

> [it is] divided into five sections: communication, conflict resolution, self-understanding, sensuality and sexuality, and contracting. Participants are taught new ways to relate and resolve conflict before they are led to increased awareness of self. Then, they learn to release anger, take responsibility for their own needs, and develop the ability to understand, hear and give to their partner. Later, they are able to work on sensuality and sexuality issues. In the final weeks participants are given a format for confronting their most difficult issues as a necessary step toward a better relationship contract. (pp. 42-43)

The exercises are experiential, paper-and-pencil questionnaires, and conversational. For example, in one exercise couples are provided with an extensive list of "inner characters" that portray different aspects of one's personality that emerge in different types of situations with different types of people (e.g., "Betty Crocker" is the homemaker character; "Hamlet" is a brooding, tragic victim; and "Rockefeller" is very wealthy and controlling). Once the spouses list their cast of characters, playful matchmaking occurs so that the husband's "Adventurer" gets along with the wife's

"Amelia Earhart." By discussing characters that clash with each other, characters that are seen too often or not often enough, or characters that frighten, couples maintain a safe, structured format for exploring and resolving a number of otherwise toxic issues.

Hendricks and Hendricks (1993) have a centering program that shares many components of the PAIRS program. In their program, the three keys to successful communication are awareness, honesty, and commitment. All of their exercises make couples aware, at a new and deeper level, of how the relationship can be strengthened. For example, one of the exercises is the "Two-Step." The rationale and instructions for this exercise are as follows:

> The mind-reading problem and ostrich problem bog down many relationships. The mind-reading problem involves not seeing or saying what we want because our partner should already know if she/he really loves us. The ostrich problem is not seeing how it is or saying how it is and pretending that others can't see either. Simply put, we don't get what we want and need because we fail to acknowledge the truth and to express our wants and needs effectively. The following exercise will help you to verbalize both how things are in your relationship and how you want them to be. Stand facing each other. You'll have a verbal ping-pong game in which you'll take turns completing the following sentences out loud.
>
> "How it is, is _____"
>
> "What I want is _____"
>
> Complete both sentences before your partner's turn. (1993, pp. 102-103)

In the course of the exercise, a lifetime of marital insights and wishes can be volleyed back and forth.

These programs all try to teach couples to break through their defensiveness and in an authentic way risk being themselves. Of the many different concise programs presented for improved marital communication, Laveman and Borck (1993) have reduced it to six simple but highly effective guidelines packaged into six simple sentences. They are as follows:

1. Learn to give "I feel" messages.
2. Stay in the present.
3. Avoid catastrophic statements and reactions.

4. Keep arguments and conflict brief—no longer than ten minutes.
5. Learn how to end an argument—admit the wrongdoing you have contributed and apologize.
6. Never assume anything.

These six guidelines are great for posting all over the house.

LEARNING AIDS

Therapeutic Dialogue (Communication)

1. What is the ideal way for you to resolve conflicts in your marriage?
2. What are the most destructive behaviors and attitudes you bring to the marital conflict?
3. What are the most constructive behaviors and attitudes you bring to the marital conflict?
4. Among your friends and family, discuss notable constructive and destructive attitudes and behaviors that are used to resolve marital conflict.
5. How can you change your ideal communication style to make it more attainable?

Self-Exploration 1: Communicating About Differences

Using a modified form of the programmed writing format developed by L'Abate (1992), couples can work on resolving the tensions caused by their differences by engaging in daily twenty-minute written dialogues with each other. Couples are presented with the eighteen polarizations listed in the Adaptability Cornerstone on pages 289 and 290. They decide, with the guidance of the therapist, to discuss a polarized issue that is only mildly troublesome to them but on which they agree they have some significant discrepancies. Then, in a graduated fashion, they discuss more and more difficult issues on subsequent days. Each written dialogue encounter begins by having each couple write down their answers to the following questions:

1. Give two examples of how your family of origin dealt with Polar Personality Trait A and then Polar Personality Trait B.
2. What happens now when you show Polar Personality Trait A and then Polar Personality Trait B?

3. Between the two extreme personality traits listed in the polar pairing you are currently working on, where would you say that you are in the relationship? Where would you say that your partner is?

1	2	3	4	5	6	7	8	9	10
Little of this trait				Moderate amount				A lot of this trait	

4. Using the same scale, circle where you would like to be on these two traits and where you would like your mate to be on these two traits.
5. What steps could you take to change your position on this scale so that it is more the way you would like it to be? Be specific.

After the writing exercise, the couple should set up an appointment sometime during the week when they can talk about their ratings. When there are discrepancies in how one spouse rated the other, see if conversation can bring consensus on actual and ideal ratings for each of them. Then the participants write down what they have learned from their talk and they exchange these observations.

Self-Exploration 2: Communication Skills Inventory

Instructions: Below is a list of communication skills. Rate each item so that it best represents the frequency with which that statement applies to your relationship. Before sharing your answers with your spouse, circle the five skills you would like to increase over the next few months. Have a brainstorming session with your spouse to see how you can increase these skills.

1	2	3	4	5
Never	Seldom	Occasionally	Frequently	Very frequently

1. How often do you and your spouse talk over pleasant things that happen during the day?
2. How often do you and your spouse talk over unpleasant things that happen during the day?
3. Do you and your spouse talk over things you disagree about or have difficulties over?
4. Do you and your spouse talk about things in which you are both interested?
5. Does your spouse adjust what he (she) says and how he (she) says it to the way you seem to feel at the moment?
6. When you start to ask a question, does your spouse know what it is before you ask it?

7. Do you know the feelings of your spouse from his (her) facial and body gestures?
8. Do you and your spouse avoid certain topics in conversation?
9. Does your spouse explain or express himself (herself) to you through a glance or gestures?
10. Do you and your spouse discuss things together before making an important decision?
11. Can your spouse tell what kind of day you've had without asking?
12. Your spouse wants to visit some close friends or relatives. You don't particularly enjoy their company. Would you tell him (her) this?
13. Does your spouse discuss matters of sex with you?
14. Do you and your spouse use words that have a special meaning not understood by outsiders?
15. How often does your spouse sulk or pout?
16. Can you and your spouse discuss your most sacred beliefs without feelings of restraint or embarrassment?
17. Do you avoid telling your spouse things that put you in a bad light?
18. You and your spouse are visiting friends. Something is said by the friends that causes you to glance at each other. Would you understand each other?
19. How often can you tell as much from the tone of voice of your spouse as from what he (she) actually says?
20. How often do you and your spouse talk with each other about personal problems?
21. Do you feel that in most matters your spouse knows what you are trying to say?
22. Would you rather talk about intimate matters with your spouse than with some other person?
23. Do you understand the meaning of your spouse's facial expressions?
24. If you and your spouse are visiting friends or relatives and one of you starts to say something, does the other take over the conversation without the feeling of interrupting?
25. During marriage, have you and your spouse, in general, talked most things over together?

Scoring Key for the Communication Skills Inventory

1. For all items except 8, 15, and 17, use the number given by the client—for example, a 5 (very frequently)—and add 5 points to the total score.

2. For Items 8, 15, and 17, the scoring process is reversed. Because these items ask for a frequency estimation of negative or nonproductive behaviors, a 5 (very frequently) would add 1 point to the total score, a 1 (never) would add 5 points to the total score.

3. The scores for Items 5, 6, 7, 9, 11, 13, 15, 21, and 24 are transposed from the spouse's questionnaire. These scores are switched because they involve a judgment of the spouse. The total communication score is a composite of self-descriptions and the judgments of one's spouse. Thus, this questionnaire can only be scored accurately if it is completed by both partners in the relationship.

4. To obtain a nonverbal score, sum the scores for Items 6, 7, 9, 11, 15, 18, and 23. Subtract this sum from the total score to calculate the verbal subscore.

Normative Data

	Total Inventory Score	Nonverbal Score	N
Happily married husbands	X = 05.1	29.3	24
Happily married wives	X = 105.4	28.9	24
Distressed husbands	X = 81.6	23.2	24
Distressed wives	X = 81.1	23.2	24

Source: Navran, L. (1967). Communication and adjustment in marriage. *Family Process, 6*(2), 173-184.

Sample Workshop Flowchart Intended for Groups of Four or Five Couples Working on Communication

I. Psychoeducational Strategies
   A. The minimum daily requirements for communication
   B. Different couple communication styles
   C. Effects of attitude on communication
   D. The autonomy of couple arguments
      1. Bodily communications
      2. Affective communications
      3. Verbal and behavioral communications

II. Self-Explorations (Done by couples in private and shared before rejoining the group)
   A. Communicating about differences
   B. Communication skills inventory

III. Therapeutic Dialogue (Done by couples in private and shared before rejoining the group)

(Proceeding in the order presented, both partners respond to each question before going on to discuss the next question)

In group, the therapist explores with couples how relationship goals can be achieved by modifying overly ambitious, pie-in-the-sky expectations. Using information about their current situation and the realities seen among friends and family, couples fine-tune expectations so they are achievable and motivate rather than discourage attempts at change.

IV. Therapeutic Interventions

Work with a couple in front of the group and apply one or more of the therapeutic interventions. Share rationale during demonstrations. Let group discuss additional interventions.

A. The Willi Method for communicating multiple explanations for a spouse's behavior and one's own behavior

B. Understanding a partner by exploring one's own personal motives

C. Creating boundaries for discussing conflict

D. Modeling positive metacommunications

E. Storytelling for symbolic healing communications

V. Finding the Motivation and Time to Make the Changes

Group discussion

Bibliotherapy

Gordon, L. (1993). *Passage to intimacy.* New York: Fireside.

Gottman, J. and Silver, N. (1994). *Two-part harmony: Why marriages succeed or fail.* New York: Simon and Schuster.

Gray, J. (1994). *What your mother couldn't tell you and your father didn't know: Advanced relationship skills for better communication.* New York: HarperCollins.

Hendricks, S. and Hendricks, C. (1993). *Centering and the art of intimacy handbook.* New York: Fireside.

Luquet, W. (1996). *Short-term couples therapy: The imago model in action.* New York: Brunner/Mazel.

Macauley, R. and Betcher, W. (1993). *The seven basic quarrels of marriage: Recognize, defuse, negotiate and resolve your conflicts.* New York: Ballantine.

Notarius, C. and Markman, H. (1994). *We can work it out: How to solve conflicts, save your marriage and strengthen your love for each other.* New York: Putnam.

Videotherapy

Mr. and Mrs. Bridge. (1991). Directed by James Ivory. Details how an
  emotionally paralyzed couple live together and communicate.
Scenes from a Marriage. (1973). Directed by Ingmar Bergman. A study in
  marital dissolution.
Two for the Road. (1967). Directed by Stanley Donen. After twelve years
  of marriage, communication is the only key to saving their happiness.

Professional Development Questions (Communication)

1. Within the therapy context, what are the critical bodily, affective, and
   verbal communications to assess between couples? How much feedback should you give couples on their communication styles and in
   what stage of therapy?

2. When do you believe it is best to work on "communication skills"
   and when do you believe it is best to work on the "negative attitude"
   underlying the communication problems?

3. What is the most helpful stance for a therapist to take concerning
   gender differences in communication needs and communication
   styles? How can one remain gender neutral and help both couples
   feel increased satisfaction with the way they communicate?

4. When one partner's communication style is filled with criticism and
   contempt and the other partner is passive and blame absorbing, how
   should the therapist proceed?

REFERENCES

Alberts, L. K. (1990). The use of humor in managing couples' conflict interactions. In D. D. Cahn (Ed.), *Intimates in conflict: A communication perspective*
  (pp. 105-120). Hillsdale, NJ: Lawrence Erlbaum.
Bach, G. and Wyden, P. (1968). *The intimate enemy.* New York: Avon.
Berg-Cross, L., Kidd, F., and Carr, P. (1990). Cohesion, affect, and self-disclosure
  in African-American adolescent families. *Journal of Family Psychology, 4*(2),
  235-250.
Fitzpatrick, M. (1988). *Between husbands and wives: Communication in marriage.* Newbury Park, CA: Sage.
Fowers, B. J., Montel, K. H., and Olson, D. H. (1996). Predicting marital success
  for premarital couple types based on PREPARE. *Journal of Marital and Family Therapy, 22*(1), 103-119.

Gottman, J. (1991). Predicting the longitudinal course of marriages. *Journal of Marriage and Family Therapy, 17*(1), 3-7.

Gottman, J. (1992). Toward a typology of marriage based on affective behavior: Preliminary differences in behavior, physiology, health and risk for dissolution. *Journal of Personality and Social Psychology, 63*(2), 221-233.

Gottman, J. (1993). The roles of conflict engagement, escalation, and avoidance in marital interaction: A longitudinal view of five types of couples. *Journal of Consulting and Clinical Psychology, 61*(1), 6-15.

Gottman, J. (1994). *Why marriages succeed or fail.* New York: Simon and Schuster.

Guerney, B. (1977). *Relationship enhancement: Skill training programs for therapy, problem prevention, and enrichment.* San Francisco: Jossey-Bass.

Heavey, C. L., Layne, C., and Christensen, A. (1993). Gender and conflict structure in marital interaction: A replication and extension. *Journal of Consulting and Clinical Psychology, 61*(1), 16-27.

Hendricks, S. and Hendricks, C. (1993). *Centering and the art of intimacy handbook.* New York: Simon and Schuster.

Hendrix, H. (1988). *Getting the love you want: A guide for couples.* New York: HarperCollins.

Howard, G. S. (1991). Culture tales: A narrative approach to thinking about cross-cultural psychology and psychotherapy. *American Psychologist, 46*(3), 187-193.

Jackson, D. (1965). Family rules: The marital quid pro quo. *Archives of General Psychiatry, 12*(6), 589-594.

Krokoff, L. (1991). Communication orientation as a moderator between strong negative affect and marital satisfaction. *Behavioral Assessment, 13*(1), 51-65.

L'Abate, L. (1992). Programmed writing: A self-administered approach for intervention with individuals, couples and families. Pacific Grove, CA: Brooks/Cole.

Lavee, Y. and Olson, D. (1993). Seven types of marriage: Empirical typology based on ENRICH. *Journal of Marital and Family Therapy, 19*(4), 325-340.

Laveman, L. and Borck, J. (1993). Relationship conflict resolution model: A short term approach to couples counseling, *Family Therapy, 20*(3), 145-163.

Lederer, W. and Jackson, D. (1968). *The mirages of marriage.* New York: Norton.

Minton, H. L. and Schneider, F. W. (1985). *Differential psychology.* Prospects Heights, IL: Waveland.

Navran, L. (1967). Communication and adjustment in marriage. *Family Process, 6*(2), 173-184.

O'Donohue, W. and Crouch, J. (1996). Marital therapy and gender-linked factors in communication. *Journal of Marital and Family Therapy, 22*(1), 87-101.

Pittman, F. (1991). The secret passions of men. *Journal of Marital and Family Therapy, 17*(1), 17-23.

Sager, C. (1976). *Marriage contracts and couples therapy: Hidden forces in intimate relationships.* New York: McGraw-Hill.

Sinclair, I. and McCluskey, U. (1996). Invasive partners: An exploration of attachment, communication and family patterns. *Journal of Family Therapy, 18*(1), 61-78.

Snyder, M. (1992). A gender-informed model of couple and family therapy: Relationship enhancement therapy. *Contemporary Family Therapy, 14*(1), 15-31.

Stein, I. and Brodsky, S. (1995). When infants wait: Frustration and gender as variables in distress disclosure. *Journal of General Psychology, 122*(1), 19-27.

Tannen, D. (1990). *You just don't understand.* New York: William Morrow.

Turner, L. and Gordon, L. (1995). PAIRS (Practical Application of Intimate Relationship Skills): An integrative approach to intimate relationship change through a psychoeducational program. *Journal of Couples Therapy, 5*(1/2), 37-53.

Vangelisti, A. and Banski, M. (1993). Couple's debriefing conversations: The impact of gender, occupation and demographic characteristics. *Family Relations, 42*(2), 149-157.

Weiss, R., Hops, H., and Patterson, G. (1973). A framework for conceptualizing marital conflict: A technique for altering it, some data for evaluating it. In L. A. Hamerlynck, L. C. Handy, and E. J. Marsh (Eds.), *Behavior change: Methodology, concepts and practice* (pp. 309-342). Champaign, IL: Research Press.

Willi, J., Frei, R., and Limacher, B. (1993). Couples therapy using the techniques of construct differentiation. *Family Process, 32*(3), 311-321.

PART IV.

THE SELF-FULFILLMENT CORNERSTONE: CREATING A SPIRITUAL CONNECTION

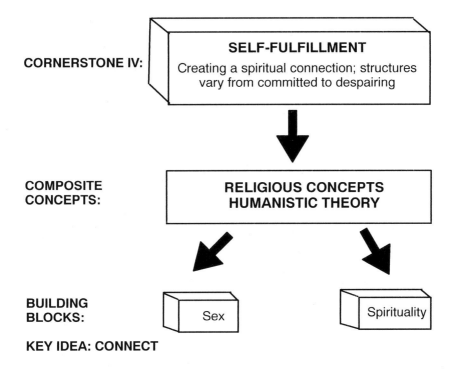

CORNERSTONE IV:

SELF-FULFILLMENT

Creating a spiritual connection; structures vary from committed to despairing

COMPOSITE CONCEPTS:

RELIGIOUS CONCEPTS HUMANISTIC THEORY

BUILDING BLOCKS:

Sex

Spirituality

KEY IDEA: CONNECT

THEORETICAL ORIENTATION: HUMANISTIC AND THEOLOGICAL

I would rather live in a world where my life is surrounded by mystery than live in a world so small that my mind could comprehend it.

Harry Emerson Fosdick

SELF-FULFILLMENT THROUGH COMMITMENT AND TRUST

Self-fulfillment through commitment to and trust in a partner is one of the primary ways that people develop their innate potentiality to become spiritually complete and satisfied with life. It is a form of self-actualization that allows for a harmonious blending of many different aspects of one's personality. Self-fulfillment through commitment and trust is part of the psychic evolution of the "self," as described by myriad personality theorists, including Jung (1939, 1965), Goldstein (1939), and Adler (1927). Committed, trusting couples can successfully blend their experiences of separateness and togetherness along with a sense of connectedness to all of life. This is my own definition of being spiritually complete within a long-lasting relationship.

If partners cannot experience self-fulfillment through commitment and trust, they will most often report a lack of loving feelings and an inability "to connect" with their partner. This seriously threatens the couple's stability and ability to effectively build the other three cornerstones.

The self-fulfillment cornerstone of couples therapy is built from a composite of three different theoretical perspectives: Eastern religious viewpoints (including Hinduism, Buddhism, Taoism, and Zen), Western religious viewpoints (Judeo-Christian theologies), and existential personality theories (such as those of Maslow, 1970; Fromm, 1966; and May, 1977). This introduction highlights how each worldview defines the relationship between couple satisfaction and individual fulfillment within its respective belief structure. Current-day researchers, theorists, and clinicians borrow liberally from all three perspectives, searching for clinically meaningful ways to map the relationship between individual growth and the marital relationship.

ORGANIZED RELIGION, SPIRITUALITY, AND MARRIAGE

> Pain makes you think, thought makes you wise, and wisdom makes pain bearable.
>
> Oriental proverb

Along with the maturing of the baby boomers, psychotherapy has matured to include issues of both religion and spirituality. This has been a difficult step. Ever since the birth of psychotherapy and the "talking cure" developed by Sigmund Freud, organized religion had been viewed, by most psychologists, as a developmental coping strategy. Instead of being the zenith of human fulfillment, religion had been seen as a stepping-stone on the road to self-fulfillment. Like Karl Marx, who thought that religion was the opiate of the people, social psychologists believed that when people with minimal inner and/or social resources needed help, they looked to religion for support. Overall, organized religion was viewed by most secular psychologists as potentially stifling of human freedom, as offering ready-made mass solutions instead of individually derived, existentially meaningful answers, and as antiscientific.

Although psychologists may have been critical of organized religion, they have traditionally embraced the potent role of theistic and nontheistic spirituality (i.e., the role of the nonmaterial world) in fostering a personal meaning to life, instilling hope, creating motivation for change, and being an integral part of the experience of self-fulfillment (James, 1890; Jung, 1939; Maslow, 1970).

Unlike most other parts of the Western industrialized world, where organized religion has declined over the past twenty-five years, the U.S. populace has continued to use religion and spirituality to strengthen the marital relationship. Bergin and Jensen (1990), for example, report that two thirds of the population of the United States feel that traditional religious beliefs are "very important" to them. Because successful marriages are cultivated in fields of values that stress the importance of family life, and because virtually every organized religion reinforces and strengthens the value of the family, couples with active religious faiths tend to highly value family life and the quality of their couple relationships. As a profession, secular couple therapists also highlight and promote family values by encouraging and rewarding both women and men for putting family commitments on par with or above their other commitments (Jensen and Towle, 1991). Increasingly, secular couple therapists are also trying to incorporate the religious and/or spiritual values of their clients into their therapeutic work.

A scientific understanding of religion and its role in an individual's life must begin with a conceptual analysis that discerns the many different definitions and meanings of the word "religious." Psychologists have built many models that highlight the different dimensions of religiosity and have tried to develop a continuum of experiences from highly organized religious rituals and beliefs to personal, evolving, nontheistic, spiritual attitudes and guidelines for living. A model developed by Batson and Ventis (1982), for example, proposed that religiosity has three central dimensions: an external dimension that refers to how much an individual uses religion to satisfy social needs for love and safety; an internal dimension that refers to how much an individual uses religion to provide clear-cut answers to existential questions (e.g., What is the purpose of marriage?); and a quest dimension in which an individual is involved in an open-ended dialogue about existential issues.

Ethical and therapeutic problems may arise when the religious or spiritual models of the therapist are disguised as secular or universal solutions or when therapists assume they share the same religious model as their clients. One of the few studies to examine the religious models of therapists found that 45 percent were primarily in the quest dimension, 32 percent were primarily in the internal dimensions, and 23 percent were primarily in the external direction (Shafranske and Malony, 1990). Assuming that a client or couple shares the same relationship to their religion and/or philosophy of life as the therapist can weaken the therapeutic alliance and create a conundrum of misunderstandings. For example, a therapist may naively assume that he or she shares the same type of religiosity with a couple because they share the same denominational affiliation. If the therapist sees specific religious documents as offering definitive answers to the "why" of marital fidelity (an internal dimension) and shares those beliefs, he or she may alienate a couple for whom the "why" of marital fidelity needs to be explored through a variety of contradictory philosophical sources (a quest dimension), or alienate a couple for whom religious readings are simply part of a social ritual (an external dimension). The therapeutic skill is understanding where the client is coming from and stretching from your own base to work within his or her framework.

The use of religion or religious concepts by secular therapists is surprisingly high. Shafranske and Malony (1990) found that although less than 20 percent of the clinical psychologists in their study stated that organized religion was a primary source of their spirituality, therapeutic interventions with a religious focus were not uncommon. Over half of the psychologists sampled reported using religious words or concepts, and over a third had recommended participation in a religion to a client. Seven percent prayed with a client, and 24 percent prayed privately for a client.

It may seem to the consumer that the pastoral counseling services offered by organized religious groups are synonymous with those offered by professional couple therapists. Both the differences and similarities between pastoral counseling and marital counseling are important to acknowledge and understand. The problem focus, on the surface, is the same for pastoral counselors and marriage counselors. Like the various schools of couple counseling, organized religions provide paradigmatic tools to resolve the major marital conflicts of the day. Sermons and couples' church groups focus on the need for intimacy, communication problems between partners, sexual fulfillment, gender roles, delay of gratification, forgiveness, and dealing with disagreements.

Yet the process of finding solutions sharply distinguishes the two approaches. Pastoral counselors find solutions within the teachings of their religious doctrines, applying universal guidelines to the specific marriage. Marital therapists, on the other hand, seek to help clients find unique, personal answers that fit in with their developmental life stage, personality needs, and cultural context. Secular marriage counselors help elicit the values and meaningful life philosophies from the couple, whereas pastoral counselors are helping couples understand the meaning of life and values inherent in a particular religious doctrine. Another way of saying this is that religious solutions are found by pastoral counselors within the context of the possibilities allowed by the religion; secular therapeutic solutions are found within the couple's personological and cultural context. When religion is part of that couple's personological and cultural context, secular therapists should maximize its benefits.

The secular marital therapist, in all cases, should be mindful of the resources available within the clients' religious community and acknowledge and incorporate the religious values important to the couple. However, when the religious doctrine is compounding the couple's problems, as will be discussed, the secular therapist must be willing to point out and confront the limiting nature of the belief system in helping the couple creatively solve their problems.

Religion, after all, is far from a panacea. Religion can create as many problems as it solves (Prest and Keller, 1993). An extensive body of research demonstrates that fundamentalist religions that take a literal, perfectionist view of human beings create totally unrealistic expectations for their adherents. Constantly finding themselves and their loved ones in the role of sinner and failure, dysfunctional moods, behaviors, and interactions proliferate.

Take, for example, the case of Bob and Joan, who after twenty years of marriage are headed for divorce. Both devout Catholics, Joan feels that she is so oppressed and abused that she will seek a divorce even though it goes against the teachings of the church. Bob spends all of his time in therapy focused on how treacherous Joan is to even contemplate divorce. Clearly, Bob believes that they must live with each other no matter how degrading and unhappy the marriage. He cannot focus on her complaints because, to him, they pale in comparison with her more hideous intentions of breaking her marital vows. He feels morally superior even though for twenty years he has verbally abused his wife, ignored his responsibilities in the home, and terrorized the children.

Sometimes, people reenact conflicts with their religion that they had with their parents or spouse. Such might have been the case with Bob. He had been brought up in a verbally abusive home that fostered independence at an early age. At seven years old, he was working at his father's auto supply store during all his free hours and was never indulged or allowed to deviate from the schedule. Although he tried to be obedient, he was never rewarded. His parents always found fault with his behavior. Adhering to the church precepts was all-important to Bob. He was driven to follow the letter of the law to appease his parents—represented now through the organized Church authority. When Bob understood the roots of his religious zealousness and dealt with his frustrated need for approval, his anger toward his wife started to soften and he was less hostile toward her. He also began to accept that a divorce could occur if he did not work on the marriage. Hence, religious zealousness was being used as a psychological defense for Bob. It protected him from the anxiety of confronting faults in himself and accepting responsibility for his own behavior. Such defenses and projections are not uncommon. Individuals often transfer frustrated dependency or nurturance needs onto their religious group.

Although secular therapists believe that there are multiple realities and multiple ways of dealing with relationships, they know they must help and guide the client to eventually select only one or two behaviors that are both adaptive and morally responsible. For example, if a person is having an affair, the issue is not simply whether he or she wants to spend time with this new force in his or her life. Therapists need to help women and men put their decisions into a social/ethical context, where they weigh the effect their decision will have on the family, the children, and the lover.

It is only through an exploration of client values that the therapist can help guide the client toward morally and psychologically satisfying behaviors. When those values are couched, for a couple, within a religious context, the therapist is aided by acknowledging that context and using it in the problem-solving process. When the values are placed in a more private, spiritual framework, it is useful to take the time to understand the value system that has been developed by the client or couple and how it came to be. Not only does an exploration of spiritual values help guide clients toward meaningful personal solutions, it pushes the therapist to understand clients in all of their humanness.

Most often, the values of the religious doctrines are in accord with humanistic values. This can work very effectively in the hands of a skilled therapist, who can help couples find affirmation for certain values from divergent sources in their life space. For example, DiGiuseppe, Robin, and Dryden (1990) elucidated how three of the irrational thought processes posited by rational emotive therapists to be at the core of psychopathology (demandingness, lack of self-worth, and low frustration tolerance) are also inconsistent with Judeo-Christian philosophy. These irrational thoughts can exist in rationally devout clients, though, because they have often misconstrued the philosophical core of their religious beliefs. By learning more rational ways of thinking, secular and religious values become more visibly consonant and personal changes more likely and durable.

Koltko (1990) provided guidelines for how the wise therapist can best incorporate the client's religious or spiritual beliefs into the treatment program. First, he stresses that it is important to know the official beliefs of a person's religion or credo as well as what the religion or credo means to the client. To illustrate, I once was treating a Buddhist couple whose faith was centralized in the bonding that occurred between the two of them during their daily meditation sessions. Understanding that Buddhism was for them, primarily, a vehicle for partner intimacy allowed me to strengthen that component of their relationship. Second, Katko highlights the importance of cultural sensitivity and realizing what the "hot buttons" are for particular religious groups. For example, Judaism is greatly concerned about intermarriage, Mormonism with the idea of free agency (an expanded notion of free will that includes solving problems by diligent work and willpower), and Jehovah's Witnesses with the ban on giving presents on traditional holidays. Cultural sensitivities can help guide an adequate assessment of how religion is affecting the couple's problems. Next, "lapsed" or "inactive" religious members may still be affected and guided by their previous religious involvement. A client who had formerly belonged to the Jehovah's Witnesses had entered a wonderfully rewarding relationship with another woman but firmly believed that she was a sinner and the cost of her happiness was that she would never get to Heaven. Therapy was focused on modifying her belief system to allow for continued appreciation of the religious values and rituals that helped her and refusing to believe those that she found intellectually and emotionally unfeasible. Finally, therapists should draw on clients' religious beliefs to promote healing, foster forgiveness, and increase partner commitment.

Ironically, a number of philosophers have categorized psychotherapy as one of the many religions of the world: It also presents a worldview with mass solutions and promises of salvation. Stander, and colleagues (1994) have described ten similarities between the goals of traditional religions and those of psychotherapy: "(a) to foster a sense of perspective, (b) to give meaning to life, (c) to provide rituals that transform and connect, (d) to provide social support networks, (e) to structure society and set ethical norms, (f) to give an identity and heritage to its members, (g) to support families, (h) to facilitate positive change in individuals, (i) to look out for the physical and emotional welfare of its members, and (j) to educate its members" (p. 29).

Organized religion and psychotherapy can both vary in their usefulness, depending on the developmental level of the individual. When children or adults are the victims of inadequate nurturing, they lack a basic sense of trust in others and confidence in their own abilities. Needing external support, adhering to religious doctrine or secular therapeutic doctrine becomes an adaptive coping skill. All dogmas promise rewards for those who follow their dictates. Adherents feel safer and less inadequate by following the letter of the law.

As people become more confident and more mature over their lifetimes many progress to a point where they feel that they have the inner resources to judge and guide their own behavior, regardless of the rewards and punishments offered by friends and family. At this point, they are able to leave the literal teachings of a particular faith or school of mental health and develop a transcendent faith. This more mature faith is characterized by a number of wonderful characteristics, including the ability to relate to something greater than oneself, a style of living that is consistent with spiritual values, the ability to make a deep commitment without having certainty, openness to spiritually diverse viewpoints, the development of social interest and humanitarian concerns, and meaning and purpose in life. These are, in fact, the highest goals expressed by the theologians of Eastern religions, the Judeo-Christian religions, and modern-day personality theory. And so all three approaches start off confronting the same issues and, ultimately, reach the same answers. The paths that they take to get there are different.

EASTERN RELIGIONS, PERSONAL FULFILLMENT, AND MARITAL FULFILLMENT

Hinduism, Taoism, Zen, and Yoga are all becoming increasingly popular with Westerners who are seeking ways to reduce stress and develop a set of values consonant with nature and capable of integrating the conflicting needs and demands pressing on modern day-couples. All of the Eastern religions are designed to help the individual find the path to self-realization. Self-realization is a deeper way of knowing the "truth" about the world—beyond the five senses. Although the Eastern religions vary widely from one another, they share the following four premises (Jagdish, 1977).

The first premise is that the ultimate truth lies in personal experience. There is no empirical test to assess the love of one person for another. The certitude that one is loved or unloved comes from a personal experience of the truth that is beyond debate or proof. Similarly, the road to marital happiness is built on personal insight—not lectures from others. Each person must take personal responsibility for finding his or her way to marital happiness. Relying on others for advice on what to do or what to say will only confound the journey. Buddha's last words to his disciple Ananda summarized this directive for staying faithful to one's personal experiences. He said, "Appa deepo bhava"—"Be thy own lamp." In a marriage, we each must find our own way to be responsive, loving, responsible spouses, and for each of us the emotional, behavioral, and philosophical path will be unique. There are no rule books or simple guidelines. Each person must develop his or her own truth of the world and truth in marriage.

It is somewhat paradoxical that personal truths are so central to Eastern religions, for they also put great stress on the role of teachers, mentors, or gurus. However, the role of the guru is to be a living example of someone who follows an inner truth and encourages disciples to do the same.

The second premise is that there is unity in diversity. Eastern religions see all things as interwoven and interconnected. The way the wife responds to the husband's dirty underwear thrown on the chair is related to the type of dinner conversation they have, which is interwoven with the way they will respond to crises on the job the next day. No simple cause and effect exists in marital relationships. All events are interconnected and part of the greater relationship.

A third axiom posits the potential divinity in each person. Everyone has the potential to experience God within himself or herself. Each of us contains the potential for achieving the awakening of the enlightened one within ourselves. The statue of the Buddha is reproduced with infinitely different faces to reinforce that very point: We are all capable of godliness. Godliness is reflected in every face. The Hindu greeting "Namaste"—"I bow to the divinity in you"—also reflects this basic assumption of human nature.

The concept of potential divinity makes the marital relationship very emotionally charged. Partners with an Eastern philosophy come to believe that the person they have chosen to spend their life with has a universal spirit or god within and that spouses can bear witness to and revere that spirit as they search for their own spirit or godliness. Believing in the spiritual goodness of a spouse makes one more respectful, more nurturing, more in awe of the potential of the relationship.

Fourth, all people are responsible for how they use their energy. Each person's energy must be released and channeled, in the right way, for personality development. In Yoga psychology, seven different types of personal energy must be channeled. These centers of psychic energy or consciousness are called chakras, and they correspond to seven points along the spinal cord. The first chakra is located at the base of the spinal chord and is connected with the individual asserting his or her separateness from other human beings. The second chakra is located a few inches above the level of the genitals and is primarily concerned with sexual actions and reactions. The third chakra is located at the level of the navel and is concerned with power, mastery, superiority, and ego control. Most people spend all their energy on these three levels.

Individual fulfillment and marital fulfillment usually require reaching the higher energy levels. The fourth chakra, located at the level of the heart, is concerned with compassion, empathy, and nurturance. The fifth chakra, located in the throat region, is focused on nurturing creativity and devotional behaviors. The sixth chakra, located between the eyebrows, has to do with developing a cosmic perspective—the energy is spent seeing the world from outside of an individual ego, thus we see the world much as an objective alien looking down on us would see us. The seventh chakra, located at the top of the head, is described as follows:

> [a] place where one has broken attachments to any one perspective. It is connected with wisdom, a place of creative intelligence, a realm of pure ideas. It is a center of integration, integrating the judgment and discriminations of the right side of consciousness and the intuitiveness of the left side of consciousness. At the center, the two modes of knowing are integrated into one. The seventh chakra is known as the thousand-petaled lotus. It is the center of the highest state of consciousness. Here the difference between the observer and the observed, the experiencer and experienced ceases. One becomes one with existence, an experience of superconsciousness. (Jagdish, 1977, p. 68)

Clearly, from the fourth chakra on, the level of spiritual fusion with the spouse can be quite astounding, and people who can expend energy at this level see no meaningful differentiation between themselves and their marriage, their spouse and themselves. Because their total consciousness has transcended the "me" orientation, the marriage has been lifted to a higher, more unified level. As we will see in a moment, Maslow's personality theory is very similar to the chakra theory of the yogis.

In summary, the Eastern religions place the marital relationship within the broader context of self-development. A strong marriage can help one to develop spiritually. Because Eastern religions stress the human union with all of nature, they are usually very encouraging of passion in the marital relationship. Indeed, the *Kama Sutra* (Burton and Muirhead-Gould, 1963) is based on the idea that enlightenment (the thousand-petaled lotus) is best achieved through different varieties of sexual intercourse with a soul mate. Similarly, in Taoism, sexual love may be transformed into a type of worship in which the spouses are, for each other, incarnations of the divine (Watts, 1959).

The Western translations of Eastern religions sometimes stress individuality over the couple or relationship. The ultimate truth becomes a private solo journey that cannot be shared with anyone else. Indeed, some might say that individuals who quest for the Americanized version of Eastern knowledge are sometimes too self-centered to focus on the tasks of marriage! Once enlightenment occurs, the divorce is probably many years old. Eastern religions, in fact, vary on the importance placed on marriage. At one extreme are the Hindus (the religion of 80 percent of the population of India), for whom marriage is almost obligatory and symbolizes the union of entire families (Mullatti, 1995). At the other extreme are Zen followers, who place no special emphasis on the couple relationship.

JUDEO-CHRISTIAN RELIGIOUS TRADITIONS,
PERSONAL FULFILLMENT, AND MARITAL SATISFACTIONS

Most couples in America still identify themselves as belonging to one of the many Judeo-Christian religions. The Judeo-Christian religions share features with the Eastern religions, but there are some very important differences as well. Most notably, although one has to personally search for the answers in Eastern religions, the Judeo-Christian tradition relies heavily on devotees' successfully implementing its dictates.

Contemporary movements in the Jewish and Christian traditions encourage and reinforce the value of a strong couple relationship. The most basic principle of Judeo-Christian religions is that there is only one God and every person is a child of God. This creates a sense of unity among all human beings. Partners are joined together by their love for each other but also by their same relationship to God, as God's children. This is related to the Eastern idea of personal divinity, albeit in a more indirect way.

Second, Judeo-Christian orthodoxy states that humans were made to serve God and, through good works, to live eternally in his light. The offer of eternal life is central to the Judeo-Christian tradition. By creating a wholesome, pure, and giving relationship, one is not only gaining joy in this lifetime but is assuring himself or herself of a place in eternity. Commitment to another person or cause is part of God's plan.

Third, the soul is an essential fact of human life. Similar to the Eastern traditions, there is a knowing beyond the five senses. The most essential part of our nature is not to be found in our soma. As God's children, we share in divine wisdom. With faith, we can elevate our comprehension of the universe to a truly cosmic level. Our soul is the repository of that divine wisdom.

Fourth, neglect of the human soul is a sin to be punished. The search for spiritual wisdom is a mandate of the Judeo-Christian tradition. The alternative to following the right path is damnation for following the wrong path. Of course, many Eastern religions believe in reincarnation of the human soul, where our next life is determined by how we behaved in this one. But many Judeo-Christian notions of sin can lead to eternal damnation. The world is populated with severely distressed couples who will not separate because divorce is a sin that can be associated with eternal damnation. This attitude of "doing right to avoid punishment" is endemic to many Western marriages. On the therapeutic side, the heavy emphasis on sin is a major motivator to think about what one is doing in a relationship. Also, the ability to be redeemed from sin creates motivation for change. It is never to late to see the light.

A fifth principle is that there is no way for an individual to affect God's plan nor can earthly wisdom fully reveal it. Many things in the Judeo-Christian tradition need to be accepted on faith. There is no way of knowing everything one wonders about. When couples face difficult times, there may not ever be a definitive answer as to why one person hurt another or why some crisis befell the family. The ability to accept what happens is akin to the Eastern notion of unity in diversity.

Therapists must carefully explore how central these types of beliefs are to individuals or couples with a current or historical affiliation with an organized religion. Such central organizing beliefs can motivate change, paralyze a person with fear, or create curative reframes for unavoidable marital strife.

PERSONALITY THEORIES, PERSONAL FULFILLMENT, AND MARITAL SATISFACTIONS

Couples therapists usually have received no academic training in the world's great religions and how they affect the marital relationship. Instead, human motivation, needs, and values are presented via the great humanistic psychologists. Without recourse to a Creator or a theology, these psychologists have tried to explain how values, spirituality, and the need to grow emotionally affect human development and marital strife. The ties between these personality theories and structured theologies are many, but there are a myriad of insights and contributions unique to the "person-centered" approach to values.

The most popular and best researched humanistic personality theory was developed by Maslow (1970). Maslow postulated that people are motivated to interact in certain ways to reduce tension. Sometimes, people are trying to satisfy needs for survival or safety ("D [deficiency] needs"). Other times, behavior is motivated by the need to self-actualize and fulfill one's potential ("B [being] needs"). D needs always take precedence over B needs. Thus, when a husband is tired, he will not be motivated to have a meaningful conversation with his wife—he will want to go to sleep.

In this way, Maslow described a hierarchy of human needs. The strongest and most compelling are the physiological needs for food, drink, sleep, oxygen, shelter, and sex. These needs will always take precedence over any other needs unless motivated by self-actualized decisions to abstain for a higher purpose. Next are the safety needs, which require creating an orderly, stable, and predictable world. A comfortable house and predictable job routine both exist at this level. The third level of needs are belonging and love needs. We all seek love and affection once we are physiologically satisfied and safe. Love and affiliation needs are satisfied primarily by our mate, but community groups, friends, and relatives are also vitally important. Next, the self-esteem needs emerge. When the lower needs are satisfied, it becomes very important to get respect, appreciation, and status from others, but particularly from one's spouse. The highest needs are the self-actualization needs. These needs vary from person to person, but they all involve having the person fulfill his or her highest potential.

Maslow believed that optimal mental health was synonymous with self-actualization. Once all our other needs are satisfied, we are capable of being fully human and motivated to use our potential, unselfishly, to further the well-being of others. The self-actualized spouse loves and accepts love in an unconditional manner. Maslow's studies of self-actualized individuals revealed that, as a group, the following personality traits were associated with optimal mental health:

1. They can see reality—they are not taken in by the phoniness in others and understand the deeper motives in other people as well as in themselves.
2. They have a freshness of appreciation—they live in the moment, filled with wonder at the sights and sounds around them.
3. They have the capacity for peak experiences—they have the experience of transcending self.
4. They have a high degree of ethical awareness and are able to distinguish good from evil.
5. They have a philosophical sense of humor.
6. They have a deep social interest and feel a kinship with other people.
7. They are capable of forming deep interpersonal relationships.
8. They have a democratic character structure, free of prejudice.
9. They have a need for privacy and are capable of being very detached from others to pursue their own inquiries.
10. Self-actualizers are autonomous and independent.
11. Self-actualizers are spontaneous, simple, and natural.
12. Self-actualizers are problem solvers and have a sense of mission about life.
13. Self-actualizers show a high degree of acceptance of themselves, others, and nature.
14. Self-actualizers are not fashion followers. In fact, they prefer to follow their own light.
15. Self-actualizers are highly creative.

Clearly, the self-actualized person is in the best position to develop a viable, healthy couple relationship. Conversely, a highly satisfying couple relationship would help fulfill a person's D needs so that he or she could more readily become self-actualized.

Much of Maslow's theory is similar to the Eastern philosophies. Both share the assumption that people have an actualizing tendency that fosters positive growth. Both see transcendence, a clearer view of reality, self-direction, and deep caring for others as the highest levels of human potential. The various levels of human need are developmentally arranged in a similar manner to that of the chakras of the yogis.

The humanistic orientation has been formally organized into a spiritual community by the Ethical Cultural Society—a humanistic (nontheistic) religion founded on the idea that individuals fulfill their spiritual destiny, directly, by having rich and meaningful relationships with other human beings.

The Ethical Cultural Society views marriage as one of the most important avenues for self-discovery and self-growth. Although we can perceive much of the world through our five senses, the Ethical Cultural Society believes that we can never directly experience ourselves. Rather, we come to understand ourselves, indirectly, through our reflected interactions with others. Intimate others, particularly spouses, are a mirror we use to see our "true selves." Through our interactions with others, we come to understand our personalities (e.g., Are we dependent, independent, funny, depressed), our needs (e.g., What are our sexual needs, intimacy needs, autonomy needs, appreciation needs), and our values (e.g., How important are children, family, ritual, commitment). These most basic components of self-discovery are found only through intense interactions with others. Sometimes, our spouses present us with a distorted mirror, and sometimes we are angry and resentful of the reflection we observe. But, overall, marriage provides a unique opportunity to learn about who we are now and to change more successfully into who we want to be. Self-actualized persons, described by Maslow above, are those who, by having successful social relationships, have made a match between what they see reflected and what they have aspired to be. Thus, success in an intimate relationship and self-fulfillment become synonymous processes for humanistically oriented people (D. Montogna, personal communication, May 1995).

Chapters 8 and 9 build on these three philosophical foundations. However, the content of the chapter on sexuality is based largely on cognitive-behavioral assessments and treatment programs. It was included because of the author's strong preference for viewing sexuality within a spiritual framework as well as an appreciation for the roles that intimacy, commitment, and devotion play in the current thinking of couple therapists.

REFERENCES

Adler, A. (1927). *The practice and theory of individual psychotherapy.* New York: Harcourt.

Batson, C. D. and Ventis, N. L. (1982). *The religious experience: A social-psychological perspective.* New York: Oxford University Press.

Bergin, A. and Jensen, J. (1990). Religiosity of psychotherapists: A national survey. Special issue: Psychotherapy and religion. *Psychotherapy, 27*(1), 3-7.

Burton, R. and Muirhead-Gould, J. (Trans.). (1963). *The kama sutra.* London: Panther.

Di Giuseppe, R., Robin, M., and Dryden, W. (1990). On the compatibility of rational-emotive therapy and Judeo-Christian philosophy: A focus on clinical strategies. *Journal of Cognitive Psychotherapy, 4*(4), 355-368.

Fromm, E. (1996). *Man for himself: An inquiry into the psychology of ethics.* New York: Holt, Rinehart, and Winston.

Goldstein, K. (1939). *The organism.* New York: American Book Publishing.

Jagdish, D. (1977). *Personality: The Eastern perspective.* Glenview, IL: Himalayan Institute.

James, W. (1890). *The principles of psychology.* New York: Henry Holt.

Jensen, L. C. and Towle, C. A. (1991). Religion and gender differences in the perception of success. *Psychological Reports, 69*(2), 415-419.

Jung, C. G. (1939). *Modern man in search of a soul.* New York: Harcourt, Brace.

Jung, C. G. (1965). *Collected works of C. G. Jung,* Volume 17. Mysterium coniunctionis. Princeton, NJ: Princeton University Press.

Koltko, M. (1990). How religious beliefs affect psychotherapy: The example of Mormonism. *Psychotherapy, 27*(1), 132-141

Maslow, A. (1970). *Motivation and personality* (Second edition). New York: Harper & Row.

May, R. (1977). *Existential psychology* (Second edition). New York: Random House.

Montogna, D. (1995). Personal communication. Ethical Cultural Society, Washington, DC.

Mullatti, L. (1995). Families in India: Beliefs and realities. Special issue: Families in Asia: Beliefs and realities. *Journal of Comparative Family Studies, 26*(1), 11-25.

Prest, L. and Keller, J. (1993). Spirituality and family therapy: Spiritual beliefs, myths and metaphors. *Journal of Marital and Family Therapy, 19*(2), 137-148.

Shafranske, E. P. and Malony, H. (1990). Clinical psychologists' religious and spiritual orientations and their practice of psychotherapy. *Psychotherapy, 27*(1), 72-78.

Stander, V., Piercy, F., Mackinnon, D., and Helmeke, K. (1994). Spirituality, religion, and family therapy: Competing or complementary worlds? *American Journal of Family Therapy, 22*(1), 27-41.

Watts, A. (1959). *Nature, man, and woman.* New York: Pantheon.

Chapter 8

Sexuality and the Couple Relationship

Same bed, different dreams.

Chinese saying

SEXUAL RELATIONSHIPS

Assessing Sexuality in the Couple Relationship

There have been two dramatically different ways of conceptualizing a couple's sexual problems: the sex therapist model and the marriage therapist model. The traditional sex therapist model views all sexual problems as belonging to the couple, not only to the obvious dysfunctional symptom bearer. Sexual problems are real and primary, meaning that one need not resolve other problems in the marital relationship to understand and treat the dynamics of the sexual relationship. The causes of sexual problems are contemporary: performance anxiety, spousal anger, health problems, and fears of intimacy. Sex therapy techniques tend to be straightforward: lots of education, desensitization, and skill learning. The focus is on the presenting problem.

Traditional marriage therapists, on the other hand, view sex as a symptom or metaphor for the more dysfunctional aspects of the marital relationship. The presenting problem may be impotency, but the real causative problems are poor communication, hostility, power manipulations, or sex role problems that invade many other areas of marital functioning. Many of these problems can be resolved only by dealing with family-of-origin issues in which the problems were rooted. All require a systemic analysis of the role each partner plays in maintaining the problem. If the sexual problem is due to a medical condition or other trauma clearly not related to the marriage, the relationship is still deeply affected by the resulting feelings of guilt and inadequacy that occur with a sexual dysfunction. These therapists work on the general marital relationship and assume that the sex problem will be resolved as other problems are worked out.

In fact, research surveys show that most distressed marriages do have problems spill over into the sexual relationship. When the primary complaint is marital distress, somewhere between 50 to 85 percent of the couples also report significant sexual difficulties (Metz and Weiss, 1992). Sexual problems, however, can often exist and arise in a healthy, nurturing marriage. It has been found that when couples have a primary, clear-cut sexual dysfunction in the marriage, one-third of the couples also have a significant contributing marital dysfunction and two-thirds have well-functioning marriages. Obviously, the happy marriages are much easier to treat for their sexual dysfunctions than the unhappy marriages.

The point of view taken in this book, and by most contemporary experts in the field, is that sexual problems are multidetermined and both models must be used, at different times with different couples, to ensure the most successful assessment and treatment of the problem.

The Nature of Sexual Satisfaction

> I began as a passion, and ended as a habit, like all husbands.
>
> George Bernard Shaw

Sexual satisfaction is important to most marriages. What constitutes sexual satisfaction is a highly individual matter. Some stereotypes have more than a grain of truth associated with them. One such image is that for men, sexual satisfaction is highly related to the frequency and nature of sexual intercourse. For women, sexual satisfaction is more highly associated with how satisfied they are with the total relationship. Woody Allen's classic line about this difference occurs when Diane Keaton says, "Sex without love is an empty experience," and Allen retorts, "Yes, but as empty experiences go, it's one of the best." Indeed, these two stereotypes reveal the two general domains that feed into sexual satisfaction for both men and women: specific sex-related behaviors and relationship variables. Most research finds that young women, however, do put greater stress on the relationship as a precondition for satisfying sexual relationships than do young men. Men find it a pleasant surprise that as positive feelings increase and marital communication increases, sex becomes a lot better for them as well as for their wives.

Oggins, Leber, and Veroff (1993) put forth a provocative cultural explanation of why middle-class women have such a strong need to have a "good relationship" before allowing themselves to have "good sex." They posit that middle-class women, in particular, are likely to idealize their marital relations because, traditionally, they were very dependent on their husbands for emotional and financial support. The marriage was the overwhelmingly important relationship in their lives and provided them with entertainment, stimulation, intimacy, and meaning in life. When you look at women who are more financially and emotionally independent of their men, you find that these women value their friendships with friends and family as much as their relationship with their spouse. The marital relationship is only one of many important relationships in their lives, and what is not forthcoming from their mates will come, they hope, from other support systems. Without the intense importance of the marital relationship, these women are better able to focus on enjoying sex even when the relationship is having problems. And indeed, the African-American women that Oggins, Leber, and Veroff studied who were financially and emotionally self-sufficient did not link relationship factors with sexual satisfaction to the same extent as African-American and Caucasian women who were financially and emotionally dependent on their spouses.

Hurlbert, Apt, and Rabehl (1993) found that women reported the following levels of sexual satisfaction associated with various sexual behaviors: 82.6 percent were very satisfied with cunnilingus, 68.4 percent with intercourse, 14.3 percent with masturbation to orgasm as part of a sexual encounter with spouse, 4 percent with masturbation to orgasm alone, 3.2 percent with partner stimulation, 8.6 percent with fellatio, and 5.3 percent with anal intercourse. The women who responded to this study were 161 women at an Army Community Center for military wives at the Fort Hood military installation. When predicting sexual satisfaction, women were more satisfied if they felt psychologically close to their husbands, were able to express what sexual acts gave them pleasure, were sexually excited by a wide range of situations, had high sexual desire, and high activity with a high proportion of the activities leading to orgasm. That is, there was not a magic number of orgasms that led to sexual satisfaction, but it was important that a significant percentage of the sexual encounters led to orgasm. The single most satisfying sexual activity for women was foreplay (compared to sex and afterplay). Overall, the relationship variables were more predictive of sexual satisfaction than the activity variables.

Clinically, this means that men must be able to answer the following questions if they are interested in their wives having a sexually satisfying relationship: What does my wife mean by closeness? What can I do to make her feel intimate with me? Do I know what specific activities are erotically charged for my wife? Do I know how to perform the activities that would bring pleasure to my wife? Is my wife satisfied with the frequency with which she has orgasms? Unfortunately, the study did not have husbands assess their levels of satisfaction for the various sexual activities. Many other researchers, however, have found that men like wilder activities than women; they like having intercourse in unusual places and at unusual times. It is the new, the different, and the forbidden that men find exceptionally exciting.

The question of how important orgasms are to women has been central to sexologists since it was acknowledged by scientists at the turn of the century that women do have orgasms. In the Hurlbert, Apt, and Rabehl study (1993), women reported having 8.8 episodes of intercourse over a three-week period. Twenty-five percent of these coital encounters resulted in the wife having an orgasm. This figure reinforces the results reported by Kinsey (1953), in which 40 percent of sexually active married women reported being orgasmic in only 10 percent of their coital encounters. By contrast, 81 percent of the time that the women reported engaging in cunnilingus, they had an orgasm. Clearly, lack of orgasm is a normal variation of female sexuality, particularly when it is restricted to coitus. The men in the current study reported a 97 percent orgasm rate via coitus over the same period. The men had 100 percent orgasm rates with anal intercourse (the women reported 0 percent), 100 percent from self-masturbation (the women reported 98 percent), and 100 percent from spouse-assisted masturbation (the women reported 83 percent). To the extent that a specific couple wants to increase the frequency with which the wife is orgasmic, the following two rules are very helpful:

1. Always remember it is "ladies first." This general good faith rule works because, very often, women need more discussion, more foreplay, and more activities besides intercourse to achieve orgasm. In addition, men, in general, are more private, noninteractive, relaxed, and sleepy after an orgasm. If men have an orgasm first, it very often makes it more of a "chore" than an erotic or spiritual adventure to have the women reach orgasm. As men age, they also need more foreplay to achieve and maintain an erection. Still, the time differential remains significant for most couples. In those instances in which the case is reversed, the man should first come to orgasm and then the woman.
2. Masturbation is an art that can be mastered by almost anyone. There are a variety of very helpful books on the market that teach masturbation skills in the context of heterosexual marriages. The classic is Heiman and LoPiccolo's *Becoming Orgasmic*. It is geared for the sophisticated layperson but can be used as a therapy guide for the practitioner wanting to know how to instruct couples to proceed.

Both men and women change their criteria for sexual satisfaction over the course of a lifetime. Men, in particular, have been noted as experiencing marked changes. A 1994 study done by researchers at Mt. Sinai Hospital in New York (Schiavi, Mandeli, and Schreiner-Engel) is one of the few to empirically examine what leads to sexual satisfaction in healthy aging men (over the age of forty-five) and compare it with the sexual satisfactions of younger men. It has long been acknowledged that as men age they report less sexual desire, less sexual arousal, and less sexual activity. Still, they do not report less sexual satisfaction. Obviously, the three factors (desire, arousal, and activity) so central to the young man for sexual satisfaction are not the only critical factors for the older man. Instead, Schiavi and colleagues found that, along with sexual functioning factors, the quality of the marital relationship and the men's overall mood were major determinants of how sexually satisfied they felt. Older men who were emotionally close to their wives and not depressed reported the highest level of sexual satisfaction. These supposedly feminine relationship factors seem to become very important to men, as well, over time.

With any one couple it is essential to determine their idiosyncratic levels of satisfaction with both sex-related behaviors and the more general relationship issues. The Sexual Satisfaction Questionnaire (see Self-Exploration 1 at the end of this chapter, p. 394) is a good starting point for exploring these issues. Therapists can modify and add to the questionnaire as they see fit.

THERAPEUTIC INTERVENTION 1:
THE HANDICAPPING METAPHOR

Most often, couples experiencing distress in their sexual relationships have one partner who wants more sex or different kinds of sexual encounters than the other partner. By letting the more aroused partner become aware of the objectively different starting points, he or she becomes motivated to change his or her own behaviors to get his or her partner to the same starting line. A helpful therapeutic metaphor that increases the compliance rate of spouses doing the recommended at-home exercises is to explain that by getting the less aroused person more aroused, the couple is ensuring the needed "handicapping advantage" to make for a successful and exciting liaison. Only by getting to the starting gate at the same time can they be mutually aroused together for some period of time during the lovemaking.

THERAPEUTIC INTERVENTION 2:
THE WRONG-TURN INFORMATION

Sex relations are often marred by one distasteful procedure. A woman may hate the way her husband slaps her thigh but she never says anything about it. Instead, it automatically and consistently reduces her satisfaction

(continued)

(continued)

level for the rest of the event. A husband may hate the way his wife tickles his chest but be afraid of making her feel bad by mentioning it. Instead, his satisfaction is permanently dampened by her consistent habit. It is very easy and important for partners to learn to give each other feedback while they are engaged in the activity. A simple "yes" gives a clear message of enjoyment. Moving the partner's hand or taking it and showing the partner what to do with it gives the clear message that another behavior would be more pleasing. If you let sexual partners take the wrong turn and refuse to tell them, they may end up at the wrong destination point, frustrated and confused that no one told them they were on the wrong road.

Once feedback is given during the lovemaking, there should be discussion about it afterward. Couples need to discuss what about it they do not like, what they do want to experience, and if they can accommodate each other's preferences, at least to some extent. This micromanaging of the sexual act is a big turnoff to many couples. It should only be suggested when couples are agreed that increasing their sexual satisfaction is a mutual goal and that negative feedback, set in a caring, cooperative climate, is an inevitable part of the learning process.

MOST COMMON TYPES OF SEXUAL PROBLEMS AND TREATMENTS

What makes for a good sexual relationship? Good sexual relationships are a function of the sexual activities the couple engages in, individual personality characteristics, and relationship factors. The biggest problems couples have with sex is that they are doing it either too little or too much for one or both of the partners; they are frustrated or angry by the conservative or bizarre nature of their partner's sexual preferences; or they have problems achieving orgasm in the preferred way or within an acceptable period of time. Each of these typical problems will be discussed below with an emphasis on self-help and skill-remediation approaches. The clinician who wants to treat these dysfunctions will find the professional bibliography at the end of the chapter helpful.

Factors Leading to Sexual Problems

Sex is an emotion in motion.

Mae West

There are five types of problems that interfere with sexual satisfaction: biological factors, dysfunctional sexual attitudes, poor sexual communication, lack of adequate sexual information, and relationship problems.

Before assuming that the problems are treatable psychologically, it is vital to rule out any physical problems or diseases (e.g., renal failure, circulatory problems, back problems, diabetes), or diseases that could affect sexual functioning. The effects of prescription drugs, recreational drugs (alcohol, marijuana, etc.), and prior surgeries need to be explored. Careful questioning in these areas is essential for the assessment.

Second, nearly all people carry around dysfunctional sexual attitudes. Some of these attitudes are out and out irrational (e.g., "Oral sex is for the young"), whereas others are more philosophically debatable (e.g., "The goal of lovemaking is to have an orgasm," or "Each person is responsible for the pleasure that their partner experiences during lovemaking"). Erroneous beliefs can ruin a sexual encounter as quickly as a summer storm can ruin a stroll on the beach.

Sexual communication, the third factor, usually focuses on four specific skills:

1. How to initiate sexual activity and how to refuse sexual activity
2. A technical or shared symbolic language to communicate specific acts or techniques
3. How to give instantaneous sexual feedback without ruining the "flow"
4. How to share sexual preferences and fantasies

Adequate sexual information requires didactic teaching, for inadequate sexual knowledge is the fourth obstacle to sexual satisfaction. It is important for all couples to know the four phases of the sexual response as elucidated by Masters and Johnson (1966, 1970): the excitement phase, the plateau phase, the orgasm phase, and the resolution phase. The excitement phase is essential for a complete sexual response. It happens whenever a person is exposed to a sexually stimulating situation (as defined by the person). It is related to feelings of pleasure, excitement, desire for more stimulation, and physiological arousal. In the plateau phase, there is increased muscular tension and an intense drive to continue the sensations until an orgasm is achieved. Orgasm consists of those few seconds when stimulation reaches its maximum intensity. In the resolution phase a lessening of sexual tensions occurs, and most men and many women find stimulation at this time very irritable. Couples should find each phase satisfying because dysfunctions can occur at any one of the phases. Sexual education also needs to cover all areas of sexual technique and sexual dysfunction.

Fifth, as mentioned above, relationship problems can spill over into the bedroom. The most prevalent relationship problems are partner rejection, lack of trust, power struggles, contractual disappointments, sexual sabotage, and a general failure of communication (Kaplan, 1974).

Sexual enhancement programs that focus on these five components have been shown to empirically increase men's ability to be affectively expressive and to more accurately perceive their wives' sexual needs and desires. Women feel more self-accepting after such programs, and both men and women report increased satisfaction with the frequency with which they have sex. Not bad for programs whose participants met once a week for three hours for a total of four sessions (Cooper, 1985; Cooper and Stoltenberg, 1987)!

Role of Abstinence in Assessing and Treating Sexual Problems

Most sexual problems that couples present at therapy are best dealt with by initiating a period of abstinence while the problem is being assessed and a treatment plan proposed. Couples with sexual dysfunctions are relieved of a great deal of anxiety when the therapist puts intercourse off-limits. Fears of having to "go all the way" once they are intimate create a number of secondary problems for couples dealing with impotency, lack of desire, or premature ejaculation. The ability to explore touching each other, flirting with each other, and creating psychological closeness without the imminent act of intercourse being the predestined goal allows couples to become much more intimate. The definition of what is sexual expands to include all types of psychological and physical "feel goods" when coitus is not allowed. Those who can remember the joys of endless nights of petting because of a hesitancy to "go all the way" will immediately understand how defocusing from coitus intensifies all other feelings and energies.

THERAPEUTIC INTERVENTION 3:
QUICKIE SEXUAL PROBLEM ASSESSMENT

The interview procedure for assessing sexual problems requires that the clinician have a good knowledge of the DSM-IV sexual problems criteria and a good understanding of how difficult it is for individuals to explain, honestly, what their sexual life is like. The mandatory, preliminary set of ten questions should include the following:

1. How satisfied are you with your sexual relationship? What are the best parts? Which parts would you like to change? What parts are repulsive to you?
2. How often is sex a duty, how often is it a physiological need, and how often is it a mutually satisfying spiritual act?
3. When you have sex with your spouse, who else would you say was metaphorically in the bedroom with you—your parents or your spouse's or both? Why?

(continued)

(continued)

4. How uninhibited are you with your sexuality? In what ways are you inhibited? Is this a problem for you or your spouse?
5. If you were to have the perfect sexual encounter with your spouse, what would it be like? Describe it in great detail.
6. If you were to have the perfect sexual encounter with somebody other than your spouse, what would it be like? Describe it in great detail.
7. Using imagery, the couple are asked to visualize the sexual conflicts that they are experiencing in a nonhuman form. For example, a wife came to therapy because the husband was a cross-dresser. He had come to the point where he needed to wear women's panties and a bra to become sexually excited. The wife was frightened and disgusted. Asked to use imagery to symbolize the current situation, she imagined herself, in the bedroom, as a petrified piece of rock and her husband as a hefty, masculine man who had a mermaid's bottom and was thrashing around looking for water. He was a feminized fish out of water and she was, dead as a rock, unable to save him by giving him his needed environment. Exploring the image, she realized she was as disgusted and disappointed in herself as her husband. She felt powerless and angry at the same time.
8. Using imagery, the couple is asked to visualize an ideal sexual encounter in a nonhuman form.
9. When is your sexual life most likely to suffer? What types of pressures and stressors do you each have to cope with that affect your ability to respond sexually to each other?
10. How important is it to you to improve your sex life? How much effort can you realistically put into making your sex life better?

Celibacy

There are many reasons why relationships become celibate and sexual intimacies of any kind disappear. Avna and Waltz (1992) found nine different categories of reasons:

1. Desire discrepancy disorder (DDD)—in which one partner has a higher or lower sex drive than the other
2. Infidelity
3. Emotional, verbal, or physical abuse
4. Illness, whether physical or mental
5. Celibacy that is freely chosen as a means toward spiritual growth
6. Loss of respect for a spouse
7. Same-sex preference acknowledged
8. Fear of intimacy
9. Low sex drive of both partners

Couples therapists should view celibacy as a red flag for other relationship problems. In particular, the therapist should carefully assess for factors that would make the celibacy secondary to a more basic relationship problem (e.g., abuse, fear of intimacy, same-sex preference).

Some people believe that sex in a long-term, committed relationship is overrated. Maybe people can live happily together without sex. Or can they? Donnelly (1993) examined a sample of 6,029 married people from the National Survey of Families and Households and found that 16 percent of them reported having no sexual activity in the past month. The characteristics that distinguished them from the sexually active group were that they were more unhappy with the marital relationship, reported increased likelihood of separating, lacked shared activities and rituals, had few arguments over sex (apparently having come to terms about not having sex), lacked physical violence, were older, had fewer children but more preschoolers, and poorer health. The only discrepancies between Avna's (Avna and Waltz, 1992) clinical findings and Donnelly's empirical study is that Avna found abuse related to celibacy and Donnelly found just the opposite. Also, Avna found that many couples had celibate marriages that "worked" for them. Obviously, more research is needed, but the differences are probably due to sampling different couples and the fact that Avna used a much more clinically realistic and encompassing definition of abuse (it included verbal, psychological, and physical abuse) than Donnelly (who looked only at physical abuse).

The Problems of Hypoactive Sexual Desire

Hypoactive sexual desire is the largest sexual complaint that marriage counselors hear. People are simply too tired, too stressed, and too angry to be interested in having sex. An essential part of treatment is the "sensate focus," where couples learn, through a series of homework assignments in massage and touch, to reawaken their senses, communicate their desires, and luxuriate in the effects of human touch.

What is too little desire or too little sex? This is the most frequent question couples have about sex. In America today, it seems that the average couple is having sex seven times a month. Income and education seem to have no bearing on the frequency of sex, but the frequency of sex definitely declines with age.

Reasons for Hypoactive Sexual Desire

Among a group of fifty-five women who came to a clinic seeking help for hypoactive sexual desire, Hurlbert (1993) found that the women had a variety of explanations for their hypoactive sexual desire. Ninety-three percent stated that they did not get enough affection from their partner, 90 percent stated that the relationship lacked romance, 85 percent lacked sexual energy or motivation, 84 percent were not easily aroused, 75 percent cited a lack of adequate foreplay, 69 percent expressed a lack of sexual satisfaction and a lack of emotional closeness, and 60 percent had problems maintaining lubrication. Less frequently cited explanations included overall poor communication in the marriage (49 percent), dissatisfaction with the marriage (47 percent), frequent arguments about sex (38 percent), low frequency of orgasms with partner (35 percent), lack of partner trust (21 percent), dissatisfaction with body (13 percent), fear of pregnancy (4 percent), problems with children (2 percent), and problems with in-laws (2 percent).

Hurlbert's (1993) study indicates that women believe that they are hyposexual because of physiological reasons and relationship reasons. Women may not be aware that lack of desire is also a function of the extent to which they are mentally deinvested or not interested in "getting into it." People who actively imagine themselves engaging in various sexual scenarios get much more physiologically aroused by audiovisual stimuli than those people who simply look at their partner and do not imagine themselves heavily involved in the passions of the moment (Mahoney and Strassberg, 1993). Desire is born from the willingness to actively engage one's mind and attention on erotic stimuli in a personalized manner. Many men and women allow themselves to make lists of chores, finish a report, or solve a thorny interpersonal work problem while they are having sex with their spouse. Then they report feeling no desire. They say having sex has become a take it or leave it mechanical activity. No wonder! One of the basic prerequisites of feeling desire is to think tempting, desirous thoughts in which the person is the star participant.

Therapists who understand how sexually excitable each partner is will have important information for treatment planning. Sexual arousal is obviously necessary (but not sufficient) for satisfying sexual relations. There are great individual differences in sexual excitability. People who have a sensation-seeking personality tend to report higher sexual desires, greater sexual arousability, and more positive attitudes toward sex. Somewhat surprisingly, men who are married to women who are high-sensation seekers have less happy marriages than those who are married to low-sensation-seeking women. Perhaps, men find such women very "demanding" or "threatening," for they are likely to want to seek out new and different experiences in many phases of their lives, not just in the sexual arena (Apt and Hurlbert, 1992).

Sexual Arousal and Sensate Focus

Mosher (1980) presents three basic modes of sexual arousal: entrancement (arousing oneself through imagery and thoughts), partner involvement (partner arouses through verbal and tactile methods), and role enactment (both partners play out a determined scene that is highly arousing). Sexual therapists rely most heavily on partner involvement, although the other modes need to be explored and developed.

Thus, when couples need to learn to reawaken their senses and tackle their hypoactive sexual desire, therapists often begin by instructing the couple in joint role enactments of pleasuring exercises (sensate focus exercises). Sensate focus exercises were developed to help couples learn to teach each other what types of touch and strokes are erotically pleasing to them. During sensate focus exercises, intercourse or sexual touching to buttocks, breasts, penis, and vaginal areas is forbidden. The goal is to learn how to awaken desires by gently massaging or rubbing various areas of the face, arms, legs, and back. Couples take turns telling their partners what they like, what feels good, and what they do not like. They use oils and lotions to relax with each other and build a climate of safe feeling. Again, a plethora of books and tapes is available explaining how to do this. Spouses take turns being the recipient of the pleasuring and the one giving pleasure. One popular format is for one partner to pleasure the other for thirty minutes and then change places. It is very important that couples do not feel sleazy or compromised by any of the self-help books and tapes. They need to find ones that they are comfortable with to be able to model the exercises they are shown.

All too often, this seemingly simply exercise of sensate focus needs to be preceded by extensive groundwork in communication, education about the destructiveness of put-downs, and insights about the vulnerabilities associated with sexual trust.

Women, somewhat more than men, are very sensitive about their body images. Chronically on diets, they have all types of self-criticisms and self-loathings. Unfortunately, men are also more likely to be centered on criticizing their wives' bodies. Women often shy away from sex because they have registered the critical looks and comments and feel they are unattractive to their mates. Many men directly or indirectly vocalize about how turned off they are to various features of their wives' anatomy. To get to the point where a middle-aged man can easily and openly admire a middle-aged woman's body would undoubtedly require a great change in the cultural values of our time. Nonetheless, loving the bowed breast that nursed the children, the extended tummy that carried them, or the cellulite thighs that have walked through a complicated life requires only a moment of spiritual insight into the meaning of life. Instead of being turned on by lust (defined as the illusionary idea that one is good enough or strong enough to have a valued "object" that other men would compete for), men can be turned on by the opportunity to momentarily lose the need to compete with other men and fuse with their other half (the female half). When the wife is turned off by her husband's aging body, which happens far more often than is commonly acknowledged, the same set of dynamics come into play.

In a way, the sexual love of longtime married couples is a potent opportunity to experience and affirm the real self, whereas lust merely grasps at an illusionary idealized self. This makes the sex of long-term couples potentially more frightening than the lustful sex of young, attractive couples.

Some years ago, I saw a couple in which the husband was refusing to have sex with his wife until she had breast surgery to reshape her breasts, which had become misshapen after having breast-fed two children. The wife was, objectively, a beautiful woman. Horrified by her husband's rejection, she quickly became self-loathing and depressed. When she started to gain a little more confidence, she decided to leave him. Before she did, she went to Florida and had the surgery. She wanted him to miss her and be remorseful when she left. She felt the only way to ensure this outcome was through this procedure. She said, "If he can miss my breasts, he'll be able to miss the rest of me." The tragedy of this case is that so many women end up rejecting their critical husbands but accepting the demeaning bodily criticisms offered by the otherwise discredited spouse.

Many couples mistakenly think that sexual arousal should begin once they are in bed and naked. However, nakedness is much less arousing than the process of becoming naked, regardless of the body that is being unveiled. That is why striptease shows are so exciting and nudist colonies are said to quickly lose their arousal value.

The payoff in terms of sexual pleasure for women who are able to enjoy undressing for their spouse is considerable. Of those who are not ashamed of nakedness and do strip to tease their spouse (about one out of every three), 62 percent report sex at least several times a week rather than 29 percent of those in the opposite category (Greeley, Michael, and Smith, 1990). Although men, in general, are more aroused by visual cues than women are, no one has yet empirically assessed the arousing effects of males undressing for their female partners.

The Hurlbert Index of Excitability (1993) (see Self-Exploration 2, p. 395) helps the therapist explore arousal levels in the husband and wife.

THERAPEUTIC INTERVENTION 4:
INCREASING SEXUAL DESIRE

For couples who want more sexual excitement but label many activities as too "kinky" or weird for them, it is essential to show how erotic and exciting the most simple behaviors can become. For example, one can use a body image exercise in which the partners take turns viewing themselves nude in the mirror. While one partner is clothed, the other looks in the mirror and shares his or her fears and desires in terms of his or her own body image. If the partner can be reassuring and complimentary, this can be a very meaningful exercise. (Metz and Weiss, 1992)

A more intense exercise requires that the partners take turns leading each other in an exploration of their bodies and genitals using a mirror and even a plastic speculum. Besides gaining comfort in touching and exploring, it allows each person to practice some sexual leadership, some period of taking charge of the situation.

Couples can also learn to give each other sensual massages using books such as Adele Kennedy and Susan Dean's 1986 book, *Touching for Pleasure: A Guide to Sensual Enhancement.*

CASE STUDY 1:
HYPOACTIVE SEXUAL DESIRE
AND THE PRIORITY LIST

Sue and Paul were twenty-eight years old and successful young lawyers. They were both on track to becoming partners at their respective firms before the age of thirty. They had one child who was two years old and being cared for by a live-in nanny. Their daily routine consisted of twelve-hour workdays. They alternated going home each workday for a two-hour lunch to play with their daughter and to do some errands. After work, they met at the gym and worked out. Home around 9 p.m., they would play with their daughter till 11:30 p.m. and then spend an hour doing wash, cleaning, and getting ready for the next day. They would collapse into bed around 1:00 a.m. and be up at 6:00 a.m.

Weekends were just as hectic. They alternated the Saturdays that they went to work but were disciplined about being home by 5:00 p.m. on Saturdays. Then they would either see one set of parents or the other. Sometimes, family events would require that they see both sets during the weekend. Then Sunday would be completely lost. Otherwise, Sunday was a decompression day. They did errands, played with their daughter, saw friends, and tried to have a normal life.

Typical of their problem, when they called for treatment, they had no immediate time in which they could be seen. We scheduled an appoint-

(continued)

(continued)

ment for a month later. Sue and Paul came in and had total unanimity about the problem. Neither of them felt sexual any more. Sue could not remember ever wanting to have sex since the birth of their daughter. Paul felt that every month or two he got in the mood. They had had sex three times in the past year, all at Paul's initiation. All three times, it was in the middle of the night. Sue was mostly asleep. Paul was sort of dreaming and having intercourse at the same time. Needless to say, they were worried about this continuing for a lifetime.

Like many couples, Sue and Paul thought they should be able to be aroused at a moment's notice, at a time convenient to their schedules. Although they realized that at 1 a.m. they were so tired they couldn't see straight, they were still disappointed in their libidinal void. Psychoeducational discussions first centered around the roles of stress, sleep deprivation, and physical fatigue on sexual arousal. We spoke a great deal about peak performance at work and how they prepared to get their best work done. Both agreed that once a piece of work was given high priority, they "saved up" their energy until they could get to that task. When they tried to place sexual intimacy on a list of priorities, both placed it under work responsibilities, child care responsibilities, exercise responsibilities, and family-of-origin responsibilities. It was ranked above social life with friends, religious responsibilities, and housecleaning responsibilities (Sue had housecleaning on the same level as sex; Paul had it right below sex).

A few sessions were devoted entirely to discussing what priorities would have to change to make sexual arousal a high-priority item. Sue eventually decided she would have to give up a daily workout to have energy to "work out" in the bedroom. Paul decided he would have to stop coming home in the afternoon and just leave an hour earlier at the end of the day to be with his daughter. As time was made for sexual arousal, we also had planned sensate focus sessions. Gradually, their sex life increased so that they were having intercourse once every two weeks and making out and enjoying each other at least once a week. Although both felt that it was not where they wanted to be, they both were satisfied, for now, with the improved state. They felt closer and connected.

THERAPEUTIC INTERVENTION 5:
LETTER WRITING TO INCREASE SEXUAL DESIRE

Ask each spouse to write a letter to the other during the week in which they describe an exceptionally fond intimate memory. It can be either a nonsexual or sexual intimate moment, or a sexual moment. The level of detail in the letter is up to the letter writer. What is most important is to convey the warm, close feelings, the images, and thoughts that remain

(continued)

(continued)

from that memory. After the letter is written, it should be given to the spouse in a sealed envelope. The receiving spouse should read the letter in private. It is essential that neither partner discusses the content of the letter before or afterward for a period of one month. This allows sharing without the possibility of analyzing, criticizing, annotating, or rewriting the shared moment. It allows time for the partner's memory to quietly "sit" with the spouse and invoke further memories over time. After a month, some clients want to discuss the letters with the therapist while some prefer to keep the moments quiet.

THERAPEUTIC INTERVENTION 6:
EXERCISE TO INCREASE SEXUAL DESIRE
BY EROTIC IMAGERY

David Treadway (1993) has developed a way to let couples explore which of three types of sexual arousal practices (communication, sensate focus, or risk taking) would be most effective for them. He begins by asking the couple to sit together on the couch so that their hips and thighs are touching. This shifts couples out of their public posture and hopefully allows for the flow of more intimate feelings. Then, he says:

> As you go through this together on the couch, with your thighs and hips touching, you may feel a full range of emotions from excitement to anxiety to embarrassment. Just let them happen. As you settle back on the sofa and make yourself comfortable, imagine you're in a movie theater and the wall behind me is the screen. Now you can do this with your eyes open, focusing intently on the wall until you see the screen, or you can do it with your eyes closed, letting yourself get lost in the privacy and darkness of the theater.
>
> I am going to project several scenes on the screen that will show different ways that couples find their own path toward emotional connection and sexual intimacy. See if you can see yourselves on the screen enacting the scenarios. You can try on each approach in the privacy of your mind, discovering the full range of your feelings. But, if you are not quite ready to put yourself on the silver screen, just let yourself imagine some other couple going through these scenarios.
>
> Now, let's begin with the first scene. It opens with a close-up shot of a crackling fire in a living room. The camera focuses on a couple sitting together on the sofa. They are surrounded by books, and the woman is reading one of them out loud to the man. The camera zooms in on the book and we see that it is about intimacy and sexuality. They begin to talk about their embarrassment as adolescents when they discovered the secret shame and delight of masturbation. They talk about feelings and thoughts that they had never shared before. As the scene fades, the woman takes the man's hand. He slides closer and puts an arm around her. (COMMUNICATION)

(continued)

> *(continued)*
> In scene two, there is a couple in the bedroom. They are taking turns giving each other a sensual, full-body massage. They are telling each other about what type of touch feels just right. There are some touching (?) moments as they learn how to give and receive, but they persist through their difficulties with a good mix of humor and tenderness. (SENSATE FOCUS)
> In the third scene, I describe a couple learning how to be playful and seductive with each other. I describe the couple making out in the car and flirting with each other when they are doing the dinner dishes. I describe them being seductive with each other and learning the gentle art of saying no in a loving manner. (RISK TAKING) (pp. 36-37)
>
> After having all three images, couples discuss which ones they felt most comfortable with, which ones they think would work for them, and how they can individualize the practice to reflect their own needs and style.
>
> *Source:* Treadway, D. (1993, March/April). In a world of their own. *Family Networker,* pp. 33-39. Used with permission.

The Problem of Sexual Addiction

Only ten years ago, it was hard to find professionals who were willing to diagnose a married man as "oversexed" or "sexually addicted." Married women who were eager to have sex on a daily basis, or more frequently, were often judged by husbands as "nymphomaniacs" and seen by therapists as "immature." Suddenly, though, the maturing of the addictions movement has raised the consciousness of the counseling community so that both husbands and wives are more likely to be assessed and diagnosed as using sex as an anxiety-reducing coping mechanism.

To be diagnosed with a sexual addiction, a person must show the following three symptoms of an addiction (Goodman, 1993):

1. The person must have uncontrollable urges. This is demonstrated by continuous unsuccessful attempts at resisting the urge to act out certain sexual behaviors, although a strong desire to reduce the occurrences of the sexual behavior is evident.
2. The person feels very anxious prior to engaging in the sexual behavior. Addiction to sexual behavior is comparable to how a drug addict desires the drug substance. Performing the sexual act becomes the person's primary focus. He or she is determined to satisfy the sexual urges, and they come second to nothing else.
3. The only way to alleviate the tension is to perform the sexual act. The sex addict returns to his or her normal state only after the craving has been satisfied.

In addition to these three cardinal symptoms, people must show five of the following eight characteristics:

1. The person's thoughts are preoccupied with sex and sex-related thoughts.
2. Sex occurs more often and for a longer duration of time than anticipated.
3. The person has made attempts at controlling, lessening, or alleviating the sexual urges and behaviors through self-help techniques.
4. The person is continously preoccupied with sex: If not engaging in a sexual act, the individual is constantly in preparation for the next sexual encounter.
5. Important social, domestic, or job-related responsibilities have been neglected because of the precedence given to sex.
6. Sexual behavior continues despite the realization of recurrent psychological, economic, social, or physical problems that are a result of the sexual behavior.
7. The individual develops a "tolerance" in which he or she feels the need to increase the occurrence or intensity of the sexual behavior to attain the desired effect.
8. The person experiences symptoms of irritability or uneasiness.

From these criteria, it is possible that a person can be sexually addicted to sexual intercourse or to any other sexual behavior. Men who need to have women dress a certain way or perform certain sexual acts can be sexual addicts. Women who need men to engage in specific behaviors or ritualized verbalizations, or have very specific fantasies, can be sexually addicted.

Much like treating other addictions, a psychologist treating sexual addictions must help clients realize the type of situations or psychological environments that are most likely to bring about their urges. Ordinarily, these are highly affective situations: situations that increase feelings of anxiety, anger, or sadness. Once the clients understand the types of situations that bring on the urges, they are able to avoid those situations or, when they are unavoidable, begin their coping responses very early. For example, many sexual addicts are particularly vulnerable to stress arising from work, family-of-origin issues, or any public blow to their self-esteem. Clients then need to learn how to cope with the urges by engaging in specific acts of thought stopping (focusing on the negative consequences of engaging in the sexual behavior), talking to someone about the urge until it goes away, and focusing on the benefits of abstinence.

In therapy, the clients need to reframe their behavior as an addiction and then work on finding more appropriate ways to achieve their emotional and social needs. As people grapple with the paradox of both needing other people and needing to protect themselves from being too vulnerable with others, they discover how to maintain a healthy equilibrium and modulate their anxiety without the use of addictions.

The idea of looking at excess sexual behavior as an addiction runs counter to the whole notion of a sexual freedom in which everything is "healthy" provided there are two consenting adults. Now, the thinking is that only by examining the context in which sex is taking place can an individual or therapist decide if a particular behavior or frequency is normal or abnormal.

Hurlbert and colleagues (1994) have argued against the notion of sexual addiction, saying that it has not been empirically proven to exist and it takes responsibility for the behavior away from the man or woman. Instead, they suggest that the problem be conceptualized as a case of sexual narcissism, a form of sexual acting out typical of people with narcissistic, histrionic, or borderline personality disorders. They found that sexual narcissism is more common among men and is very common among physically abusive husbands. These men have traditional sex role attitudes, low self-esteem, and have great difficulty experiencing satisfying sexual relations with their wives. Often, they are promiscuous and frequently complain about being sexually bored at home.

The spouse with a narcissistic personality disorder is interpersonally exploitive, has great feelings of entitlement ("I want, so I should have," "It is a husband's right to have sex when he wants it"), feelings of self-importance, an inability to experience emotional intimacy, and a lack of empathy (keenly focused on getting his or her own needs satisfied without a desire to satisfy the spouse). These characteristics are also central to the person with a sexual addiction. The basic fear of rejection, and feelings of worthlessness underlying these defensive attitudes, leads these men to overcompensate and bolster their self-esteem with grandiose fantasies and a constant use of manipulative power. Only as the men work on developing better relationships and reworking the developmental sources of their behavior will they be able to be more responsive sexual partners (Hurlbert et al., 1994). Empirical studies conducted by Hurlbert and colleagues found that, true to their expectations, individuals with a narcissistic personality disorder displayed many of the traits associated with sexual narcissism (or addiction).

However, there is some empirical evidence that sex can and is used as a coping mechanism by nearly everyone. Morokoff and Gillilland (1993) found that the more daily hassles people have, the more sexual desire they report feeling. This relationship was found for both men and women. It suggests that sex as a "pleasurable distraction" and a form of "exercise" could successfully be used to reduce tension. Of course, correlation does not prove causation, and an equally likely interpretation of these findings is that people interpret the elevated arousal that accompanies chronic stress as a signal that they are sexually aroused.

CASE STUDY 2:
HYPERSEXUALITY IN A CROSS-DRESSER—
USING COMMUNICATIONS TRAINING
AND FAMILY-OF-ORIGIN WORK

Tom and Alison were both high school teachers in their early thirties. They had two children. Actively involved in their church, their careers, and parenthood, they seemed to have a wonderful, efficient marriage. In reality, they rarely spoke to each other other except to coordinate schedules. They never fought.

They had sex constantly. They could count the nights in a year when they did not have sex. On the weekends, they would always have intercourse at least twice a day (morning and night). They felt that this was a normal routine for happily married couples.

When Tom was caught cross-dressing by Alison, she freaked out and demanded that he seek help. He was frantic and even suicidal. He had dressed in ladies bras and panties to masturbate ever since he was twelve years old. He was deeply ashamed and wanted to be rid of the compulsion. He was too afraid to share this habit with his wife and went on year after year hiding it from her. He entered a sexual disorders clinic as an inpatient soon after "coming out" and there began to explore all aspects of his sexuality. It became clear to him that he had used intercourse as a Band-Aid, a cocktail, a weapon against Alison, and a security blanket. He was addicted to sex, just like an alcoholic is addicted to drink. He realized that whenever he wanted to fight with Alison, he simply had sex with her instead. Instead of finding out what was happening with Alison and talking to her, he had intercourse with her. Alison quickly realized that she also used sex in this compulsive manner.

After the inpatient treatment, Tom and Alison entered marital therapy. For a year and a half, they practiced communicating with each other, learning to express anger and fear to each other. They did extensive family-of-origin work. They each traced back and discovered childhood experiences and family lifestyles that taught them to be afraid to express themselves verbally. Together they explored ways they could help each

(continued)

> *(continued)*
> other grow as individuals. Each was encouraged to explore new activities and new friends. They looked for ways to bond together sexually. Finding out how to be in a romantic mood at the same time took many weeks, particularly because a romantic mood was never needed for sexual relations in the past.
>   It was very difficult for the Tom and Alison to stop using sex in a compulsive manner. Nine months into treatment they decided to try a period of abstinence. Six months of experimentation followed, during which they tried to learn what were the cues for positive intercourse and what were the cues they had been using during their ritualized, addictive relations. The most difficult thing they needed to learn was how to say "No" to each other. Instead of using and being used by each other sexually, they needed to learn to make it a mutually satisfying, spiritual experience.
>   Treatment was terminated by unanimous agreement.

The Problem of Infidelity

Although statistics on extramarital affairs are hard to come by, a number of research reports concur that within the United States (Hurlbert, 1992):

1. At least 25 to 50 percent of men report having had at least one affair; the numbers for women range from 20 to 45 percent.
2. The primary motive for men and women in having an affair seems to be, not surprisingly, sexual fulfillment. Women also seek friendship, freedom, and independence through an affair. Men seek excitement and change, as well as the desire to be needed (Lawson, 1989).
3. Most extramarital sex does not involve love, and sexual intercourse usually does not occur more than five times a year.
4. There are three types of affairs: sexual but not emotional, emotional but not sexual, and both emotional and sexual. Men tend to have more affairs that are just sexual, women more that are just emotional.
5. The fewer the affairs people have, the more stress they put on the emotional meaning of the liaison (Lawson, 1989).

Hurlbert's studies showed a very skewed distribution for the length of women's affairs. Over a third of the women had no further contact one month or less after the first sexual contact. A little less than one-third of the women had affairs that lasted for one year or more.

By definition, an affair involves secrecy. If the spouse is aware of the lover, then the relationship is an "arrangement" or some sort of "ménage à trois." An affair involves deception, lies, and the automatic distancing of couples from each other. Although some actually believe that the affair will "help" the marriage, most are aware of the self-destructive nature of their behavior. They want an affair the same way that a person on a diet wants a Big Mac or a hot fudge, double chocolate sundae. They know it is probably one of the worst things they can have, and still they crave it.

Yet the motivations fueling affairs vary from person to person. Brown's (1991) typology of affairs describes well the different types of affairs encountered by therapists. The first type of affair is called the "conflict-avoidance affair." Participants are pleasing and self-sacrificing couples for whom the affair is motivated by a desire on the part of one partner to let go of the facade of a model marriage. These partners want their spouses to know about the alienation and pain they feel. These folks still love their partners and always manage to find a way to let the affair become known. The affair is not the real threat to the marriage, rather, it is the avoidance of conflict. When the affair becomes known, these couples can often face very sticky issues and resolve to have a stronger marriage.

The second type of affair is the "intimacy-avoidance affair." Participants' marriages are characterized by a lack of cooperation and many arguments and disagreements. One or both partners find it very threatening to become intimate. They are desperately afraid to put energy and commitment into the relationship. The arguments are used to avoid empathizing or being honest and, on the surface, they justify the affair. Once these couples learn how to be intimate with each other and risk being vulnerable and dependent, they can become faithful to each other.

The "sexual-addiction affair" is found among emotionally deprived, abused, or overwhelmed individuals who seek personal power and validation by proving they can win the affections of attractive, wealthy, young, or otherwise desirable "trophies." They often go from one affair to the next, motivated by the pursuit. The spouse of someone involved in a sexual-addiction affair is often willing to look the other way until it becomes a public embarrassment. Men are more likely to get into these types of affairs.

"Empty-nest affairs" are common among middle-aged men and women who are with people they no longer love and are trying to recapture a meaningful, intimate relationship. The prognosis for these marriages is quite poor. The relationship is usually too tortured or too empty to create a satisfying emotional union. The spouse who has been betrayed is most often completely devastated by the total rejection, and it often takes years to rebuild any self-esteem, optimism, or faith.

"Out-the-door affairs" are similar to empty-nest affairs in that those participating have marriages that are no longer vibrant or satisfying any emotional needs. Yet the unfaithful spouse is afraid to leave and be alone. Instead, he or she tries putting only one foot out the door by having a comfortable affair. Usually, such spouses like to talk to their newfound buddy about all of their mate's deficiencies and problems. They seek support to take the big step. Sometimes, when these affairs become known, they are seized by the faithful spouse because there is now an objective "bad guy" to explain why the marriage is dissolving (e.g., he stole her away from me). Quite often, these affairs die a natural death after the unfaithful partner has been successfully shepherded out the door.

Extramarital involvements can present at three different phases in therapy: Couples can come in after the affair has been terminated and as they are trying to rebuild their trust; couples can come during the crisis period when the affair is in the process of being unearthed; or they can start therapy when it is still a big, haunting secret. It is in this third instance that therapists have the most problems.

Although space does not permit an expanded discussion of these issues, it should be quite clear that both the treatment strategies and prognosis will vary according to the type of affair. For example, a couples format is most appropriate for conflict-avoiders, intimacy-avoiders, and out-the-door types. Individual work is initially most appropriate with sexual addicts and empty-nesters.

Regardless of the type of affair or the therapeutic approach used to deal with the exposed crisis, extramarital relationships have an overwhelmingly negative influence on marriages. A recent clinical study of sixty-two marriages affected by infidelity found that 34 percent (twenty-one) ended in divorce, 43 percent (twenty-seven) remained intact but in an overall negative atmosphere, 6 percent (four) stayed intact with a "blah" or empty marital quality, and only 14 percent (nine) couples blossomed and improved through the ordeal (Charney and Parnass, 1995).

Very often, marital infidelity is exposed as part of the therapy process. Usually, this occurs in an individual session, after one or two joint sessions, and before the therapeutic goals and contract have been finalized. With confidentiality guaranteed within the individual session, a spouse will confess to an old or ongoing extramarital involvement. This puts therapists in a very compromising situation: They cannot share this privileged information with the betrayed spouse, and by not sharing this information, they are in collusion with the unfaithful spouse. Some therapists advocate limiting confidentiality only to those issues that do not affect the health and well-being of the marriage. In short, this means forewarning individuals, up front, that disclosing an affair is not a piece of information that will be kept confidential. Because few will disclose such information under these conditions, I prefer to tell the couple that after the individual sessions, I will either make a recommendation for individual therapy for one or both of them (in which case I will refer them both to different therapists) or agree that couples therapy is indicated. I explain that there are many reasons for seeking individual therapy over couples therapy. The primary reason is that personal issues need to be resolved before working on the marriage. The personal issues can range from existential insecurities to depression to marital infidelities to personality disorders of various types. I explain that I can share the recommendation but that confidentiality will prevent me from sharing my reasoning. If both partners agree to this procedure, which they always do, I proceed. Then, the sharing of an affair in the individual session prompts a recommendation for individual therapy or a discussion of ways for the unfaithful spouse to share his or her actions with his or her mate (inside a therapy session or outside of one). Sometimes, depending on the situation, I will recommend that the unfaithful spouse and the lover seek counseling to resolve their situation. I do not believe it is possible to work on a marriage, in therapy, when one partner is having an extramarital involvement that is secret. The message that couples therapy is contraindicated at this point, indicates to the betrayed spouse that the marital situation is dire and basically out of his or her control.

If the affair is disclosed or was disclosed before the couple came to therapy, it is important for the therapist to understand how it affected both the unfaithful and the betrayed spouse. Important questions to ask include: How long was the affair? How often did you see your lover? What was your emotional connection to the lover? Have there been other extramarital involvements in the past? How was the affair discovered (if it was not voluntarily disclosed)? What history of extramarital involvements are there on both sides of the family tree? What were the emotional costs of the affair? The answers to these questions can reveal how corrosive the affair was to the marriage and the potential difficulties in reconciliation and forgiveness.

Although sexual infidelity is focused on the sexual act between the lover and the spouse, very often there is no sexual dissatisfaction or dysfunction in the marriage. After the affair is disclosed, however, the betrayed spouse develops deep sexual resentments or inhibitions. Sex becomes the stimulus for painful comparisons, memories, and doubts. Learning to sexually reconnect becomes an important focus of therapy even though it was not a problem prior to the sharing of the secret.

Problems in Orgasmic Timing and Frequency

Female Orgasmic Disorder

There are many varieties of orgasmic failure. In lifelong orgasmic failure, the woman has never achieved an orgasm of any type by any means. In acquired orgasmic failure, the woman most likely does not achieve an orgasm when she is having sexual relations with her husband but can achieve orgasm by masturbation or with other men or women. This is called the situation type. In the generalized type, the woman loses all ability to achieve orgasm, whether by masturbation, oral sex, or coitus (Kaplan, 1987).

The primary treatment for orgasmic failure involves enabling the female client to feel comfortable with exploring her own body, in her own time frames, without the husband present. Admiring oneself in the mirror, stroking oneself for pleasure, and playing with arousing fantasies are all encouraged. Learning to be orgasmic via masturbation is an essential component. Once the woman can masturbate herself to orgasm, she learns to masturbate in front of her husband as part of their lovemaking. Eventually, she teaches her husband how to pleasurably masturbate her. Often, the man is instructed to place his hand lightly over his wife's hand, like a light glove, so that he can learn to model how much pressure she likes, the movements she likes, and the locations she likes. The most helpful book on this technique is Julia Heiman and Joseph LoPiccolo's (1988) *Becoming Orgasmic: A Sexual and Personal Growth Program for Women.*

Lately, therapists have been questioning the uncritical use of masturbation in treating orgasmic failure as well as the other sexual dysfunctions. Therapists have noted that for some couples masturbation practices may actually further damage the trust and openness necessary for interpersonally meaningful sexual encounters (Christensen, 1995). These masturbation-wary practitioners believe that many sexual dysfunctions serve a defensive purpose and that until safety, respect, and intimacy are restored in the relationship, it may not even be advisable to seek improved sexual relations. This harkens back to the sex therapist/couple therapist split discussed in the beginning of this chapter. Respecting the uniqueness of each couple's sexual difficulties should keep therapists from giving blanket prescriptions of masturbation. However, it should also encourage therapists to use such strategies when there are no strong reasons to suggest that it would not help.

Male Erectile Disorder

There are also many varieties of male erectile disorder. In lifelong erectile disorders, the man has never achieved an erection—not even a morning erection (almost universal during REM sleep). This type of impotency is very hard to treat and almost always biological in nature. In acquired erectile dysfunctions, if the man has problems getting an erection only on specific occasions, such as when he is trying to have sexual relations with his wife, the disorder is situational. Here, the man can achieve an erection in the shower, or with a prostitute or lover. In generalized erectile disorder, the man has lost the ability to attain and maintain an erection in all situations.

Men develop situational erectile disorder whenever they are under extreme stress or feeling extreme anxiety. Stressors such as unemployment, criminal and legal proceedings, extreme fatigue, active combat, diabetes, heart conditions, and marital strife are all related to the inability to attain an erection (Morokoff and Gillilland, 1993).

The primary treatment for erectile dysfunction is systematic desensitization in which the couple is taught to pleasure each other during a period of coital abstinence. Although the length of abstinence varies according to the progress of the treatment, during that period they are forbidden to have intercourse regardless of how hard an erection is achieved or how long it remains. The wife is taught how to masturbate her husband to have an erection. She is instructed in the art of handriding, where she gently places her hand over her husband's hand while he masturbates himself to get an erection. In this way, she can model the degree of pressure and the type of thrust that is exciting for the man.

Premature Ejaculation

Premature ejaculation is one of the most common types of sexual dysfunction. Many men fear that they suffer from premature ejaculation because they are not having coitus for at least thirty minutes before ejaculating. The reality is that although this disorder is, in part, self-defined, the average man in treatment for premature ejaculation is unable to delay orgasm for thirty seconds. Although the majority of premature ejaculators are young men with new partners, some married men lose the ability to delay orgasm after years of adequate functioning. Often, this follows a period of sexual inactivity. Sometimes, men who were heavy drinkers develop premature ejaculation when they become abstinent because they have not learned how to delay orgasm independent of alcohol.

Treatment consists of systematic desensitization and teaching both partners the "squeeze technique." In this procedure, a simple squeeze at the base of the penis can cause the urge to ejaculate to disappear. It is important for the couple to learn to squeeze from front to back so as not to rupture any veins (Kaplan, 1989).

Male Orgasmic Disorder

This is a rare problem in which the man gets excited, gets an erection, maintains an erection, but is unable to ejaculate and reach orgasm during coitus even when the stimulation is intense, focused, and of a long duration. In the most common form of this disorder, the man can reach orgasm by manual or oral stimulation. Women often find this problem very diffi-

---

CASE STUDY 3:
A ONE-SESSION SEXUAL EDUCATION CURE
FOR ERECTILE FAILURE

Karin and Cory were both in their early forties and had been married for twenty years. They had a strong, satisfying relationship, but the past two years had been exceedingly stressful. Cory lost his job as an aeronautical engineer and was forced to be a "jobber." He had to commute three hours a day and had no health benefits or job security. He felt he was too old to be rehired as a full-time engineer and was busy looking for small-business opportunities. Karin's sister, divorced and with four children, developed breast cancer. Karin became a weekly visitor, running errands, watching the kids, and taking her sister for her chemotherapy treatments. In addition, Karin's mother was diagnosed with Alzheimer's during this period. Karin was helping her dad make plans and deal with the day-to-day agony of the disease. Six months ago, Karin and Cory decided to stop trying to get pregnant and accept that they would be childless. This was a difficult decision for both of them, but they had been trying for ten years and were totally depleted of enthusiasm for any more high-tech solutions.

With all of these stressors and losses, it was no surprise that three months prior to making the appointment, Cory had developed an impotency problem. He would get an erection, but as soon as he tried to enter Karin, he would go soft. The therapist met with the couple for one session and explained how erectile failures are treated. It was stressed that Cory must stop watching himself mentally during sexual activity, monitoring to see when he would fail. Karin would have to stop worrying about Cory's sexual abilities also. Sensate focus was described as was the philosophy of "giving to get" (by giving pleasure to the partner one gets very aroused and sexual). Most important was the idea of teasing—that Karin was to stimulate Cory to have an erection, then stop arousing him and lie quietly in his arms until the erection went away. Then she was to tease him again

(continued)

(continued)

and again wait for the erection to disappear. They were instructed to play this way for about thirty minutes. Lastly, the therapist discussed how manual and oral stimulation of the penis would help Cory maintain an erection and have an orgasm. It was suggested that during the next week they restrict their sex to noncoital methods. The history was not at all complete and details of the program had to be worked out.

The next week the therapist had to cancel. When Karin and Cory were seen two weeks later, they could not believe how easy it had been to solve the problem, even before they were thoroughly assessed! They had gone home the night of the session and Karin had oral sex with Cory to the point of orgasm. Afterward, she teased him once or twice. The next night, they manually stimulated each other to orgasm. The third night, Cory was shocked to find himself waking up in the middle of the night with an erection that would not go away. They had tried to have intercourse three times during the next eleven days and were successful on all three occasions.

This is a very typical successful treatment of erectile failure.

cult because they get physically raw from all the thrusting. They often attribute the inability to reach orgasm to their own deficiencies in being an appropriately erotic lover.

Dyspareunia

Both men and women can experience recurrent and persistent genital pain associated with intercourse, although the condition is far more common among women. The condition is usually chronic unless treated. For women dyspareunia is due to vaginal infections, vaginal sensitivity (often to chemical contraceptives), or tears in the ligaments that hold up the uterus. The most common forms of treatment are medical interventions that clean up the infection or repair the damaged tissue.

Vaginismus

Vaginismus is a condition in which involuntary spasms of the musculature of the outer third of the vagina severely constrict the opening so that a penis cannot penetrate or can penetrate only with extreme pain to the woman. It does not take long for a woman with vaginismus to develop strong conditioned fear responses to intercourse. This strengthens the spasm response and makes intercourse a horrible thought and a torturous act.

The most successful treatments involve systematic desensitization, in which plastic rod devices of varying circumferences are inserted by the woman into her vaginal opening. She begins with very thin rods and when she is relaxed and successful with one level rod, she proceeds onward.

Despite the success of such a mechanical treatment, whenever a woman presents with dyspareunia or vaginismus, the therapist should first carefully assess for a history of sexual abuse because these conditions are frequently associated with a traumatic sexual history. Although desensitization techniques would still be required, additional sexual anxieties would need to be addressed as well, to maximize sexual enjoyment and prevent relapse.

Paraphilia

Paraphilias include recurrent, intense sexual arousal involving (1) nonhuman objects (shoes, panties, bras, etc.), (2) the suffering or humiliation of oneself or one's partner (sadomasochistic sexual practices, exhibitionism), and (3) children or other nonconsenting persons (pedophiles, frotteurs [those who rub against or touch nonconsenting adults]). Although most people realize that a pedophile or a frotteur is legally out of bounds and in need of help, the average mental health professional is much more confused about the first two classes of paraphilias.

Cross-Dressing

Cross-dressing is on the rise and quickly coming out of the closet. Movies such as *Tootsie, The Crying Game, Even Cowgirls Get the Blues, Yentl,* and *Kiss of the Spider Woman* focus on cross-dressers. MTV is filled with videos of cross-dressers. The International Foundation for Gender Education found that 6 percent of the U.S. population are cross-dressers (individuals of one gender who like to wear the clothes of the opposite gender) and 1 percent are transsexuals (feel that their cross-dressing is matching their true psychological gender identity). Cross-dressing has been celebrated in politically correct circles. Those with "politically correct" views believe cross-dressers should be defined as the "third gender," not an aberration of either maleness or femaleness but true to their own otherness.

Historically, cross-dressing was used for political purposes—to symbolically bridge two disparate worlds. Little Richard, the early rock star, used flamboyant costumes and makeup, very similar to that of singer Michael Jackson. Both were trying to cross over from the black music world to the white marketplace. Liberace, another high fashion cross-dresser, was trying to blend classical music with easy listening fare. The most famous cross-dresser of all, the Big Bad Wolf in *Little Red Riding Hood,* is perhaps symbolic of how aggression can masquerade as nurturance (Garber, 1992). However, the local husband who is dressing in his wife's panties and bras assuredly has no grand political goal. Rather, he is compulsively driven to cross-dress in order to become sexually aroused.

Those men who are lucky enough to find sensitive wives nearly always choose to continue cross-dressing. Although cross-dressing is not a violent crime, most women find it so unnatural and such a turnoff that the marriage cannot survive the crisis unless the husband learns to inhibit that behavior. Women whose husbands are cross-dressers need to be reassured that it has nothing to do with their husband's love, devotion, or attraction toward them. It is usually a long-term, developmental habit that started in adolescence and can be broken only with extreme discipline, a supportive family, and cognitive-behavioral types of therapy. There have been recent reports that medications traditionally used with obsessive-compulsive disorders have been very successful with some cross-dressers.

Sadomasochism

Sadomasochistic propensities can exist in one or both partners. Sometimes, these couples enter therapy because one partner is pushing for S/M enactments and the other stubbornly refuses. Other times, the S/M enactments have become out of hand and couples are frightened by their own behavior.

Here, also, there is uncertainty about how healthy such behaviors are. Some analytic clinicians have posited that playful fantasies of dominance or submission, when enacted, can be healthy and reassure some people that their mate can survive the full expression and power of his or her sexual desire (Bader, 1993). Others try to explain the appeal of S/M as providing an emotional means of overcoming the primitive splitting of love and hate that occurs in all intimate relationships. S/M enactments are rare opportunities to express love and hate at the same time (Kernberg, 1991). Most therapists believe that ritualized S/M enactments are, ultimately, degrading and destructive in a marital relationship.

Couples who engage in S/M scenes are not particularly different from other couples. The Institute of Psychiatry in London compared eighty-seven women who used S/M in their sex life with fifty more sexually traditional women. The S/M women were more extroverted, stable, lower in neuroticism, and higher in psychotism than the traditional women. The S/M women were also more sexually active in both fantasy and behavior (Gosselin, Wilson, and Barrett, 1991). It is not clear what makes one person want to be a masochist and one a sadist, but a variety of sources indicate that there are more masochists around than sadists. (I guess this should be reassuring.)

According to the 1986 Attorney General's Commission on Pornography report, 25 percent of the magazines and books they surveyed were concerned with sadomasochism. This might explain, in part, why the report found pornography to be related to sexual offenses. Sadomasochistic behaviors are entirely oriented toward domination and the infliction of pain.

Such paraphiliacs are responsive to treatment if both partners are motivated. Treatment usually involves a period of abstinence, sensate focus training, and learning new, nondominating ways of enjoying sex. Most couples I have worked with needed to work out feelings of impotency and powerlessness in the nonsexual aspects of their marriage as well.

The Role of Pornography

The passion of a new romance is unforgettable. The closeness that comes with long-term sexual intimacy is sustaining but almost always goes through long periods of great boredom and totally forgettable evenings. Pornography is often used as an antidote, to give zip to the everyday sexual routine of married couples. Despite its popularity in practice, commercial pornography (versus the self-generated fantasy type) is under attack.

Pornography has become less acceptable over the past twenty years for two reasons. First, it has become increasingly violent and vulgar. Material that could be obtained only at midnight on 42nd Street in New York City is now available at every convenience store countertop. This hard-core pornography is characterized by themes of violence, submission, degradation of women, and male narcissism.

Pornography's bad reputation was officially recognized in the 1986 Attorney General's Commission Report on Pornography, which concluded that exposure to sexually explicit material increased the likelihood of committing sexual offenses. Although that report has been severely criticized by scientific sexologists and psychologists, it remains the official point of view and is accepted by many experts in the field. Antagonists point out that for every study that shows a deleterious association between pornography use and violence, there is a study showing that no such relationship exists (Gentry, 1991). However, the evidence, I believe, is to the contrary.

There seems to be a clear consensus that men who are heavy alcohol abusers and watch pornography are more likely to be violent sexually (Attorney General's Commission on Pornography, 1986). A high percentage of nonincarcerated rapists and child molesters have admitted that their crimes were incited by pornography. Large numbers of males, as young as junior high age, report imitating X-rated movies within a few days of exposure. Numerous studies have shown that the viewing of violent pornography increases male aggression toward women (Russell, 1995).

The problems with hard-core pornography come from the fact that there are no socially redeeming behaviors or personalities portrayed in the films. Brosius, Weaver, and Staab (1993), at the German Institut für Publiziistik, conducted a thematic analysis of fifty randomly chosen modern porno-graphic movies to find out exactly what were the hot themes in pornogra-phy. Their results were as follows.

Women were portrayed as more sexually active with a greater variety of partners than were men. A strong age bias (i.e., only young women) was apparent for female but not for male characters. Essentially all sexual scenes involved at least one woman with almost a quarter of the scenes portraying female characters only. Women were far more expressive than men during sexual interactions, with most dialogues consisting of verbal and nonverbal expressions of delight and pleasure. In scenes involving heterosexual couples, women typically initiated sexual interactions through penile fondling or fellatio. Furthermore, fellatio was usually per-formed with the female in a subordinate posture (i.e., kneeling before rather than over her partner). The experience of orgasm was clearly the domain of the male and typically involved extravaginal ejaculation onto the body, face, or mouth of the female. In other words, although always the focus of attention, women were, as a group, portrayed as promiscuous sexual creatures who were subordinate and subservient to men.

The hard-core pornographic reality frequently depicted sexual behav-ior, in general, and female sexuality, in particular, as occurring outside the bounds of the cultural norms of most Western societies.

> More than half of all sexual scenes involved casual sex, while sex between committed partners was quite rare. Sexual narcissism was the primary reason for engaging in the sexual acts as opposed to a desire to express affection. (Brosius, Weaver, and Staab, 1993, p. 168)

Some themes appeared to change over the time period of the study: Recent porno films showed more of the females as powerful and initiating the sex.

This study confirms that what turns men on is the unusual. Most of the time, men have sex with their mate, ejaculate inside of her, initiate the sexual encounter, and are more vocal and expressive. But do these types of images work on women as well as men?

In an intriguing study by Laan and colleagues (1994), a traditional male-oriented pornographic movie was compared with a new age female-oriented pornographic movie. In the female-oriented movie, the female initiated the sexual encounter, the partners were clearly attracted to each other and had equal roles as far as sexual desire and sexual pleasure were concerned, and there was a prolonged emphasis on foreplay (four minutes). The male-oriented movies had the woman being of inferior status (prostitute in a brothel), the activity was initiated by the male and focused on male pleasures, and the emphasis was on coitus (there was no foreplay). Subjects ranged in age from eighteen to forty-five. All the people in the study had their genital responses recorded with a vaginal photoplethysmograph that measured blood volume and pulse amplitude (both measures of sexual arousal). Besides having physiological measures of arousal, the participants rated how sexually aroused they consciously felt. Interestingly, both the male and female films were highly effective in creating a physiological sexual arousal response (this might explain why men like to have women watch such films with them as a prelude to lovemaking). Intellectually and consciously, though, the women reported feeling much more excited by the female-oriented movie. The male-dominated movies gave them feelings of shame, guilt, and aversion. Thus, although sexual stimuli of all types may arouse the vasoconstriction response system, the meaning of that arousal is dependent upon intellectual factors.

Despite male interest and drive for hard-core pornography, most women do not identify with or admire the interpersonal interactions portrayed in such material. Rather than being turned on, they are turned off mentally. We know the opposite situation is true for many men.

So what about soft porn? Is it bad to use erotica to get in the mood? Erotic literature stands apart from hard-core pornography because the sexually explicit material is nondegrading, nonviolent, and consensual. In these cases of mutually agreed-on sex, partners pleasure each other with tenderness and love. It is well known that many couples like to read erotic literature aloud or to make love while watching a sexually explicit, erotic film. Edward Brecher (1984) found that 37 percent of women and 56 percent of men over age fifty say that they have read sexually explicit material, and the overwhelming majority have liked it.

In therapy, couples are sometimes encouraged to use erotica to spice up their sex life. The preceding discussion should make the clinician wary about giving any general directive. Rather, material known to the therapist to be tasteful and nonoffensive should be recommended. Also, the occasional use of erotica seems much more effective for most couples than heavy use of such materials to elicit or maintain arousal. However, sparingly used and with knowledgeable selection, erotica can dramatically increase sexual interest and satisfaction for many long-term married couples.

CASE STUDY 4:
PORNOGRAPHY AND MARITAL STRIFE

Jerry and Patty had been married for twelve years and had two children, nine and eight years old. Patty had a full-time job with the government as a grants specialist and was the primary breadwinner. Her job provided the health benefits, the consistent paycheck, and the greater income. Jerry had shifted from job to job but was currently working installing gas fireplaces. His real love was to build homemade airplanes, and he spent much of his free time in the air park working with a group of fellow aficionados. Jerry was an excellent father and loved taking care of the children, playing with them, and including them in his activities. Patty dealt fairly well with Jerry's carefree ways and consuming pastimes. They sought treatment because Jerry was threatening to leave Patty if they did not increase the amount of sex they were having.

Patty was very turned off to sex with Jerry—primarily because she did not like the type of sex that Jerry pushed for. He had a huge collection of pornographic films. Before sexually approaching his wife, he would sit in the basement and watch films for an hour or two. He would beg Patty to watch them with him, but she found them degrading and disgusting. After watching the films, he would want to reenact scenes that he had watched. He was particularly insistent that Patty perform fellatio in certain positions and in a certain way.

In the sessions, it became clear that Jerry had no sensitivity for his wife's likes and dislikes and no desire to compromise his desires. He had come from an abusive home with an alcoholic father and older brother. His older brother was particularly brutal to him when drinking. Both his father and older brother exposed Jerry to pornography, and both had multiple girlfriends throughout their lives. His mother had deserted the family when he was five years old. Jerry was highly resistant to discussing any of his family-of-origin issues, and just wanted the therapist to loosen Patty up so she wasn't such a "tight ass." He saw nothing wrong in any of his behaviors and refused to enter a period of sexual abstinence while therapy was getting under way. He also refused to stop watching the pornography.

Patty wanted to spend the sessions problem solving, focusing on finding sexual routines that were satisfying for both of them. After four weeks, Patty decided to terminate therapy because no progress was being made. She decided to try to have more sex, and if she could not do it, she would just have to allow him to leave. Jerry refused to be in treatment without Patty.

This failure case highlights the confusion of the role of pornography in complicated couple interactions. Jerry contributed many marital stressors to the relationship. His sexual behavior was oriented toward being pleased; he was not interested in pleasing. His basic desire to use women was obvious in his nonsexual marital life as well as in the type of pornogra-

(continued)

(continued)

phy he found attractive. Yet he was not a total monster. He was very proud of Patty's career success and was a caring, involved father. The failure of therapy to engage this couple was in large part due to an inability to come to a common understanding about the effects pornography was having on restricting Jerry's sexual repertoire and turning his wife off. The therapeutic strategy was to have Jerry learn to explore other sexual arousal methods because his violent pornographic films were not arousing to his wife and restricted his creativity in exploring nondegrading sexual play. Of course, Jerry felt the focus of therapy should have been to treat Patty's pornophobia and allow her to enjoy what he enjoyed.

LEARNING AIDS

Therapeutic Dialogue (Sex)

1. How satisfied are the husband and the wife with their sexual relationship? Using the Sexual Satisfaction Self-Exploration Questionnaire (1), clarify the areas of satisfaction and dissatisfaction for each partner.
2. How satisfied are most of the people they know with their sexual relationships? Use the stories of satisfaction and dissatisfaction that they relate to build a community model of sexual satisfaction. With how many people have they been able to sit down and openly discuss sexual issues? What are the similarities and differences between this couple's situation and the average couple that they know?
3. What is the ideal sexual relationship for which they are striving? How obtainable is that ideal in the near future? In the far future?
4. How can the ideal sexual relationship be modified to make it more attainable?
5. What issues bother each spouse in terms of their own sexual behaviors and attitudes? Do they suffer from any problems in orgasmic timing and frequency? Do they have any paraphilias? What are their attitudes toward pornography? Is the use of pornography an issue between the partners? What problems does each partner see in the other's behaviors and attitudes?
6. What are the ideal sexual practices and attitudes of each spouse? How can the ideal image of sexuality be modified to make it more attainable?

Self-Exploration 1: Sexual Satisfaction Questionnaire

Each partner should answer the questionnaire, and then the couple should discuss each of the items together.

1. Are you satisfied with the frequency of sexual relations?
2. Are you satisfied with the length of foreplay?
3. Are you satisfied with the type of foreplay?
4. Are you satisfied with the variety of behaviors in your sexual relationship?
5. Are you satisfied with the frequency of your orgasms?
6. Are you satisfied with the type of afterplay?
7. Are you satisfied with the length of afterplay?
8. Are you satisfied with how frequently you are interested in having sex?
9. Are you satisfied with how frequently your spouse is interested in having sex?
10. Are you satisfied with how sexually assertive you are?
11. Are you satisfied with how sexually assertive your spouse is?
12. Are you satisfied with how uninhibited you are in your sexual relationship?
13. Are you satisfied with how uninhibited your spouse is in your sexual relationship?
14. Are you satisfied with how much self-disclosure there is between your spouse and yourself?
15. Are you satisfied with how much your spouse can understand your needs?
16. Are you satisfied with the degree of sacrifice your spouse exhibits in the relationship?
17. Are you satisfied with the amount of noncoital sexual affection between you and your spouse?
18. Are you satisfied with how well you and your spouse function as a "couple" in the community, with your friends, and with your family?
19. Are you satisfied with the amount of time you have with your spouse to discuss issues?
20. Are you satisfied with the goals you and your spouse have set for yourselves?

Couples should share their answers with each other. All areas of joint dissatisfaction should be discussed first. Then, individual concerns can be explored. There is no way to score this test, and it is not intended to identify sexually troubled couples. The goal is to explore contentment with the various areas defining one's sexuality.

Self-Exploration 2: The Hurlbert Index of Sexual Excitability

Instructions: Use the following scale to rate each question:

All of the time = 0
Most of the time = 1
Some of the time = 2
Rarely = 3
Never = 4

1. I quickly become sexually excited by foreplay (R).
2. I find sex with my partner to be exciting (R).
3. When it comes to having sex with my partner, I have orgasms (R).
4. It is difficult for me to become sexually aroused.
5. During sex, I seem to lose my initial level of sexual excitement.
6. I feel I take too long to get sexually aroused.
7. It is hard for me to be sexually exciting.
8. Sex is boring.
9. I quickly become sexually excited when my partner performs oral sex on me (R).
10. Just thinking about sex turns me on (R).
11. I find anal sex to be exciting (R).
12. When it comes to sex, I am easily aroused by my partner touching me (R).
13. I find masturbation to be sexually stimulating (R).
14. I seem to lose my sexual excitement too fast.
15. Kissing is sexually arousing for me (R).
16. Even when I am in the mood, it is difficult for me to get excited about sex (R).
17. Sexual foreplay is exciting for me (R)
18. When it comes to sex, it seems to take too long to get me sexually aroused.
19. Pleasing my partner is sexually exciting for me (R).
20. I have difficulty maintaining my sexual excitement.
21. I find sexual intercourse to be exciting (R).
22. When it comes to sex, I think my level of sexual excitement is low.
23. Even when I desire sex, it seems hard for me to become excited.
24. Giving my partner oral sex is sexually exciting for me (R).
25. In general, sex is satisfying for me (R).

R = reverse-scored item. For the reverse scored items, a 0 becomes a 4; a 1 becomes a 3; a 2 becomes a 2; a 3 becomes a 1; and a 4 becomes a 0. After performing the appropriate reverse scoring procedures, add all the scores to get a sexual excitability index. Low scores are associated with increased problems with sexual excitability. This test has been used in clinical practice since 1988. It has a test retest reliability coefficient of .87 over a seven-day period and a Chronbach's alpha coefficient of .83, indicating good internal consistency.

Scores on this scale serve to highlight differences in arousability between the partners and can serve as a stimulus for a discussion of how to increase arousability to a desired level.

Source: Hurlbert, D. F., Apt, C., and Rabehl, S. (1993). Key variables to understanding female sexual satisfaction: An examination of women in nondistressed marriages. *Journal of Sex and Marital Therapy, 19*(2), 154-165. Copyright 1993 from the *Journal of Sex and Marital Therapy*. Reproduced by permission of Taylor & Francis, Inc., <http://www.routledge-ny.com>.

Sample Workshop Flowchart Intended for Groups of Four or Five Couples Working on Sex

I. Psychoeducational Strategies
   A. Explaining the four phases of the human sexual response: the excitement phase, the plateau phase, the orgasmic phase, and the resolution phase
   B. Explaining the wide range of "normal" sexual behaviors and frequency of intercourse (hyposexuality and hypersexuality)
   C. Discussing the relationships between marital satisfaction and sexual satisfaction
   D. Teaching ways to increase arousal and desire
   E. Specific treatment programs for specific sexual dysfunctions

II. Self-Explorations (Done by couples in private and shared before rejoining the group)
   A. Sexual Satisfaction Questionnaire
   B. The Hurlbert Index of Sexual Excitability

III. Therapeutic Dialogue (Done by couples in private and shared before rejoining the group)
   (Proceeding in the order presented, both partners respond to each question before progressing to discuss the next question)
   In group, the therapist explores with couples how relationship goals can be achieved by modifying overly ambitious, pie-in-the-sky expecta-

tions. Using information about their current situation and the realities seen among friends and family, couples fine-tune expectations so they are achievable and motivate rather than discourage attempts at change.

IV. Therapeutic Interventions
Work with a couple in front of the group and apply one or more of the therapeutic interventions. Share rationale during demonstrations. Let group discuss additional interventions.
   A. The handicapping metaphor (to increase compliance for sensate focus)
   B. Wrong-turn information
   C. Quickie sexual problems assessment
   D. Image exercises to increase sexual desire
   E. Letter writing technique to increase sexual desire

V. Finding the Motivation and Time to Make the Changes
   Group discussion

Bibliotherapy

Comfort, A. (1994). *The new joy of sex: A gourmet guide to lovemaking in the nineties.* New York: Crown.
Griffin-Shelley, E. (1991). *Sex and love: Addiction, treatment and recovery.* Westport, CT: Greenwood. (Professional book).
Janus, S. and Janus, C. (1994). *The Janus report on sexual behavior.* New York: John Wiley and Sons. (The first broad-scale scientific national survey on sex since Kinsey).
McCormack Brown, K. (1994). *Sexuality workbook.* New York: Brown and Benchmark.
O'Donohue, W. and Gear, J. (1995). *Handbook of sexual dysfunctions: Assessment and treatment.* Needham Heights, MA: Allyn & Bacon. (Professional book).
Renshaw, D. (1995). *Domeena Renshaw's Rx for good sex: A seven-week program for a more enriching sex life.* New York: Random House.

Videotherapy

Falling in Love, Again. (1990). A ninety-minute videotape created by Lonnie Barbach, PhD, that comes with a his-and-her guidebook and two audiocassettes that present skills and exercises designed to enhance communication and intimacy. The program consists of five steps: knowing oneself, knowing one's mate, verbal communication, intimate communication, and loving together. Available from Focus International, 1160 East Jericho Turnpike, Huntington, New York 11743.

Loving Better. (1985). A five-part series from Dr. Sheldon Kule at the New School for Osteopathic Medicine. Each tape is approximately one hour long, and the topics include the basics (anatomy, partner examination, communication), communication through touch, variations to lovemaking, marital aids and fantasies, and sexual problems. Available from Focus International, 1160 East Jericho Turnpike, Huntington, New York 11743.

Sex: A Lifelong Pleasure. (1991). A five-part series from Holland that offers a comprehensive look at sexual relationships. The material is presented by two psychologists: Dr. Goedele Liekens and Dr. Michael Perry. The expert advice is interspersed with tasteful scenes of explicit lovemaking. Each title is one hour long. Topics include: enjoying sex, harmony, the female orgasm, the male orgasm, and erection. Available from Focus International, 1160 East Jericho Turnpike, Huntington, New York 11743.

Professional Development Questions (Sex)

1. How would you assess if insufficient sexual desire was an important clinical issue? How would you go about treating the problem? How would your approach vary if both partners were not interested versus if the female was not interested versus if the male was not interested?

2. What clinical options are appropriate for dealing with a couple in which one of the partners is hooked on pornography and the other is disgusted by it?

3. What are your own feelings about the role of orgasm in sexual relations? How would that affect your working with couples who have problems with secondary erectile failure or orgasmic failure?

4. Three couples come to you with sexual problems. Couple 1 are newlyweds who work in different cities and are together only on the weekends. They found that after the wedding all interest in sex ceased for both of them. Couple 2 have a terminally ill child and the husband is frustrated that the wife has been totally uninterested in sex for over a year. Couple 3 are in their sixties. The husband is not interested in sex anymore. He attributes this to his high blood pressure medication and the boredom of his wife as a stimulus. What aspects of treatment would be in common for all three couples? How might your approach vary for each couple?

REFERENCES

Apt, C. and Hurlbert, D. (1992). The female sensation seeker and marital sexuality. *Journal of Sex and Marital Therapy, 18*(4), 315-324.

Attorney General's Commission on Pornography. (1986). Final report. Washington, DC: Government Printing Office.

Avna, J. and Waltz, D. (1992). *Celibate wives: Breaking the silence.* Los Angeles: Lowell House.

Bader, M. (1993). Adaptive sadomasochism and psychological growth. *Psychoanalytic Dialogues, 3*(2), 279-300.

Brecher, E. (1984). *Love, sex, and aging.* Boston: Little-Brown.

Brosius, H. B., Weaver, J. B., and Staab, J. (1993). Exploring the social and sexual reality of contemporary pornography. *Journal of Sex Research, 30*(2), 161-170.

Brown, E. (1991). *Patterns of infidelity and their treatment.* New York: Brunner/Mazel.

Charney, I. and Parnass, S. (1995). The impact of extramarital relationships on the continuation of marriages. *Journal of Sex and Marital Therapy, 21*(2), 100-115.

Christensen, C. (1995). Prescribed masturbation in sex therapy: A critique. *Journal of Sex and Marital Therapy, 21*(2), 87-99.

Cooper, A. (1985). "An evaluation and comparison of a sexual enhancement and a communication training program for their effects on sexual and marital satisfaction." Unpublished doctoral dissertation, Texas Tech University.

Cooper, A. C. and Stoltenberg, C. D. (1987). Comparison of a sexual enhancement and a communication training program on sexual and marital satisfaction. *Journal of Counseling Psychology, 34*(3), 309-314.

Donnelly, D. (1993). Sexually inactive marriages. *Journal of Sex Research, 30*(2), 171-179.

Garber, M. (1992). *Cross-dressing and cultural anxiety.* London: Routledge.

Gentry, C. (1991). Pornography and rape: An empirical analysis. *Deviant Behavior, 12*(3), 277-288.

Goodman, A. (1993). Diagnosis and treatment of sexual addiction. *Journal of Sexual and Marital Therapy, 19*(3), 225-251.

Gosselin, C., Wilson, G., and Barrett, P. (1991). The personality and sexual preferences of sadomasochistic women. *Personality and Individual Differences, 12*(1), 11-15.

Greeley, A. M., Michael, R. T., and Smith, T. W. (1990). Almost monogamous people: Americans and their sexual partners. *Society, 27*(1), 36-42.

Heiman, J. R. and LoPiccolo, J. (1988). *Becoming orgasmic: A sexual and personal growth program for women.* Englewood Cliffs, NJ: Prentice-Hall.

Hurlbert, D. (1992). Factors influencing a woman's decision to end an extramarital sexual relationship. *Journal of Sex and Marital Therapy, 18*(2), 104-109.

Hurlbert, D. (1993). A comparative study using orgasm consistency training in the treatment of women reporting hypoactive sexual desire. *Journal of Sex and Marital Therapy, 19*(1), 41-49.

Hurlbert, D., Apt, C., Gasar, S., Wilson, N., and Murphy, Y. (1994). Sexual narcissism: A validation study. *Journal of Sex and Marital Therapy, 20*(1), 24-34.

Hurlbert, D., Apt, C., and Rabehl, S. (1993). Key variables to understanding female sexual satisfaction: An examination of women in nondistressed marriages. *Journal of Sex and Marital Therapy, 19*(2), 154-165.

Kaplan, H. (1974). *The new sex therapy: Active treatment of sexual dysfunctions.* New York: Brunner/Mazel.

Kaplan, H. S. (1987). *The illustrated manual of sex therapy.* New York: Brunner/Mazel.

Kaplan, H. S. (1989). *How to overcome premature ejaculation.* New York: Brunner/Mazel.

Kennedy, A. and Dean, S. (1986). *Touching for pleasure: A guide to sensual enhancement.* Chatsworth, CA: Chatsworth Press.

Kernberg, O. (1991). Sadomasochism, sexual excitement, and perversion. *Journal of the American Psychoanalytic Association, 39*(2), 333-362.

Kinsey, A. (1953). *Sexual behavior in the human female.* Philadelphia: W. B. Saunders.

Laan, E., Everaerd, W., Bellen, G., and Hanewald, G. (1994). Women's sexual and emotional responses to male and female produced erotica. *Archives of Sexual Behavior, 23*(2), 153-169.

Lawson, A. (1989). Greener pastures. *Family Networker,* (May/June), 40-43.

Mahoney, J. and Strassberg, D. (1993). Self-involvement via self-schema activation during sexual arousal. *Journal of Sex Research, 30*(1), 70-74.

Masters, W. H. and Johnson, V. E. (1966). *Human sexual response.* Boston: Little-Brown.

Masters, W. H. and Johnson, V. E. (1970). *Human sexual inadequacy.* Boston: Little-Brown.

Metz, M. and Weiss, K. (1992). A group therapy format for the simultaneous treatment of marital and sexual dysfunctions: A case illustration. *Journal of Sex and Marital Therapy, 18*(3), 173-195.

Morokoff, P. and Gillilland, R. (1993). Stress, sexual functioning and marital satisfaction. *Journal of Sex Research, 30*(1), 43-53.

Mosher, D. L. (1980). The psychological dimensions of depth of involvement in human sexual response. *Journal of Sex Research, 6*(1), 1-42.

Oggins, J., Leber, D., and Veroff, J. (1993). Race and gender differences in black and white newlyweds' perceptions of sexual and marital relations. *Journal of Sex Research, 30*(2), 152-160.

Russell, D. (1995). Pornography and rape: A causal model. *Prevention in Human Services, 12*(2), 49-51.

Schiavi, R., Mandeli, J., and Schreiner-Engel, P. (1994). Sexual satisfaction in healthy aging men. *Journal of Sex and Marital Therapy, 20*(1), 3-13.

Treadway, D. (1993). In a world of their own. *Family Networker,* March/April, 33-39.

Chapter 9

Spirituality and the Couple Relationship

WHAT IS SPIRITUALITY?

Life is not a problem to be solved. It is a mystery to be loved.

Kierkegaard

As marriages and relationships evolve, so do individuals. The development of a fulfilled partnership is paralleled, in part, by the development of spirituality in both the individuals. This chapter will try to operationalize what spirituality is and describe how marriage can foster this ultimate goal of personal development.

Spirituality can be described as a transcendent understanding of the meaning and purpose of life. It is the desire to underpin a lifetime of objective experience on articles of faith. Cosmic philosophies can guide and support people through the toughest crises in their lives.

Spirituality is viewed here as a cognitive developmental task of adulthood. If we have mastered the lower tasks of personal identity formation, generativity, and intimacy, the specter of spiritual development comes to the foreground as a pressing personal task. When all goes as it should, people want to understand a grander purpose for their lives than material acquisitions and sensory pleasures.

Although spiritual development is a private affair, spiritually mature persons tend to share certain characteristics. They are compromisers, open-minded, and nondogmatic. There is a commitment to ideals. The spiritually mature person sees life in a rich palette of subtle shades. The stark black-and-white, right-and-wrong judgments of an earlier age seem artificial and untextured. The many struggles, compromises, and crises of married life help individuals reach these deeper, more subtle levels of understanding.

A long-term marriage commitment provides a number of unique paths for spiritual discovery and development. Of course, the meaning of life can be discovered only by an individual. But a spouse can help one tread a path of self-discovery or put up gates before inviting but misleading paths.

Sometimes, the meaning of life is found right within the marital union. This becomes the basis of a totally spiritual marriage, that is, a life-to-life relationship. Such people come to believe, without a shadow of a doubt, that the purpose of life is to be with and care for this other life with whom one was matched. Although marriage is the answer for only a very few individuals, nearly all spiritually evolved married people revere the marital union and their partner for the part she or he plays in creating purpose and meaning in their life. The meanings for living are as varied as life itself. Yet spiritually evolved couples tend to have marriages with distinct characteristics. Most important, they are happy and satisfied with their marriage.

In a way, this becomes a chicken-and-egg problem. Are these individuals satisfied with their marriage because they are mature, principled individuals who have the discipline and emotional energy to bring to a relationship? Or does a strong marriage cultivate these characteristics? Although each clearly influences the other, in this chapter we are interested in trying to trace the latter road. We are interested in exploring the marital characteristics that encourage, promote, and maintain individual growth and development.

All of the other sections of this book slant a bit more toward explaining how an individual can act or react in ways that strengthen the marital relationship. This section slants a bit more toward explaining how a strong, happy marriage can enrich an individual's life.

PROMOTING SPIRITUAL DEVELOPMENT BY FEELING LOVED

> A relationship I think is . . . is like a shark. You know it has to constantly move forward or it dies.
>
> Woody Allen in *Annie Hall*

Spiritual husbands and wives report feeling loved by their spouse. What does this really mean? Bell, Daly, and Gonzalez (1987) tried to operationally define "love" in a landmark study that asked 144 married women and eighteen individuals cohabiting with their romantic partner to describe, in writing, the things they said and did within their relationships to maintain "liking and solidarity."

The responses from the study were analyzed by a panel of judges, and twenty-eight strategies were identified:

1. *Be altruistic.* Example: Doing the partner's household chores when the partner is sick.
2. *Be willing to concede control.* Example: Allowing the spouse to decide what the two of them should do for socializing and recreation over the weekend.
3. *Speak to the partner with the same level of politeness usually reserved for work colleagues.* Example: No interrupting, shouting, screwy faces, etc.
4. *Be dynamic.* Example: Client is physically and vocally animated when interacting with partner.
5. *Encourage partner to share thoughts and feelings.* Example: Client asks partner's opinions on a variety of world, community, work, and personal topics.
6. *Treat partner as an equal.* Example: Client should inhibit desire to act superior by bragging, issuing orders, or playing "one-upsmanship" games.
7. *Make as many interactions pleasurable as possible.* Example: Client tells jokes and interesting stories to partner.
8. *Be faithful.* Example: Client does not engage in physical or emotional unfaithfulness.
9. *Be honest and sincere.* Example: The client should not lie, cheat, or engage in pretense. White lies should be acknowledged and discarded in favor of risking a more authentic communication.
10. *Engage in joint social activities.* Example: Clients should ask their spouses to go with them on shopping errands, walks, athletic events, or other such activities that have, over time, become "solo" or "nonspousal" activities.
11. *Find different ways to express closeness.* Example: Psychological closeness can be expressed in many ways. People use pet names, say "we" instead of "I" when talking, and share supportive glances with each other. Touch is the most popular method of expressing closeness, whether it be a squeeze on the shoulder, a pat on the behind, or a full, embracing bear hug.
12. *Listen and pay attention to what the partner says.* Example: Client can demonstrate listening by keeping eye contact, asking for clarifications, and remembering things the spouse has shared.
13. *Self-disclose.* Example: Client must risk disclosing feelings, fears, and insecurities.
14. *Be optimistic.* Example: The client should try to show how the cup is half full instead of half empty and how the lemons can, with joint effort, turn into lemonade.

15. *Be physically affectionate.* Example: Clients should attend to their sex life and try to make it more pleasurable for both partners.

16. *Take care of one's self.* Example: Paying attention to how attractive one looks certainly helps most people feel better about themselves. Spouses also appreciate, within bounds, the thoughtfulness and care that the partners give themselves. However, clients already narcissistically bound up with their appearance may need to take less care of themselves to be more appreciated by their spouse.

17. *Be interesting to spouse.* Example: Most people enjoy spontaneous acts of joy, going to a special restaurant without a special reason, having sex on the deck under a chilly autumn moon, or asking some friends over for tea and conversation.

18. *Carry out responsibilities to the partner and family.* Example: Clients should do the chores they have agreed to do, on time, without complaining.

19. *Give nice presents.* Example: Clients can treat partners to a nice dinner and then present them with a gift, for no reason other than that they want the marriage to be stronger and more beautiful. Such presents need not cost any money—a coupon book filled with back rubs, chore relief, and a choice of TV shows is often most appreciated.

20. *Build partner's self-esteem.* Example: The client should find behaviors and traits that deserve sincere compliments and give them liberally.

21. *Improve one's self.* Example: Some time and energy needs to be spent on improving one's self, independent of the marriage. Not only does that help put the marital problems into perspective, it makes one a more interesting, attractive, and likable mate.

22. *Join in the partner's activities.* Example: The client should try to introduce himself or herself into the mate's hobbies and leisure time pursuits. Many a husband is shocked to learn that his wife would be willing to learn to play golf or go hunting. Wives are shocked when their husbands are willing to go shopping or take an exercise class with them. Like all deep sexist attitudes, the segregation of leisure pursuits is far more a matter of cultural conditioning than genetic destiny.

23. *Be warm, caring, and empathic.* Example: Ah, these are three tired adjectives. What we mean here is that when a spouse faces a problem or setback, the client should try to be there emotionally three times: once to say "You're not alone. I will stick by you and see this through with you," once to ask, "How can I help?" and once to share the

emotions and thoughts the client has had because of the spouse's setback. This triple conversation method is very effective if the conversations are spaced and both partners are receptive to a good interaction.

24. *Share spiritual activities.* Example: Go to church, join in a community service together, meditate together, or simply marvel at the joys of nature together.

25. *Stress the similarities, not the differences.* Example: As discussed in other parts of this book, it is important to have similar attitudes, reactions, and interests with a mate. Clients who want to improve their marriage need to stress the similarities. Although forcing similarities where none exist will only cause more alienation, shifting the focus from true differences to true similarities is very fruitful.

26. *Stick up for the partner in public.* Example: Very often, when spouses are in front of children or other extended family members, mates are criticized or made fun of by other family members. Clients can choose to overtly or covertly join in on the "put-downs" or to defend their spouse. Open defense of a spouse is a treasured moment in a marriage. Encourage clients to try it.

27. *Love whom the partner loves.* Example: People should be wise enough to realize that when they get married they are forming an allegiance with every person whom their spouse admires and loves. Few realize that because most people, deep down, really do love their parents, they want and need their partner to love them also.

28. *Use words of affection.* Example: Using words of affection is the most cost-effective method of maintaining a loving relationship. It appears that many people drift away from "I love you," "You are wonderful," and "I'm glad I'm with you" because they fear that their mate no longer feels that way toward them. Forget it. Words of affection work on a one-way street. Clients who get hung up with "She never says she loves me back" need to be told that reciprocity, though wonderful, is not necessary for both partners to feel good about the words of affection that are expressed.

Research showed that marital satisfaction was clearly and positively related to the use of these twenty-eight strategies. Not all twenty-eight strategies were found to be equally important to the women in the study. The nine most central strategies were honesty, listening, openness, physical and verbal affection, physical attractiveness, self-concept confirmation, sensitivity, and supportiveness.

Wives most desired their husbands to be faithful, honest, physically attractive, sensitive, and confirming of their self-concept. Wives believed

that their husbands wanted them to be faithful, honest, physically affectionate, sensitive, and physically attractive. These are frequency counts set
by a group of women who were attending graduate classes and teaching
kindergarten. What is important for any particular couple is to find out
how important each of the twenty-eight behaviors is in their relationship.

A smaller but similar study was conducted on fifteen couples who were
married at least thirty years to find out what "long-timers" felt contributed
to their ability to stay married (Robinson and Blanton, 1993). These snow
leopards of the social contract have much to teach us, and too few researchers are attending to their lessons. The twenty-eight characteristics
found by Bell, Daly, and Gonzalez (1987) fell nicely into the following
five factors found in Robinson and Blanton's work: intimacy, sexual compatibility, commitment, congruence, and religious orientation.

This chapter will explore how each of these five factors can help an
individual in his or her spiritual quest. (Note that religious orientation will
be subsumed under the discussion of congruence.)

PROMOTING SPIRITUALITY BY FOSTERING INTIMACY

A relationship is placing one's heart and soul in the hands of another
while taking charge of another in one's soul and heart.

Kahlil Gibran

Couples want and need "intimacy" to have a great relationship. Yet really
understanding the ingredients that go into intimacy has occupied many researchers for many years. Moss and Schwebel (1993) recently reviewed all
the various definitions of intimacy in the literature and found over sixty-one
unique definitions. Analyzing all the different definitions, they found five
components that kept on cropping up in the various definitions. First was the
feeling of commitment. In intimate marriages, spouses know that they can
rely on each other to be there for them, sharing their joys and sorrows, and
helping out in whatever ways they can. Next was affective intimacy, the
desire to talk on the phone when kept apart, to go shopping together instead
of apart, to think about the partner during the day, and generally being
attracted to and caring about that person. Third was cognitive intimacy. This
involved knowing and sharing dreams, values, day-to-day happenings, fears,
and prejudices. The fourth component, physical intimacy, included the hugs,
touches, kisses, and tender love that most people associate with the word
intimacy. Last was mutuality. Couples experienced mutuality when there was
an equitable give-and-take in the relationship, sharing in both the spoils and

the toils. Thus, having your wife save you a piece of cheesecake from the office party can be an important act of intimacy.

The definition of intimacy ends up reading as follows: "Intimacy in enduring romantic relationships is determined by the level of commitment and positive affective, cognitive, and physical closeness one experiences with a partner in a reciprocal relationship" (Moss and Schwebel, 1993, p. 33). Although we have chosen to treat commitment and congruence as distinct from intimacy, it is clear that the concepts intertwine and overlap, and the distinction is made, primarily, for ease of reading and the clinical applicability of each concept.

Intimacy and Communication

> The marriage state, with and without the affection suitable to it, is the completest image of Heaven and Hell we are capable of receiving in this life.
>
> Sir Richard Steele

Intimacy involves spending time together, talking to each other, listening to the other's needs—communicating with each other.

Self-disclosure is the most essential factor in creating intimacy. Although we can love and understand someone just by watching his or her behavior, self-disclosure ensures that we understand the intentions, hopes, and fears that surround this behavior and make it personally meaningful to us.

Self-disclosure is a very reciprocal action. The more one person discloses, the more the other person is likely to disclose. So, as a husband allows his wife to know what he thinks and feels, she will become freer to share what she thinks and feels. The value of self-disclosure has been noted since the beginning of time. In the Old Testament it is written,

> And you should choose someone whom you have tested, at least according to your ability, to see that he wants nothing but to reach the truth, and wants with all his heart to escape from the snares of evil—from illusionary desires and from falsehood. Then you should converse together every day for about half an hour, where each one should disparage his own bad traits in front of the other, exposing them before his friend. Then when you have become accustomed to this and your friend sees something ugly in you and rebukes you for it, you will not be ashamed before him and you will be able to admit the truth. As a result, falsehood will fall and the truth will begin to emerge. (Avot 1:6, 39:27:4; Rabbi Menahem Mendel of Vitebsk, in Or ha-Emet, 1967, II, p. 52)

Thus, when openness is an everyday occurrence, constructive criticism becomes a possibility. Without the free flow of innermost thoughts, feelings of secrecy and shame make most people too defensive to hear what their mate is saying to them during a conflict.

Are There Gender Differences in the Communication of Intimacy?

With so much talk about different gender styles in communication, is it possible that self-disclosure is only describing the female definition of intimacy? Or are men also seeking affirmation and validation in their communications? As discussed in detail in the chapter on communication, most males are socialized to show their empathy by being problem solvers. They want to fix and master the situation. When confronted with a wife who cannot stand her demanding and demeaning boss, the typical husband talks about finding another job or how to circumvent the boss. Wives want to talk about feelings, not solutions. Which one is the more intimate communicator? The answer is that neither of them is, because in intimate communications each partner must participate equally in the creation of meaning. Understanding the bad job situation is a question of neither feelings nor solutions. It is a task of taking from each perspective to generate a shared new vision of the experience.

When one assumes that intimate communications involve the creation of shared meaning, stereotyped male and female communication modes become no more than any other individual difference variable in communication. A husband and wife struggling to become closer must learn to create their own unique communication casserole. For example, his way of expressing anger must be perceived, accepted, and integrated with her way of expressing being the recipient of anger. Although each style will continue to be identifiable, if they are successful in their intimacy efforts, the two styles will blend and create a harmonious conversational duet. Elements of each communication style are used by the other to expand and enlarge their expressive and receptive vocabularies. Such intimate, jointly crafted communications are the indigenous language of lovers. Outsiders may never understand the innuendoes, but fluent speakers feel it is the most natural and effective way to communicate.

Of course, culture affects the meaning of intimacy. Individuals who seek emotional intimacy primarily from their own family of origin, from friends, or from work settings will not have the same need for such intimate conversations with their spouse.

THERAPEUTIC INTERVENTION 1:
INCREASING INTIMACY BY STRUCTURED ASSIGNMENTS

One of the most popular techniques for increasing intimacy between couples is the Alternative Day Technique in which individuals take responsibility for initiating intimacy with each other on alternate days of the week. The procedures here were developed by Stuart (1980), but many other therapists use similar variants of this technique.

The instructions are simple: One partner takes responsibility on Monday, Wednesday, and Friday. The other partner has Saturday, Tuesday, and Thursday. Sunday is a day off and no one is responsible. On days when partners are in charge, they must make one, and only one, intimacy request from their partners. It may be asking for a kiss, to make love, to discuss a problem they have been having, or to hold the partner's hand. It has been agreed on, beforehand, that no matter what the one request is, it will be honored. The requests are not allowed to be cosmic, like asking the partner to "Never leave me," and should be doable in a short amount of time. Many couples decide to exclude matters of sex and money because these are two of the most difficult areas couples have to negotiate.

After a few months of this arrangement, when it feels natural and is working well, up the ante from one to two intimacy requests, and later to three requests. Of course, a person does not need to use all of his or her allotted request opportunities and may ask for intimacy that is not part of the game. However, when the game is being played, each spouse must deliver the required number of intimacy requests that are actually requested.

The last part of the game occurs when there are unlimited requests and the noninitiating partners have the opportunity to refuse any request. However, once they refuse one request, the game is over for the day. This allows both partners to have control for regulating the intimacy in their relationship (Stuart, 1980).

PROMOTING SPIRITUALITY
THROUGH SEXUAL RELATIONSHIPS

As mentioned in the chapter on sexuality, there are three problems that interfere with sexual satisfaction in married life: dysfunctional sexual attitudes, poor sexual communication, and a lack of adequate sexual information.

First, nearly all people carry around dysfunctional sexual attitudes. Some of these attitudes are out and out irrational (e.g., "Foreplay is for the young"), whereas others are more philosophically debatable (e.g., "The goal of lovemaking is to have an orgasm," or "Each person is responsible for the pleasure that his or her partner experiences during lovemaking").

Second, poor sexual communication invariably interferes with a rewarding sex life. Learning to communicate openly about sex requires mastering four skills: learning how to initiate and refuse sexual activity in a nonoffensive manner, developing a shared language to communicate specific techniques, learning how to give sexual feedback without ruining the "flow," and sharing sexual preferences and fantasies.

Third, ignorance or misinformation can hamper a couple's sexual relationship for years on end. Therapists who can openly share information (e.g., the arousal stages or creating a sense of desire), provide good bibliotherapy sources, and debunk dysfunctional myths held by the couple can pave the way for a spiritually satisfying sexual relationship.

Sexual enhancement programs that focus on these three areas (attitudes, communication, and information) have been shown to empirically increase men's ability to be affectively expressive and to more accurately perceive their wives' sexual needs and desires. Women feel more self-accepting after such programs, and both men and women report increased satisfaction with the frequency with which they have sex.

Still, better sex is not the same as great sex. Great sex is intimate and revealing. It requires more than communication and technique. It requires that individuals be willing to have a spiritually transcendent experience with their partner. Fear of sharing so intensely with a spouse can lead to routinized sex, boredom, and hypoactive sexual desire.

Schnarch (1993), in fact, traces the increased incidence of hypoactive sexual desire to the increased fear of intimacy and spiritual contact with one's spouse. People experience dull sex because they are apprehensive about displaying the intense emotion that is involved. It has been shown that adult eroticism has considerably more to do with a person's emotional maturity than with physiological reactivity. Personal growth and maturity can be obtained through sexual intimacy. In the crucible, people develop an ambivalent respect that ultimately requires them to view the spouse as an individual who is totally independent. Finally they must come to the realization that they will not be unconditionally loved by their partner until they have established a foundation of trust and respect. Couples that have taken responsibility for themselves in this manner show a thorough understanding of intimacy: They are individuals who are taking a risk in a relationship that has the potential to both flourish or cease (Schnarch, 1993).

However, great sex is not simply a matter of letting it all hang out. It is a delicate art that requires sharing what is most difficult to share at a sacred time. This is why so many religions have found that placing restrictions on sex make it more pleasurable. For example, extremely orthodox Jews restrict sex only to the Shabbat (Friday evening) because the Shabbat is so holy it helps raise the sexual act into the realm of the spiritual (Buxbaum, 1990, p. 589).

Similarly, spiritual sexual relationships are fostered by the development of tsnius, a Hebrew concept that involves respect, a reciprocal sense of propriety, delicacy, and good taste. One of the reasons that religion is helpful in fostering spiritually satisfying marriages is that it provides the guidelines for how to recognize and join in the tsnius. Women who mask their femininity under robes and scarves are practicing age-old customs of tsnius. Not going into the bathroom when it is occupied, not having intercourse during menstruation, keeping the lights off during lovemaking, and saving certain sexual acts for special occasions are all examples of tsnius in today's world (Buxbaum, 1990).

CASE STUDY 1:
SUBURBAN SADOMASOCHISM
AND SPIRITUAL HEALING

Helen and Jerry were a very attractive couple with two children, ages eight and ten. Jerry was a mechanical engineer and often traveled. Helen had a catering business serving high-end "open houses" for local real estate offices. Both were practicing Buddhists, although Helen was brought up Jewish and Jerry was brought up Methodist. Helen and Jerry felt that their sex life was "out of control" and had consulted a teacher at their temple. He had recommended that they seek professional help.

A detailed history revealed that they had had a very traditional sex life until after the birth of their second son. One day they were sharing sexual fantasies, and Jerry confided how he always wanted to be tied up and "yelled at." Helen thought it was funny and innocent enough and offered to enact the fantasy with him. Jerry found the experience unbelievably satisfying, and after they had played the scene for ten minutes or so, they proceeded to have fantastic sex. Jerry immediately wanted to replay the scenario the next night, but they waited about two weeks until Helen consented. Again, the sex afterward was the best they had ever had—full of passion and abandon. Pretty soon, it was a fixture of foreplay. Then, every few months, Jerry would introduce a new element. One day he brought home a whip. Helen got excited and went out and bought high black leather boots. Very gradually the rituals and sadomasochistic behavior became more and more extreme. At the point of treatment, the ritual consisted of first going out to the mall to walk for an hour. Jerry would wear a dog collar with a leash, hidden under his shirt. Helen would take him for a walk through the mall, directing him wherever the mood took her and yanking at the collar at the least sign of resistance. After this, they would

(continued)

(continued)

return home and she would tie him to the bed or tie his hands to a rail along the bedroom wall. Then she would proceed to smack him with her hands. At first he would have to beg for her to hit him with the whip, but finally she would get aroused enough to want to whip him. She would strike hard, until he had giant welts on his thighs, back, and backside. When he was limp, she would untie him and make him lie on the floor for some "April showers" (urinating on his face). After this, he would curl up in a corner and just space out for an hour or two. Helen would sometimes rub against him until she had an orgasm but recently would just go to the shower, wondering how they were going to get out of this cycle. They had not had sexual intercourse for over four months and were aware of the deep physical and psychological harm they were inflicting on each other and the relationship.

Treatment began by having the couple make a joint decision to go "cold turkey" and not engage in any S/M scenarios. If one spouse made an innuendo or subtle cue for preengagement, the other spouse was to loudly say "No" and go to another room. All the leather and boots and whips were thrown into the trash.

After the couple meditated together each night, they were asked to spend several minutes becoming verbally intimate with each other, sharing what was frustrating during the day, what competencies they wanted to develop to deal with such frustrations better, and how the spouse could help, if at all. In the sessions, we focused on issues of commitment, development of new rituals, and the shame they both felt. Issues of power and how to feel recognized and loved in the marriage were also major themes. In addition, they met with their Buddhist teacher once a month.

After three months of dealing with mutual feelings of empowerment, the couple began a sensate focus program. Seven months after becoming abstinent, they had sexual intercourse. They described it as their true wedding night; they approached each other as emotional virgins, ready to be vulnerable and close and confident, all at the same time. Both felt cleansed of the S/M experience and felt no recurrent urges.

PROMOTING SPIRITUALITY
BY FOSTERING COMMITMENT

Acts of Dedication and Obligation

Finally, the joy of marriage is the joy of giving. To the jaded, it may sound trite and hackneyed, like some middle-brow bromide from the advice columns on the women's pages, but it's true: It's more blessed, or at least more satisfying to give than to receive. For in giving, we tap those parts of our being that make us special, noble, transcendent. In giving, we exercise the most glorious powers of human nature. In giving, we dispense grace. We dignify ourselves, we become almost divine.

Art Carey

Marriage was as deep as a well, as rich as the Bayeaux tapestry, and with as many stitches and as much detail. Married people suffered and rejoiced over and over and over again. Marriage was a trench dug by time, a straight furrow, the mighty oak that has grown from a tiny acorn. Lovers were, by comparison, little scratches in the ground.

Laurie Colwin

Commitment has two possible meanings: It can be an act of dedication or it can be an act of obligation. Marital satisfaction often hinges on what the ratio of dedication commitments are to obligation commitments. Personal dedication involves a desire not only to continue in the marriage but to improve it, sacrifice for it, invest in it, and make the partner's needs and desires on an equal par with one's own. It refers to the positive passions we feel toward the spouse. Obligatory commitments, on the other hand, are the external constraints that keep one anchored to the marriage. Obligatory commitments usually include the economic investments, social investments with joint friends and extended family, and the psychological benefits of being able to count on old, comfortable routines. Nathaniel Branden (1981), in *The Psychology of Romantic Love,* encompasses both meanings in his own discussion of commitment:

> the ability to know that we can love our partner deeply and nonetheless know moments of feeling enraged, bored, alienated, and that the validity and value of our relationship is not to be judged by moment-to-moment, day-to-day, or even week-to-week fluctuations in feeling. There is a fundamental equanimity, an equanimity born of the knowledge that we have a history with our partner, we have a context, and we do not drop that context under the pressure of immediate vicissitudes. We remember. We retain the ability to see the whole picture. (p. 27)

The commitment of dedication requires a high level of energy and work. It includes the ardent desire to maintain or improve the quality of the relationship for the benefit of both partners. Personally committed spouses, ideally, have the following characteristics: The spousal relationship has a higher priority over all other activities, the person thinks of the couple as a "team" with joint values and goals, and the person is happy and satisfied doing things that are largely or solely for their partner's benefit.

Unfortunately, at the end of a few short years, many marriages are at the polar opposite of the ideal. Yet the marriages go on and on. Why? These couples have shifted to a marital commitment based on obligations and constraint. That is, they are committed to the marriage because the economic, social, personal, and psychological costs of leaving the marriage are too high. Individuals with a commitment of constraint do not value the "we"—they value the "me" in the current arrangement and do not want to upset the proverbial apple cart. The rationales of people with only obligatory commitments are varied. Some believe that they would suffer economically if they left the partnership. Some do not want to change their style of living, their place of residence, or the freedoms they enjoy in the current situation. Others do not feel that they would be able to attract a better partner, or they feel a divorce would be too hurtful to the children. Some people just do not want to live alone, or they believe it is amoral or wrong to divorce.

The personal and societal costs of divorce are so high that therapists are searching for innovative ways to rekindle personal dedication while hanging on to any type of commitments they can find. Gray (1995) suggests some very unorthodox methods to give couples time to explore what they can give to the relationship and what personal needs must be met to make the relationship viable. For example, she suggests that couples who feel as if they have no space should try setting up separate bedrooms. She reminds us that "total sharing" is hard to maintain and that throughout history and across cultures, men and women have set up private dens, parlors, libraries, and bedrooms to create psychological and physical space for themselves. In a similar vein, she suggests separate vacations for partners who no longer agree on what is exciting, relaxing, or a needed change of pace. The idea is that by having some important personal needs met, anger will subside and feelings of altruism or personal dedication will again come to the fore.

The most dramatic of her suggestions is the use of a marriage sabbatical for couples whose personal dedications are totally depleted. The sabbatical involves living separately for a period of three months to one year. Each partner develops individual goals for growth during the sabbatical. Boundaries are set about other relationships and sexual conduct. The couple continues to meet with the therapist to discuss their individual growth, what they need from the relationship, and what they want to give to the relationship. Ideally, at the end of the sabbatical, each partner has rekindled some personal dedication for the other—by seeing the partner change, by changing oneself, and by having the opportunity to miss each other. When the couple still wants a divorce, it usually is more amicable because both understand, by this time, exactly why they are divorcing.

Commitment: Caring or Codependency?

In today's world, it is getting more and more difficult to expect psychological, economic, physical, or emotional support from a spouse. Marital equity is translated to include individual responsibility and a single life raft philosophy. Indeed, in this age of narcissism, many therapists and laypeople label helpful spouses as weak, addicted "codependents." Inasmuch as I place so much importance on spousal help and compensation, when needed, it is important to place the issue of codependency in some perspective.

Much has been written about the concept of codependency. Codependent people have partners with visible addictions, obsessions, or dysfunctions. The codependent partner is hypothesized to be addicted to his or her "sick" spouse and the spouse's problem. In fact, identified "troubled" spouses are capable of maintaining their troublesome behavior only because they have helpers who enable them to maintain their problem. By having codependent spouses who compensate and cover for their irresponsibility, addicts are able to avoid the natural but noxious, constraining consequences others would bestow on them.

The addiction problem of the codependent partner is less obvious but just as compelling. The codependent partner devotes his or her life to enabling the visibly troubled partner to function more effectively in the world while still retaining the addiction. If a woman is married to an alcoholic man, she may make excuses for him when he does not carry out his family responsibilities; she may be forgiving after he has created embarrassing and distressing scenes at home in an effort to restore family order; and she may take on extra jobs to compensate for the money that is being spent on the addiction. Rationalizations, repeated acts of forgiveness, and compensatory behaviors are hallmark signs of the codependent personality. The codependent person is trapped in a helping, sacrificing mode that has been shaped and reinforced by the pathology of his or her mate. To make the relationship work and get through the day, the codependent spouse becomes emotionally pinned, with his or her back to the wall, continually distorting the truth and denying the problem.

In the world of codependency, the road to health requires learning how to stop sacrificing to cover for the mate's screwups. It involves learning how to be assertive and how to put one's own healthy needs before the pathological needs of others.

Although codependency is clearly a useful construct that has helped many men and women disentangle themselves from murky, dead-end relationships, the universal application of the concept to normally functioning couples appears a bit bizarre.

Increasingly, professionals are voicing their concerns about the codependency label even when used with couples in which one partner has a drug or alcohol problem (Troise, 1993). Mostly used to label women, the concept is seen as sexist and antiquated. More important, the validity of the concept has not been supported by empirical research. No evidence supports the idea that women have a masochistic tendency to enjoy or get their pathological needs met by suffering with a dysfunctional, addicted spouse. Indeed, research supports an interactive model in which personality disturbance is greatest among the spouses of active addicts and significantly lower among spouses who have become abstinent or recovered (Paolina and McGrady, 1977). If anything, the alcoholic's illness seems to be driving the spouse's dysfunction and not the other way around!

Normally functioning couples, in our society, still fare the best when they embrace the concept of "univocal reciprocity." This high-flown phrase is used by family ethnologists to describe societies in which there are strong expectations of reciprocity between people, but the terms of the reciprocity are embedded in an endless time capsule, bounded only by the life of the relationship. For example, consider the woman who asks her husband to drive her to see her mother who lives 500 miles away. He complies. Family psychologists would say that she is becoming indebted to him and he will "cash in" on his favor when he needs to or feels like it. If he finds himself banking too many such favors, he will get to feel "underbenefited," as if he is giving too much and getting too little. He should, according to social psychological theory, become dissatisfied with the marriage. However, we know that although this is often is the case, just as often it does not happen.

We all know many couples in which one partner objectively is giving much more to make the relationship work than the other partner. Yet both of them seem pleased with the marriage and each other. Why does this happen? Is it always codependent behavior? Why doesn't the partner who is giving so much more inevitably explode from the unfairness of the entire situation? The reason is that for many couples univocal reciprocity is a guiding value in the relationship. What is important is not equal benefits but faith that if and when it ever became necessary, the overbenefited partner would gladly take on the role of the underbenefited partner. This faith in possible reciprocity is spiritual nourishment to the marriage.

Thus, marital support is not a quid pro quo contract in which one good deed is balanced by another. Marital support is more of a socialist pact that guarantees that partners will give according to their abilities and be free to take according to their needs. Only when the kindness is being used to maintain a destructive, out-of-control habit is codependency an appropriate label for spousal support and cause for concern.

PROMOTING SPIRITUALITY
BY FOSTERING FORGIVENESS AND ACCEPTANCE

The one spiritual characteristic that strengthens marriages is the ability to truly forgive one's mate for hurtful and inconsiderate behavior. Forgiveness refers to the ability to dissipate the ill will and extinguish the anger toward people after they have intentionally or unintentionally harmed you. Forgiveness does not necessitate forgetting, but it does, in the truest sense of the word, entail reinstituting a sense of trust. The inability to forgive is probably at the root of most divorces. The ability to forgive is truly divine, because it allows one to reconnect on a deeper, more humane level.

Forgiveness is a major theme in dramatic works about the family. For example, in the movie *The Best Years of Our Lives,* the mother displays this wisdom of forgiveness as she tries to explain to her daughter that she also knows about the tribulations and tortures of love. She looks to her husband and says, "We never had any trouble? How many times have I told you that I hated you—and believed it in my heart? How many times have you said that you were sick and tired of me—that we were all washed up? How many times have we had to fall in love all over again?"

Even better than the art of forgiveness, though, is the art of acceptance. Acceptance is the ability not to be hurt or offended or slighted by our partners. It is the ability to tolerate and accept, in good spirit, who they are, where they are, and how they relate to us, without compromising our own well-being and personal development. Obviously, when partners are being consistently abused (physically, emotionally, or verbally), their well-being and personal development are threatened and what may appear as acceptance is really a form of battered spouse syndrome, a dependent or avoidant personality disorder, or a codependent style of relating. True acceptance can occur only when both spouses are functioning moderately well together and as individuals.

No one has found a foolproof way to teach forgiveness or acceptance. Moore (1994) proposes that an acceptance of fate is critical for both acceptance and forgiveness. He urges people to look at a committed relationship as "being occasionally blissful and occasionally mortifying, with a mixture of all possibilities between. [Then] we might not be so surprised when challenging difficulties appear" (p. 59). If the challenging difficulties and unexpected turns in a marriage were accepted as inevitable occurrences, out of the control of either partner to predict or prevent, they could be faced with solidarity and a respect for the mysteriousness of life and destiny. Instead of harboring an "It's your fault" attitude, the goal should be to give sanctuary to "the mystery of life and the challenges it is presenting us with on our journey." Like Odysseus, life's voyage is filled with unexpected problems that must be approached with bravery and confidence.

Moore (1994) expands on how accepting the element of fate can take the sting out of conflictual situations and orient a couple toward productive problem solving:

> The fatefulness of a relationship may appear not only in extraordinary circumstances or synchronicities, but also as an element in the most ordinary events when it isn't appropriate to take full credit for what has happened. If a person's career goes off in a certain direction, that development may be due in part to decisions and conscious choices, but also in part to a gradual unfolding of the soul; unknown forces and deeper motivations are involved. Couples sometimes spend a great deal of energy and time arguing over choices that have been made, whereas they might be better off, examining together, with a degree of humility and receptivity, the mysterious elements that have entered their lives. (p. 61)

Thus, acceptance of uncontrollable elements entering one's life is a big key to forgiving one's partner for acting or thinking in ways that we did not predict and do not personally embrace. Such an acceptance allows us, in the most distressing of situations, to positively connect with our partner, stretch our own capacities for growth, and humanely look for ways to be effective in any given situation. Instead of screaming, "Why did you . . . ?" energy is focused on "How can we proceed, given where we find ourselves?"

THERAPEUTIC INTERVENTION 2: TOLERANCE TRAINING

Tolerance training has been an essential part of many therapeutic approaches, most notably rational-emotive psychotherapy (Ellis, 1962), Hayes's (1987) Acceptance Commitment Therapy, the positive reframing used by systemic therapists, and the twelve-step programs.

Jacobson and Christenson (1995) have developed an integrative behavior couple therapy based on the premise that it is just as important to foster "acceptance" as to promote "change" when working with distressed couples. Learning to accept noxious or insensitive spousal behaviors often requires deeper and more pervasive personality changes than manipulating the spouse to accommodate to the complaining partner. To truly accept previously annoying behavior, one has to "let go of the struggle to change

(continued)

(continued)

and in some cases even embrace those aspects of a partner which have traditionally been precipitants of conflict" (Jacobson, 1992, p. 497).

Teaching tolerance is part psychoeducational, part redefinition of self-growth, and part spiritual. Jacobson (1992) uses three primary strategies when helping couples learn tolerance: He tries to externalize the problem, he changes the context in which the negative behaviors occur, and he promotes self-care.

First, by externalizing the problem, neither spouse becomes responsible for the pain and both are responsible for finding a solution. Instead of saying, "You never have time for me," the problem is reframed and externalized to "The job is creating problems for us having time together."

Second, by changing the context, the couple is negotiating a win-win situation. So, instead of arguing if the wife can get to sleep only with the windows open all night, they may decide to change the focus to the husband and rearrange the furniture so he is not exposed to so much breeze.

Third, by promoting self-care, each spouse becomes less dependent on the other. The wife who realizes that she can spend her time alone getting reacquainted with old friends, going to a pottery class, or helping out in local politics may find that the husband's busy work schedule is giving her a rare opportunity to grow as a person.

Dreikurs (1968) talks about how couples need to learn to tolerate pain and tensions during stressful periods:

"Hardly any marriage can avoid a serious crisis; but most crisis situations would not need to lead to a marital breakup if the people involved knew how to extricate themselves or had the courage to let themselves be pulled down by the whirlpool of life and be spilled out safely, if they only could hold their breath and wait" (p. 502).

PROMOTING SPIRITUALITY BY FOSTERING CONGRUENCE

> Life has taught us that love does not consist in gazing at each other but in looking outward together in the same direction.
>
> Antoine de Saint-Exupéry

Spiritually evolved individuals tend to have partners with similar values and attitudes. This congruence in basic life outlook is a product of shared rituals, similar problem-solving strategies, and a shared history based on evolving values.

Rituals and Marital Bonding

There is magic to spending time together doing the same types of activities in the same way, week after week. My own research (Berg-Cross, Daniels, and Carr, 1992) showed that at different points in the couple's history, different types of rituals were important: For the newlyweds it was very important to develop nesting rituals—going out shopping for food together, cleaning the house together, doing the yard together, and visiting relatives together. Couples who nested together stayed together. Couples who spent their together time going out to parties, nightclubs, and hanging out with friends were far, far more likely to get divorced. Other researchers report similar results. Smith, Snyder, and Monsma (1988), for instance, found that time spent in individual activities and hobbies or with people other than the spouse was significantly correlated with marital distress. Women were twice as likely to feel the detrimental effects of time apart as were the men, suggesting strong gender differences on the meaning and function of couple ritual.

Ritual implies obligation (Stein, 1992), many obligations. If we have a ritual of eating dinner at 8 p.m., my spouse is obliged to restructure his day so that he will be there at that time. There is the obligation to help get it ready, if necessary, when he comes home. There is the obligation not to bring up toxic issues that would ruin the mealtime ambiance. There is an obligation to listen and be interested in the daily activities described by each of the family members. There is an obligation to personally share in a meaningful way his own day with the rest of the family. So many obligations for such a little ritual! One of the reasons some people abhor rituals is that the obligatory aspects of the ritual overwhelm the bonding aspects of the ritual. Balancing obligation with bonding is a difficult act in today's world. Those who succeed have the strongest families in America.

Children are also very sensitive to family rituals. Children value family rituals more than school rituals (Gruber and McNinch, 1993). High family ritual activity is associated with high levels of self-esteem and low levels of anxiety in adolescents (Fiese and Kline, 1993). A recent study from Toronto demonstrated that children from alcoholic families who managed to deliberately plan and execute family rituals and valued family relationships were less likely to evidence behavioral or emotional problems compared with children from alcoholic families who did not have that positive glue for building a family identity.

Roberts (1992) has termed the phrase "knowledge by acquaintance" to explain the powerful, affective knowledge of another that comes from doing things together. When working with couples, homework assignments are given that have the couple engage in affectively bonding activities. Instead of focusing on talking it out, focus is on creating different types of feelings by engaging in new activities that directly promote those feelings (Roberts, 1992). When the couple finds activities that deepen their emotional connectedness to each other, they have to find a new way to incorporate the new experience into a ritual. In this way, the rituals become "canonized."

But rituals can and do have dramatically different meanings for husbands and wives. Shaw (1992) examined so-called family time (leisure ritual time) to see how much of it was actually leisure and how much of it was actually work. Women, in particular, found time with the husband and children and/or time with the children alone to most often involve "work." Men were more likely to see these times as leisure and treat them as such. If the family is taking a trip to visit relatives, most husbands clearly put this in the leisure category. Women were the ones most likely to be involved in orchestrating the event: dressing the kids, making the sandwiches for the car trip, calling and negotiating the time of arrival and agenda with the relatives, and acting as facilitators during the visit. They tended to see this as "work."

Marital conversations can be framed as a type of ritual for couples. Routinely talking after dinner or on Saturday morning before getting out of bed can prevent conflict and hostility from getting out of control. Some couples find it helpful to ritualistically avoid certain topics on certain days of the week or after a certain hour in the evening. Many couples use special ritualistic phrases to signify when a conversation has reached a point when either person is too angry to continue, such as "The red alert light just went on" or "Time for dessert." Some even designate specific places (e.g., certain chairs or rooms of the house) to have emotionally intimate conversations.

CASE STUDY 2:
DIARY ENTRY ON RITUALS
AND THE DESTRUCTION OF A MARRIAGE

Different rituals are really what ruined my marriage of five and a half years. We had different rituals from the word "go." My mother-in-law and I never could accommodate each other or ignore each other on these issues. The best example and the most disastrous issue revolved around that good old wedding ritual. Larry and I had been dating for a year when we got engaged. His parents seemed to approve of the relationship at that time and we all got along well. Then, after we had been engaged for half a year, he got orders to go to Vietnam. He was not going to return until about one month before the wedding. After Larry was gone about three months, I started making preparations for the wedding. It was then that I started getting bad vibes from his mother and father. Suddenly, they did not think it

(continued)

(continued)

was such a good idea for Larry to get married right after returning home. What really turned them off was that the rituals we had for marriage were very different from the rituals that they had.

In my family, weddings are a very upbeat and formal affair and model themselves after the Church of England. Princess Di might have had more guests, but the wedding I planned and the wedding I had was every bit as elegant as hers was. Larry's parents lived in a large, beautiful home and his dad was a patent lawyer so they were solidly middle-class. Yet their idea of a wedding was a small, simple ceremony at the church and then a platter of cold cuts and a cake at the house. Anything else was viewed as crass social climbing. I think that the real issue was that his mother felt socially inadequate. She did not know how to dress or speak when she was out with strangers. She did not understand any cuisine that didn't have "Swanson's" written across the carton. It was that sort of thing. Well, regardless of the real reasons for her discomfort, it got so bad they refused to take part in any of the planning. When Larry came home, five weeks before the wedding, they begged him to cancel it and do something simple. Eventually, the situation became so volatile that he moved out of the house two weeks before the wedding. He moved into the apartment we were going to live in after the wedding. His mother refused to go to the wedding and then said that if she went, she was going to wear black. On the day of the wedding we were still not sure if they were going to attend.

Finally, things sort of normalized, but then the differing rituals kept getting in the way, again and again. When I was pregnant with Tina, my mother-in-law could not understand why my brother's wife was going to give a baby shower. She felt it was bad luck to have a shower. After all, who knew if the baby was going to live or come out terribly deformed and not need regular sleepers! I thought such superstitions were crazy, but her daughter thought pretty much the same way as her mother. Well, I had my shower and she and my mother-in-law came and made me miserable.

Once Tina was born, I very much wanted to have her baptized. It was not a big religious event—to me it was not religious at all. It was just a family ritual that I wanted my daughter to experience. My mother-in-law was from a very long line of nonobservant Protestants and she thought that I was acting like a heathen. I told her that I did not want to insult her, so I was not going to invite her to this "heathen" event. A year later, she saw pictures of the christening and was furious that we had had her christened. She swore that we had never told her about it and demanded to know how we could have not invited her.

Every time these rituals came up, there was a terrible scene. It would take half a year to bury the hatchet and then it would never be buried very deep. Our attitudes toward each other got worse and worse. My mother-in-law and father-in-law would make very large cash gifts to us and then if we did not ritualistically reciprocate with an out-of-this-world anniversary present or Christmas present, they would be very insulted.

Probably, most stressful were the phone call rituals. She told me very early on that the only way women can keep close to their sons was if their

(continued)

(continued)

daughters-in-law were willing to keep them informed. So twice a week she would call when Larry was still at work and I had just arrived home and she would want a thirty-minute report on how her dear son was doing and what I had fed him the night before and what we were planning to do over the weekend. I liked the fact that she was interested in Larry. I hated the fact that this was the time that she chose to socialize with me and this the manner that she chose to do it in. But once the ritual gets started you cannot get out of it and we kept that up all five and a half years of the marriage. I hated each of the more than 500 phone calls I had with that woman.

When we were splitting up, I asked Larry, on one of our more cordial days, what his parents had said when he told them that we were splitting. He said they each said the same thing, "I told you so."

I don't know if Larry and I would still be together if we had been able to have the appropriate rites of passage with both families joyously helping us celebrate our union, step by step. It just seemed that every time we were trying to ceremonially glue ourselves together, they ripped into our holiday or ritual, trying to demean it and in so doing demeaned the relationship.

Anonymous

THERAPEUTIC INTERVENTION 3:
REENACTMENTS OF EARLY RELATIONSHIP MEMORIES

One of the most romantic exercises a couple can be given for homework is to make an appointment with each other to discuss what originally attracted them to each other. They are not to discuss what happened to those wonderful traits and behaviors, only to itemize what they were and flesh out the circumstances under which they occurred. Then they are asked to pick out one or two interactions that they both agree were fun activities and very bonding. They should try to adapt that behavior and re-create it during the week. So often the attraction is based on how people felt holding each other's hands, making love a certain way, or having certain meals or friends with whom to share a lighter moment.

Ritualistically reenacting these early memories can rekindle old feelings, but they are far more likely to ignite new, deeper, and different feelings that match the more mature stage of the marital relationship.

LEARNING AIDS

Therapeutic Dialogue (Spirituality)

1. Ideally, how do you think a husband and wife should show their love for each other?

2. What are the things that your mate feels are important for you to say or do to show your love?
3. How do your friends and family show their love for their spouses?
4. How can you change your ideal model of showing love to make it more attainable in your marriage?
5. Ideally, do you believe that commitments of restraint are useful to the institution of marriage?
6. What are your commitments of constraint and obligation?
7. What commitments of constraint and obligation do you see operating among your friends and extended family in their marital relationships?
8. Is there any way that the commitments of constraint and obligation help strengthen the commitments of dedication in your marriage?
9. Ideally, what type of rituals would you like to share with your spouse?
10. What type of rituals do you share with your spouse?
11. Among other couples you know, what type of ritual activity do you see occurring?
12. How could you change or modify your ideal model of shared ritual to make it more attainable in your marriage?

Self-Exploration 1: The Love Expression Scale for Spouses

Rate how important it is to you for your spouse to increase the frequency with which he or she shows the following traits and behaviors.
Use the following scale:

1 = Not at all important
2 = Slightly important
3 = Moderately important
4 = Very important
5 = Extremely important

If your partner displays enough of any one trait, you should give it a "1," indicating that it is not at all important for him or her to increase the frequency with which he or she displays that trait. Remember, the higher the rating, the more change you are seeking.

1. Help me more with my chores and responsibilities.
2. Allow me to make more decisions that are important to me.
3. Be more polite in our conversations.
4. Be more active and enthusiastic when we are together.
5. Encourage me more to share my thoughts and feelings.
6. Treat me more as your equal.
7. Try to make the times we have more light and enjoyable.

8. Be more emotionally and sexually faithful to me.
9. Be more honest and sincere in our interactions.
10. More frequently, invite me to be part of your social activities.
11. Let me know more often that we are special to each other by giving me sweet reminders and special moments.
12. Show more attention when I am talking to you.
13. Share more of your thoughts and feelings with me; do not keep them so much inside yourself.
14. Be more optimistic and cheerful.
15. Be more physically affectionate.
16. Spend more time making yourself attractive in how you dress and look.
17. Try to be more daring and risk-taking so our life is more interesting.
18. Be more responsible in carrying out your responsibilities to me and the family.
19. Increase how often you give me something nice and special.
20. Compliment me more often and help me overcome my own self-doubts with realistic reassurances.
21. Take more interest in activities outside of our family.
22. Get more involved with my hobbies and activities.
23. Be more warm, caring, and empathic toward me.
24. Share in religious rituals with me more often.
25. Find more interests and values that we have in common and let's talk more about these areas.
26. Defend me in front of family and friends more often instead of putting me down in front of them.
27. Be friendlier to my family and friends.
28. Tell me you love me more frequently and be verbally affectionate in other ways.

Have your partner go over the five or six areas that are most important to him or her and then switch roles. The two most important questions to ask are "Can you tell me more about it?" and "How can I improve?"

Self-Exploration 2: Values Inventory

Read the following list of thirty values. Decide which ten of the values would be the most important to you. Rank order the ones you choose from 1 to 10 (1 being the most important). Place these numbers in the appropriate spaces under "You" at the left of the value. Next, decide which ten of the values you think your spouse would choose. Rank order these and place the numbers in the appropriate spaces under "Your Spouse."

You   Your Spouse

                  A secure and comfortable retirement
                  A sense of equality in relationships
                  Emotional and sexual intimacy
                  A sense of accomplishment in life
                  A sense of independence and self-reliance
                  A meaningful love relationship
                  Financial security for the family
                  Happiness
                  A meaningful relationship with God
                  Achieving feelings of self-confidence
                  Achieving social recognition and community
                      status
                  A fulfilling marriage
                  A life with meaningful purpose
                  Helping the poor, sick, and disadvantaged
                  A sense of family togetherness
                  Learning, gaining knowledge continually
                  Honesty and personal integrity
                  Being in good health and physically fit
                  Having close relationships with relatives
                  Traveling and quality vacations
                  Companionship, spending time together as a
                      couple
                  Success in a job or career
                  Freedom to live life as you choose
                  New experiences and adventures
                  Being outdoors; away from city life
                  Satisfying friendships
                  Living in the city: access to restaurants
                      and entertainment
                  Having alone time
                  Having nice things, for example, cars, boat,
                      furniture
                  Emotional security, freedom from stress.

Where are your strongest areas of agreement? Which areas cause conflict and is there some common ground that you share even in these areas?

Sample Workshop Flowchart Intended for Groups of Four or Five Couples Working on Spirituality

  I. Psychoeducational Strategies
    A. Definition of spirituality
    B. Activities people describe doing to create a loving marriage

    C. How to cultivate the different types of intimacy that exist in a marriage

    D. Sex and the spiritual experience

    E. Commitments of dedication and obligation: an important part of a spiritual marriage

    F. Role of forgiveness

    G. Rituals and marital bonding

II. Self-Explorations (Done by couples in private and shared before rejoining the group)

    A. The Love Expression Scale for Spouses

    B. Values Inventory

III. Therapeutic Dialogue (Done by couples in private and shared before rejoining the group)

    (Proceeding in the order presented, both partners respond to each question before going on to discuss the next question)

    In group, the therapist explores with couples how relationship goals can be achieved by modifying overly ambitious, pie-in-the-sky expectations. Using information about their current situation and the realities seen among friends and family, couples fine-tune expectations so they are achievable and motivate rather than discourage attempts at change.

IV. Therapeutic Interventions

    Work with a couple in front of the group and apply one or more of the therapeutic interventions. Share rationale during demonstrations. Let group discuss additional interventions.

    A. Increasing intimacy by structured assignments

    B. Symbolic demonstrations of a commitment of dedication

    C. Tolerance training

    D. Reenactment of early relationship memories

V. Finding the Motivation and Time to Make the Changes

    Group discussion

Bibliotherapy

McCarthy, B. and McCarthy, E. (1992). *Intimate marriage.* New York: Carroll and Graf.

Rosenbaum, S. and Rosenbaum, M. (1994). *Celebrating our differences: Living two faiths in one marriage.* New York: White Main.

Ruszczynski, S. and Fisher, J. (1995). *Intrusiveness and intimacy in the couple.* New York: Brunner/Mazel.

Schwarz, P. (1994). *Peer marriage: How love between equals really works.* New York: Free Press.
Spirituality and couples [Special issue]. (1995). *Journal of Couples Therapy, 3*(1).

Videotherapy

Breathing Lessons. (1994). Directed by John Erman. On a daylong car trip, a couple reconstructs the past to face the future.
Pontiac Moon. (1994). Directed by Peter Medak. A family takes a historic car trip to learn the meaning of family loving and inevitable change.
The War. (1994). Directed by Jon Avnet. A Vietnam vet symbolizes every man who tries to heal his own wounds and resolve his problems while still trying to fulfill the family's dream.

Professional Development Questions (Spirituality)

1. What is your own definition of spirituality? Can you invent an exercise that would allow couples to develop their own definition of spirituality?

2. Discuss how a therapist can use the concepts of commitment and dedication to foster spirituality between a couple.

3. Forgiveness is one of the most difficult processes to achieve in a marriage. Can you think of secular approaches (e.g., cognitive or experiential) that would help individuals learn how to forgive? What are the components of forgiveness? Are they teachable?

4. What is the role of rituals in creating a spiritually fulfilling marriage? How can the therapeutic process enhance the development, maintenance, and remembrance of bonding rituals?

REFERENCES

Bell, R. A., Daly, J. A., and Gonzalez, M. C. (1987). Affinity-maintenance in marriage and its relationship to women's marital satisfaction. *Journal of Marriage and the Family, 49*(2), 445-454.
Berg-Cross, L., Daniels, C., and Carr, P. (1992). Marital rituals among divorced and married couples. *Journal of Divorce and Remarriage, 18*(1), 1-32.
Branden, N. (1981). *The psychology of romantic love.* New York: Bantam.
Buxbaum, Y. (1990). *Jewish spiritual practices.* Hillsdale, NJ: Jason Aronson.
Colwin, L. (1983). Swan song. *The New Yorker,* April 18.

Dreikurs, R. (1968). Determinants of changing attitudes. *Individual Psychology,* *49*(3-4), 488-505. Also in S. Rosenbaum and I. Alger (Eds.), *The marriage relationship: Psychoanalytic perspective.* New York: Basic Books, 1993.

Ellis, A. (1962). *Reason and emotion in psychotherapy.* New York: Lyle-Stuart.

Fiese, B. and Kline, C. (1993). Development of the family ritual questionnaire: Initial reliability and validation studies. *Journal of Family Psychology, 6*(3), 290-299.

Gray, D. (1995). Divorce or a room of your own: Options for a troubled marriage. *Family Therapy, 22*(3), 143-156.

Gruber, E. and McNinch, G. (1993). Home versus school: Parents' perceptions of the development of rituals leading to young children's self-esteem. *Journal of Instructional Psychology, 20*(2), 102-110.

Hayes, S. C. (1987). A contextual approach to therapeutic change. In N. S. Jacobson (ed.), *Psychotherapists in clinical practice: Cognitive and behavioral perspectives* (pp. 327-387). New York: Guilford.

Jacobson, N. S. (1992). Behavior couple therapy. A new beginning. *Behavior Therapy, 23,* 493-506.

Jacobson, N. S. and Christenson, A. (1995). *Couple therapy: An integrative approach.* New York: Norton.

Moore, T. (1994). *Soul mates: Honoring the mysteries of love and relationship.* New York: HarperCollins.

Moss, B. and Schwebel, A. (1993). Romantic relationships: Defining intimacy in romantic relationships. *Family Relations, 42*(1), 31-37.

Or ha-Emet (1967). *The Maggid of Mezritch.* Bnei Brak, Israel: Yahadut.

Paolina, T. J., Jr., and McGrady, B. (1977). *The alcoholic marriage: Alternative perspectives.* New York: Grune and Stratton.

Roberts, T. (1992). Sexual attraction and romantic love: Forgotten variables in marital therapy. *Journal of Marital and Family Therapy, 18*(4), 357-364.

Robinson, L., and Blanton, P. (1993). Marital strengths in enduring relationships. *Family Relations, 42*(1), 38-45.

Schnarch, D. (1993). Inside the sexual crucible. *Family Networker,* (March/April), 40-48.

Shaw, S. (1992). Dereifying family leisure: An examination of women's and men's everyday experiences and perceptions of family time. *Leisure Sciences, 14(4),* 271-286.

Smith, G., Snyder, D., and Monsma, B. (1988). Predicting relationship satisfaction from couples' use of leisure time. *American Journal of Family Therapy, 16*(1), 3-13.

Stein, C. (1992). Ties that bind: Three studies of obligation in adult relationships with family. *Journal of Social and Personal Relationships, 9*(4), 525-547.

Stuart, R. (1980). *Helping couples change: A social learning approach to marital therapy.* New York: Guilford.

Troise, F. (1993). An overview of the historical and empirical antecedents in the development of the codependency concept. *Journal of Couples Therapy, 1*(1/2), 89-104.

Chapter 10

Finishing Touches:
Frequently Asked Professional
and Ethical Questions

1. Many studies cited in this text demonstrate that couples therapy is beneficial in treating many particular types of problems. But overall, has couples therapy been shown to be more effective than no treatment at all?

Neil Jacobson and Michael Addis (1993) have reviewed the outcome and process research on marital therapy. More than twenty-four studies demonstrated that behavioral couples therapy (which was primarily a combination of behavioral exchange and communication training) led to increased marital satisfaction compared to couples who were in a control group. This treatment has received the lion's share of outcome research because it was developed by the same family researchers who tested its effectiveness.

There are, in addition, three studies supporting the effectiveness of emotion-focused couple therapy (Greenberg and Johnson, 1988). This is a combination of gestalt and systemic perspectives that tries to have couples cleanse themselves of negative emotions and elicit positive emotions. Also, positive changes in couples were reported from one study that assessed strategic couples therapy and one analytic model that tested insight-oriented couples therapy. In all, about 50 percent of couples who finish treatment report being "happily married." It is not known at this time which treatments work for which couples with which problems.

In general, it appears that the most likely couples to benefit from therapy are those who are: only moderately distressed, younger, flexible in their gender role preferences, and emotionally committed to their partner (Jacobson and Addis, 1993).

Outcome research on couples therapy is in its infancy. Ideally, therapists will eventually be able to rely on empirical information to guide them in deciding which techniques work best for which couples struggling from which problems. Until then, the art of choosing the right technique and using it in an effective manner will remain, in large part, an art that is perfected by practice and a spirit of experimentalism.

2. What is the best way to conduct an initial assessment of a couple?

The thrust of this book was that each of the four cornerstones must be carefully assessed before treatment begins and monitored throughout treatment. The many therapeutic interventions and self-explorations should help therapists tailor their own set of cornerstone assessments that are relevant to any one particular couple.

However, it is important to supplement any individualized assessments with a standardized intake package of couple assessment measures. Such a measure serves four distinct purposes (Bray, 1995).

First, a comprehensive objective assessment can be conducted routinely prior to the first therapy session. Thus, it can be used to develop initial hypotheses about which cornerstones have the most problems and which have the most strengths. With minimal use of the clinician's time, the clients can highlight pressing issues and have an initial airing of their personal concerns.

Second, a questionnaire focused on couple functioning immediately helps orient both individuals toward looking at the relationship instead of looking to "fix" the other person.

Third, national norms, particularly those that are normed for different couple structures (traditional, remarriages, homosexual, dual career, etc.) help place any one couple in perspective and one's entire couple practice in a larger perspective.

Fourth, an objective initial assessment instrument can be compared with posttreatment assessments to document the extent and type of changes that have taken place. Although it would be ideal to routinely individualize appropriate pre- and post-therapy assessments, the reality of time constraints makes standard protocol procedures essential.

Given the importance placed on such a general checkup measure, what are the best ones available? Clearly, a number of assessments are included in this text that are appropriate for such an intake package. However, many other simple and very effective measures may be found in the public domain (free and reproducible). For example, O'Leary (1987) recommends the following battery:

1. The Marital Adjustment Test (Locke and Wallace, 1959).
2. Daily Checklist of Marital Activities (Broderick, 1980).

3. Positive Feelings Questionnaire (O'Leary and Arias, 1983).
4. Relationship Beliefs Inventory (Eidelson and Epstein, 1982).
5. Sexual History Form (LoPiccolo, 1987).

All five of these self-report measures, with validation and normative data, are provided in the appendixes of *Assessment of Marital Discord: An Integration for Research and Clinical Practice* (O'Leary, 1987).

3. How does one know when it is "too late" to work on the relationship? What is the advisable course when one partner wants to work on the marriage and the other partner refuses treatment?

Quite frequently, one partner will want to try couples therapy as a way of improving the relationship and the other partner comes as a reluctant participant. Reluctant partners sometimes have already made the decision to separate or divorce; at other times, they feel personally uncomfortable with the disclosure styles required in therapy, and sometimes they are happy with the status quo and do not want to change anything but their partner's constant complaining about the relationship.

Within the first one or two sessions, however, therapists often feel pressed to make an assessment of whether or not the relationship is "workable" or "salvageable." As mentioned in the communication chapter, assessments such as PREPARE can indicate the level of divorce risk, but other clinical signs are useful to the therapist. For example, once an individual has contacted an attorney, moved out of the family home, told extended family about a possible separation, or started to develop new friendships and leisure activities, the prospects for working things through drops dramatically. Individual sessions, as part of the assessment process, very often lead to unmistakable signs: confessions about wanting out and having no desire to repair or work on the relationship (Walsh, Jacob, and Simons, 1995).

To assess the likelihood of therapy helping restore marital happiness, it is essential to know the "relationship story" of each of the partners, and this is another vital reason to conduct individual sessions. The stories are virtually never the same, and buying into only one version of the story can make a therapist blind to the irreconcilable differences in the relationship. Hetherington and Tryon (1989) found that the personal accounts of the marital history and breakup of divorced partners were so discrepant that blind raters could not match ex-spouses; they were unable to recognize who had even been in the same marriage! Indeed, the more discrepant the two marital stories are, the more dire the probability for success in therapy might be.

However, I feel it is important to work with anyone who wants to try to save his or her relationship, regardless of the initial probability assessment of success. On an individual basis, some of the most anguished relationships find the proper balm for their woes, and some of the most intimate relationships find their futures are not meant to be in tandem. Even when only one partner is willing to come to therapy, marital work within each of the cornerstones can be done. The most important task is for the therapist to work out an explicit therapy contract that specifies which issues need to be addressed to make the relationship healthier and happier. The decision on how to proceed with one's life after such work has been attempted can appropriately be a therapeutic task but is a separate and distinct task that must be negotiated independently.

4. How long should a couple be in treatment? What are the special termination issues?

I have found that for the typical couple coming to my practice, exploring and working on the four cornerstones takes six to nine months, meeting once a week. Some couples find it useful to be in therapy for a year or two, and many like to use the therapy format for general relationship maintenance work. Working with clients on managed care insurance contracts often means finding ways of reducing that time to three months. However, a distressed marriage or relationship is not responsive to a minute intervention. A careful assessment, joint goal-setting, breaking through resistances, and practicing new ways of dealing with old problems simply takes a great deal of time.

Termination is trickier in couples therapy because three different parties are trying to reach consensus instead of the usual two. Termination is usually a process of "fading" out sessions over a month or two instead of going "cold turkey." Couples often find it easier to terminate knowing the therapist encourages them to call on an as-needed basis or to return for a booster session once or twice a year.

During the termination process, partners are often told that they are free to contact the therapist for individual consultations in the future but that the potential conflict of interest issues are best avoided if they inform the partner of that decision. Some couple therapists feel that once a couple's therapist, always a couple's therapist, and that it is unethical to develop an individual therapist-patient relationship with either one of the partners. Although this argument certainly has merit, the realities are that each partner has invested an enormous amount of time and energy in the therapy process, and if one needs assistance at some later point, it is usually in his or her best interest to see their couples therapist if he or she so desires.

It saves time in building rapport and the telling of the story. In addition, the knowledge of the significant other is often invaluable for therapeutic success of individual issues. Clearly, many therapists will think through this issue differently with each couple, depending on the particular dynamics in a particular situation.

5. *What are the benefits of a couples group?*

The sample group formats provided at the end of each chapter attest to the value and importance this author places on group work with couples. The sample group formats presented in this book are part psychoeducational, part family-systems oriented, and part group-process oriented. There are, of course, as many different ways to run a couples group as there are to run any other type of therapeutic group. However, one of the most exciting and coherent models has been developed by Judith Coche (1995). The Coche model works well with a cornerstone perspective on relationships.

In the Coche model, groups are closed (meaning that no couples are allowed in once the group starts), limited to four couples, convene over a period of one year for twenty-two sessions on a bimonthly basis, and last for two and one-half hours per session. There is an emphasis on each partner taking responsibility for his or her actions and making life choices. The level of analysis varies, as in the cornerstone approach, from focusing on personal issues, to focusing on couple issues, to focusing on interpersonal issues that involve different members of the group, and finally to focusing on group-as-a-whole issues (e.g., dealing with tone of the sessions, people who monopolize sessions).

Each group session contains structured and unstructured portions. The first half is unstructured and resembles traditional groups in which couples are free to discuss whatever they choose. The second half, though, always involves a structured exercise relevant to the issues being discussed. For example, exercises may focus on anger, fear of intimacy, exploring anxiety over death, expectations, equality, or many other topics. Couples are also seen individually and as a family unit on a regular, as needed basis.

The Coche model involves giving a structured initial assessment (including the Couples Assessment Inventory, the Symptom Checklist, and the Myers-Briggs Questionnaire) that serves as the basis for the final, formal evaluations. Often, the whole group will evaluate how far a couple has come in achieving their goals; at other times the assessments are done in private sessions.

Coche (1995) makes the point that therapists wanting to do couples work need to be grounded in both family therapy skills and group therapy skills to be effective.

6. How important is a male-female cotherapist team?

Many couples therapists believe that it is essential to have a male and female therapist in each session to remain gender sensitive and to prevent partner-therapist collusion. From a psychodynamic perspective, having both male and female therapists present facilitates the transferences and brings characterological issues into the open more quickly and blatantly. From a systems perspective, it allows one therapist to process the interactions while the other is orchestrating an intervention or interaction. From a learning viewpoint, sharing ideas about how therapy should proceed and what would work is almost always beneficial to the couple. In short, I see many, many advantages to cotherapy models.

The drawbacks to cotherapy are primarily availability and cost. It is difficult for therapists to find colleagues to work with routinely whose hours and schedules match one's own. Most important, it is difficult to justify charging couples twice as much for having two therapists present when such a technique has not been empirically tested and found to be twice as effective or indeed, any more effective than one therapist.

7. How much self-disclosure from the therapist is appropriate in couples therapy?

Therapist self-disclosure is generally inappropriate in couples therapy. However, even here, there are many times and situations in which a limited, humane self-disclosure on the therapist's part can facilitate treatment. For example, a wife who finds her husband's spending habits out-of-hand may be more willing to reevaluate her judgments if the therapist shares that his or her own marriage needed to work on money issues and found that a particularly rough area in which to maintain tolerance. However, when a therapist does choose to self-disclose, it should be with one or more of the following goals: (1) to facilitate self-disclosure in the client; (2) to reduce client anxiety or shame over a particular behavior, attitude, or feeling; (3) to demonstrate the universality of a particular issue; (4) to model more effective coping strategies; and (5) to create a sense of optimism about overcoming a difficulty. Therapist disclosures should always be brief and related to an issue that is historical and long resolved.

8. Where can I find information on other specific programmatic approaches to couples therapy?

The most established "schools" of couples therapy are in the following list along with a text that gives a detailed description of the conceptualizations and techniques used by that particular school:

- Cognitive-Behavioral Couples Therapy: A. Ellis, J. L. Sichel, R. J. Yaeger, D. J. DiMattia, and R. DiGiuseppe, *Rational-Emotive Couples Therapy* (New York: Pergamon, 1989).
- Bowen Family Systems: D. V. Papero, *Bowen Family Systems Theory* (Boston: Allyn & Bacon, 1990).
- Integrative Behavioral Couples Therapy: N. S. Jacobson and A. Christensen, *Integrative Behavioral Couples Therapy* (New York: Norton, 1996).
- Ego Analytic Couples Therapy: D. B. Wile, *After the Fight: A Night in the Life of a Couple* (New York: Guilford, 1993).
- Emotionally Focused Couples Therapy: S. Johnson and L. Greenberg, *The Heart of the Matter: Perspectives on Emotion in Marital Therapy* (New York: Brunner/Mazel, 1994).
- Solution Focused Couples Therapy: S. deShazer, *Putting Differences to Work* (New York: Norton, 1991).
- Psychoanalytic Couples Therapy: D. Scharff and J. S. Scharff, *Object Relations Couples Therapy* (Northvale, NJ: Jason Aronson, 1991).

9. What are the ethical issues in couples work?

The three ethical issues most commonly faced by couples therapists are confidentiality, dual relationships, and the use of the *Diagnostic and Statistical Manual of Mental Disorders* (DSM-IV) (American Psychiatric Association, 1994).

Confidentiality

The most common problems of confidentiality in couples work concern whether one can keep information that is received by one of the partners confidential from the other partner.

When one partner wants to keep a secret with the therapist from the other partner, the confidentiality requirements of the revealing partner are pitted against the need for the therapist to be honest and maintain his or her integrity to the partner being kept in the dark. Most of the time these secrets emerge in individual sessions, but often they are conveyed by special letters sent in between sessions or in phone messages. Although many of the secrets have to do with infidelity, there are a myriad of other secrets that couples keep from each other, including sexual paraphilias (e.g., cross-dressing), financial debts, troubles at work or with the family of origin, issues with the children, and even health concerns.

Of course, most therapists try to avoid this problem by telling the couple, beforehand, that although everything they say is confidential within the session, secrets shared in individual sessions may be communicated to the partner by the therapist if she or he finds that it is necessary for the progress of the therapy. Once the disclosure is made, however, most therapists realize that, regardless of their warnings, they are in a catch-22 in which there is no right answer: A terribly damaging disclosure may wreak havoc on the relationship, but not disclosing it will wreak havoc on the therapy.

Sometimes, the decision to break confidentiality pivots on the extent to which the secret betrays the basic trust on which the unknowing partner is predicating his or her feelings and actions. The general consensus confirms a need to respect disclosures about private information (e.g., a brother's request for money that was denied), which, although emotionally shameful or difficult for a person, do not affect the couple's relationship. On the other hand, an equally compelling need exists to share secret information that is being withheld because it violates the core expectancy of trust and relevancy (e.g., lending a brother money from one's retirement account without telling the partner). Consider the issues facing Bill and Gary's therapist.

Bill and Gary had been a couple for ten years. They were open about their relationship and had been the entire time. They had consulted a therapist because Gary was worried that Bill was seeing someone else. Bill had assured Gary that this was not the case and complained that he was getting tired of Gary's "paranoia." In individual sessions, Bill confessed to seeing someone with whom he was having unprotected sex. He was afraid to tell Gary because he was sure that this breach of trust would lead to their breakup.

Here, most would agree that the therapist must disclose the information to Gary because he or she has a "duty to warn" (due to the risk of AIDS) as well as a need to avoid colluding in withholding secret information. If Bill had been having protected sex with his lover, he might have been judged as presenting only an "intermediate" level of risk to Gary. Since he was having unprotected sex, he was engaging in "high-risk" behaviors. Either way, in this situation a therapist can identify a potential victim (Gary), has a special relationship of trust with the client (Bill), and can see that Gary's health may be at risk. The same analysis would hold true for infidelity with any heterosexual couple (Knapp and VandeCreek, 1990).

For couples therapists to ensure that confidentiality is maintained outside the therapy process, they must explain to each new couple, orally and in writing, the nature and extent of the confidentiality of their sessions. In couples therapy, confidentiality must be extended to include both people present in the room. Indeed, most couples will assume that anything they say will never be divulged without their permission. Unfortunately, that is often not the case.

Take the case of Marcie and Eitan, who had been in couples therapy for two years when they decided to divorce. Eitan's attorney later requested all the notes and records that pertained to the therapy. He stated that the material would be subpoenaed if he did not receive it within a week's time. Meanwhile, Marcie had called the therapist and told him that she adamantly refused to give him permission to release any of the information about their therapy. In many such cases, depending on the particular issues discussed and the state in which one resides, the judge may eventually require that the therapist share records or be held in contempt of court.

Regardless of who is asking for information and under what pretense, the therapist's first job is to ask that the requesting partner put the request in writing and authorize release of the information. The therapist's second job, in this scenario, involves telling the partner, in writing, that she or he is unable to release any of the record because the record belongs to the couple, as a unit, and unless they both agree to release the material, it must remain private.

The legal standing on what is confidential in couples work varies from state to state, with some states protecting a nonconsenting spouse's right to confidentiality and other states assuming that there is no confidentiality, as it is commonly understood, because the conversations did not take place in private but were made in the presence of a spouse and were therefore public (Huber, 1987). Therapists should become familiar with the laws of their state on the statutory protection of communication in multiperson therapies. Some therapists have suggested that couples who enter therapy together sign an agreement that neither will seek court disclosures of therapy communications (Gumper and Sprenkle, 1981).

When a document or record is subpoenaed, the therapist is still legally able to go to court and argue, with counsel, as to why he or she wants to keep the information confidential. A subpoena means only that one is legally required to appear at the courthouse on the appointed day. If, after hearing an argument from the therapist or therapist's counsel, the judge still finds the material necessary, the therapist must legally supply it or be found in contempt of court.

Confidentiality issues are becoming more and more prominent in the workplace as well as the legal arena. As employee-assistance personnel and human resource administrators use success in therapy as part of probationary or disciplinary actions, the therapist will increasingly be put in a number of compromising situations. The case of Jennifer is typical.

Jennifer worked in a large corporation and felt that she had been sexually harassed by her immediate supervisor. She brought a legal suit against him, and her work and home life began to deteriorate. The human resource manager told Jennifer that she must go into therapy because she was not functioning well on the job. When Jennifer went to the recommended therapist, she and the therapist soon realized that couples therapy was indicated. Although Jennifer signed a release of information allowing the therapist and human resource manager to communicate about her progress, she was shocked to find that the human resource manager knew about specific marital problems she was working on in therapy. She felt that these issues had nothing to do with her job performance and that the therapist had acted unethically with this breach of confidentiality.

The guidelines in such situations are very unclear, and what could be judged as facilitative and appropriate by one party can easily be viewed by the other as inappropriate and embarrassing. The best way for any therapist to proceed in such cases is to consult with two or more colleagues on the specific situation and discuss what will be revealed with the client beforehand.

Dual Relationships

Dual relationships occur when a therapist maintains a second distinct role relationship simultaneously or sequentially with one or both members of the couple. Ideally, the only relationship one would ever have with any client is that of doctor-patient. However, the realities of community life are such that clear-cut boundaries are not always possible. For example, if you have a couple in therapy and come September your child is placed in the husband's history class, you are suddenly in a dual relationship.

Dual relationships are troublesome when they disturb the expectancies or priorities of the therapy relationship. The most heinous dual relationships are those that directly use the therapy relationship to help satisfy the social, sexual, or psychological needs of the therapist. Like all ethical quandaries, though, the most common situations are the least clear-cut ones. The case of Dr. Robb represents such a common dilemma.

Dr. Robb has been using the same dentist for five years. Although Dr. Robb and the dentist do not have a social relationship, they do chat when they see each other at community events. The dentist contacts Dr. Robb and asks her to please see her and her long-term partner. She has just become pregnant and they are in a crisis mode deciding whether they should get married before the birth of the baby. The dentist assures the doctor that all they really want is to sit down for one or two sessions with someone they are comfortable with who can help them gather their thoughts.

Does the fact that the therapist has a prior relationship with the doctor create a "dual relationship" problem and does it prevent the therapist from objectively working with the couple? The answer to this depends partly on the comfort level of Dr. Robb. Would she feel comfortable seeing this couple? Would she feel awkward going to the dentist after having had her as a patient? Are there other therapists to whom she can refer the dentist? Although I believe most therapists would refer the dentist on, it could be ethical and responsible to accept such a case.

Use of Diagnostic and Statistical Manual of Mental Disorders (DSM-IV)

In most clinics, hospitals, and group practices, for the clinical records to be complete, the identified patient must be given a diagnosis based on the DSM-IV. For insurance reimbursement, such an "illness" code is mandatory. However, the DSM-IV potentially raises some ethical issues for couples therapists.

Most notably, couples therapists, by and large, do not look for individual pathologies when explaining the malaise of the clients that they see. Rather, significant emphasis is placed on seeing difficulties in relationships as being the cause for the malaise. When a therapist gives a client a diagnosis that he or she does not believe in just to make the paperwork complete or collect insurance benefits, the therapist is undoubtedly on the slippery slope of an ethical violation. Labeling a patient with a disorder one does not believe that he or she has raises questions about the integrity of the provider.

Traditionally, most therapists end up giving the partner who initiated the therapy, or the partner who has the better insurance policy, a diagnosis of some type of "adjustment disorder" (309.XX). This diagnosis is a "catchall" category in which a person needs to show marked distress from some identifiable stressor and have a significant impairment in occupational (academic) or social functioning.

Although this is a very useful start, there are at least two problems with this diagnosis. First, many insurance companies will not reimburse for this "condition." Second, many therapists feel that, inasmuch as all couples would receive this diagnosis, it does not say much about diagnosing the relationship problem.

For a fuller discussion of ethical issues, the reader is encouraged to read Huber's (1987) *Ethical, Legal and Professional Issues in the Practice of Marriage and Family Therapy.*

REFERENCES

American Psychiatric Association. (1994). *Diagnostic and statistical manual of mental disorders* (Fourth edition). Washington, DC: Author.

Bray, J. H. (1995). Family assessment: Current issues in evaluating families. *Family Relations, 44*(4), 469-477.

Broderick, J. (1980). Attitudinal and behavioral components of marital satisfaction. Unpublished doctoral dissertation, State University of New York at Stony Brook.

Coche, J. (1995). Group therapy with couples. In N. S. Jacobson and A. S. Gurman (Eds.), *Clinical handbook of couples therapy* (pp. 197-211). New York: Guilford.

Greenberg, L. S. and Johnson, S. M. (1988). *Emotionally focused therapy for couples.* New York: Guilford.

Gumper, L. L. and Sprenkle, D. H. (1981). Privileged communication in therapy: Special problems for the family and couple therapist. *Family Process, 20*(1), 11-23.

Hetherington, E. M. and Tyron, A. S. (1989). His and her divorces. *Family Therapy Networker, 13*, 58-61.

Huber, C. (1987). *Ethical, legal and professional issues in the practice of marriage and family therapy* (Second edition). New York: Macmillan.

Jacobson, N. and Addis, M. (1993). Research on couples and couple therapy: What do we know? Where are we going? *Journal of Consulting and Clinical Psychology, 61*(1), 85-93.

Knapp, S. and VandeCreek, L. (1990). *What every therapist should know about AIDS.* Sarasota, FL: Professional Resource Exchange.

Locke, H. and Wallace, K. (1959). Short marital adjustment and prediction tests: Their reliability and validity. *Marriage and Family Living, 21*(2), 251-255.

LoPiccolo, J. (1987). Sexual history form. In K. O'Leary (Ed.), *Assessment of marital discord: An integration for research and clinical practice.* Hillsdale, NJ: Lawrence Erlbaum.

O'Leary, K. D. (Ed.). (1987). *Assessment of marital discord: An integration for research and clinical practice.* Hillsdale, NJ: Lawrence Erlbaum.

O'Leary, K. and Arias, I. (1983). The influence of marital therapy on sexual satisfaction. *Journal of Sex and Marital Therapy, 9*(3), 171-181.

Walsh, F., Jacob, L., and Simons, V. (1995). Facilitating healthy divorce processes: Therapy and mediation approaches. In N. Jacobson and A. Gurman (Eds.), *Clinical handbook of couple therapy* (pp. 340-365). New York: Guilford.

Name Index

Subject Index

Social disgrace, 133-135
Social skill model, 80-81
Social support, 87-90, 155. *See also*
    Networks
Sociocognitive theory, 157-167
Solution-focused couples therapy,
    435
Spillover, 233, 234-239, 240-243
Spirituality, 399-427
Splitting, 284
Spouse-assisted therapy, 94-103,
    140-146
Squabbles, 53
Stepparents, 204-205
Stonewalling, 318-320
Storytelling, 327-328
Stress, 82
Structural job stressors, 236-238
Stubbornness, 48-49
Symmetry (in relationships), 91
Systems theory, 289-294

Teenagers, drug abuse and, 190-191
Termination, 432-433
Therapeutic dialogue
    for anger, 65
    for anxiety, 146-147
    for communication, 331
    for depression, 103
    for in-laws, 271-272
    for parenting, 208
    for sex, 391
    for spirituality, 421-422
    for work, 242
Therapeutic effectiveness, 5
Ties that stress, 167
Time, 37-39, 131-132
Time-out, 51-53
Tolerance training, 416-417
Touch, 99
Traditional couples, 300, 301
Transactional work, 228
Treatment (effectiveness), 93-94,
    266-267, 429-430

Triangles
    detouring, 195-196
    with in-laws, 266-267
    parent-child, 195, 196, 197
    split loyalties, 195, 197
Triangulation, 195-197
Trust, 341
Twelve-step program, 140

Univocal reciprocity, 414

Vaginismus, 384
Validating couples, 318, 325
Values inventory, 423-424
Videotherapy
    for anger, 71
    for anxiety, 150
    for communication, 336
    for depression, 106
    for in-laws, 274
    for parenting, 212
    for sex, 390
    for spirituality, 426
    for work, 250
Violence, 54-65
Vitalized couples, 318, 301
Volatile couples
    gender, 57-58
    physical abuse, 56, 58-60
    psychological abuse, 56, 60-61
    verbal abuse, 56

Weddings, 162
Who Takes Responsibility for the
    Children?, 179, 210
Willi method, 306-308
Withdrawal, 48-49
Work addiction test, 246-248
Wrong turn information, 361-362
Work-family relationships
    effects on health, 238
    in relation to culture, 158-161

Order Your Own Copy of
This Important Book for Your Personal Library!

COUPLES THERAPY, SECOND EDITION

_____ in hardbound at $89.95 (ISBN: 0-7890-1453-X)

_____ in softbound at $49.95 (ISBN: 0-7890-1454-8)

COST OF BOOKS _____

OUTSIDE USA/CANADA/
MEXICO: ADD 20% _____

POSTAGE & HANDLING _____
(US: $4.00 for first book & $1.50
for each additional book
Outside US: $5.00 for first book
& $2.00 for each additional book)

SUBTOTAL _____

IN CANADA: ADD 7% GST _____

STATE TAX _____
(NY, OH & MN residents, please
add appropriate local sales tax)

FINAL TOTAL _____
(If paying in Canadian funds,
convert using the current
exchange rate. UNESCO
coupons welcome.)

☐ **BILL ME LATER:** (\$5 service charge will be added)
(Bill-me option is good on US/Canada/Mexico orders only;
not good to jobbers, wholesalers, or subscription agencies.)

☐ Check here if billing address is different from
shipping address and attach purchase order and
billing address information.

Signature _____

☐ **PAYMENT ENCLOSED: \$** _____

☐ **PLEASE CHARGE TO MY CREDIT CARD.**

☐ Visa ☐ MasterCard ☐ AmEx ☐ Discover
☐ Diner's Club ☐ Eurocard ☐ JCB

Account # _____

Exp. Date _____

Signature _____

Prices in US dollars and subject to change without notice.

NAME _____

INSTITUTION _____

ADDRESS _____

CITY _____

STATE/ZIP _____

COUNTRY _____ COUNTY (NY residents only) _____

TEL _____ FAX _____

E-MAIL_____

May we use your e-mail address for confirmations and other types of information? ☐ Yes ☐ No
We appreciate receiving your e-mail address and fax number. Haworth would like to e-mail or fax special
discount offers to you, as a preferred customer. **We will never share, rent, or exchange your e-mail
address or fax number.** We regard such actions as an invasion of your privacy.

Order From Your Local Bookstore or Directly From
The Haworth Press, Inc.
10 Alice Street, Binghamton, New York 13904-1580 • USA
TELEPHONE: 1-800-HAWORTH (1-800-429-6784) / Outside US/Canada: (607) 722-5857
FAX: 1-800-895-0582 / Outside US/Canada: (607) 772-6362
E-mail: getinfo@haworthpressinc.com
PLEASE PHOTOCOPY THIS FORM FOR YOUR PERSONAL USE.
www.HaworthPress.com

BOF00

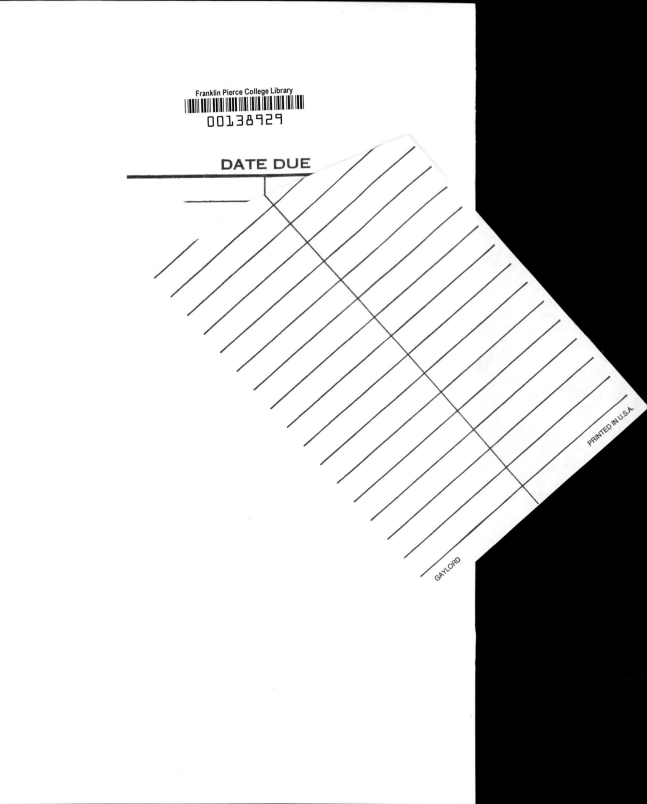

DATE DUE

GAYLORD   PRINTED IN U.S.A.